Welcome to
Amazing
ANSWERS
to Curious
QUESTIONS

Hungry for knowledge? Then The How It Works Book Of Amazing Answers To Curious Questions is here to help you feed your mind full of fascinating facts and figures and indispensable information. No subject is too small or too big – from what's inside a tiny mosquito to how the universe began. With answers to questions from six all-encompassing subject areas, including science, the environment, history, technology, transport and space, The How It Works Book Of Amazing Answers To Curious Questions is a fun, accessible companion for inquisitive minds with each section featuring intricate cutaway diagrams that detail the workings of everyday items and massive mechanisms. From how time works to what's inside a black hole, inside are the amazing answers to all the curious questions you could ever ask about the world in which we live.

Enjoy the book

HOW IT WORKS
BOOK OF
Amazing
ANSWERS
to Curious
QUESTIONS

Imagine Publishing Ltd
Richmond House
33 Richmond Hill
Bournemouth
Dorset BH2 6EZ
☎ +44 (0) 1202 586200
Website: www.imagine-publishing.co.uk

Editor in Chief
Dave Harfield

Design
Charles Goddard, Andy Downes

Photo Studio
Studio equipment courtesy of Lastolite (www.lastolite.co.uk)

Printed by
William Gibbons, 26 Planetary Road, Willenhall, West Midlands, WV13 3XT

Distributed in the UK & Eire by
Imagine Publishing Ltd, www.imagineshop.co.uk. Tel 01202 586200

Distributed in Australia by
Gordon & Gotch, Equinox Centre, 18 Rodborough Road, Frenchs Forest,
NSW 2086. Tel + 61 2 9972 8800

Distributed in the Rest of the World by
Marketforce, Blue Fin Building, 110 Southwark Street, London, SE1 0SU.

How It Works Annual © 2011 Imagine Publishing Ltd

ISBN 9 781908 222343

IMAGINE
PUBLISHING

Contents

AMAZING ANSWERS TO CURIOUS QUESTIONS

Science

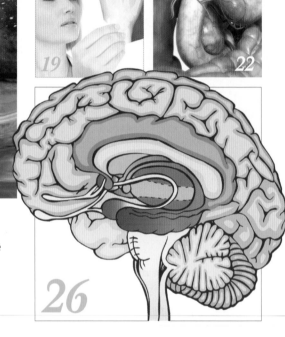

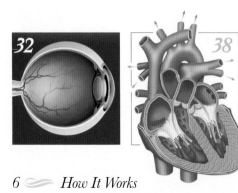

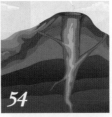

54

62

50

74

65

History

Environment

Technology

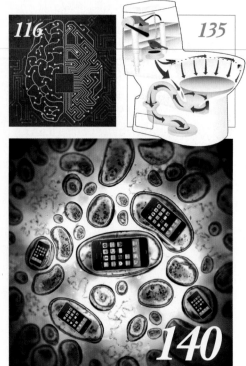

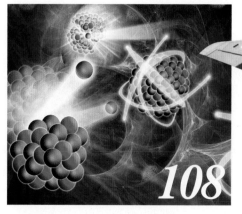

Transport

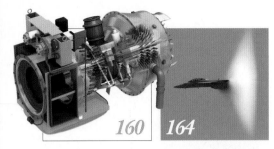

160 *164*

165

156

Space

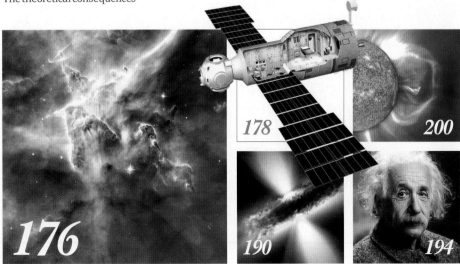

176 *178* *200* *190* *194*

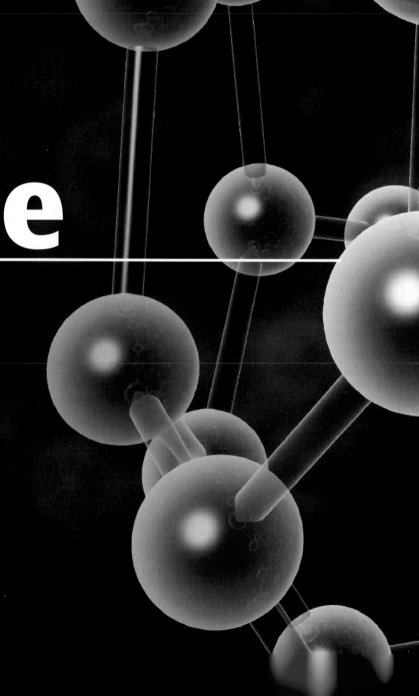

Science

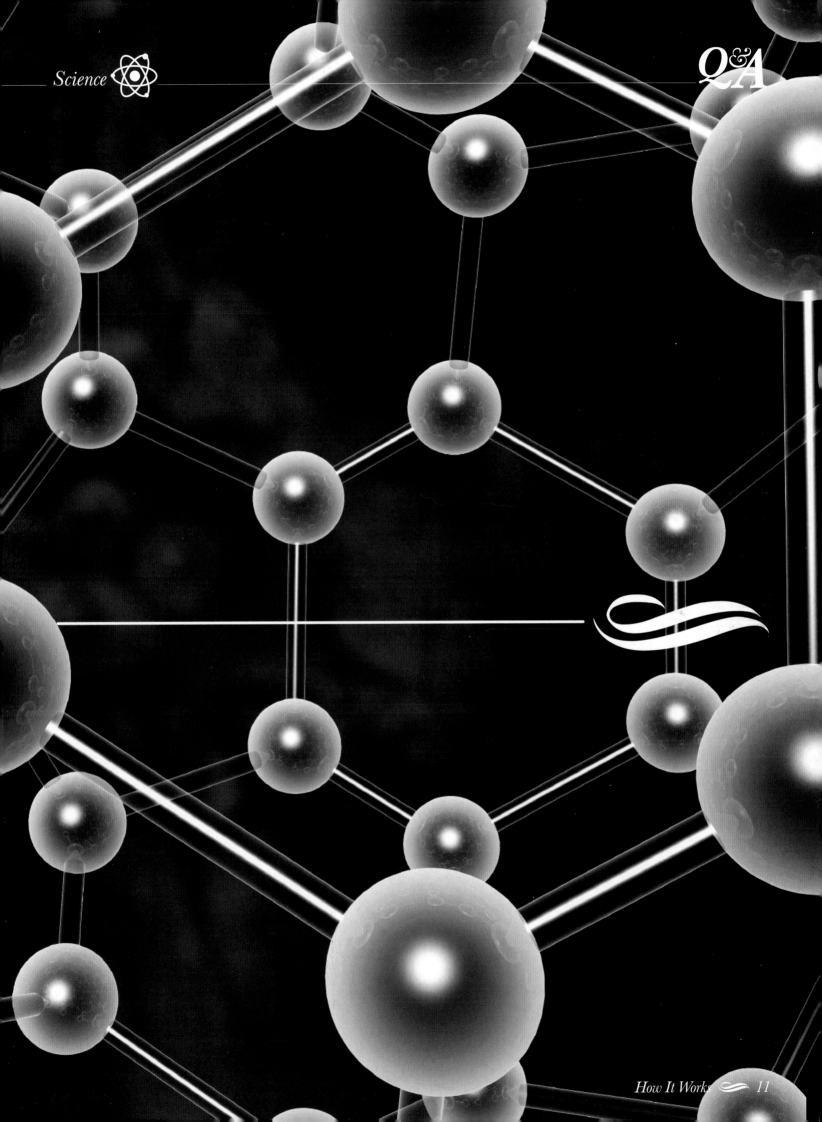

© Science Photo Library

How does time work?

Tick by tick, second by second, minute by minute, time has moved on in a seemingly constant manner from the beginning of the universe to the present day. It's one of the few things we regard as regular and unchanging, but is it really so constant?

You may want to sit down to read this feature. When considering time, it's easy to quickly get lost in the complexity of the topic. Time is all around us, ever present, and is the basis of how we record life on Earth. It's the constant that keeps the world, the solar system and even the universe ticking. Civilisations have risen and fallen, stars have been born and extinguished, and our one method of keeping track of every event in the universe and on Earth has been comparing them to the present day with the regular passing of time. But is it really a constant? Is time really as simple as a movement from one second to the next? We're about to find out.

13.7 billion years ago the universe was born, and since then time has flown by to the present day, overseeing the creation of galaxies and the expansion of space. But when it comes to comparing time, it's daunting to realise just how little of time we've actually experienced. The Earth might be 4.7 billion years old, but we modern humans have inhabited it for no

> ❝ *You would have to relive your life 150,000 times just to match the age of the youngest known star in the universe* ❞

more than 400,000 years, just 0.003% the age of the universe. Feeling small yet? It gets worse. You've experienced so little time on Earth that in astronomical terms you're entirely negligible. You would have to relive your life 150,000 times just to match the age of the youngest known star in the universe.

In the 17th Century Newton saw time as an arrow fired from a bow, travelling in a direct straight line and never deviating from its path. To Newton, one second on Earth was the same length of time as that same second on Mars, or Jupiter, or in deep space. He believed that absolute motion could not be detected, which meant that nothing in the universe had a constant speed, even light. By applying this theory he was able to assume that, if the speed of light could vary, then time must be constant. Time must tick from

What is special relativity?

How Einstein changed our perception of time

Einstein's theory of special relativity relies on one key fact: the speed of light is the same no matter how you look at it. To put this into practice, imagine you are travelling in a car at 32km/h (20mph), and you drive past a friend who is standing still.

As you pass them, you throw a ball out in front of the car at 16km/h (10mph). To your friend, the ball's speed combines with that of the car, and so appears to be travelling at 48km/h (30mph). Relative to you, however, the ball travels at only 16km/h (10mph), as you are already travelling at 32km/h (20mph).

Now imagine the same scenario, but this time you pass your stationary friend while travelling at half the speed of light (theoretically, of course). Through some imaginary contraption, your friend can observe you as you travel past. This time you shine a beam of light out of the car windscreen. Previously, we added together the speed of the ball and the car to find out what your friend saw, so in this instance, does your friend see the beam of light travelling at one and a half times the speed of light? According to Einstein, the answer is no. The speed of light always remains constant, and nothing can travel faster than it. Therefore, on this occasion, both you and your friend observe the speed of light travelling at its universally agreed value c, roughly 299,792,458 metres per second. This is the theory of special relativity, but why is it important when talking about time? Read below...

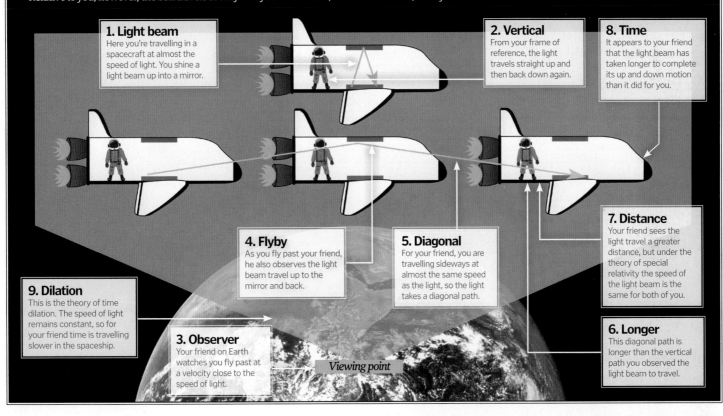

1. Light beam
Here you're travelling in a spacecraft at almost the speed of light. You shine a light beam up into a mirror.

2. Vertical
From your frame of reference, the light travels straight up and then back down again.

8. Time
It appears to your friend that the light beam has taken longer to complete its up and down motion than it did for you.

4. Flyby
As you fly past your friend, he also observes the light beam travel up to the mirror and back.

5. Diagonal
For your friend, you are travelling sideways at almost the same speed as the light, so the light takes a diagonal path.

7. Distance
Your friend sees the light travel a greater distance, but under the theory of special relativity the speed of the light beam is the same for both of you.

9. Dilation
This is the theory of time dilation. The speed of light remains constant, so for your friend time is travelling slower in the spaceship.

3. Observer
Your friend on Earth watches you fly past at a velocity close to the speed of light.

6. Longer
This diagonal path is longer than the vertical path you observed the light beam to travel.

Viewing point

one second to the next, with no difference between the length of any two seconds. This is something that you probably think to be true. Every day has roughly 24 hours; you don't have one day with 26 and another with 23.

However, in 1905, Einstein asserted that the speed of light doesn't vary, but rather it was a constant (roughly 299,792,458 metres per second). He postulated that time was more like a river, ebbing and flowing depending on the effects of gravity and space-time. Time would speed up and slow down around cosmological bodies with differing masses and velocities, and therefore one second on Earth was not the same length of time everywhere in the universe. This posed a problem. If the speed of light was really a constant, then there had to be some variable that altered over large distances in the universe. With the universe expanding and planets and galaxies moving on a galactically humongous scale, something had to give to allow for small fluctuations. And this variable had to be time.

It was ultimately Einstein's theory that was not only believed to be the

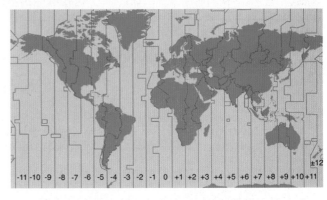

-11 -10 -9 -8 -7 -6 -5 -4 -3 -2 -1 0 +1 +2 +3 +4 +5 +6 +7 +8 +9 +10 +11   ±12

Time zones are separated by a distance of 15° longitude extending from pole to pole, but for political reasons some countries and provinces have chosen to belong to a different time zone than the one in which they are geographically located

truth, but also proved to be entirely accurate. In October 1971, two physicists named Hafele and Keating set about proving its validity. To do this, they flew four caesium atomic clocks on planes around the world, eastwards and then westwards. According to Einstein's theory, when compared with ground-based atomic clocks (in this instance at the US Naval Observatory in Washington DC), Hafele and Keating's airborne clocks would be about 40 nanoseconds slower after their eastward trip and about 275 nanoseconds faster after travelling west, due to the gravitational effects of the Earth on the velocity of the planes. Incredibly, the clocks did indeed register a difference when travelling east and west around the world, about 59 nanoseconds slower and 273 nanoseconds faster respectively when compared to the US Naval Observatory. This proved that Einstein was correct,

specifically with his theory of time dilation and that time did indeed fluctuate throughout the universe.

Newton and Einstein did agree on one thing, though – that time moves forward. So far there's

> **If the universe were to contract then time would reverse, a paradox for scientists and astronomers**

no evidence of anything in the universe that is able to dodge time and move forwards and backwards at will. Everything ultimately moves forward in time, be it at a regular pace or slightly warped if approaching the speed of light. Can we answer why time ticks forwards, though? Not quite, although there are several theories as to why it does. One of these brings in the laws of thermodynamics, specifically the second law. This states that everything in the universe

wants to move from low to high entropy, or from uniformity to disorder, beginning with simplicity at the Big Bang and moving to the almost random arrangement of galaxies and their inhabitants in the present day. This is known as the 'arrow of time', coined by British astronomer Arthur Eddington in 1927. He suggested that time was not symmetrical, stating: "If as we follow the arrow we find more and more of the random element in the state of the world, then the arrow is pointing towards the future; if the random element decreases, the arrow points towards the past." For example, if you were to observe a star in almost uniformity, but later saw it explode as a supernova and become a scattered nebula, you would know that time had moved forwards from equality to chaos.

Another theory suggests that the passage of time is due to the expansion of the universe. As

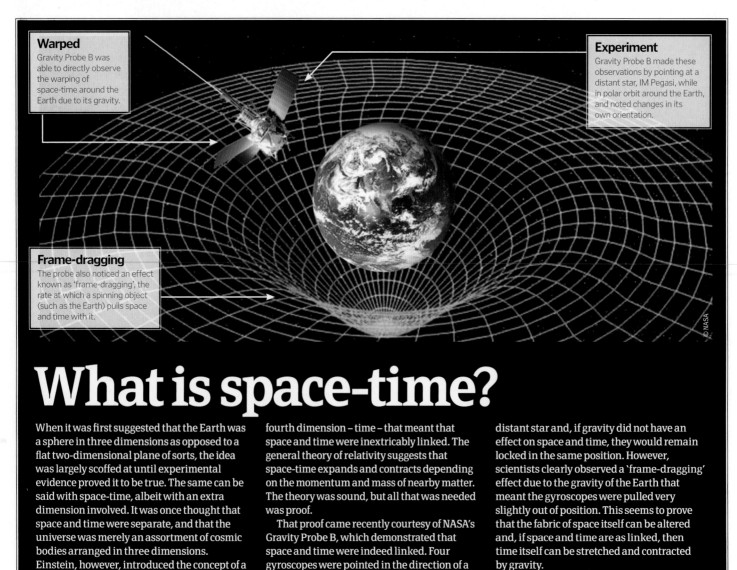

Warped
Gravity Probe B was able to directly observe the warping of space-time around the Earth due to its gravity.

Experiment
Gravity Probe B made these observations by pointing at a distant star, IM Pegasi, while in polar orbit around the Earth, and noted changes in its own orientation.

Frame-dragging
The probe also noticed an effect known as 'frame-dragging', the rate at which a spinning object (such as the Earth) pulls space and time with it.

© NASA

What is space-time?

When it was first suggested that the Earth was a sphere in three dimensions as opposed to a flat two-dimensional plane of sorts, the idea was largely scoffed at until experimental evidence proved it to be true. The same can be said with space-time, albeit with an extra dimension involved. It was once thought that space and time were separate, and that the universe was merely an assortment of cosmic bodies arranged in three dimensions. Einstein, however, introduced the concept of a

fourth dimension – time – that meant that space and time were inextricably linked. The general theory of relativity suggests that space-time expands and contracts depending on the momentum and mass of nearby matter. The theory was sound, but all that was needed was proof.

That proof came recently courtesy of NASA's Gravity Probe B, which demonstrated that space and time were indeed linked. Four gyroscopes were pointed in the direction of a

distant star and, if gravity did not have an effect on space and time, they would remain locked in the same position. However, scientists clearly observed a 'frame-dragging' effect due to the gravity of the Earth that meant the gyroscopes were pulled very slightly out of position. This seems to prove that the fabric of space itself can be altered and, if space and time are as linked, then time itself can be stretched and contracted by gravity.

the universe expands it pulls time with it, as space and time are linked as one (see below), but this would mean that if the universe were to reach a theoretical limit of expansion and begin to contract then time would reverse, a slight paradox for scientists and astronomers. Would time really move backwards, with everything coming back to an era of simplicity and ending with a 'Big Crunch' (as opposed to the Big Bang)? It's unlikely we'll be around to find out, but we can postulate on what we think might happen.

It's incredible to think of the progress we have made in our understanding of time over the past century. From ancient sundials to modern atomic clocks, we can even track the passing of a second more closely than ever before.

Time remains a complex topic, but thanks to scientific visionaries, we are getting closer to unlocking the secrets of this not-so-constant universal constant. ❁

How do different lengths of time compare?

13.7 BILLION YEARS
Age of the universe

4.5 BILLION YEARS
Age of the Earth

65 MILLION YEARS
Time since extinction of dinosaurs

365.242 DAYS
Earth's orbit around the Sun

1 SECOND
Average length of a heartbeat

ONE HUNDREDTH OF A SECOND (CENTISECOND)
Eyes blinking

ONE TENTH OF A SECOND (DECISECOND)
Lightning strike

ONE TRILLIONTH OF A SECOND (PICOSECOND)
Shortest measurable length of time

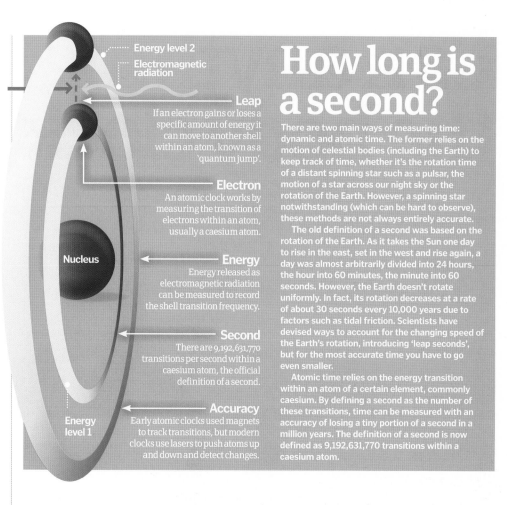

Energy level 2
Electromagnetic radiation

Leap
If an electron gains or loses a specific amount of energy it can move to another shell within an atom, known as a 'quantum jump'.

Electron
An atomic clock works by measuring the transition of electrons within an atom, usually a caesium atom.

Nucleus

Energy
Energy released as electromagnetic radiation can be measured to record the shell transition frequency.

Second
There are 9,192,631,770 transitions per second within a caesium atom, the official definition of a second.

Accuracy
Early atomic clocks used magnets to track transitions, but modern clocks use lasers to push atoms up and down and detect changes.

Energy level 1

How long is a second?

There are two main ways of measuring time: dynamic and atomic time. The former relies on the motion of celestial bodies (including the Earth) to keep track of time, whether it's the rotation time of a distant spinning star such as a pulsar, the motion of a star across our night sky or the rotation of the Earth. However, a spinning star notwithstanding (which can be hard to observe), these methods are not always entirely accurate.

The old definition of a second was based on the rotation of the Earth. As it takes the Sun one day to rise in the east, set in the west and rise again, a day was almost arbitrarily divided into 24 hours, the hour into 60 minutes, the minute into 60 seconds. However, the Earth doesn't rotate uniformly. In fact, its rotation decreases at a rate of about 30 seconds every 10,000 years due to factors such as tidal friction. Scientists have devised ways to account for the changing speed of the Earth's rotation, introducing 'leap seconds', but for the most accurate time you have to go even smaller.

Atomic time relies on the energy transition within an atom of a certain element, commonly caesium. By defining a second as the number of these transitions, time can be measured with an accuracy of losing a tiny portion of a second in a million years. The definition of a second is now defined as 9,192,631,770 transitions within a caesium atom.

What is the world's most accurate clock?

The most accurate clock in the universe would probably be a rotating star like a pulsar (although this is debatable), but on Earth it's atomic clocks that provide an accurate track of time.

The entire GPS system in orbit around the Earth uses atomic clocks to accurately track their position and relay data to the Earth, while entire scientific centres are set up to calculate the most accurate measure of time, usually by measuring transitions within a caesium atom. While most atomic clocks rely on magnetic fields, modern clocks are using lasers to more accurately track and detect energy transitions within caesium atoms and keep a more definite measure of time.

Although caesium clocks are currently used to keep time around the world, strontium clocks (strontium atoms inside a laser grid) promise twice as much accuracy, while an experimental design based on charged mercury atoms could reduce discrepancies even further to less than one second lost or gained in 400 million years.

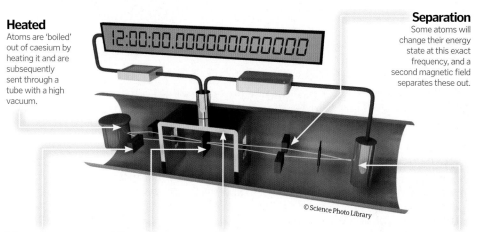

Heated
Atoms are 'boiled' out of caesium by heating it and are subsequently sent through a tube with a high vacuum.

Separation
Some atoms will change their energy state at this exact frequency, and a second magnetic field separates these out.

© Science Photo Library

Magnet
A magnetic field is able to discern between atoms of varying energy states and pick the ones that are at the right level.

Microwaves
The selected atoms are passed through a microwave field of high intensity that has a fluctuating frequency.

Frequency
A crystal oscillator allows the microwave field to accurately reach 9,192,631,770 Hertz, the resonant frequency of a caesium atom.

Count
A detector measures the number of atoms changing their state at this frequency and, once it detects 9,192,631,770 of these transitions, a second is said to have passed.

Can anything stop the body clock?

How the circadian cycle affects our lives

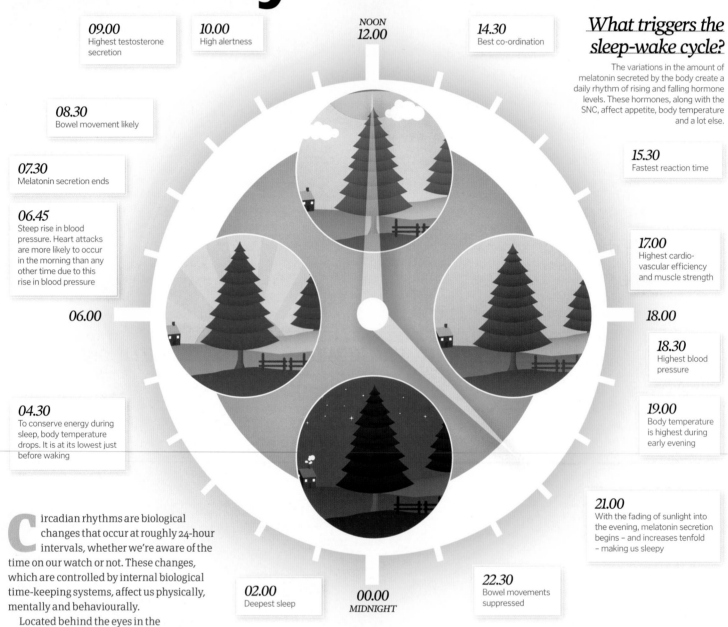

09.00
Highest testosterone secretion

10.00
High alertness

NOON
12.00

14.30
Best co-ordination

What triggers the sleep-wake cycle?

The variations in the amount of melatonin secreted by the body create a daily rhythm of rising and falling hormone levels. These hormones, along with the SNC, affect appetite, body temperature and a lot else.

08.30
Bowel movement likely

07.30
Melatonin secretion ends

15.30
Fastest reaction time

06.45
Steep rise in blood pressure. Heart attacks are more likely to occur in the morning than any other time due to this rise in blood pressure

17.00
Highest cardio-vascular efficiency and muscle strength

06.00

18.00

18.30
Highest blood pressure

04.30
To conserve energy during sleep, body temperature drops. It is at its lowest just before waking

19.00
Body temperature is highest during early evening

21.00
With the fading of sunlight into the evening, melatonin secretion begins – and increases tenfold – making us sleepy

02.00
Deepest sleep

00.00
MIDNIGHT

22.30
Bowel movements suppressed

Circadian rhythms are biological changes that occur at roughly 24-hour intervals, whether we're aware of the time on our watch or not. These changes, which are controlled by internal biological time-keeping systems, affect us physically, mentally and behaviourally.

Located behind the eyes in the hypothalamus is a region of the brain called the suprachiasmatic nucleus. No larger than a grain of rice, the SCN is a kind of master body clock that controls all our other internal clocks, which in turn control our circadian rhythms, or daily wake-sleep cycles. Circadian rhythms respond mainly to light and dark cues but even if the body was monitored under conditions devoid of day or night signals, our circadian rhythms still cycle in a period of around 24 hours. The retina in the eye senses light level information, which is relayed to the SCN, which sends a signal to the pineal gland. This pea-sized gland, located beneath the thalamus, is responsible for the secretion of melatonin – a hormone that tells the body to sleep – and so at night when light levels fall, the production of melatonin increases, telling us to head to bed. ✱

Are you a lark or an owl?

We all know that our genes make us different, and this also affects our individual natural rhythms. Some people have a body clock that lasts longer than 24 hours, which means they tend to stay up later: these people are referred to as owls. Other people with shorter body clocks, meanwhile, tend to rise earlier in the morning: people like this are larks.

How do boats stay afloat?

Displacement enables huge ships to stay above the water

Unladen
The ship sinks until the water it displaces equals its own weight

Fully loaded
It will continue to displace more and more water as it's loaded with cargo

At first displacement appears to be far from fascinating. Simply put, the volume of an object, when submerged in water, pushes aside the same volume of water. This simple process allows anyone to measure the precise volume of any object by then measuring the amount of fluid that either spills out of the top of the container or rises by said amount in a measuring cylinder. It's all very 'science textbook'.

It becomes a little more interesting when you consider that it's this effect that enables enormous supertankers weighing up to 400,000 tons to float. For example, when a supertanker is launched into the sea it will sink if the water it displaces is equal to or exceeds the weight of the ship itself. However, if when launched its weight is less than that of the water it displaces and its shape allows it to displace the weight faster than the water will reach the tanker's submerging point, no matter how large or full of cargo, then it will float.

Of course, if you were to drop a solid iron bar into a swimming pool, it would sink straight away because: firstly, its weight far outweighed that of the water it was displacing and secondly, even if its weight was less than that of the water, its shape would not allow it to displace the weight fast enough. This is why ships' hulls are shaped how they are.

So while the scientific principle might lack wow factor, it does enable fantastic feats of engineering like the TI class supertankers, the largest ocean going-ships in the world. They're an incredible 379 metres long, 68 metres wide and have a deadweight of some 441,585 metric tons and float thanks to the law of displacement discovered by Archimedes in the original Eureka moment. ☼

How do fish breathe underwater?

They don't 'breathe' the water – it's much cooler than that

The process of absorbing oxygen and the release of carbon dioxide is called 'gas exchange'. Fish need oxygen in the same way humans do, they just go about getting it in a different way.

A fish has gills behind its mouth, on the side of the head (unless you're a bottom dweller like a stingray, then your gills are on the top of your head). Each gill begins with a gill arch which then splits into two filaments, much like a wishbone. Those filaments are lined with lamellae, which are little discs that are filled with capillaries. Those capillaries have oxygenated blood running through them, which is why the inside of gills are red. The more active a fish is, the more oxygen it needs, and the more lamellae it has.

As a fish swims, the water moves into the mouth and flows through the gills. When a fish is stationary, it can still push water through the gills by opening and closing its mouth. When water passes over the lamellae, the oxygen in the water diffuses into the capillaries, oxygenating the blood.

Fish have a 'countercurrent system of flow', which means that the blood flows in the opposite direction of the water. They need this clever little trick because the diffusion only works if there is less oxygen in the blood than there is in the water. So, the blood with the least amount of oxygen is meeting the 'oxygen depleted' water first, taking what's left, and then moving on to fresher, more oxygenated water.

Like humans, fish must get rid of the carbon dioxide created by absorbing and using oxygen. Gills are multi-taskers – they diffuse the carbon dioxide out of the body and into the water. Fish are then free to focus on swimming. ☼

Water flows over gills, then out

Fish gill

Water flows in through mouth

How do you perform CPR?

The proper way isn't exactly the Hollywood method, but it's no less dramatic

On television, cardiopulmonary resuscitation (CPR) is like the Fonz hitting the jukebox on *Happy Days*: whack a dying person in the right spot and his or her heart will start beating again.

However, this hardly ever works in real life, and it isn't actually the point of administering CPR. The real goal here is to buy some valuable time until it's possible to revive a normal heartbeat, typically by using an electric jolt from a defibrillator.

The cells in your body need oxygen to convert food into usable energy. Your heart delivers the goods. It pumps oxygenated blood from the lungs out to the body, and pumps deoxygenated blood back to the lungs. If your heart isn't pumping sufficient blood – a condition called cardiac arrest – your body's cells will fail. Most significantly, your brain cells (neurons) will start dying four to six minutes after cardiac arrest begins. Ten minutes without resuscitation efforts and the chances of revival are almost nil.

The idea of CPR is to hold off death by forcing the lungs and heart to provide oxygenated blood to the brain. Exhaling air into the victim's lungs provides the oxygen, and regularly compressing the chest forces the heart to pump blood. ❁

CPR, step by step

Authorities differ on exact recommendations. The procedure described here is based on guidelines from the Resuscitation Council (UK). To ensure you administer CPR correctly, it's essential to take a training course with a qualified instructor. If you believe someone has suffered cardiac arrest, gently shake their shoulders and shout, "Are you okay?" If the victim responds, he has not suffered cardiac arrest and does not need CPR. If the victim doesn't respond, yell for help.

1. Clear the airway
Carefully roll the victim on his back. Gently press his forehead to tilt his head back, while lifting his chin. This will clear the airway. Watch chest movement and listen for normal breathing. If the victim is breathing normally, do not administer CPR. If you aren't sure whether the victim is breathing normally, assume he is not.

2. Prepare for compressions
Before beginning the process, you must ask someone to call an ambulance. If you're alone, call one yourself. Kneel beside the victim and place one hand over the other, interlocking your fingers. Place the heel of your lower hand in the centre of the victim's chest, but not above the ribs.

3. Begin chest compressions
With your arms straight, press down 4-5 cm on the sternum, and then release. Continue compressing and releasing at a rate of a little less than two full compressions every second (a rate of 100 compressions per minute). Oddly enough, timing compressions to the beat of the Bee Gees' *Stayin' Alive* works perfectly.

4. Administer rescue breaths
After 30 compressions, reopen the victim's airway and pinch his nose closed. Take a breath, place your lips around the victim's mouth, and blow into the victim's mouth. Watch for his chest to rise, then remove your mouth, allowing air to escape again. Repeat the process for a second breath, then administer 30 more chest compressions. Continue the cycle until help arrives.

Disclaimer
CPR should only be performed in emergencies. These instructions are a guide to how CPR works – professional first aid training is always recommended.

How does exercise work?

Warming up
To prepare for increased demand from the muscles, stretching and light exercise raise heart rate, blood flow and muscle temperature.

Jogging
For light exercise or long distance running, muscles use oxygen to fully break down glucose into useful energy during aerobic respiration (with oxygen).

Sprinting
When the muscles require a large amount of energy, for sprinting, for example, they break down glucose with no oxygen to produce energy faster, but for a limited duration.

Fatigue
Anaerobic respiration (no oxygen), unlike aerobic respiration, produces excess lactic acid quickly that slows the muscles and may lead to cramp.

Discover how your muscles convert energy into power

When resting or performing light exercise, such as jogging, the body uses aerobic respiration – with the aid of oxygen – to break down energy-rich fuels such as glucose. This produces usable energy in the form of adenosine triphosphate (ATP) for the muscles. This results in some waste being produced, such as water and carbon dioxide, which leave the body via sweating and breathing respectively. As a person gets fitter their muscles increase in size so they need to do less work to perform an action, expelling less waste products.

When performing an extremely strenuous activity, such as sprinting, the muscles need energy faster than the heart can pump blood around the body. Instead of using oxygen from the blood the muscles use a large amount of glucose to produce the required ATP. This is known as anaerobic respiration and takes place in the absence of oxygen. While this increases the speed at which the muscles can work, it also decreases the amount of time they can stay active before muscle fatigue hits, when excess waste products are produced. ❁

What is 'brain freeze'?

Technically called sphenopalatine ganglioneuralgia, ice cream headaches are related to migraines

Ophthalmic

The Ophthalmic branch carries sensory messages from the eyeball, tear gland, upper nose, upper eyelid, forehead, and scalp.

Mandibular

The Mandibular branch carries sensory messages from the skin, teeth and gums of the lower jaw, tongue, chin, lower lip and skin of the temporal region.

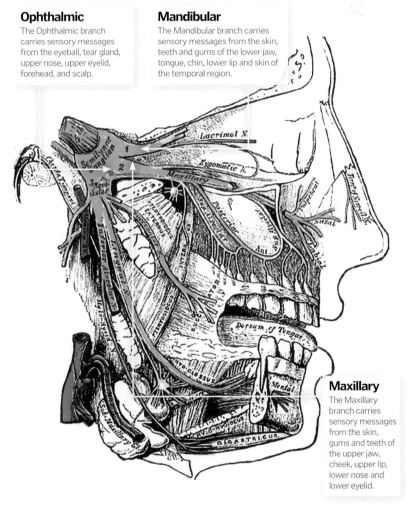

Maxillary

The Maxillary branch carries sensory messages from the skin, gums and teeth of the upper jaw, cheek, upper lip, lower nose and lower eyelid.

The pain of a brain freeze, also know as an ice cream headache, comes from your body's natural reaction to cold. When your body senses cold, it wants to conserve heat. One of the steps it takes to accomplish this is constricting the blood vessels near your skin. With less blood flowing near your skin, less heat is carried away from your core, keeping you warm.

The same thing happens when something really cold hits the back of your mouth. The blood vessels in your palate constrict rapidly. When the cold goes away (because you swallowed the ice cream or cold beverage), they rapidly dilate back to their normal state.

This is harmless, but a major facial nerve called the trigeminal lies close to your palate and this nerve interprets the constriction/dilation process as pain. The location of the trigeminal nerve can cause the pain to seem like its coming from your forehead. Doctors believe that this same misinterpretation of blood vessel constriction/dilation is the cause of the intense pain of a migraine headache. ⚙

How safe are x-rays?

With a small dose of x-ray energy, your doctor can examine your bones or circulatory system – too high of a dose and you're doomed to a painful death from cancer

An x-ray is a form of energy within a certain range of wavelengths. Any radiation between 3×1016 Hz to 3×1019 Hz (30 petahertz to 30 exahertz) is considered x-ray radiation. These are very short wavelengths, just below the ultraviolet region of the spectrum. The actual wavelength is about 10,000 times smaller than the wavelength of visible light. Short wavelength rays have high energy, which is why x-rays pass through most things. The high energy level of an x-ray photon doesn't 'fit' with others atoms' electron orbits, making it difficult for atoms to absorb x-rays unless the atom is large enough to accommodate the x-ray photon's energy.

The x-ray machine at your doctor's office generates x-rays by cranking a bunch of electrons up to a very high speed using a highly charged cathode. These electrons are then drawn to an anode made of tungsten. There, the electrons strike tungsten atoms and are either deflected or knock other electrons out of orbit. The collisions emit photons at the wavelength of x-rays which are channelled using a small window and lots of lead shielding.

From there, the rays are passed through some portion of your anatomy. Many of the them go right through, but your bones are made from larger atoms (calcium, mostly) than your other bits, and these atoms have a greater chance of absorbing some x-rays. On the other side of you, the rays strike a photosensitive plate. The more x-rays that strike the plate, the darker that portion of the plate. That's why the resulting image is a negative, with your bones the brightest: they absorbed the most x-rays. Doctors can x-ray image your blood vessels or other soft tissue by injecting or making you drink a special contrast dye that absorbs x-rays.

The x-rays that are absorbed by your body aren't entirely harmless. The x-ray photons can knock electrons away from their atoms, creating ions and starting a minor chain reaction. Ricocheting ions alter substances in your body at the atomic level, destroying or altering the DNA of your cells. This 'ionising radiation' is what did the damage suffered by those who endured unshielded, very long or frequent x-ray exposures in the days before the dangers of x-rays were understood. Today's medical x-rays are very safe when used properly, and vastly superior to being cut open every time a doctor needs a look inside you. ⚙

How do kidneys function?

Find out what your kidneys are doing to keep you alive

Kidneys are bean-shaped organs situated halfway down the back just under the ribcage, one on each side of the body, and weigh between 115 and 170 grams each, dependent on the individual's sex and size. The left kidney is commonly a little larger than the right and due to the effectiveness of these organs, individuals born with only one kidney can survive with little or no adverse health problems. Indeed, the body can operate normally with a 30-40 per cent decline in kidney function. This decline in function would rarely even be noticeable and shows just how effective the kidneys are at filtering out waste products as well as maintaining mineral levels and blood pressure throughout the body. The kidneys manage to control all of this by working with other organs and glands across the body such as the hypothalamus, which helps the kidneys determine and control water levels in the body.

Each day the kidneys will filter between 150 and 180 litres of blood, but only pass around two litres of waste down the ureters to the bladder for excretion. This waste product is primarily urea – a by-product of protein being broken down for energy – and water, and it's more commonly known as 'urine'. The kidneys filter the blood by passing it through a small filtering unit called a nephron. Each kidney has around a million of these, which are made up of a number of small blood capillaries, called glomerulus, and a urine-collecting tube called the renal tubule. The glomerulus sift the normal cells and proteins from the blood and then move the waste products into the renal tubule, which transports urine down into the bladder through the ureters.

Alongside this filtering process, the kidneys also release three crucial hormones (known as erythropoietin, renin and calcitriol) which encourage red blood cell production, aid regulation of blood pressure and help bone development and mineral balance respectively. ✱

What's inside a kidney?

As blood enters the kidneys, it is passed through a nephron, a tiny unit made up of blood capillaries and a waste-transporting tube. These work together to filter the blood, returning clean blood to the heart and lungs for re-oxygenation and recirculation and removing waste to the bladder for excretion.

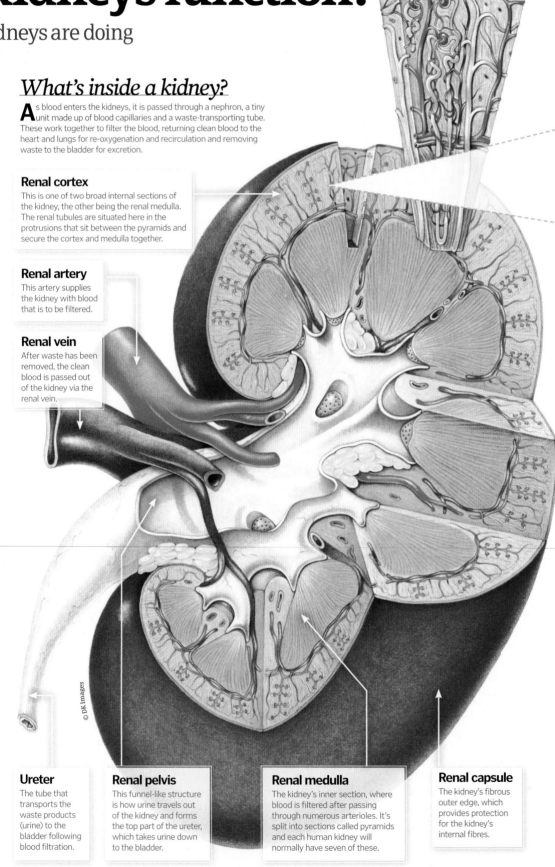

© DK Images

Renal cortex
This is one of two broad internal sections of the kidney, the other being the renal medulla. The renal tubules are situated here in the protrusions that sit between the pyramids and secure the cortex and medulla together.

Renal artery
This artery supplies the kidney with blood that is to be filtered.

Renal vein
After waste has been removed, the clean blood is passed out of the kidney via the renal vein.

Ureter
The tube that transports the waste products (urine) to the bladder following blood filtration.

Renal pelvis
This funnel-like structure is how urine travels out of the kidney and forms the top part of the ureter, which takes urine down to the bladder.

Renal medulla
The kidney's inner section, where blood is filtered after passing through numerous arterioles. It's split into sections called pyramids and each human kidney will normally have seven of these.

Renal capsule
The kidney's fibrous outer edge, which provides protection for the kidney's internal fibres.

Nephrons – the filtration units of the kidney

Nephrons are the units which filter all blood that passes through the kidneys. There are around a million in each kidney, situated in the renal medulla's pyramid structures. As well as filtering waste, nephrons regulate water and mineral salt by recirculating what is needed and excreting the rest.

Proximal tubule
Links Bowman's capsule and the loop of Henle, and will selectively reabsorb minerals from the filtrate produced by Bowman's capsule.

Collecting duct system
Although not technically part of the nephron, this collects all waste product filtered by the nephrons and facilitates its removal from the kidneys.

Glomerulus
High pressure in the glomerulus, caused by it draining into an arteriole instead of a venule, forces fluids and soluble materials out of the capillary and into Bowman's capsule.

Bowman's capsule
Also known as the glomerular capsule, this filters the fluid that has been expelled from the glomerulus. Resulting filtrate is passed along the nephron and will eventually make up urine.

Distal convoluted tubule
Partly responsible for the regulation of minerals in the blood, linking to the collecting duct system. Unwanted minerals are excreted from the nephron.

Renal artery
This artery supplies the kidney with blood. The blood travels through this, into arterioles as you travel into the kidney, until the blood reaches the glomerulus.

Renal vein
This removes blood that has been filtered from the kidney.

Loop of Henle
The loop of Henle controls the mineral and water concentration levels within the kidney to aid filtration of fluids as necessary. It also controls urine concentration.

Renal tubule
Made up of three parts, the proximal tubule, the loop of Henle and the distal convoluted tubule. They remove waste and reabsorb minerals from the filtrate passed on from Bowman's capsule.

The glomerulus

This group of capillaries is the first step of filtration and a crucial aspect of a nephron. As blood enters the kidneys via the renal artery, it is passed down through a series of arterioles which eventually lead to the glomerulus. This is unusual, as instead of draining into a venule (which would lead back to a vein) it drains back into an arteriole, which creates much higher pressure than normally seen in capillaries, which in turn forces soluble materials and fluids out of the capillaries. This process is known as ultrafiltration and is the first step in filtration of the blood. These then pass through the Bowman's capsule (also know as the glomerular capsule) for further filtration.

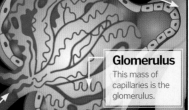

Afferent arteriole
This arteriole supplies the blood to the glomerulus for filtration.

Proximal tubule
Where reabsorption of minerals from the filtrate from Bowman's capsule will occur.

Glomerulus
This mass of capillaries is the glomerulus.

Efferent arteriole
This arteriole is how blood leaves the glomerulus following ultrafiltration.

Bowman's capsule
This is the surrounding capsule that will filter the filtrate produced by the glomerulus.

What is urine and what is it made of?

Urine is made up of a range of organic compounds such as proteins and hormones, inorganic salts and numerous metabolites. These by-products are often rich in nitrogen and need to be removed from the blood stream through urination. The pH-level of urine is typically around neutral (pH7) but varies depending on diet, hydration levels and physical fitness. The colour of urine is also determined by these factors, with dark-yellow urine indicating dehydration and greenish urine being indicative of excessive asparagus consumption.

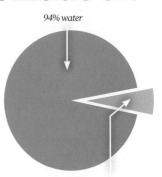

94% water

6% other organic compounds

What does the liver do?

The human liver is the ultimate multitasker – it performs many different functions all at the same time without you even asking

The liver is the largest internal organ in the human body and has over 500 functions. In fact, it is the second most complex organ after the brain and is involved in almost every aspect of the body's metabolic processes. Its main functions are energy production, removal of harmful substances and the production of proteins. These tasks are carried out within liver cells called hepatocytes, which sit in complex arrangements to maximise efficiency.

The liver is the body's main powerhouse, producing and storing glucose as a key energy source. It is also responsible for breaking down complex fat molecules and building them up into cholesterol and triglycerides, which the body needs but in excess are bad.

The liver makes many complex proteins, including clotting factors which are vital in arresting bleeding. Bile, which helps digest fat in the intestines, is produced in the liver and stored in the adjacent gallbladder.

The liver also plays a key role in detoxifying the blood. Waste products, toxins and drugs are processed here into forms which are easier for the rest of the body to use or excrete. The liver also breaks down old blood cells, produces antibodies to fight infection and recycles hormones such as adrenaline. Numerous essential vitamins and minerals are stored in the liver: vitamins A, D, E and K, iron and copper.

Such a complex organ is also unfortunately prone to diseases. Cancers (most often metastatic from other sources), infections (hepatitis) and cirrhosis (a form of fibrosis often caused by excess alcohol consumption) are just some of those which can affect the liver. ✿

What is the hepatobiliary region?

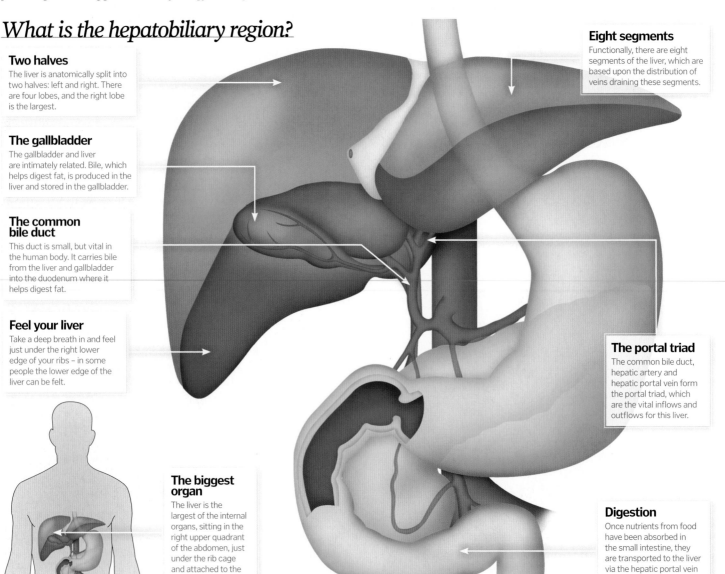

Eight segments
Functionally, there are eight segments of the liver, which are based upon the distribution of veins draining these segments.

Two halves
The liver is anatomically split into two halves: left and right. There are four lobes, and the right lobe is the largest.

The gallbladder
The gallbladder and liver are intimately related. Bile, which helps digest fat, is produced in the liver and stored in the gallbladder.

The common bile duct
This duct is small, but vital in the human body. It carries bile from the liver and gallbladder into the duodenum where it helps digest fat.

Feel your liver
Take a deep breath in and feel just under the right lower edge of your ribs – in some people the lower edge of the liver can be felt.

The portal triad
The common bile duct, hepatic artery and hepatic portal vein form the portal triad, which are the vital inflows and outflows for this liver.

The biggest organ
The liver is the largest of the internal organs, sitting in the right upper quadrant of the abdomen, just under the rib cage and attached to the underside of the diaphragm.

Digestion
Once nutrients from food have been absorbed in the small intestine, they are transported to the liver via the hepatic portal vein (not shown here) for energy production.

Blood vessels
Blood vessels infiltrate liver tissue, supplying lobules with blood.

Why is the liver a 'high demand' organ?

The liver deals with a massive amount of blood. It is unique because it has two blood supplies. 75 per cent of this comes directly from the intestines (via the hepatic portal vein) which carries nutrients from digestion, which the liver processes and turns into energy. The rest comes from the heart, via the hepatic artery (which branches from the aorta), carrying oxygen that the liver needs to produce this energy. The blood flows in tiny passages in between the liver cells where the many metabolic functions occur. The blood then leaves the liver via the hepatic veins to flow into the biggest vein in the body – the inferior vena cava. ✿

Liver lobules
The functional unit that performs the liver's tasks

The liver is considered a 'chemical factory,' as it forms large complex molecules from smaller ones brought to it from the gut via the blood stream. The functional unit of the liver is the lobule – these are hexagonal-shaped structures comprising of blood vessels and sinusoids. Sinusoids are the specialised areas where blood comes into contact with the hepatocytes, where the liver's biological processes take place. ✿

3. Sinusoids
These blood-filled channels are lined by hepatocytes and provide the site of transfer of molecules between blood and liver cells.

1. The lobule
This arrangement of blood vessels, bile ducts and hepatocytes form the functional unit of the liver.

2. The hepatocyte
These highly active cells perform all of the liver's key metabolic tasks.

4. Kupffer cells
These specialised cells sit within the sinusoids and destroy any bacteria which are contaminating blood.

9. Central vein
Blood from sinusoids, now containing all of its new molecules, flows into central veins which then flow into larger hepatic veins. These drain into the heart via the inferior vena cava.

5. Hepatic artery branch
Blood from here supplies oxygen to hepatocytes and carries metabolic waste which the liver extracts.

6. Bile duct
Bile, which helps digest fat, is made in hepatocytes and secreted into bile ducts. It then flows into the gallbladder for storage before being secreted into the duodenum.

7. Portal vein
This vein carries nutrient-rich blood directly from the intestines, which flows into sinusoids for conversion into energy within hepatocytes.

8. The portal triad
The hepatic artery, portal vein and bile duct are known as the portal triad. These sit at the edges of the liver lobule and are the main entry and exit routes for the liver.

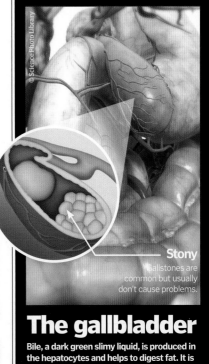

© Science Photo Library

Stony
Gallstones are common but usually don't cause problems.

The gallbladder

Bile, a dark green slimy liquid, is produced in the hepatocytes and helps to digest fat. It is stored in a reservoir which sits on the under-surface of the liver, to be used when needed. This reservoir is called the gallbladder. Stones can form in the gallbladder (gallstones) and are very common, although most don't cause problems. In 2009, just under 60,000 gallbladders were removed from patients within the NHS making it one of the most common operations performed; over 90 per cent of these are removed via keyhole surgery. Most patients do very well without their gallbladder and don't notice any changes at all.

How do we get drunk?

How does drinking alcohol make people drunk, and why do they suffer from the side effects?

There are actually many kinds of alcohol in the chemical world, but the one we drink the most is ethanol. It's the particular shape of an ethanol molecule that gives a glass of beer or a shot of the hard stuff its specific effects on the human brain. The molecule is very tiny, made up of just two carbon atoms, six hydrogen atoms, and one oxygen atom. Ethanol is water soluble, which means it enters the blood stream readily, there to be carried quickly to all parts of the body (most notably the liver and the brain). It's also fat soluble; like an all-access pass through various cell membranes and other places that are normally off limits.

A certain portion of the ethanol you drink passes through your stomach to your small intestine, then absorbed into your bloodstream and carried to your brain. That's what we're really concerned with. Research has not conclusively determined exactly how ethanol accomplishes all of its various effects in the brain, but

there are some well-supported theories. The slow reactions, slurred speech and memory loss of a drunk are probably caused by ethanol attaching to glutamate receptors in your brain's neural circuitry. These receptors normally receive chemical signals from other parts of the brain, but instead they get an ethanol molecule. This disrupts the flow of signals and generally slows the whole brain down.

Ethanol also binds to GABA (gamma-aminobutyric acid) receptors, which normally serve to slow down brain activity. Unlike glutamate receptors, ethanol actually makes GABA receptors more receptive, causing the brain to slow down even more. But alcohol isn't simply a depressant, because it also stimulates the production of dopamine and endorphins, chemicals that produce feelings of pleasure. Research hasn't yet revealed the exact mechanism involved, but it may be similar to the way ethanol stimulates the GABA receptors. ✿

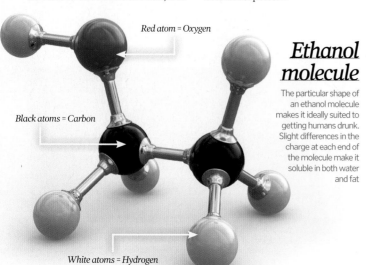

Red atom = Oxygen

Black atoms = Carbon

White atoms = Hydrogen

Ethanol molecule

The particular shape of an ethanol molecule makes it ideally suited to getting humans drunk. Slight differences in the charge at each end of the molecule make it soluble in both water and fat

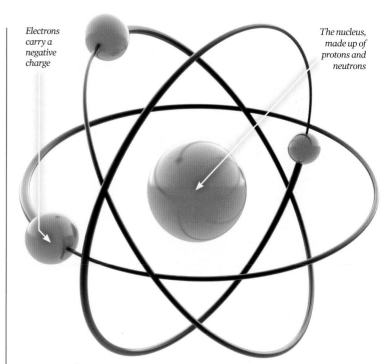

Electrons carry a negative charge

The nucleus, made up of protons and neutrons

What are atoms?

It's the little things in life that make the biggest difference

The big bang has a lot to answer for. The astonishing cosmic forces hypothesised to have created the universe formed all known types of atom. Atoms that have since gone on to do great things; creating stars, planets, us, and indeed the pen and paper used by Russian chemist Dmitri Mendeleev in his 1869 publication of the first universally recognised form of the periodic table, which was essentially a tabular list of the atomic weights of all 117 known chemical elements.

Of course, depending on the way atoms are bonded together they are the very substance of everything we see and know. Just as it's mind-boggling to contemplate the size of the universal macrocosm as we look out into the cosmos, the microcosm is equally astounding.

Atoms are made up of various numbers of protons, neutrons and electrons.

But just like the expanding understanding of the universe, smaller and smaller sub-atomic particles are being discovered all the time. This quest has led particle physicists to build the Large Hadron Collider, a particle accelerator with the primary purpose of smashing atoms with such force as to either confirm or rule out the existence of the Higgs boson, a particle that could explain the origin of the universe's mass.

Atoms hold the key to understanding where it all started; where we're from in the truest sense and therefore render much pre-existing philosophy redundant. Apparently, the answer to life isn't out there as we once thought, it's in here! ✿

> ❝ *Smaller and smaller sub-atomic particles are being discovered all the time* ❞

What exactly is a knee-jerk reaction?

Why does your leg kick out when the doctor taps just below your knee?

Doctors often test the knee-jerk, or patellar reflex, to look for potential neurological problems. Lightly tapping your patellar tendon just below the kneecap stretches the femoral nerve located in your thigh, which in turn causes your thigh muscle (quadriceps) to contract and the lower leg to extend. When struck, impulses travel along a pathway in the dorsal root ganglion, a bundle of nerves in the L4 level of the spinal cord. Reflex actions are performed independently of the brain. This allows them to happen almost instantaneously – in about 50 milliseconds in the case of the knee-jerk reflex. This reflex helps you to maintain balance and posture when you walk, without having to think about every step you take.

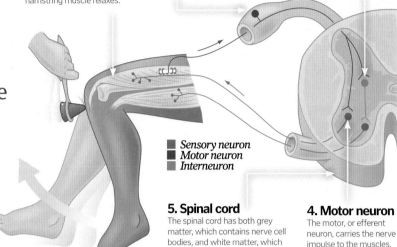

1. Quadriceps and hamstring muscles
The knee-jerk reflex means that the quadriceps muscles contract at the same time the hamstring muscle relaxes.

2. Sensory neuron
The sensory, or afferent neuron, receives an impulse from the femoral nerve.

3. Interneuron
The interneuron provides a connection between the sensory and motor neurons.

■ *Sensory neuron*
■ *Motor neuron*
■ *Interneuron*

5. Spinal cord
The spinal cord has both grey matter, which contains nerve cell bodies, and white matter, which contains the nerve fibres.

4. Motor neuron
The motor, or efferent neuron, carries the nerve impulse to the muscles.

> « *This reflex helps you to maintain balance and posture when you walk* »

Why do we get spots?

Find out what causes pimples to form on the surface of human skin

Pimples are caused by sensitivity to the testosterone hormone present in both males and females, which can trigger the overproduction of an oily substance called sebum. Sebum, which is produced by sebaceous glands attached to hair follicles in the dermis, helps keep hair and skin waterproof.

Your skin is constantly renewing itself, and while new cells are produced in the lower layers of skin, the old dead cells are sloughed away from the surface. This, together with excessive sebum production, can lead to acne and pimples.

Sebum normally travels through the hair follicle to the surface of the skin. However, if a pore becomes blocked by a few dead skin cells that haven't been shed properly, the sebum builds up inside the hair follicle. This oily buildup is a breeding ground for bacteria, which then accumulate and multiply around the area, making the skin inflamed and infected. This results in the pimple.

Whiteheads and blackheads are types of acne pimples known as comedones. Blackheads are open comedones, which means the blockage of sebum is exposed to the air, causing oxidation of the sebum (similar to when an apple browns). Whiteheads, on the other hand, are closed comedones and are not exposed to air as they're covered by a layer of skin.

Inflammation
The trapped sebum attracts bacteria that build up and cause a pustule, which can grow sore and inflamed.

Whitehead
Blockages can occur beneath a layer of skin that prevents air from coming into contact with the sebum which results in it staying white.

Epidermis
Sebum helps slough away the cells on the surface of the skin as they die to make room for the fresh cells generated in the dermis.

Blackhead
When the blockage is nearer the surface, the accumulation of sebum can be exposed to the air, causing oxidation which turns the substance black.

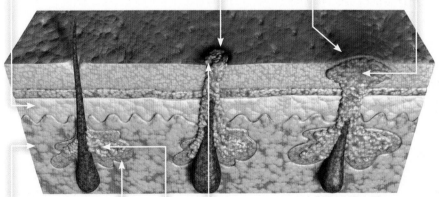

© Science Photo Library

Dermis
New skin cells are created in the lower layers of skin.

Sebaceous gland
Attached to the hair follicle, the sebaceous gland produces an oily, waxy substance called sebum.

Sebum
The sebum travels up the hair follicle to waterproof the hair and protect the surface of the skin.

Blockage
If dead skin cells fail to be shed properly, they can become blocked inside pores. When this happens sebum is plugged behind a barrier, which can lead to a spot forming.

How does the brain think?

The human brain is the most mysterious and complex entity in the known universe

It's a computer, a thinking machine, a fatty pink organ, and a vast collection of neurons – but how does it actually work? The human brain is amazingly complex – in fact, more complex than anything in the known universe. The human brain effortlessly consumes power, stores memories, processes thoughts, and reacts to danger.

In some ways, the human brain is like a car engine. The fuel – which could be the sandwich you had for lunch or a sugar doughnut for breakfast – causes neurons to fire in a logical sequence and to bond with other neurons. This combination of neurons occurs incredibly fast, but the chain reaction might help you compose a symphony or recall entire passages of a book, help you pedal a bike or write an email to a friend.

Scientists are just beginning to understand how these brain neurons work – they have not figured out how they trigger a reaction when you touch a hot stove, for example, or why you can re-generate brain cells when you work out at the gym.

The connections inside a brain are very similar to the internet – the connections are constantly exchanging information. Yet, even the internet is rather simplistic when compared to neurons.

There are ten to 100 neurons, and each one makes thousands of connections. This is how the brain processes information, or determines how to move an arm and grip a surface. These calculations, perceptions, memories, and reactions occur almost instantaneously, and not just a few times per minute, but millions. According to Jim Olds, research director with George Mason University, if the internet were as complex as our solar system, then the brain would be as complex as our galaxy. In other words, we

have a lot to learn. Science has not given up trying, and has made recent discoveries about how we adapt, learn new information, and can actually increase brain capability.

In the most basic sense, our brain is the centre of all input and outputs in the human body. Dr Paula Tallal, a co-director of neuroscience at Rutgers University, says the brain is constantly processing sensory information – even from infancy. "It's easiest to think of the brain in terms of inputs and outputs," says Tallal. "Inputs are sensory information, outputs are how our brain organises that information and controls our motor systems."

Tallal says one of the primary functions of the brain is in learning to predict what comes next. In her research for Scientific Learning, she has found that young children enjoy having the same book read to them again and again because that is how the brain registers acoustic cues that form into phonemes (sounds) to become spoken words.

"We learn to put things together so that they become smooth sequences," she says. These smooth sequences are observable in the brain, interpreting the outside world and making sense of it. The brain is actually a series of interconnected 'superhighways' or pathways that move 'data' from one part of the body to another.

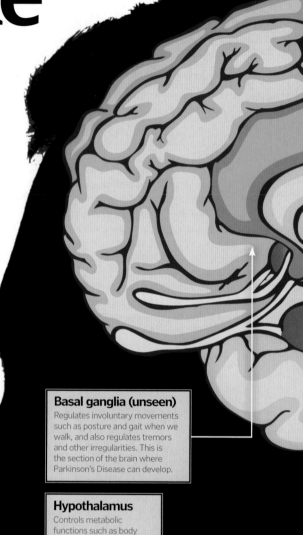

Basal ganglia (unseen)
Regulates involuntary movements such as posture and gait when we walk, and also regulates tremors and other irregularities. This is the section of the brain where Parkinson's Disease can develop.

Hypothalamus
Controls metabolic functions such as body temperature, digestion, breathing, blood pressure, thirst, hunger, sexual drive, pain relays, and also regulates some hormones.

What are the parts of the brain?

According to Olds, there are almost too many to count – perhaps a hundred or more, depending on who you ask. However, there are some key areas that control certain functions and store thoughts and memories.

> " In a sense, the main function of the brain is in ordering information – interpreting the outside world and making sense of it "

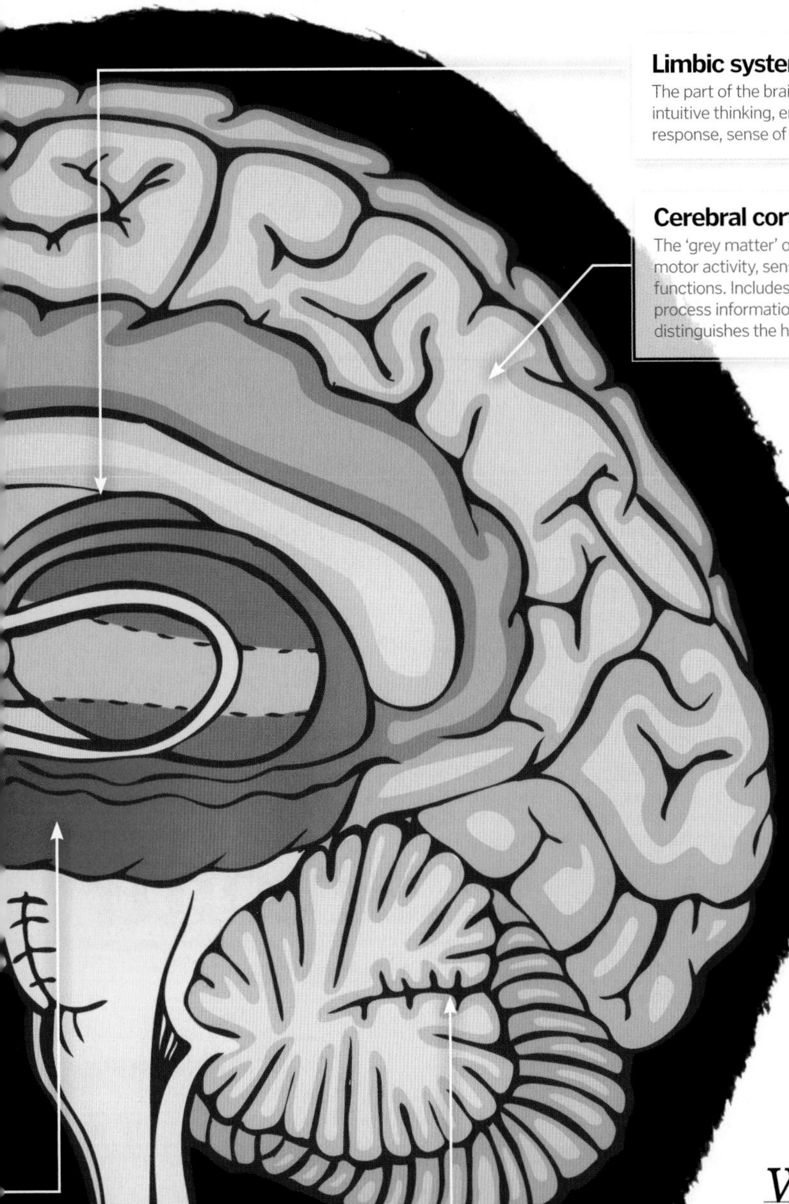

Limbic system

The part of the brain that controls intuitive thinking, emotional response, sense of smell and taste.

Cerebral cortex

The 'grey matter' of the brain controls cognition, motor activity, sensation, and other higher level functions. Includes the association areas which help process information. These association areas are what distinguishes the human brain from other brains.

> " *This combination of neurons might help you compose a symphony or pedal a bike* "

Tallal says another way to think about the brain is by lower and upper areas. The spinal cord moves information up to the brain stem, then up into the cerebral cortex which controls thoughts and memories.

Interestingly, the brain really does work like a powerful computer in determining not only movements but registering memories that can be quickly recalled.

According to Dr Robert Melillo, a neurologist and the founder of the Brain Balance Centers (www. brainbalancecenters.com), the brain actually predetermines actions and calculates the results about a half-second before performing them (or even faster in some cases). This means, when you reach out to open a door, your brain has already predetermined how to move your elbow and clasp your hand – maybe even simulated this movement more than once, before you even perform the action.

Another interesting aspect to the brain is that there are some voluntary movements and some involuntary. Some sections of the brain might control a voluntary movement – such as patting your knee to a beat. Another section controls involuntary movements, such as the gait of your walk – which is passed down from your parents. Reflexes, long-term memories, the pain reflex... they are all controlled by sections in the brain. ✿

Cerebellum

Consists of two cerebral hemispheres that control motor activity, the planning of movements, co-ordination, and other body functions. This section of the brain weighs about 200 grams (compared to 1,300 grams for the main cortex).

What role does the cerebral cortex play?

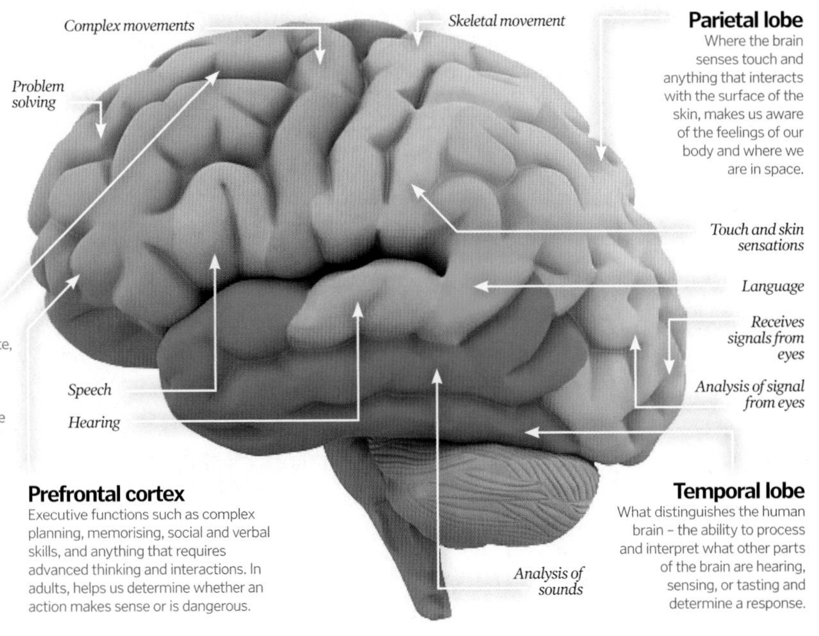

Complex movements

Problem solving

Skeletal movement

Parietal lobe

Where the brain senses touch and anything that interacts with the surface of the skin, makes us aware of the feelings of our body and where we are in space.

Touch and skin sensations

Language

Receives signals from eyes

Analysis of signal from eyes

Frontal lobe

Primarily controls senses such as taste, hearing, and smell. Association areas might help us determine language and the tone of someone's voice.

Speech

Hearing

Prefrontal cortex

Executive functions such as complex planning, memorising, social and verbal skills, and anything that requires advanced thinking and interactions. In adults, helps us determine whether an action makes sense or is dangerous.

Analysis of sounds

Temporal lobe

What distinguishes the human brain – the ability to process and interpret what other parts of the brain are hearing, sensing, or tasting and determine a response.

What's a neuron?

Neurons fire like electrical circuits

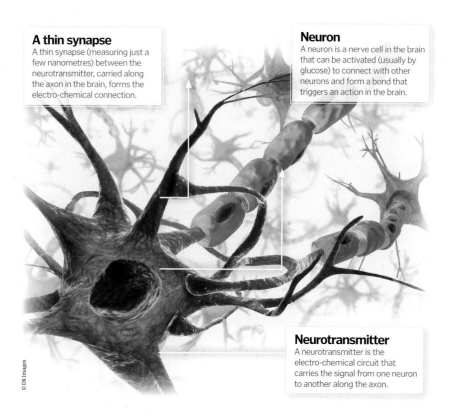

A thin synapse
A thin synapse (measuring just a few nanometres) between the neurotransmitter, carried along the axon in the brain, forms the electro-chemical connection.

Neuron
A neuron is a nerve cell in the brain that can be activated (usually by glucose) to connect with other neurons and form a bond that triggers an action in the brain.

Neurotransmitter
A neurotransmitter is the electro-chemical circuit that carries the signal from one neuron to another along the axon.

© DK Images

Neurons are a kind of cell in the brain (humans have many cells in the body, including fat cells, kidney cells, and gland cells). A neuron is essentially like a hub that works with nearby neurons to generate an electrical and chemical charge. Dr Likosky of the Swedish Medical Institute says another way of thinking about neurons is that they are like a basketball and the connections (called axons) are like electrical wires that connect to other neurons. This creates a kind of circuit in the human body.

Dr Paula Tallal explained that input from the five senses in the body causes neurons to fire: "The more often a collection of neurons are stimulated together in time, the more likely they are to bind together and the easier and easier it becomes for that pattern of neurons to fire in synchrony as well as sequentially."

How important is the spinal cord?

It's actually part of the brain and plays a major role in how your body works

Scientists have known for the past 100 years or so that the spinal cord is actually part of the brain. According to Dr Melillo, while the brain has grey matter on the outside (protected by the skull) and protected white matter on the inside, the spinal cord is the reverse: the grey matter is inside the spinal cord and the white matter is outside.

Grey matter cells
Grey matter cells in the spinal cord cannot regenerate, which is why people with a serious spinal cord injury cannot recover over time. White matter cells can regenerate.

White matter cells
White matter cells in the spinal cord carry the electro-chemical pulses up to the brain. For example, when you are kicked in the shin, you feel the pain in the shin and your brain then tells you to move your hand to cover that area.

Neuroplasticity
In the spinal cord and in the brain, cells can rejuvenate over time when you exercise and become strengthened. This process is called neuroplasticity.

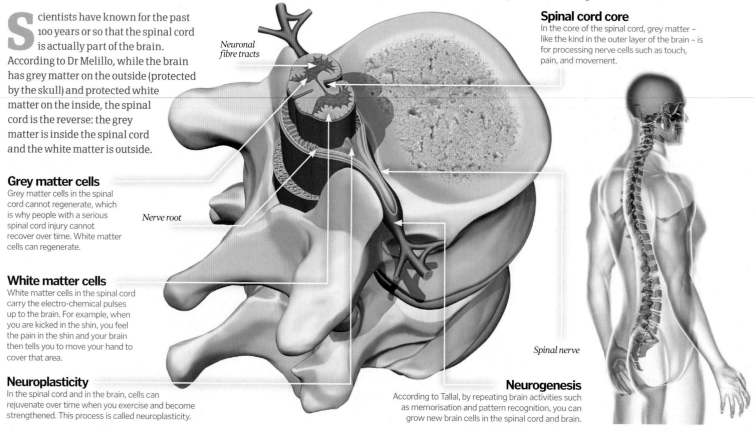

Neuronal fibre tracts

Nerve root

Spinal cord core
In the core of the spinal cord, grey matter – like the kind in the outer layer of the brain – is for processing nerve cells such as touch, pain, and movement.

Spinal nerve

Neurogenesis
According to Tallal, by repeating brain activities such as memorisation and pattern recognition, you can grow new brain cells in the spinal cord and brain.

What's inside a nerve?

"Nerves are the transmission cables that carry brain waves in the human body," says Sol Diamond, an assistant professor at the Thayer School of Engineering at Dartmouth. According to Diamond, nerves communicate these signals from one point to another, whether from your toenail up to your brain or from the side of your head.

Nerve transmissions

Some nerve transmissions travel great distances through the human body, others travel short distances – both use a de-polarisation to create the circuit. De-polarisation is like a wound-up spring that releases stored energy once triggered.

Nerve triggers

When many neurons are activated together at the same time, the nerve is excited – this is when we might feel the sensation of touch or a distinct smell.

Myelinated and unmyelinated

Some nerves are myelinated (or insulated) with fatty tissue that appears white and forms a slower connection over a longer distance. Others are un-myelinated and are un-insulated. These nerves travel shorter distances.

How do patches help smokers?

Quitting smoking is tough, but the nicotine patch can wean people off cigarettes

Transdermal patches are non-invasive medicated sticking plasters that are used daily to dispense a steady dose of medication through the skin and into the bloodstream. Nicotine is the addictive element of a cigarette that makes you want to keep smoking.

While a cigarette delivers the nicotine that a smoker craves straight to their brain, this nicotine fix can be replaced with a much lower dose that can be released slower to reduce the cravings associated with trying to give up smoking, and without chemicals found in tobacco smoke. The drug is sandwiched in a reservoir between an impermeable backing layer and an adhesive permeable membrane that sticks to the skin.

Although our skin is designed to keep chemicals out, the molecules of the drug used in a patch are so tiny they can permeate it. The drug is diffused from the reservoir to a drug-release membrane and adhesive membrane, then from the adhesive membrane to the outer-most layer of skin. The drug is taken up by the capillaries and takes effect on the brain. ✿

The patch
A small disc measuring about 2.5cm in diameter.

Backing layer
The impenetrable backing layer forms a barrier, preventing the drug from leaking.

Drug-release membrane
This component controls the rate at which nicotine passes through the membranes to the skin.

Microscopic nicotine
Nicotine is a liquid, which means it can penetrate the skin. The amount of nicotine in the compound can be between 5-50 per cent. The drug is stored in a reservoir between the backing and the membranes.

Adhesive membrane
The adhesive used must be medicated, pressure-sensitive, non-irritating, water-resistant and cohesive. It should be resilient enough that it doesn't degrade.

How do glow sticks glow?

What's going on inside these popular light sticks?

Inside a glow stick is a thin glass vial containing chemicals. When you bend the stick you're breaking this vial open, releasing the chemicals into the rest of the glow stick, where other chemicals react with them and release light.

Some chemical reactions produce light, known as 'chemiluminescence'. Usually the vial contains a solution phenyl oxalate ester and a fluorescent dye – which will determine the colour of the glow stick – while the surrounding tube contains a solution of hydrogen peroxide. Mixing these compounds causes the electrons to rise to a higher energy level and return to their normal state, releasing energy as light as they do. ✿

1. Snap
When the glow stick is bent or snapped, the glass vial breaks and releases its chemicals into the surrounding chemical-containing tube.

2. Oxidise
The phenyl oxalate ester in the vial is oxidised by the hydrogen peroxide in the tube, producing a chemical called 'phenol' and unstable peroxyacid ester.

3. Decompose
The unstable peroxyacid ester decomposes, which creates additional phenol and another peroxy compound, which decomposes to carbon dioxide.

4. Energy
The decomposition to carbon dioxide releases energy into the dye, which causes the electrons in the atoms to move to a higher energy level.

5. Light
The electrons will then fall back down to their original energy level by releasing this additional gained energy in the form of light.

Why do boomerangs come back?

Learn the principles that make this flying stick return to sender

A boomerang is basically a single-winged aircraft propelled through the air by hand. Boomerangs have two 'wings' joined in a V-shape. Both wings have an airfoil-shaped cross-section just like an aircraft wing. An airfoil is flat on one side but curved on the other with one edge thicker than the other – this helps the boomerang stay in the air due to lift.

Lift is generated as the air flowing up over the curved side of the wing has further to travel than the air flowing past the flat side. The air moving over the curved surface must therefore travel quicker in order to reach the other edge of the wing.

Because the two sides of a boomerang have different air speeds flowing over them, as it spins the aerodynamic forces acting upon it are uneven. This causes the section of the boomerang moving in the same direction as the direction of forward motion to move faster through the air than the section moving in the opposite direction. These uneven forces make the boomerang start to turn in and follow a circular route, eventually heading back to the thrower. ✿

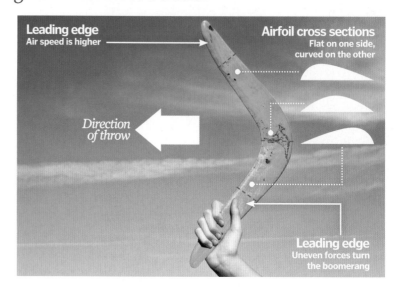

Leading edge
Air speed is higher

Airfoil cross sections
Flat on one side, curved on the other

Direction of throw

Leading edge
Uneven forces turn the boomerang

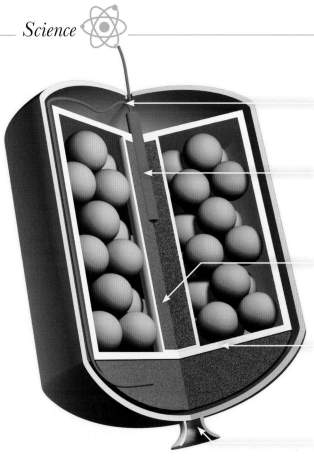

1. Fuse
The first fuse sets everything in motion. After the shell is in the mortar, the fuse is lit and the flame makes its way to the lifting charge.

3. Time-delayed fuse
While the shell soars up into the air, the time-delayed fuse continues to burn, buying enough time to get the shell at its highest point before reaching the bursting charge.

4. Bursting charge
The bursting charge is more black powder, stored higher up the shell. Once the time-delayed fuse reaches the bursting charge, the combustion sets off the stars.

5. Stars
The stars begin their heat-induced chemical reactions. The shell can no longer contain the power of the combustion, and the stars are sent flying, creating the traditional fireworks shapes.

2. Lifting charge
Black powder (also called gunpowder) is ignited by the fuse, and the explosion can send a shell up to 1,000 feet into the air.

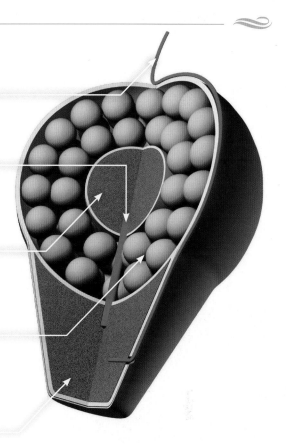

Italian-style shell
Creates more elaborate bursts

Oriental-style shell
Produces spherical bursts

How do fireworks explode?

These bright and festive chemistry experiments have been delighting people for hundreds of years

Despite their different colours, shapes, speeds and sounds, all fireworks have the same basic components. Aerial fireworks consist of a shell made of heavy paper that holds the 'lift charge', the 'bursting charge', and the 'stars'. All of these glittery spectacles come from good old-fashioned combustion.

Combustion is a chemical reaction between two substances (a fuel and an oxidant) that produces light and heat. The heat causes gasses to expand rapidly, building pressure. The shells are tightly wrapped cylinders, which provide good resistance to this pressure, giving it a short time to build in intensity. Then, when the reaction overpowers the shell, you get the explosive firework effect.

It all starts when the shell is placed into a mortar (a cylinder the same size as the shell, which holds the firework in place while the fuse burns). The lift charge, at the bottom of the shell, is basically concentrated black powder (charcoal, sulphur, and potassium nitrate).

When lit by the dangling fuse, the lift charge sends the shell into the air. Basic firecrackers are just paper-covered black powder: you light the fuse and listen to the popping sound. The bursting charge is another round of black powder with its own time-delayed fuse higher up in the shell. The bursting charge creates the heat to activate the stars that surround it and explode them outward from the shell. The stars are where the magic happens.

What makes the colours?

Colours involve different measurements and combinations of oxygen producers, fuels, binders, and colour producers. You can make colour through incandescence – light created through heat (orange, red, white), or luminescence – light created from a chemical reaction without extreme heat (blue, green). It's all about temperature control and balance.

- **Orange** – *Calcium*
- **Red** – *Strontium and lithium*
- **Gold** – *Incandescence of iron, charcoal or lampblack*
- **Yellow** – *Sodium*
- **Electric white** – *Magnesium or aluminium*
- **Green** – *Barium plus a chlorine producer*
- **Blue** – *Copper plus a chlorine producer*
- **Purple** – *Strontium plus copper*
- **Silver** – *Aluminium, titanium or magnesium powder/flakes*

Stars are balls made up of fuels, oxidisers, colour-creating combinations of different kinds of metals, and a binder to hold everything together. The stars can be arranged within the firework shell to create shapes. The shapes can be things like hearts, stars, and circles. Hundreds of stars can be used in a single firework shell.

More complex fireworks – ones that produce a shape like a smiley face, have multiple phases of different colours, or make extra sounds like whistles, for example – have shells with a more intricate infrastructure. In these types of fireworks, there are more time-delayed fuses linked to various bursting charges with their own surrounding stars. Each of these may sit in its own individual interior shell. These are called 'multi-break shells'.

While a sight to behold, fireworks are individually wrapped chemistry experiments. Tapping one too hard or creating a static electricity shock with your synthetic-material clothing could be deadly and one exploding near to your face could result in horrific burns and even blindness. They don't have the word 'fire' in them for nothing.

How does our vision work?

An eye-opening look at how we see…

The biology of the eye is extremely complex, especially when you consider that the human eye only has the rough diameter of 2.54cm and weighs approximately 7.5 grams. It is made up of around 15 distinct parts, which all have different roles to play in receiving light into the eye and transmitting the electrical impulses, which ultimately relay image information to our brains, out of the eye, so that we can perceive the world we live in.

The eye is often compared to a basic camera, and indeed the very first camera was designed with the concept of the eye in mind. We can reduce the complex process that occurs to process light into vision within the eye to a relatively basic sequence of events. First, light passes through the cornea, which refracts the light so that it enters the eye in the right direction, and aqueous humour, into the main body of the eye through the pupil. The iris contracts to control pupil size and this limits the amount of light that is let through into the eye so that light-sensitive parts of the eye are not damaged.

The pupil can vary in size between 2mm and 8mm, increasing to allow up to 30 times more light in than the minimum. The light is then passed through the lens, which further refracts the light, which then travels through the vitreous humour to the back of the eye and is reflected onto the retina, the centre point of which is the macula.

The retina is where the rods and cones are situated, rods being responsible for vision when low levels of light are present and cones being responsible for colour vision and specific detail. Rods are far more numerous as more cells are needed to react in low levels of light and are situated around the focal point of cones. This focal gathering of cones is collectively called the fovea, which is situated within the macula. All the light information that has been received by the eye is then converted into electrical impulses by a chemical in the retina called rhodopsin, also known as purple visual, and the impulses are then transmitted through the optic nerve to the brain where they are perceived as 'vision'. The eye moves to allow a range of vision of approximately 180 degrees and to do this it has four primary muscles which control the movement of the eyeball. These allow the eye to move up and down and across, while restricting movement so that the eye does not rotate back into the socket. ✿

2. Optic nerve
After the retina has processed light into electrical impulses, the optic nerve transports this information to the brain.

1. Retina
The retina is the light-sensitive area which processes light admitted into the eye and converts it into electrical impulses which are transmitted to the brain via the optic nerve.

Rods and cones

Rods are the light-sensitive cells in our eyes that aid our vision in low levels of light. Rods are blind to colour and only transmit information mainly in black and white to the brain. They are far more numerous with around 120 million rods present in every human eye compared to around 7 million cones. Cones are responsible for perceiving colour and specific detail. Cones are primarily focused in the fovea, the central area of the macula whereas rods mainly surround the outside of the retina. Cones work much better in daylight as light is needed to perceive colour and detail.

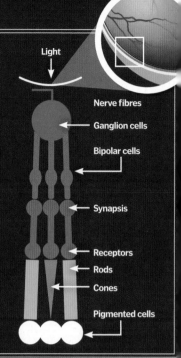

Light

Nerve fibres
Ganglion cells
Bipolar cells
Synapsis
Receptors
Rods
Cones
Pigmented cells

4. Lens
The lens is a transparent disc in the eye which, with the cornea, refracts light that enters the eye so that it is received by the retina.

3. Sclera
This is the fibrous, white exterior of the eye that is an important protective layer for the more delicate insides of the eye.

6. Cornea
The cornea is a transparent layer, covering the pupil, iris and aqueous humour. It helps refract the light towards the retina so that light is received in the correct area.

5. Iris
The iris is the coloured part of the eye which contracts to control the level of light admitted into the eye. The hole which light enters through is called the pupil.

How do we see in colour?

Colour is not actually inherent in any object. We only see colour because objects absorb some colour from light, and reflect others. It is the reflected ones that we see and that give an object a set 'colour'. Therefore, for example, grass is not green, it purely absorbs all other colours in light and reflects back green. I an object reflects all colours we will see it as white, if it absorbs all colours we see it as black. We use cones to perceive colour as rods are blind to colour.

The pupil can vary in size between 2mm and 8mm, increasing to allow up to 30 times more light in than the minimum

What makes chillies hot?

The secret behind the fiery fruit

There's a kind of machismo attached to eating the spiciest food known to man, and there's a reason so many people enjoy the powerful flavours associated with chilli peppers.

The tingling sensation on the tongue when you try a chilli is caused by a substance called capsaicin, which tricks the brain into thinking you're burning. The body then secretes natural painkilling chemicals called endorphins, which send out a rush of pleasure. The heat of a chilli, also referred to as its piquancy, is measured in Scoville heat units (SHU), after Wilbur Scoville who developed a hotness test for chillies in 1912. His scale measured the concentration of capsaicin found in a chilli by taking chilli extract and diluting it in water until a human taste test panel could no longer detect any heat from the solution.

The problem with Scoville's scale was that it relied on subjectivity, so today hotness is calculated using liquid chromatography to identify the concentration of heat-producing chemicals in chillies.

Which are the hottest chillies?

1. Dorset Naga
Heat rating: 923,000 SHU
Facts: Related to the Scotch bonnet, this devilishly hot chilli is grown in polytunnels by a couple in Dorset.

2. Red Savina habanero
Heat rating: 577,000 SHU
Facts: According to the *Guinness Book Of World Records*, this was the world's hottest chilli until 2006.

3. Scotch bonnet
Heat rating: 100,000-325,000 SHU
Facts: Used mainly in Caribbean cuisine, the Scotch bonnet is a small chilli similar to the habanero.

What's inside a hand sanitiser?

How do these cleansers keep your hands germ free without soap and water?

Unlike hand washing with soap and water, hand sanitisers are designed to cleanse hands of potentially damaging bacteria, rather than mainly dirt and detritus. Hand sanitiser dispensers deliver gel, foam or liquid solutions in which the active ingredients include isopropanol, ethanol, n-propanol and povidone-iodine. These alcohol bases are then added to a host of non-active ingredients such as plant oils, thickening agents and scent enhancers.

The alcohol base is the key for keeping your hands clean, killing 99.9 per cent of bacteria, fungi and some viruses within 30 seconds of application. As such, the dispensers are considered antiseptic devices that can be used to avoid the transmission of pathogens, and are installed in hospitals to reduce the chance of spreading infectious diseases like tuberculosis. Less common, non-alcohol-based hand sanitisers use other active agents, such as the biocide benzalkonium chloride and the organic compound triclosan, to kill germs.

© Kenn Kiser

Why do we sweat?

As your doctor may tell you, it's glandular...

Sweat is produced by dedicated sweat glands, and is a mechanism used primarily by the body to reduce its internal temperature. There are two types of sweat gland in the human body, the eccrine gland and the apocrine gland. The former regulates body temperature, and is the primary source of excreted sweat, with the latter only secreting under emotional stresses, rather than those involved with body dehydration.

Eccrine sweat glands are controlled by the sympathetic nervous system and, when the internal temperature of the body rises, secrete a salty, water-based substance to the skin's surface. This liquid then cools the skin and the body through evaporation, storing and then transferring excess heat into the atmosphere.

Both the eccrine and apocrine sweat glands only appear in mammals and, if active over the majority of the animal's body, act as the primary thermoregulatory device. Certain mammals such as dogs, cats and sheep only have eccrine glands in specific areas – such as paws and lips – warranting the need to pant to control their temperature.

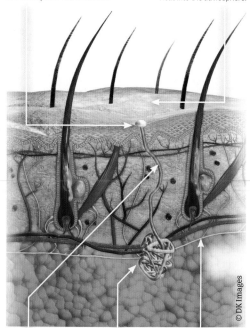

Pore
Sweat is released directly into the dermis via the secretary duct, which then filters through the skin's pores to the surface.

Skin
Once the sweat is on the skin's surface, its absorbed moisture evaporates, transferring the heat into the atmosphere.

© DK Images

Secretary duct
Secreted sweat travels up to the skin via this duct.

Secretary part
This is where the majority of the gland's secretary cells are located.

Nerve fibres
Deliver messages to glands to produce sweat when the body's temp rises.

> *This liquid cools the skin and the body through evaporation, storing and then transferring heat into the atmosphere*

How does diabetes work?

What is this metabolic condition and how is it controlled?

After eating food, our bodies naturally secrete a hormone called insulin into the blood, which enables us to turn the sugar (glucose) from food into energy. Diabetes mellitus is a long-term metabolic disorder caused by an inability to produce this hormone. This leads to excessive glucose remaining in the blood, where it cannot be used for energy. Insulin, which is produced in the pancreas, lowers blood sugar levels by turning glucose into glycogen for storage in the body's cells (liver, muscles and fat) where it can be broken down into energy. The other hormone produced in the pancreas is glucagon, which does the reverse. If there's too little glucose in the blood, glucagon stimulates the body to release glucose from the liver into the blood, raising the blood sugar level.

There are two main types of diabetes, called type one and type two. Depending upon the type from which the individual suffers, they will either need to take insulin injections for the rest of their lives, or closely control their blood sugar levels through a strict diet respectively.

Of the two main types of diabetes, type one – also known as 'insulin dependent' diabetes – is by far the least common, occurring in just 10 per cent of diabetics in the UK. Type one diabetics do not produce their own insulin, so they must inject themselves with the correct dose of the hormone in order to get it into their blood stream. This type usually occurs in children and before the age of 40.

Type two diabetes is far more prevalent. People with this condition are known as 'insulin resistant', because they either do not produce enough insulin (which encourages the liver to release its stored glucose into the blood) or their cells don't react to it in the way they should. Type two diabetes can be controlled through healthy eating and closely monitoring blood sugar levels, but often tablet medication may also need to be taken. Overweight people are more at risk of developing type two diabetes, because fat around the belly releases chemicals that disrupt the metabolic system. ✿

Pancreas
As well as producing digestive enzymes the pancreas also secretes the hormones insulin and glucagon, which regulate blood glucose levels.

Digestive enzymes
Digestive enzymes pass from the pancreas through the pancreatic duct and into the intestine for the breakdown of food.

Beta cells
The beta cells in the pancreas secrete insulin into a capillary to the blood stream, turning glucose into glycogen to reduce blood glucose levels.

Alpha cells
These cells secrete glucagon, which turns glycogen into glucose to increase blood glucose levels.

Islet of Langerhans
Groups of hormone-making cells – alpha and beta – gather in the pancreas. These cells are collectively called the Islets of Langerhans.

© Science Photo Library

How does the pancreas produce insulin?

The pancreas is a long, tapered gland located deep inside the abdomen, behind the stomach. Not only does this organ produce enzymes for the breakdown of food during digestion, it also produces the hormones insulin and glucagon, which regulate the body's blood sugar levels if they get too high or too low. After eating, when blood sugar levels are high, insulin causes the cells in the body to absorb glucose for fuel, thereby bringing the level of sugar in the blood down. After exercising or going without food, however, blood sugar levels will be low and so the body stimulates the release of glucose stored in the liver in order to raise it.

In diabetics the pancreas is either not producing insulin, or the body cannot use it properly. Subsequently the body's blood sugar levels rise dangerously high as unused sugar accumulates in the blood and urine.

> ❝ *Overweight people are more at risk of developing type 2 diabetes, because fat around the belly releases chemicals that disrupt the metabolic system* ❞

What's inside your nervous system?

Lovely as you may be, you could be considered an organisation of not especially talented cells

Like any organisation, your success depends on communication between your individual members. In a sense, you actually are this communication, since it is the magic that makes you a single, clever creature. Your built-in communications network, known as the nervous system, perceives the outside world, keeps all body parts working in harmony, and forms the thoughts and memories that make you unique.

The nervous system comprises hundreds of billions of specialised cells called neurons. A typical neuron consists of a compact cell body, protruding filaments called dendrites, and a long single fibre called an axon. The axon can transmit signals to other neurons and to muscle cells, while the dendrite can receive signals from other neurons and sensory cells. A neuron's axon may extend across the brain or body and branch off hundreds of times.

When something excites a neuron, the cell body will send an electrical charge down the length of an axon, triggering axon terminals to release chemicals called neurotransmitters. These neurotransmitters can travel to receptors on dendrites of an adjoining neuron, across a small gap called a synapse. Depending on the type of neurotransmitter and receptor, the signal may excite the adjoining neuron to fire an electrical charge down its own axon, or the signal may inhibit the neuron from firing. The complex connections and signal patterns among the hundreds of billions of neurons in your brain form thoughts, memories and all other mental activities.

Similarly, axons that extend out from your brain and spinal column into your body can release neurotransmitters to trigger muscle movement and organ activity. This is how your brain controls the rest of your body. Neurons also carry signals from the body back to the brain. You perceive sights, sounds, smells and taste when sensory cells in your eyes, mouth, nose and ears excite nearby neurons. The neurons send an electrical signal up to the brain, which interprets them. Sensory neurons near your skin and other parts of the body fire an electric signal in response to pressure, which your brain perceives as the sense of touch.

> **Like any organisation, your success depends on communication between your individual members**

1. Cerebellum
Latin for "little brain," the cerebellum co-ordinates and fine-tunes skilled movements, based on incoming sensory information. It's also involved in maintaining balance and posture.

2. Facial nerve
Branching sensory fibres run to the taste buds and the front of the tongue, while motor nerves connected to your salivary glands and muscles form facial expressions.

3. Vagus nerve
A critical nerve running from the brain to the neck, throat, chest and abdomen, the vagus is key to controlling your heart rate, swallowing, digestion and respiration.

4. Ganglion
Bundles of tightly packed neurons that serve as key connection hubs in the body's complex network of nerves.

5. Spinal cord
A bundle of long axons that run from the brain to the lower spinal column, forming the key connection between the brain and body.

6. Radial nerve
A nerve that carries muscle motor commands that move your elbow, wrist and fingers.

7. Ulnar nerve
A key nerve involved in bending your fingers and wrist.

8. Lumbar plexus
A plexus is a point where many spinal nerves intersect. The lumbar plexus is the meeting point for nerves controlling the abdomen, lower back, and legs.

How does our automatic nervous system keep us running?

The automatic nervous system (ANS) works behind the scenes to keep your body running smoothly. The ANS is part of your peripheral nervous system, made up of sensory nerve fibres that constantly relay information about the state of your body and the motor nerves that relay commands from the brain and spinal cord to various glands, the involuntary smooth muscles in organs and blood vessels, and the cardiac muscles that control your heart.

The ANS's chief function is homeostasis – adjusting bodily processes to maintain internal stability. The ANS does this through two opposing, yet complementary sub-systems: the sympathetic division and parasympathetic division. The sympathetic division is like the accelerator in your car. The motor neurons excite your body, by increasing your heart rate and producing stress hormones, among other things. The parasympathetic division is like the brakes. The motor neurons can relax your body, by doing things like decreasing heart rate, constricting the trachea and bronchial tubes, and relaxing the bladder sphincter.

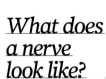
What does a nerve look like?

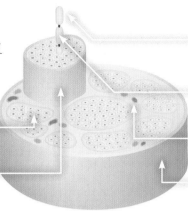

Nerve fascicle
A bundle of axons.

Perineurium
Sheath of connective tissue that protects each fascicle.

Axon
The neural fibre that carries electrical signals representing motor commands and sensory information.

Myelin sheath
Fatty insulation that keeps axons from short-circuiting.

Blood vessels
Supply of blood that provides neurons with energy.

Epineurium
Outer connective tissue that protects the nerve.

Why is the funny bone not at all funny?

Most of the larger nerves in your body are insulated by muscle, bones and tissue. The big exception is the ulnar nerve, which runs down your arm, by way of your elbow. The nerve carries motor commands to your ring and pinkie fingers and relays sensory information back to the central nervous system. If you bang your elbow, the humerus bone bumps the nerve, jarring the axons inside, which your brain interprets as a tingling sensation.

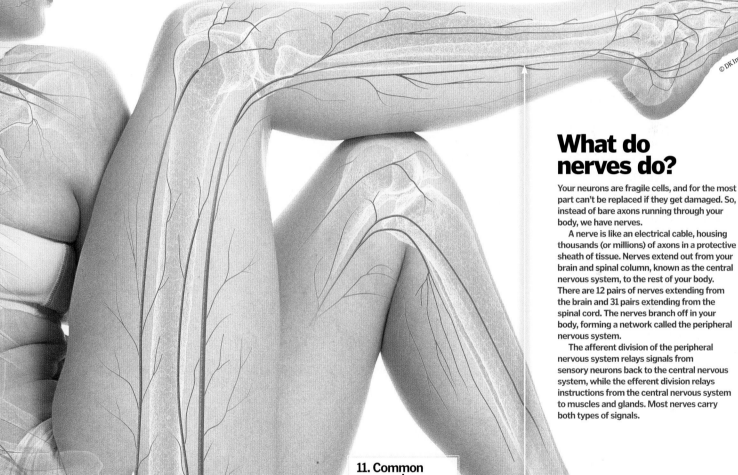

© DK Images

What do nerves do?

Your neurons are fragile cells, and for the most part can't be replaced if they get damaged. So, instead of bare axons running through your body, we have nerves.

A nerve is like an electrical cable, housing thousands (or millions) of axons in a protective sheath of tissue. Nerves extend out from your brain and spinal column, known as the central nervous system, to the rest of your body. There are 12 pairs of nerves extending from the brain and 31 pairs extending from the spinal cord. The nerves branch off in your body, forming a network called the peripheral nervous system.

The afferent division of the peripheral nervous system relays signals from sensory neurons back to the central nervous system, while the efferent division relays instructions from the central nervous system to muscles and glands. Most nerves carry both types of signals.

11. Common peroneal nerve
Connects to muscles in your lower leg, which lift your foot.

10. Sciatic nerve
Your longest nerve, which carries motor signals to muscles that bend your leg.

9. Femoral nerve
A key nerve with many smaller nerve branches that carry motor commands to leg muscles, as well as sensory information from the thigh and lower leg.

What's inside the heart?

Your heart is a turbocharged double-pumping muscle that beats more than 40 million times every year

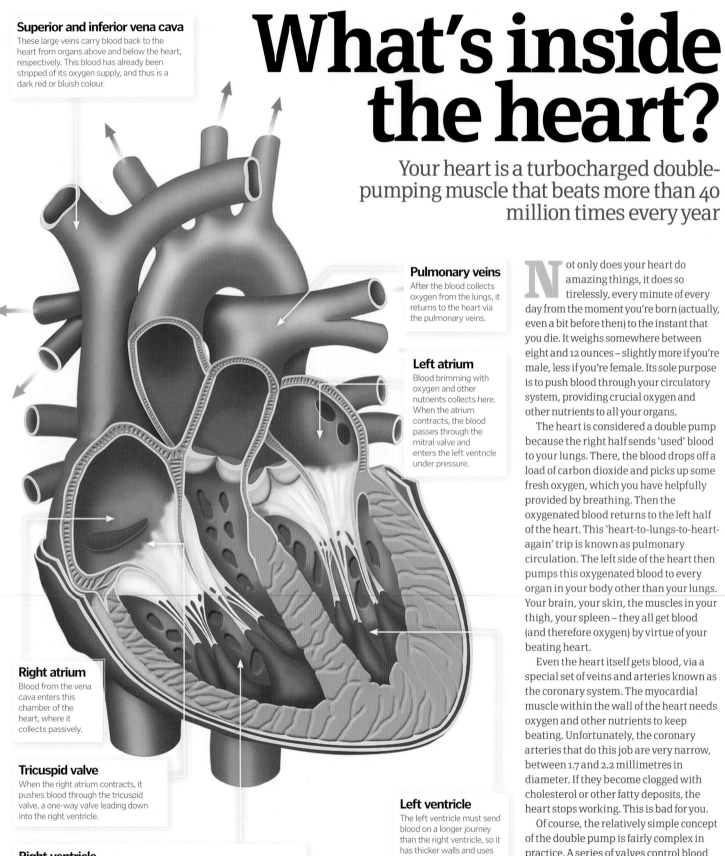

Superior and inferior vena cava
These large veins carry blood back to the heart from organs above and below the heart, respectively. This blood has already been stripped of its oxygen supply, and thus is a dark red or bluish colour.

Pulmonary veins
After the blood collects oxygen from the lungs, it returns to the heart via the pulmonary veins.

Left atrium
Blood brimming with oxygen and other nutrients collects here. When the atrium contracts, the blood passes through the mitral valve and enters the left ventricle under pressure.

Right atrium
Blood from the vena cava enters this chamber of the heart, where it collects passively.

Tricuspid valve
When the right atrium contracts, it pushes blood through the tricuspid valve, a one-way valve leading down into the right ventricle.

Left ventricle
The left ventricle must send blood on a longer journey than the right ventricle, so it has thicker walls and uses about three times as much energy. Luckily, the left atrium's contraction gives the left ventricle's output a 20 per cent boost.

Right ventricle
Blood enters the right ventricle under pressure from the atrium's contraction, giving it a boost much like the turbocharger in a high-performance car. The ventricle contracts and pumps blood through the pulmonary valve, into the pulmonary artery and toward the lungs.

Not only does your heart do amazing things, it does so tirelessly, every minute of every day from the moment you're born (actually, even a bit before then) to the instant that you die. It weighs somewhere between eight and 12 ounces – slightly more if you're male, less if you're female. Its sole purpose is to push blood through your circulatory system, providing crucial oxygen and other nutrients to all your organs.

The heart is considered a double pump because the right half sends 'used' blood to your lungs. There, the blood drops off a load of carbon dioxide and picks up some fresh oxygen, which you have helpfully provided by breathing. Then the oxygenated blood returns to the left half of the heart. This 'heart-to-lungs-to-heart-again' trip is known as pulmonary circulation. The left side of the heart then pumps this oxygenated blood to every organ in your body other than your lungs. Your brain, your skin, the muscles in your thigh, your spleen – they all get blood (and therefore oxygen) by virtue of your beating heart.

Even the heart itself gets blood, via a special set of veins and arteries known as the coronary system. The myocardial muscle within the wall of the heart needs oxygen and other nutrients to keep beating. Unfortunately, the coronary arteries that do this job are very narrow, between 1.7 and 2.2 millimetres in diameter. If they become clogged with cholesterol or other fatty deposits, the heart stops working. This is bad for you.

Of course, the relatively simple concept of the double pump is fairly complex in practice. A series of valves control blood flow to the heart's four chambers, allow for the build-up of enough blood pressure to get the job done, and direct the blood to the correct veins and arteries. ◉

What makes paint dry?

Pivotal to its application, the drying mechanism of paint tells us much about its formulation

The majority of paints dry through evaporation, a process that allows its pigmentation to be set onto a chosen surface purely by being exposed to the surrounding atmosphere. However, the drying process can vary and is often complicated and altered between different paint types.

Paints usually contain three key components: pigments, binders and additives. Pigments are dry, insoluble powders that by wavelength-selective absorption (ie they only reflect certain wavelengths) change the colour of reflected or transmitted light, giving paint its colourisation. They can be ascertained either naturally or produced synthetically.

The pigments of paint are given their paint structure by binders, synthetic or natural resins such as acrylics, polyesters or oils that impart adhesion and influence durability and flexibility. Crucially, though, binders can also play a role in how paint dries, curing it as well as supplying it with adhesion. It is important to note that curing is a different process to drying – which, as mentioned before, is caused by evaporation of a solvent – with cure adhesion attained by polymerisation (molecules bonding together in a chemical reaction). Binders are arguably the key component of paint, as without them it would never stick to a surface long enough to dry.

Finally, paint additives help to conjoin the other components and aid application, structure and drying. Certain additives are often used as catalysts for polymerisation, while others are included to prevent the clumping of paint or in order to alter its viscosity. ✿

How do blood transfusions work?

Whether it's a patient haemorrhaging to death or a 'top up' for life-long diseases, blood transfusions are vital procedures

A blood transfusion takes place when a patient is given components of blood from a donor when their own blood levels are too low. Having enough blood is essential because it carries oxygen around the body and returns carbon dioxide to the lungs to be exhaled as a waste product.

When a doctor decides a patient needs blood, they are 'cross-matched' with donor blood. A few millilitres of their blood is collected into a small bottle which must be hand-labelled to prevent confusion between patients. In the lab the blood is matched with donor blood of the same group (either A, B or O). The unit of donor blood is then transfused via a drip into the patient's vein over two to three hours.

During this time the nurse keeps close observation of the patient to look for transfusion reactions. These can be mild (such as a fever, chills or a rash), which are solved by slowing down the rate of flow, to severe, life-threatening allergic reactions. ✿

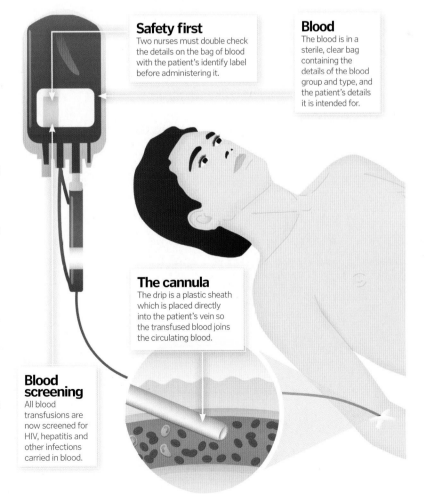

Safety first
Two nurses must double check the details on the bag of blood with the patient's identify label before administering it.

Blood
The blood is in a sterile, clear bag containing the details of the blood group and type, and the patient's details it is intended for.

The cannula
The drip is a plastic sheath which is placed directly into the patient's vein so the transfused blood joins the circulating blood.

Blood screening
All blood transfusions are now screened for HIV, hepatitis and other infections carried in blood.

What's in your blood?

RED BLOOD CELLS
Red blood cells are the most abundant cells in blood and give it a red colour. They carry oxygen from the lungs around the body, bound to a protein called haemoglobin.

PLASMA
Plasma is a straw-coloured watery fluid that carries all of the cells and proteins in blood, including the vital clotting factors.

PLATELETS
Platelets are tiny fragments of blood that are crucial in stopping bleeding, along with clotting factors, by forming a platelet plug.

WHITE BLOOD CELLS
These are your infection-fighting cells; they circulate in the blood so they can quickly multiply and be transported to an area where there's an infection flaring.

LYMPHOCYTES
Lymphocytes are a type of white blood cell that directs the body's immune system. They have a memory for invading bacteria and viruses.

What's in our ears?

The ear performs a range of functions, sending messages to the brain when a sound is made while also providing your body with a sense of balance

The thing to remember when learning about the human ear is that sound is all about movement.

When someone speaks or bangs a drum or makes any kind of movement, the air around them is disturbed, creating a sound wave of alternating high and low frequency. These waves are detected by the ear and then interpreted by the brain as words, tunes or sounds.

Consisting of air-filled cavities, labyrinthine fluid-filled channels and highly sensitive cells, the ear has external, middle and internal parts. The outer ear consists of a skin-covered flexible cartilage flap called the 'auricle', or 'pinna'. This feature is shaped to gather sound waves and amplify them before they enter the ear for processing and transmission to the brain. The first thing a sound wave entering the ear encounters is the sheet of tightly pulled tissue separating the outer and middle ear. This tissue is the eardrum, or tympanic membrane, and it vibrates as sound waves hit it.

Beyond the eardrum, in the air-filled cavity of the middle ear, are three tiny bones called the 'ossicles'. These are the smallest bones in your entire body. Sound vibrations hitting the eardrum pass to the first ossicle, the malleus (hammer). Next the waves proceed along the incus (anvil) and then on to the (stapes) stirrup. The stirrup presses against a thin layer of tissue called the 'oval window', and this membrane enables sound waves to enter the fluid-filled inner ear.

The inner ear is home to the cochlea, which consists of watery ducts that channel the vibrations, as ripples, along the cochlea's spiralling tubes. Running through the middle of the cochlea is the organ of Corti, which is lined with minute sensory hair cells that pick up on the vibrations and generate nerve impulses that are sent to the brain as electrical signals. The brain can interpret these signals as sounds. ✿

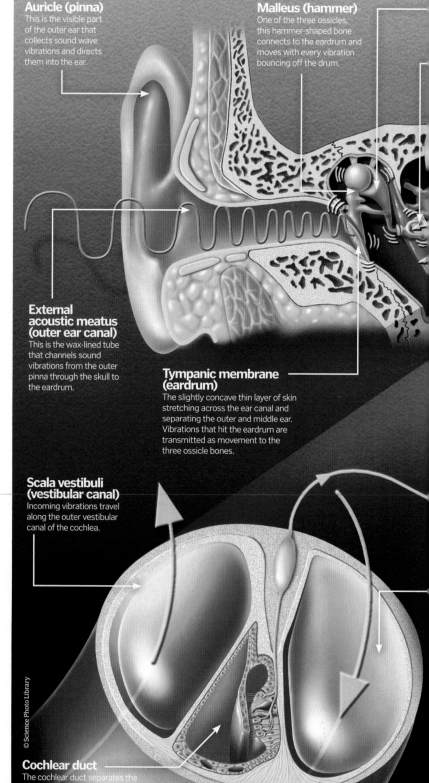

Auricle (pinna)
This is the visible part of the outer ear that collects sound wave vibrations and directs them into the ear.

Malleus (hammer)
One of the three ossicles, this hammer-shaped bone connects to the eardrum and moves with every vibration bouncing off the drum.

External acoustic meatus (outer ear canal)
This is the wax-lined tube that channels sound vibrations from the outer pinna through the skull to the eardrum.

Tympanic membrane (eardrum)
The slightly concave thin layer of skin stretching across the ear canal and separating the outer and middle ear. Vibrations that hit the eardrum are transmitted as movement to the three ossicle bones.

Scala vestibuli (vestibular canal)
Incoming vibrations travel along the outer vestibular canal of the cochlea.

Cochlear duct
The cochlear duct separates the tympanic and vestibular canals. The organ of Corti is found here.

© Science Photo Library

What is the vestibular system?

Inside the inner ear are the vestibule and semicircular canals, which feature sensory cells. From the semicircular canals and maculae, information about which way the head is moving is passed to receptors, which send electrical signals to the brain as nerve impulses.

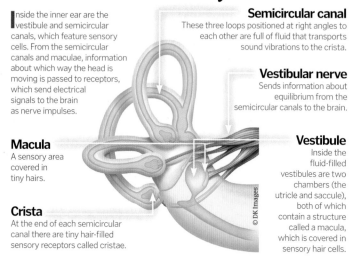

Semicircular canal
These three loops positioned at right angles to each other are full of fluid that transports sound vibrations to the crista.

Vestibular nerve
Sends information about equilibrium from the semicircular canals to the brain.

Macula
A sensory area covered in tiny hairs.

Crista
At the end of each semicircular canal there are tiny hair-filled sensory receptors called cristae.

Vestibule
Inside the fluid-filled vestibules are two chambers (the utricle and saccule), both of which contain a structure called a macula, which is covered in sensory hair cells.

© DK Images

Rumbling is louder the less food present in the small intestine, which is partly why people associate rumbling tummies with hunger

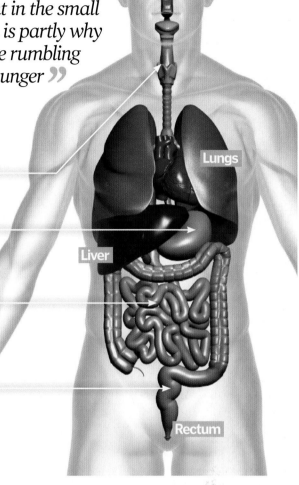

Incus (anvil)
Connected to the hammer, the incus is the middle ossicle bone and is shaped like an anvil.

Stapes (stirrup)
The stirrup is the third ossicle bone. It attaches to the oval window at the base of the cochlea. Movements transferred from the outer ear to the middle ear now continue their journey through the fluid of the inner ear.

Cochlea
A bony snail-shaped structure, the cochlea receives vibrations from the ossicles and transforms them into electrical signals that are transmitted to the brain. There are three fluid-filled channels – the vestibular canal, the tympanic canal and the cochlear duct – within the spiral of the cochlea.

Organ of Corti
The organ of Corti contains rows of sensitive hair cells, the tips of which are embedded in the tectorial membrane. When the membrane vibrates, the hair receptors pass information through the cochlear nerve to the brain.

Cochlear nerve
Sends nerve impulses with information about sounds from the cochlea to the brain.

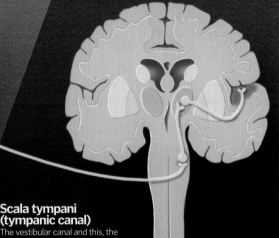

Scala tympani (tympanic canal)
The vestibular canal and this, the tympanic canal, meet at the apex of the cochlear spiral (the helicotrema).

The thing to remember when learning about the human ear is that sound is all about movement

Oesophagus
This muscular pipe connects the throat to the stomach.

Stomach
Food is churned and mixed with gastric juices to help it to break down.

Small intestine
Here, liquid food combined with trapped gasses can make for some embarrassing noises.

Large intestine
Food passes from the small intestine to the large intestine where it is turned into faeces.

Lungs

Liver

Rectum

What makes our tummies rumble?

Discover how the small intestine is really to blame...

Waves of involuntary muscle contractions called peristalsis churn the food we eat to soften it and transport it through the digestive system. The contractions are caused by strong muscles in the oesophagus wall, which take just ten seconds to push food down to the stomach. Muscles in the stomach churn food and gastric juices to break it down further.

Then, after four hours, the semi-digested liquefied food moves on to the small intestine where yet more powerful muscle contractions force the food down through the intestine's bends and folds. This is where the rumbling occurs. Air from gaseous foods or air swallowed when we eat – often due to talking or inhaling through the nose while chewing – also ends up in the small intestine, and it's this combination of liquid and gas in a small space that causes the gurgling noise.

Rumbling is louder the less food present in the small intestine, which is partly why people associate rumbling tummies with hunger. The other reason is that although the stomach may be clear, the brain still triggers peristalsis at regular intervals to rid the intestines of any remaining food. This creates a hollow feeling that causes you to feel hungry.

What does a human spine look like?

The human spine is made up of 33 vertebrae, but how do they support our bodies while allowing us such flexibility?

The human spine is made up of 33 vertebrae, 24 of which are articulated (flexible) and nine of which normally become fused in maturity. They are situated between the base of the skull to the pelvis, where the spine trails off into the coccyx – an evolutionary remnant of a tail our ancestors would have displayed.

The primary functions of the vertebrae that make up the spine are to support the torso and head, which protect vital nerves and the spinal cord and allow the individual to move. By sitting closely together, separated only by thin intervertebral discs which work as ligaments and effectively form joints between the bones, the vertebrae form a strong pillar structure which holds the head up and allows for the body to remain upright. It also produces a base for ribs to attach to and to protect vital internal organs in the human body.

Vertebrae are not all fused together because of the need to move, and the vertebrae themselves are grouped into five types – cervical, thoracic, lumbar, sacral and coccygeal. The sacral vertebrae fuse during maturity (childhood and teenage years) and become solid bones towards the base of the spine. The coccygeal vertebrae will fuse in some cases, but studies have shown that often they actually remain separate. Collectively they are referred to as the coccyx (tail bone). The rest of the vertebrae remain individual and discs between them allow them to move in various directions without wearing the bones down. The cervical vertebrae in the neck allow particularly extensive movement, allowing the head to move up and down and side to side. The thoracic are far more static, with ties to the rib cage resisting much movement. The lumbar vertebrae allow modest side-to-side movement and rotation. A particular feature of the spine is how it is actually curved to allow distribution of the body's weight, to ensure no one vertebrae takes the full impact. ✿

C1 (atlas)
This is the vertebrae which connects the spinal column with the skull. It is named 'atlas' after the legend of Atlas who held the world on his shoulders.

Cervical vertebrae
These are the smallest of the articulating vertebrae, and support the head and neck. There are seven vertebrae, with C1, C2 and C7's structures quite unique from the others. They sit between the skull and thoracic vertebrae.

C2 (axis)
C2 is the pivot for C1 (atlas), and nearly all movement for shaking your head will occur at this joint – the atlanto-axial joint.

Thoracic vertebrae
The thoracic vertebrae are the intermediately sized vertebrae. They increase in size as you move down the spine, and they supply facets for ribs to attach to – this is how they are primarily distinguished.

Intervertebral discs
These discs form a joint between each vertebrae and, effectively, work as ligaments while also serving as fantastic shock absorbers. They facilitate movement and stop the bones rubbing together.

Spine curvature

As you look at the human spine, you can see some distinct curves. The primary reasons for these are to help distribute weight throughout the spine and support aspects of the body. The curve most familiar to us is the lumbar curve, between the ribs and pelvis. This develops when we start to walk at about 12-18 months and helps with weight distribution during locomotion. Prior to this we develop the cervical curve, which allows us to support the weight of our head at around three to four months, and two smaller less-obvious curves in the spine (the thoracic and pelvic curves) are developed during gestation.

Spinal cords and nerves

The human spinal cord is an immensely complex structure made up of nerve cells and a large amount of supporting, protective tissue. It splits into 31 different sections and stretches 43-45cm, down from the brain to between the first and second lumbar vertebrae. Although more commonly referred to in respect of the brain, there is both white and grey matter present in the centre of the spinal cord. White matter contains axons tracts surrounded by fats, and blood vessels to protect them. The grey matter contains more of the neural cell bodies, such as dendrites, more axons and glial cells.

Spinal cord injuries are normally caused by trauma. If the trauma causes intervertebral discs and vertebrae to break, they can pierce the spinal cord, which can result in loss of feeling. Cord severance may result in paralysis.

How is the skull attached to the spine?

The skull is connected to the spine by the atlanto-occipital joint, which is created by C1 (atlas) and the occipital bone situated at the base of the cranium (skull). This unique vertebra has no 'body' and actually looks more like a ring than any other vertebra. It sits at the top of the cervical vertebrae and connects with the occipital bone via an ellipsoidal joint, allowing movement such as nodding or rotation of the head. An ellipsoidal joint is where an ovoid connection (in this case the occipital bone) is placed into an elliptical cavity (C1 vertebrae). The rest of the cervical vertebrae also work to support the weight of the head.

The human spinal cord is an immensely complex structure

Lumbar vertebrae
Lumbar vertebrae are the largest of the vertebrae and the strongest, primarily because they withstand the largest pressures. Compared with other vertebrae they are more compact, lacking facets on the sides of the vertebrae.

Sacral vertebrae
We have five sacral vertebrae at birth, but by maturity they will have fused to form a solid bone, which helps support the lumbar vertebrae and connect the coccyx to the spine.

Coccyx (tailbone)
The coccyx can display between three and five vertebrae. They're commonly thought to be fused, but often are not. Although these vertebrae are a vestigial remnant of a tail, they have several uses, such as supporting weight when sitting.

© SPL

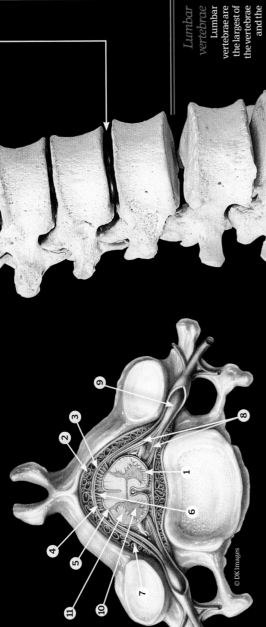

© DK Images

Spinal column cross-section

1. Spinal cord
This is an immensely important pathway for information to transfer between the brain and the body's nervous system. It is heavily protected by tissue and vertebrae, as any damage to it can be fatal.

2. Epidural space
This is the space between the outer protective tissue layer, dura mater and the bone. It is filled with adipose tissue (fat), while also playing host to numerous blood vessels.

3. Dura mater
This is the tough outer layer of tissue that protects the spinal cord. The three layers of protection between the vertebrae and the spinal cord are called the spinal meninges.

4. Arachnoid mater
Named for its spider web appearance, this is the second layer of the tissue protection provided for the spinal cord.

5. Pia mater
This thin, delicate layer sits immediately next to the spinal cord.

6. Subarachnoid space
This is the space between the pia mater and the arachnoid mater, which is filled with cerebrospinal fluid.

7. Blood vessels
Four arteries, which form a network called the Circle of Willis, deliver oxygen-rich blood to the brain. The brain's capillaries form a lining called the 'blood-brain barrier,' which controls blood flow to the brain.

8. Dorsal and ventral roots
These connect the spinal nerves to the spinal cord, allowing transition of information between the brain and the body.

9. Spinal nerves
Humans have 31 pairs of spinal nerves all aligned with individual vertebrae, and these communicate information from around the body to the spinal cord. They carry all types of information – motor, sensory and so on – and are commonly referred to as 'mixed spinal nerves'.

10. Grey matter
Within the horn-like shapes in the centre of the spinal cord, sit most of the important neural cell bodies. They are protected in many ways, including by the white matter.

11. White matter
This area that surrounds the grey matter holds axon trails, but is primarily made up of lipid tissue (fats) and blood vessels.

Why is radiation so dangerous?

There are many different types of radiation; for example, visible light is a form of radiation. Some are more harmful than others, however, as there are on average 15,000 radioactive particles travelling through your body every second! With all this radiation exposure, why aren't we all dying of cancer? Well, it is not the amount of radiation which you come into contact with, as every single one of these particles has the potential to cause cancer, it's just the probability of that occurring is about one in 30 quadrillion!

Only approximately one per cent of fatal human cancer is caused by these 30 trillion radioactive particles which pass through our bodies in a typical lifetime. Ionising radiation has the energy to detach electrons from their associated atoms, therefore causing the atom to become positively charged. These charged particles are referred to as radicals and are highly reactive due to their unstable nature.

Radicals are very important for certain processes in the body such as the killing of bacteria. However, many unwanted effects such as mutation of cells can be a problem. Scientists have found lots of evidence to suggest that these radicals cause mutations in cells which can give rise to cancer.

Can you see light if travelling at the speed of light?

If you were travelling at the speed of light, the light would still appear to you to be going at the speed of light, therefore theoretically it would look completely normal. This is an effect that is described by Einstein's special theory of relativity. Putting it into perspective, we are orbiting our Sun at an immense speed, our Sun is orbiting the galaxy at an immense speed, while all the time our galaxy is accelerating at an even more immense speed! Yet when we turn a light on it still travels at the speed of light regardless of all this motion.

How do painkillers cure headaches?

We all feel pain differently, depending on the severity of the injury or ache, as well as our health and our pain threshold. When you are in pain, nerve endings transmit the pain signal to the brain via the spinal cord. The brain then interprets the level of pain.

There are two key types of painkillers that are commonly used. The first include ibuprofen and paracetamol, which block the body's 'prostaglandins' (chemicals that produce swelling and pain) at the source of the pain, reducing swelling in the area and reducing the intensity of pain. These 'aspirin medicines' are used frequently for mild to moderate pain, but they can only work up to a certain intensity of pain. There are different types of painkillers within this group, such as anti-inflammatory medicines, like ibuprofen, which are commonly used to treat arthritis, sprains and strains. Aspirin is used to help lower the risk of blood clots when used in a low dosage, as they thin the blood. Paracetamol is what's known as an analgesic, which is used for reducing pain and lowering a temperature.

The second type of painkillers include morphine and codeine (narcotic medicines), which block the pain messages in the spinal cord and the brain. This is for much more severe pain. As both types of painkillers use slightly different methods to treat pain, they can be combined, such as in co-codamol, which blends codeine and paracetamol.

Why does ice have the energy to burst pipes?

Water is different to most other substances as upon turning into ice, its volume expands by roughly nine per cent causing it to become less dense. This is due to nature of the bonds between the molecules and the shape of those molecules. Upon changing state, a substance needs to absorb or release a certain amount of energy to undergo the phase transition. For a solid turning into a liquid, this energy is needed to break the bonds in the solid therefore needs to be absorbed by the system. For a liquid turning into a solid, this energy is released as the bonds form.

For 1kg of water at freezing point to change into ice, it must give off 333.55kJ to the surroundings, just to undergo the phase transition. This large amount of energy is normally given off as heat, which means it gives the molecules in the atmosphere more kinetic energy. However, if water is contained in a steel pipe at freezing point, the energy given off will be passed on to the molecules and bonds in the pipe, causing the pipe to burst.

Why does mint taste 'cold'?

We're sure you have all experienced the 'cool' sensation induced by eating a mint, and the reason why this happens is due to the active ingredient called menthol. When we perceive something to be hot or cold, this is due to electrical signals from the nerves which come into contact with the hot or cold 'thing'. Our brain then interprets these electrical signals as instructions such as – 'that is hot, don't touch!' or 'that is cold'.

Mints usually contain menthol. Menthol has the ability to affect the pores on our nerve cells which changes the electrical activity of the cell. This change in electrical activity corresponds to the same change that would take place if something cold came into contact with the cell. The cell interprets the change in activity due to menthol as a change in temperature and sends that information to the brain. This accounts for the 'coldness' which we experience when eating a mint.

Can glass be made from lightning hitting sand?

This is indeed possible as glass and sand are both made from the same chemical, silicon dioxide. Silicon dioxide has an extremely high melting point, so first the sand has to be heated past this for it to become a liquid. In sand the silicon and oxygen atoms are arranged in a very orderly way. When the sand is heated to very high temperatures, this arrangement breaks down and the position of the atoms becomes disorderly and random. If the sand is cooled quick enough then the atoms of oxygen and silicone don't have enough time to revert back to their nice orderly arrangement so they form the substance we know as glass.

When lightning occurs, the strike point can reach temperatures of up to 30,000°C, which is much hotter than the surface of the Sun. Providing the sand is of the right kind then it is possible that glass will form. Fulgurite is the term given to what is left over, which is a hollow glass tube and can sometimes penetrate up to 15 metres below the surface of the sand.

The type of sand the lightning strikes is a major factor as to whether it will turn into glass or not. Meteorite impacts have also been known to release a large enough amount of energy to convert sand into glass.

Due to the unpredictable nature of lightning strikes and given that they can be highly dangerous, it might be a risky business opportunity in more than just the financial sense. On average there can be more than 100 lightning strikes happening every second across the globe, but the chances of these being over the right type of sand at exactly the right moment are very low, so don't get your hopes up!

At what temperature is water at its densest?

Density is a measure of how much mass a material has in a specific volume of space. Therefore the more atoms per unit volume a material has and the more mass those atoms have, the higher the density will be. When you heat something up, it takes up more space and therefore becomes less dense. Most materials will be at their densest when they are a solid, ie when their atoms are closest together. Water does not follow this rule as we all know that ice floats on water therefore ice is less dense than water! So when is water at its densest? Well, it turns out this happens to be around 4°C. This is when the water molecules are closest together. Cooling water further than 4°C causes the density to decrease up to the point where it becomes a solid which is less dense than the liquid. This happens due to the unusual way that the water molecules arrange themselves when turning into a solid, it is known as a crystalline structure and it is such an arrangement that the molecules are further apart from each other as a solid than when they were a liquid.

How are ball bearings made?

There are few different parts that make up a ball bearing, including races, a cage, and then the covering to protect the bearing. The first stage in the process is a cold or hot forming operation; a thick piece of wire is fed into a machine where it is cut down by slicing sections off each side.

The machine then slams two hemisphere cavities (a bit like a mould) into the piece of wire to make a ball shape. As a result of this process, the ball will have a ring of excess metal around it, called a flash, which needs to be removed. The ball also needs further polishing to make it perfectly round and smooth. The ball with the flash is then fed into another machine which rolls the ball around between two rill plates. Rill plates are two hard plates of steel which wear away the flash and smooths the surface of the ball. The ball is then heated to harden it after which it undergoes a grinding process similar to that of the rill plates until it is ground down to its final, very accurate measurements which often require tolerances as small as a millionth of an inch.

The last process is called lapping, which requires a similar machine that exerts less pressure combined with a polishing paste to give the balls their perfect shiny finish without further reducing their size.

> **❝ It is ground down to its final, very accurate measurements which often require tolerances as small as a millionth of an inch ❞**

How does de-icer work?

De-icers work by lowering the freezing point of water causing it to turn back from ice into liquid water. Usually this is due to the addition of a chemical compound such as sodium chloride (often called rock salt) or calcium chloride. Most de-icers aren't designed to melt every piece of ice they come into contact with – they break the bond between the ice and the surface allowing for easier manual removal of the ice.

How does honey and lemon cure a sore throat?

Honey and lemon can be drank warm as a comfort remedy when suffering from a sore throat or cold. The idea behind this is that honey coats the throat and therefore any inflamed or sore areas will become 'protected' by a layer of honey. This means it will feel less painful when these areas come into contact with other surfaces like when you eat a meal or swallow. Lemon helps to settle the stomach as it contains acid. This can be particularly helpful when experiencing an upset stomach from the effects of a cold.

How much electricity does the brain produce?

The brain requires a relatively low power to operate – around 20 watts, which would be enough to power a weak light bulb. 20 watts corresponds to 20 joules of energy per second. The generation of electricity in the brain results from the movement of ions (charged atoms) through the brain, as opposed to electrons moving through a wire.

What are brain tumours?

A brain tumour is an abnormal growth of cells within the brain which is created from abnormal, uncontrolled cell division. These dividing cells can be of many different types and can arise from random mutation or from cancerous cells spreading to the brain from other parts of the body.

How do the holes get in Swiss cheese?

To make cheese you need the help of bacteria. Different types of bacteria in different combinations give rise to the distinct variety of flavours in many cheeses. There are various different types of bacteria used for making Swiss cheese, the one responsible for the holes is called Propionibacterium shermanii. Once this bacteria is heated slightly it reacts, forming bubbles of carbon dioxide that become the final holes in the product.

The technical term for these holes is 'eyes'. The size of these eyes can be controlled by the cheesemakers by altering the acidity, temperature and curing time of the mixture. Generally, in most foods which require fermentation, bubbles of carbon dioxide will be formed but most of the time they escape. The procedure which goes into making Swiss cheese means those bubbles remain trapped inside which means there will be 'eyes' in the final product.

How do boomerangs stay airborne?

So we've covered why they come back, but how do boomerangs stay up in the first place? The two arms of the boomerang are like the wings of a plane in that the faster they move through the air the more lift they generate. Unlike plane wings they spin as they move through the air and this combination of spin and movement means that some parts of the boomerang are moving quicker. Because the boomerang is spinning the aerodynamic lift occurs at different rates on different parts of the boomerang, as the wings of the boomerang are thrown at an angle the net lift is towards the centre of the circle that the boomerang moves on.

Why do we hiccup?

There are over 100 physiological reasons as to what sets hiccups off, the most common being expansion of the stomach and movement of stomach acid into the oesophagus. After this then it could be an irritation of the thorax or the phrenic nerve (the nerve to the diaphragm).

The mechanism of a hiccup usually involves a strong contraction of the diaphragm, the neck muscles and some other surrounding muscles. Just after the contraction begins we start to inhale, at which point the glottis (a kind of fleshy trap door which separates the food and air tubes in your throat) shuts off the windpipe and this produces the 'hic' noise.

Scientists are trying to find the purpose of hiccups. One theory is that they may have been useful for an ancestor of ours. Standing on two legs gives us the advantage of using gravity to help digest our food, but four-legged creatures have to digest horizontally which means it's easier for food to get stuck. Some scientists think the lodged food could have hit a nerve responsible for triggering the hiccup allowing the food to be swallowed. If this is the case then hiccups could have been highly useful rather than just making you look daft!

> "*One theory is that hiccups may have been useful for an ancestor of ours*"

Why use salt to melt ice on the roads?

Salt lowers the freezing/melting point of water/ice. The melting point of ice under normal conditions is zero degrees Celsius. Sea water, however, freezes/melts at -2.2 degrees Celsius due to its high salinity.

As to why salt lowers the melting/freezing point of water, this is a bit more difficult to explain without going into some complex chemistry. Basically water is made from H_2O, and anything else which gets in there, such as sodium in the case of salt, gets in the way and makes it harder for the H_2O to bond as ice.

Upon sprinkling salt onto ice, the salt first dissolves into the liquid water surrounding the ice causing the ice to melt. The salt can only lower the melting/freezing point of water up to around -16 degrees. If the temperature is below this point then salt is ineffective and it would be better to pour sand over the ice to help increase traction.

Why do we sometimes remember our dreams?

This is a very good question and it is one for which there is no satisfactory answer based on our current understanding of the brain. One thing studies have told us, though, is that dreams seem to happen more vividly and frequently during the REM (Rapid Eye Movement) stage of the sleep cycle, which tends to occur roughly four to five times in a normal night's sleep.

It has been reported by several studies that you are much more likely to remember the dream you were having if you are woken in the middle of this REM cycle. So if you would like to remember your dreams more frequently, you could try setting your alarm clock to go off in the middle of your REM sleep cycle (likely to be near the end of your night's sleep) and write down what you remember.

❝ *Flash floods are the result of intense periods of rainfall that form into walls or waves of water* **❞**

Environment

Which are the world's fastest animals?

The arms race of hunter and hunted is a ferocious battleground, with different species furiously evolving to remain one step ahead of the competition

Tail
The cheetah's long tail acts as a counterweight, maintaining balance during sharp turns at high speed.

Spine
The spine is incredibly flexible and has evolved so it curves with each stride, acting akin to a spring for the cheetah's hind legs.

Paws
The paws are blunt and sport exposed claws that provide superior grip, increasing the forward thrust of each stride.

Eyes
The cheetah's eyes are long to provide a wide-angle view of its surroundings. This provides them with excellent vision when stalking and chasing prey in the native habitat of open plains.

Lungs
Engorged lungs and nostrils allow for a fast and deep air intake. Maintaining a high level of oxygen is critical when the cheetah is on a chase as its breath-rate increases three-fold.

Heart
The heart is enlarged compared to other animals of its size, pumping a colossal amount of blood around the cheetah's body, especially during a chase.

Build
The average weight of a cheetah is 57kg (125lb) and its build is slender. It has a small head, flattened rib cage and long, thin legs that all minimise air resistance.

Cheetah

Accelerating to speeds of 70mph, the cheetah is the quickest on four legs!

Cheetahs are one of the fastest animals on Earth and have a terrifyingly quick 0-60 time of a mere three seconds. Cheetahs are unique in the fact they have evolved to such a degree in order to maximise their speed, that they regularly risk brain damage and starvation due to the great physical demands it places on their anatomy. The cheetah is fast, the fastest land animal on Earth, but that speed comes at a great price.

For example, lungs, nostrils and heart are all enlarged within the cheetah to ensure it can process enough oxygen and blood to maintain its explosive speed. However, it can only process this for short periods of time and at the close of a lengthy chase not only does it skirt dangerously close to oxygen deprivation but it must rest post-kill before it eats, leaving plenty of time for scavengers to surround it. In addition, while its muscle fibre is honed and holds superb elasticity, its physique is slender and lightweight, leaving it vulnerable to broken limbs and completely defenceless against a larger and heavier rival such as a lion or tiger.

Due to these facts – as well as through human-caused habitat loss and predation – cheetah numbers are dwindling and it is currently an endangered species in many African countries.

0-40mph in three strides

Check out the three stages a cheetah undertakes to reach 40mph in just three strides

1. Brace
The cheetah employs its hard, ridged footpads and blunt, non-retractable claws to maximise traction with the ground. Its spine curves, coil-like, and head drops a fraction.

2. Snap
The spine uncoils and snaps straight, driving the hind legs into the earth and pushing the cheetah forward. The honed, slender muscles expand in conjunction, adding greater elasticity and drive to the forward thrust.

3. Kick
The combined spine and leg muscles give the cheetah an incredibly broad swing range and propel it 7.6 metres (25 feet) through the air in a colossal bound. At the culmination of the bound one foot is replanted onto the earth and the process is repeated. The cheetah completes three strides a second.

© DK Images

Long nose
The sailfish's elongated bill is similar to a swordfish's and marlin's, placing it in the category of billfish.

The sailfish can rapidly turn its body light blue with stripes when excited, confusing its prey and making capture easier

Sailfish

Capable of swimming for long periods of time at over 40mph, and with a recorded top speed of over 70mph, the sailfish is the ocean's fastest animal

With a top speed on par with that of a cheetah, the sailfish is lightning fast and one of the most difficult-to-catch fish in the world.

Thanks to its stiffened, tapered body and scissor-shaped caudal fin, the sailfish is built for speed – a speed that comes courtesy of a rapid and ferocious flicking of its tail. Indeed, during a chase to consume fish, crustaceans or cephalopods, the sailfish will flick its tail back and forth hundreds of times, utilising the powerful muscles which run down its compressed body.

As with a peregrine falcon, the sailfish's speed is also aided by its ability to retract parts of its body, in this instance its various fins (notably the large dorsal fin that adds over a foot on to its overall height). This feature helps it reduce the effects of drag and minimise resistance to its movements.

Its spine is also very flexible and as with the cheetah allows it to generate increased thrust through the rapid curves it bends its torso into while swimming.

Sight
Prey is spotted while soaring and then the peregrine begins to draw its wings into its body. It also retracts its tail and tucks its feet into its body.

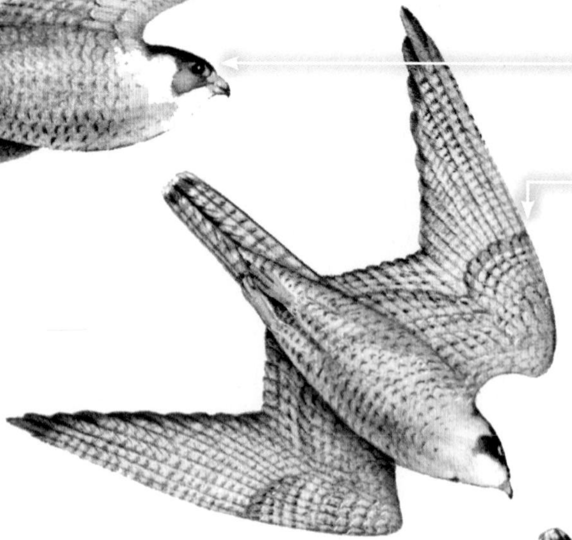

Streamline
The wings are brought right into the falcon's sternum and, thanks to their pointed, slim, stiff and unslotted feathers, it begins to rapidly reduce its air resistance.

Velocity
Speed is increased as the falcon bombs down with little-to-zero drag, soon reaching speeds up to 200mph. Its strong keel helps maintain structural solidity during the dive and its eyes are kept clear by nictitating membranes, which act like a third eyelid.

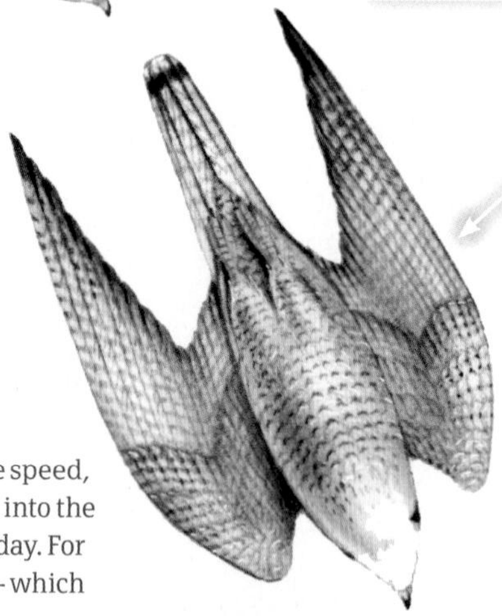

Contact
Prey is both struck and captured in mid-air. The peregrine strikes its prey with a clenched foot, which due to the immense speed either stuns or kills it, before then swooping round to catch it with its large claws. Prey is always consumed on the ground.

Peregrine falcon

When in free fall, the peregrine falcon is incredibly quick

If you thought the cheetah was fast, then think again. The peregrine falcon blows its top speed out of the water by over 130mph. Capable of hitting a monumental 200mph during a stoop (dive), the falcon has the highest top speed of any animal on Earth.

The peregrine's speed is caused by a combination of factors. Firstly it makes use of gravity, diving upon its prey from great height, even when they themselves are airborne. Secondly, its anatomy – as with the cheetah's – has been finely honed to maximise speed, evolving over millions of years into the swift and efficient killer it is today. For example, the peregrine's keel – which is located at its breastbone – is significantly larger than average birds', allowing for bigger muscles and a greater number to attach its wings to its body. This allows it to generate far more power per thrust when building speed. Further, the peregrine's wings have evolved to be incredibly pointed, with slim, stiff and unslotted feathers, which helps streamlining and reducing air resistance significantly.

Unlike the cheetah, however, arguably the peregrine handles its awesome speed much better. Firstly, while having the same enlarged heart and lungs, the peregrine does not suffer damage from oxygen deprivation at the close of its stoop. This is partly due to gravity's beneficial aid in generating its killer speed but also due to the peregrine's ability to absorb oxygen through its red muscle fibres, of which it has many. This allows it to keep a steady oxygen flow at all times and means that, consequentially, it does not need to rest post-kill, reducing its vulnerability to scavengers.

© Keven Law 08

© DK Images

> ❝ *If you thought the cheetah was fast, then think again* ❞

What is the muscle contraction cycle?

Muscle power is common to all these creatures, so here's an explanation of how muscles provide the power that in turn provides the speed

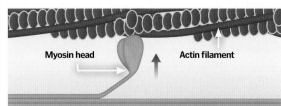

1. Attachment

Firstly a myosin head (akin to an organic hook) attaches itself to an exposed binding site on the muscle filaments, gripping it in a cross bridge.

Myosin head **Actin filament**

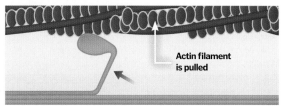

2. Power stroke

The myosin head then pulls the filament by pivoting backwards and dragging it into a compressed position.

Actin filament is pulled

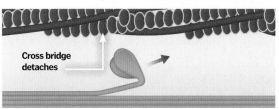

3. Detachment

A molecule of ATP (adenosine triphosphate) then binds to the myosin, releasing its grip of the filament so that the cross bridge detaches.

Cross bridge detaches

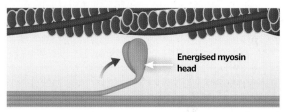

4. Energy release

Finally, the ATP releases energy to convert the myosin head from its bent, low-energy position back to its initial high-energy configuration ready for the next cycle.

Energised myosin head

Physique
Tall height, balanced weight and powerful muscles.

Metabolism
Converting 'fuels' like glucose into power, producing adenosine triphosphate.

Usain Bolt

The fastest human alive, Usain Bolt recently broke the world 100-metre record with a staggeringly quick time of 9.58 seconds

One of the most successful species of animal on the planet, Homo sapiens have evolved over the last 120,000 years into creatures with formidable physical abilities. Currently, the fastest human is Usain Bolt, a Jamaican-born sprinter who has won the world 100 and 200-metre gold medals.

Bolt epitomises the ideal human anatomy needed to produce such high speeds: a tall height (1.95m), balanced weight (93.9kg) and long, powerful muscles with an excellent metabolism – muscles cannot utilise energy-rich 'fuels' such as glucose, instead they must convert it into ATP (adenosine triphosphate) with the amount of ATP a muscle produces directly correlating to the amount of power it can generate.

The fastest animals on Earth are...

Here's a list of the most super-fast critters on the planet

FASTEST FISH	
Sailfish	68mph (110kph)
Marlin	50mph (80kph)
Wahoo	48mph (78kph)
Tunny	46mph (74kph)
Bluefish tuna	44mph (70kph)

FASTEST LAND INSECTS	
Tiger beetle	5.6mph (8.4kph)
Cockroach	3.4mph (5.4kph)

FASTEST REPTILES	
Spiny-tailed iguana	21mph (34kph)
Black mamba	12mph (20kph)

FASTEST BIRDS	
Peregrine falcon	200mph (322kph)
Spine-tailed swift	106mph (171kph)
Frigatebird	95mph (153kph)
Spur-winged goose	88mph (142kph)
Red-breasted merganser	80mph (129kph)

FASTEST MAMMALS	
Cheetah	71mph (114kph)
Pronghorn antelope	57mph (95kph)
Springbok	50mph (80kph)
Blue wildebeest	50mph (80kph)
Lion	45mph (72kph)

Sources: American Journal of Zoology, University of Michigan, Seattle Zoo, American Journal of Physiology, National Geographic, US Fish and Wildlife Service, Forest Preserve of Illinois

How does a volcano erupt?

Breathtaking and often devastating reminders that
the Earth's surface is actively evolving

Volcanoes are rare locations on the Earth's crust where molten rock (magma) spews to the surface as lava, often accompanied by superheated gas and debris.

Geologists see volcanoes as outward evidence of the inner workings of plate tectonics, the theory that the crust is fragmented into 15 oceanic and continental plates that diverge, converge and slide beneath one another over time.

Approximately 400 of Earth's 500 known active volcanoes lie atop subduction zones, places where an oceanic plate slips beneath another oceanic or continental plate. The 'Ring of Fire' traces a circle of highly active subduction zones around the Pacific Ocean.

In a subduction volcano, magma is formed 100 to 200km beneath the surface when water and carbon dioxide seep from the sinking oceanic shelf, lowering the melting point of the surrounding rock.

This fresh magma, which is lighter than solid rock, percolates upward through fissures in the crust, eventually exploding to the surface when trapped gasses in the magma rush to escape.

Rift volcanoes form along the great seams of two separating plates. The mid-Atlantic ridge, which separates the North American and African plates, is one of these seams. As the plates pull apart, magma bubbles up through hundreds, even thousands, of small volcanoes to fill the cracks, creating new ocean floor.

Five per cent of volcanoes are located far from the seams of tectonic plates. So-called hot spot volcanoes are fuelled by deep sources of magma pumped to the surface through powerful convection currents in the molten mantle. Since the deep fuel source remains fixed while the plate slides above, the result is often a string of volcanoes, much like the Hawaiian Islands. ✿

What are the different types of volcano?

Shield
Wide, shallow-sloped volcanoes formed by layers of slow-oozing lava (Mauna Loa in Hawaii).

Cinder
Small, single-vent volcanoes composed of a pile of shattered volcanic rock and ash (Paricutín in Mexico).

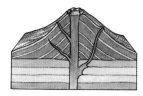

Composite
Tall, steep-sloped volcanoes made from alternating layers of cooled lava and debris like ash and lava bombs (Mt Fuji in Japan).

Fissure
Flat fields of lava that emerge from long cracks along the Earth's rift zones (Las Pilas in Nicaragua).

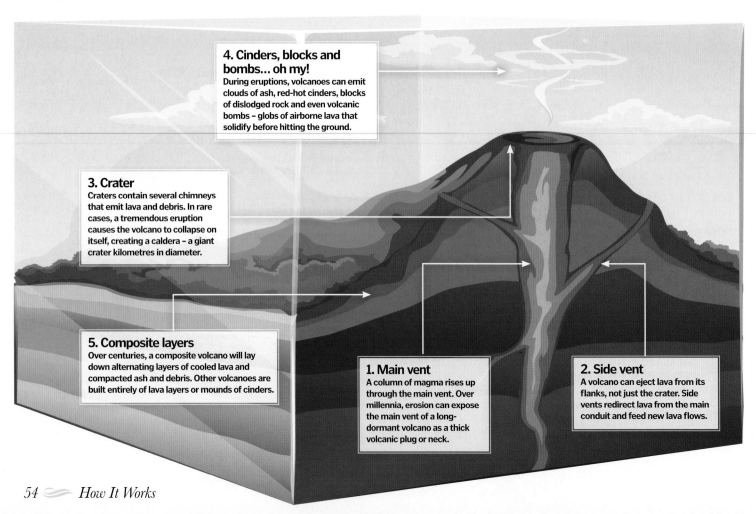

4. Cinders, blocks and bombs... oh my!
During eruptions, volcanoes can emit clouds of ash, red-hot cinders, blocks of dislodged rock and even volcanic bombs – globs of airborne lava that solidify before hitting the ground.

3. Crater
Craters contain several chimneys that emit lava and debris. In rare cases, a tremendous eruption causes the volcano to collapse on itself, creating a caldera – a giant crater kilometres in diameter.

5. Composite layers
Over centuries, a composite volcano will lay down alternating layers of cooled lava and compacted ash and debris. Other volcanoes are built entirely of lava layers or mounds of cinders.

1. Main vent
A column of magma rises up through the main vent. Over millennia, erosion can expose the main vent of a long-dormant volcano as a thick volcanic plug or neck.

2. Side vent
A volcano can eject lava from its flanks, not just the crater. Side vents redirect lava from the main conduit and feed new lava flows.

Why are geysers so rare?

What drives these fountains of superheated water, and why aren't there more of them?

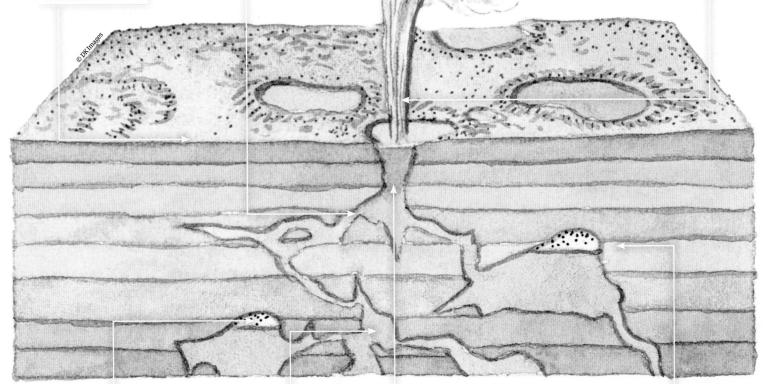

8. Sky-high water
The colder water above the superheated water is thrown up into the air as a jet. The pressure lifts, causing the superheated water to turn into steam.

1. Water trickles underground
Snow, rain or river water takes hundreds of years to trickle through fractured rocks to depths of two to three kilometres.

6. Silica seal
Silica dissolved from rhyolite – a volcanic rock – can slowly build up on the pipe walls causing a bottleneck.

7. A sudden rush
Water pressure mounts below the bottleneck until it can overcome the weight of overlying, colder water and rush to the surface.

© DK Images

3. Superheated water
The water is heated to very high temperatures, but it can't boil because of the pressure of the overlying water and rock. This is called superheating.

4. Plumbing system
The heated water circulates upwards via a complex, natural system of underground pipes and passages. As it does, the overlying pressure lessens and it can expand and boil.

5. High-pressure area
For a geyser to form, there must be a tight spot in the underground pipe system. This acts like a giant pressure cooker.

2. Hot rocks
The water comes in contact with hot rocks surrounding partially molten rock lying only a few kilometres below the Earth's surface.

Geysers form when water is superheated by volcanic activity underground, but can't move freely as it circulates towards the surface. Instead, pressure builds up until the water explodes upwards in a giant gush.

Since water needs to encounter hot rock, some geyser fields are found above upwellings of hot rock from deep within the Earth. Others are found near crustal plate boundaries where there is volcanic activity and broken, fractured rock. Rivers, snow or rainwater trickling through the Earth can provide a constant source of water.

Most geysers form where there's a silica-rich rock known as rhyolite. Rising hot water dissolves the silica in the rhyolite and carries it upwards through natural pipes in the rock where it's then deposited as a rock called geyserite. The silica seals the pipe against water pressure and narrows its walls.

Every geyser has a different plumbing and reservoir system, but there are two main types. 'Cone' or 'column' geysers like Old Faithful erupt in a steady column from a beehive-shaped nozzle of geyserite. They tend to have one reservoir of

water with a single pipe leading from it to the surface. 'Fountain' or 'pool' geysers erupt from a large pool of water in a series of powerful bursts. They are thought to have a reservoir fed by two water sources – descending shallow, cold water and hot water rising from below.

As geysers need a rare combination of geological conditions to form, they're found in just a handful of places. There are around 50 geyser fields worldwide and most have just a few geysers. The biggest – Yellowstone, USA – has almost half the world's geysers.

How do blue

What's as long as three London buses and as heavy as 112 giraffes?

The blue whale isn't just the largest animal alive, it is the largest animal ever to have lived. Even the largest dinosaurs are topped by this leviathan. Everything about the blue whale is huge. It has a heart the size of a small car, a tongue that weighs 2.7 tons and lungs that can hold 5,000 litres of air.

Blue whales spend most of their lives swimming alone or in pairs, unlike other baleen whales such as the humpback. The female gives birth every two or three years to a single calf that weighs as much as an adult hippopotamus. For the first seven months, the calf drinks more than 400 litres of milk a day to enable it to put on 90kg of weight every 24 hours.

Blue whales aren't really very blue. The top half of their body is a bluish grey and the underside is a lighter colour to make them harder to see when viewed from below, against the sky.

Blue whales are also extremely fast swimmers. They cruise at 20kph and can sprint at 50kph. This makes it virtually impossible for

Baleen plates
The blue whale doesn't have teeth. Instead the baleen plates hang down to create a colander made of keratin.

Rostrum bulge
This oil and wax-filled chamber focuses sonar pulses, used for echolocation.

Ventral pleats
60 to 90 folded grooves expand the mouth to six times its size after a huge gulp of water and krill.

Pectoral fin
Three metres long and used like the diving planes in a submarine to adjust depth and for steering.

Huge size...

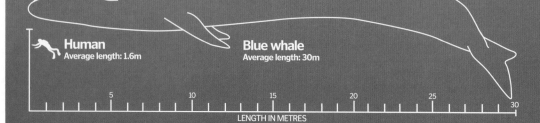

Human Average length: 1.6m

Blue whale Average length: 30m

LENGTH IN METRES

5   10   15   20   25   30

Amazing!
TYPE: Mammal
DIET: Carnivore
AVERAGE LIFE SPAN: 80 years
WEIGHT: 180 tons
Size: 30m

whales live?

barnacles and other parasites to attach themselves. In spring, however, a thin film of diatom algae growing on the skin can sometimes give them a yellow-orange hue and 19th Century whalers referred to them as 'sulphur bottoms'.

Despite their size, blue whales are preyed upon by orcas (killer whales) and 25 per cent of adult blue whales show orca bite scars. ✿

© DK Images

Tail flukes
Like all whales, the tail flukes are horizontal, unlike a fish's vertical tail. Capable of propelling the whale at 50kph.

Baleen plates
Made of keratin, these filter out the krill.

Tongue
The giant tongue pushes the water through the baleen plates.

Blubber
Up to half a metre thick in places. It conserves body heat and keeps a rigid shape to reduce drag.

Dorsal fin
Tiny, compared to sharks and many other whales. In some blue whales, it is barely more than a slight bulge.

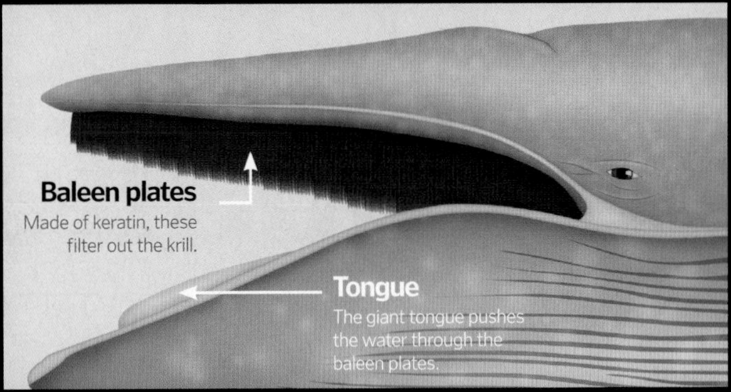

How does the largest animal feed on one of the smallest?

Blue whales don't eat plankton. Instead they eat krill, which are one step up from plankton in the food chain. Krill resemble small shrimp, except that they swim in open water in huge swarms. Most krill are only a couple of centimetres long and since a blue whale needs around 1.5 million calories every day, that means it needs to eat a lot of krill – up to 40 million a day, in fact.

To catch them, a blue whale swims at speed towards a swarm and opens its mouth to gulp in 90 tons of water at a time. It then uses its massive tongue to force the water back through the baleen plates. These are 300 feathery bars, each one a metre long, that are attached to the upper jaw. They are made of keratin, like your fingernails. The krill get sieved out by the baleen and then swallowed.

> *" The blue whale isn't just the largest animal alive, it is the largest animal ever to have lived "*

Normal fault
The rock slab lying above the sloping fault line slides downwards as the plates separate. You get the same effect removing the bookend from a shelf of sloping books.

Normal fault

Reverse or thrust fault
Slabs lying above the sloping fault line lift up along a reverse fault. Plate collisions push a rock slab up and over another along a thrust fault.

Reverse or thrust fault

Mountains
Thrust faults are common in huge mountain ranges like the Himalayas, where two continental plates are colliding.

Split river
This river basin has been split in two by the rock slabs on either side of the fault, moving in opposite directions.

Plates sliding horizontally
Crustal plates can slide past each other, causing straight cracks called strike-slip faults. The two plates move horizontally in opposite directions along the fault line.

Strike-slip fault

Basins and ranges
Steep mountain ranges and flat valley basins form where rock blocks are lifted and lowered by normal faulting. Death Valley, California in the western United States is a good example.

Plates moving apart
Crustal plates are moving apart fracturing the Earth's brittle crust along fault lines – cracks where slabs of broken rock grind past each other.

Plates colliding
Crustal plates are colliding, putting pressure on the Earth's crust. As the plates slowly crunch together, the crust bends, folds and fractures like a car bonnet in a crash.

Inside the fault
Inside California's famous San Andreas Fault are small fractures, faults and pulverised rock. The fault is 30 to 1,600m wide, 1,300km long and around 16km deep.

© Science Photo Library

What causes earthquakes?

How a sudden release of pressure flattens cities and spawns tsunamis

Even if you've never felt an earthquake, you'll know they can be devastating. Films like *2012* feature 'mega quakes', where gaping fissures swallow people and buildings. Real-life earthquakes are less dramatic than those in the movies, but they're still one of nature's worst natural hazards. Unstoppable and terrifying, big quakes strike with little or no warning, flattening cities and killing tens of thousands of people.

Most of the world's earthquakes occur at the boundaries between the Earth's huge crustal plates. These boundaries are called faults, and the plates – of which there are 15 of varying different sizes here on Earth – jostle on the planet's surface like the pieces of a giant, floating jigsaw puzzle. In some parts of the world, these crustal plates grate past each other. In other

places, they collide or are pulled apart. Faults break open as these rigid plates move and exert forces great enough to crush and tear solid rock.

As the plates move about, the rock slabs at either side of faults are dragged past each other. But rocks are jagged and uneven, meaning there's lots of friction between them. This friction causes the rocks to become locked together. Pressure builds along the fault as the plates grind along, squeezing and stretching the rocks until, eventually, they break and lurch forward. Huge amounts of pent-up energy are unleashed, and it's the resulting snap that is an earthquake.

The point at which the Earth's crust first breaks is called the earthquake focus. This is usually many miles below the Earth's surface. The epicentre is the point on the surface located directly above the focus.

The released energy speeds through the Earth in the form of shock waves. There are three main types of shock wave: primary, secondary and surface waves. Primary waves radiate fastest from the earthquake focus. Secondary waves arrive later and surface waves arrive last. The surface waves travel near the Earth's surface, rocking the ground and causing the widespread devastation wrought by the largest earthquakes. People barely feel primary or secondary waves.

The size of an earthquake is defined by its magnitude – this is a measure of the energy released. Magnitude isn't a simple measurement of the relationship between earthquake size and energy. Increasing the magnitude by one increases shock wave size by ten times and total energy released by about 30 times. So for example, a magnitude eight earthquake is a billion times

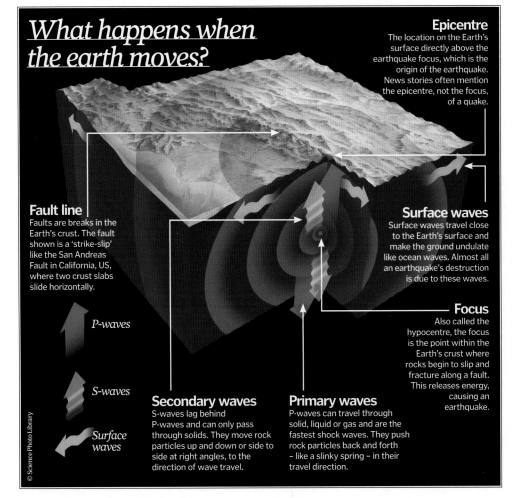

What happens when the earth moves?

Epicentre
The location on the Earth's surface directly above the earthquake focus, which is the origin of the earthquake. News stories often mention the epicentre, not the focus, of a quake.

Fault line
Faults are breaks in the Earth's crust. The fault shown is a 'strike-slip' like the San Andreas Fault in California, US, where two crust slabs slide horizontally.

P-waves

S-waves

Surface waves

© Science Photo Library

Secondary waves
S-waves lag behind P-waves and can only pass through solids. They move rock particles up and down or side to side at right angles, to the direction of wave travel.

Primary waves
P-waves can travel through solid, liquid or gas and are the fastest shock waves. They push rock particles back and forth – like a slinky spring – in their travel direction.

Surface waves
Surface waves travel close to the Earth's surface and make the ground undulate like ocean waves. Almost all an earthquake's destruction is due to these waves.

Focus
Also called the hypocentre, the focus is the point within the Earth's crust where rocks begin to slip and fracture along a fault. This releases energy, causing an earthquake.

What is the Richter scale?

An earthquake's size can be calculated on the familiar Richter scale, which makes use of logarithms for comparing the scale of one earthquake to another, or the more scientific Moment Magnitude scale, which uses sophisticated seismology equipment to measure an earthquake's actual energy.

CATASTROPHIC
Richter magnitude: >8
Moment magnitude: N/A
Affects areas thousands of miles across. Complete devastation.

VERY DISASTROUS
Richter magnitude: 8
Moment magnitude: N/A
Damage over hundreds of miles. Masonry destroyed, bridges down, large cracks appear in the ground.

DISASTROUS
Richter magnitude: 7-8
Moment magnitude: N/A
Major damage to buildings caused (masonry and frames destroyed). Ground subsidence, rails bent, pipes broken, landslides possible.

VERY DESTRUCTIVE
Richter magnitude: 7
Moment magnitude: 7.0
Serious damage possible over large areas. Structures and ground shifted.

DESTRUCTIVE
Richter magnitude: 6
Moment magnitude: 6.9
Moderate to major damage to buildings. Heavy furniture moved around.

VERY STRONG
Richter magnitude: 5-6
Moment magnitude: 6.0
Possible structural damage to buildings in populated areas. Noticed by people driving.

STRONGER
Richter magnitude: 5
Moment magnitude: 5.9
Felt by everyone. Minor to moderate damage caused.

STRONG
Richter magnitude: 4
Moment magnitude: 5.0
Felt by most people. Possible damage occurs. Windows and crockery likely to break and trees disturbed.

MODERATE
Richter magnitude: N/A
Moment magnitude: 4.9
These are often felt indoors, resulting in crockery being disturbed. Cracks may appear in walls.

SLIGHT
Richter magnitude: 3
Moment magnitude: 4.0
Noticeable vibrations indoors.

NEGLIGIBLE
Richter magnitude: 2
Moment magnitude: 3.9
Can be felt on upper floors in tall buildings.

INSTRUMENTAL
Richter magnitude: 2
Moment magnitude: 1.0-3.0
A microearthquake detected by instrumentation. Barely felt by humans.

---

more powerful than a magnitude two. Quite an unimaginable thought.

It's interesting to note that earthquake damage isn't directly related to magnitude. Deep, distant earthquakes shake the ground less than close, shallow earthquakes because the energy released at the focus has had a chance to disperse. Big earthquakes often cause longer tremors. For example, an earthquake in 1949, which had a magnitude of 7.1, shook the ground for 30 seconds, while a magnitude 8.3 earthquake in 1964 lasted five minutes.

The majority of the shuddering during an earthquake is caused by Rayleigh waves. These surface waves roll along, convulsing the Earth's crust. The ground heaves up and down and from side to side much like water waves in the ocean. Earthquakes can shake the ground violently enough to open large fissures but, unlike in the movies, these don't crunch closed around people's bodies and legs.

Big, long-lasting surface waves created by large earthquakes can topple buildings, crack roads and buildings and even trigger landslides. Well-built, earthquake-proof buildings on solid bedrock usually suffer substantially less damage

than urban areas built on loose debris and sediments. Water-saturated sediments can behave like quicksand when shaken, where loose grains move apart and flow like a liquid. In Niigata, Japan, 1964, earthquake-resistant buildings tumbled onto their sides when the ground underneath liquefied. The population faces additional hazards once the shaking stops.

> **" *Unstoppable and terrifying, big quakes strike with little or no warning* "**

Fires break out where the ground convulsions sever gas and electricity lines or destroy flammable objects. Nearly 90 per cent of the damage in the 1906 San Francisco earthquake was due to fire. Lives can be endangered and rescue efforts thwarted by collapsed bridges, burst water pipes, broken containers of hazardous chemicals and aftershocks.

Aftershocks are the less powerful earthquakes following the main tremor, when faults shift and readjust after the release of energy and stress. You could think of a tremor as the ground breathing a big sigh of relief. Major earthquakes are usually followed by several noticeable aftershocks within the first hour or so. The number of aftershocks

drops over time. However they can happen months, years or decades after the quake.

Undersea earthquakes can be as devastating as those on land, if not more. Fault movements can displace huge volumes of water, which crash to shore as killer waves called tsunamis. An undersea earthquake near northern Indonesia triggered the Indian Ocean tsunami in 2004 – the world's biggest for at least 40 years. At least 120,000 people in Indonesia alone were killed by the giant waves. Rescue teams cleared up bodies for weeks afterwards. The final death toll was over 200,000.

Tsunamis can reach speeds of 970 kilometres per hour in the deep ocean, depending on water depth. As the tsunami races into shallower water, it slows down and can reach a mammoth 30m high when it hits shore. The first sign may be water rushing out to sea, sometimes beyond the horizon, leaving the sea floor bare. The sea pours back onshore as a series of towering waves or a rapidly rising tide. Warning signs such as these can save lives. A ten-year-old British girl saw the sea hurtling away from the beach at a resort in Phuket, Thailand in 2004 and warned her mother and staff that a killer wave was coming. She'd learned about tsunamis in school a fortnight before. ❊

What is the Parkfield Experiment?

Subject to an earthquake of magnitude 6.0 or higher on average every 22 years, Parkfield in California is one of the most seriously affected places on Earth for tectonic activity. Lying straight across the epic San Andreas Fault, one of the longest and most active faults in the world, the town has seen massive destruction since its formation in the 19th Century. So much so, in fact, that the United States Geological Survey has instigated a state-of-the-art experiment in Parkfield, to better understand the physics and potential of earthquakes. Take a look at the activities going on at Parkfield…

Laser to measure surface movement by bouncing beams on reflectors

A hilltop laser near Parkfield measures movement of the Earth's crust. Red and blue laser light is fired at 18 reflectors located several kilometres away. The system converts the time the light takes to bounce back into distance travelled. It can measure movements of 1mm over about 6km.

Satellite relaying data to US Geological Survey

The US Geological Survey, which monitors natural hazards, constantly receives data from the Parkfield sensor network. Scientists can be aware of an earthquake within minutes. Sensor measurements are recorded on computer and transmitted to a satellite. There's no need to visit the instruments on foot, except for maintenance.

Sensors in water well to monitor groundwater level

Fluctuating groundwater levels can indicate that rocks are being squeezed or stretched. Monitoring pressure on rocks helps scientists monitor the risk of an earthquake. Groundwater levels are monitored in eight wells around Parkfield. Water level, air pressure and rainfall measurements are made every 10 to 15 minutes.

PARKFIELD
Pop 34

Arrows show crustal plate movements along the San Andreas Fault

The Pacific plate and North American plate are grinding past each other at a rate of about 3.5cm each year along California's San Andreas Fault. At current rates, San Francisco will lie next to Los Angeles in 15 million years.

Seismometer in hole to record microquakes

Seismometers are instruments for measuring ground movements. Nine seismometers sit in boreholes a few hundred metres underground near Parkfield. They can detect smaller earthquakes than surface instruments because they're less exposed to noise.

Magnetometer to record magnetic field

As the Earth's magnetic field alters before a quake, magnetometers measure changes in local magnetic fields. There are magnetometers located at seven sites around Parkfield.

Near-surface seismometer to record larger shocks

Seismometers can detect ground movements during earthquakes and turn them into electrical signals. The Parkfield region is bristling with seismometers, with 14 arranged in a T-shape around 1-2km across, monitoring how shock waves travel during earthquakes.

VIBROSEIS truck that probes the earthquake zone

A 14-ton truck is used to map rock layers underground without a hole being dug. The truck concentrates its weight on a short pole and shakes for several seconds. Scientists record vibrations bouncing back to the surface. How the vibrations are reflected underground vary with rock type and thickness.

Creepmeter to record surface movement

Creepmeters detect fault movement by measuring the distance between two pillars standing at either side of a fault. Measurements are made electronically by calculating the angle of a wire stretched between the pillars. There are 13 creepmeters in the Parkfield area, with one in the epicentre of past Parkfield earthquakes.

Strainmeter to monitor surface deformation

Strainmeters spot changes in the shape or size of rocks placed under pressure by movements in the Earth's crust. They can detect the crust stretching by 2.5cm in more than 25,000km by monitoring changes in the volume of liquid in a borehole, or calculating the distance between two points.

© Science Photo Library

How does the ozone work?

We may hear about it a lot, and mainly how we're slowly destroying it, but just what is the ozone layer?

The ozone layer is essentially Mother Earth's safety net, residing some 50 kilometres above the planet's surface. Created from O3, or ozone gas, it is up to 20 kilometres thick and 90 per cent of this gas can be found up on the Earth's stratosphere. This protective gas is vital to the nurturing of life on our planet, and here's why.

Ozone gases act as a shield against ultra violet, or UVB, radiation. These harmful emissions are sent through the Sun's rays, and without the ozone would severely affect the planet's ecological balance, damaging bio-diversity. UVB rays reduce plankton levels in the ocean, subsequently diminishing fish stock. Plant growth would also diminish in turn disrupting agricultural productivity. This would in turn affect the human populace, who would be exposed to an increase in skin-related diseases such as cancer.

So how does the ozone protect us? Ozone molecules consist of three oxygen atoms, hence the chemical formula O3. Stratospheric ozone absorbs UVB high-energy radiation, as well as energetic electrons, which in turn splits the O3 into an O atom and an O2 molecule. When the O atom soon encounters another O2 molecule they re-merge and recreate O3. This means that the ozone layer absorbs the UVB without being consumed. The ozone layer absorbs up to 99 per cent of the Sun's high frequency UV light rays, transforming this into heat after its combustible atomic reaction, therefore creating the stratosphere itself. This effectively incubates life on Earth.

But ozone doesn't reside only in the world above. This gas is also present in the layer around the Earth's surface. Ten to 18km above us, this is known as the tropospheric ozone or 'bad ozone', comparative to the function of the stratosphere.

This ozone occurs naturally in small doses, initiating the removal of hydrocarbons, released by plants and soil, or appearing from small amounts of stratospheric ozone, which occasionally migrate down to the Earth's surface.

However, it gets a bad reputation due to its interaction of ultraviolet light, with volatile organic compounds and nitrogen oxides, emitted by fossil-fuel powered machines and internal combustion engines. This produces high levels of ozone, which are formed in high temperature conditions, ultimately toxic to all forms of organic life.

A whole lot of hole

The area of depletion over the Antarctic, known as the ozone hole, is estimated at between 21 and 24 million square kilometres – enough to fit England in 161 times over!

The structure of the Earth's atmosphere

How the ozone extends from the Earth's surface

Tropospheric ozone
Starts at ground level, with an altitude of up to 15 kilometres. Energy transfer from the surface heats it.

The lowest part of this is the warmest with temperature decreasing with altitude. This heat and CFC intervention produces turbulent diffusion, producing great levels of ozone, harmful to organic life.

5 10 15 20
Altitude (km)

Typical cloud altitude

Stratospheric ozone
Between ten and 50 kilometres up from the stratopause. It contains up to 90 per cent of Earth's ozone.

The stratosphere contains the highest level of ozone on the planet, with two to eight parts per million. This reacts with UVB to produce what we know as the ozone layer.

The stratosphere is layered in temperature due to UVB absorption. Heat increases with altitude, with the top of the stratosphere has a temperature up to -3°C.

How big is the hole in the ozone layer?

The ozone hole refers to an area of depletion over the Antarctic region of Earth. The planet's ozone records a decline of four per cent per decade in total volume but much larger loses are recorded in the stratospheric ozone over Earth's polar region, however this is seasonal condition. These areas' unique atmospheric conditions see the most impact. Strong winds blow around the continent forming a polar vortex, isolating the air over Antarctica from the rest of the world. This allows special polar stratospheric clouds to form at about 80,000 feet altitude. These concentrate atmosphere pollutant.

When spring returns after the sunless winter period the ozone is depleted causing the ozone hole. The largest ever recorded ozone hole occurred in 2006, at 20.6 million square miles. At present the ozone hole is recorded at between 21 and 24 million square kilometres.

What's a supercell?

Find out how this phenomenally powerful and deadly thunderstorm forms

In this image we can see the culmination of a highly organised thunderstorm, commonly referred to as a 'supercell'. Supercells are incredibly rare, with significantly fewer sightings than singlecell or multicell variants, but their unique properties make them incredibly dangerous when they do occur.

A supercell thunderstorm is similar to a singlecell storm and tornado in that it has a single main updraft. However, unlike the latter it is phenomenally strong, reaching estimated speeds of 240-280km/h (150-175mph). It is so strong that it can easily upturn cars, uproot trees and even destroy entire buildings.

The main difference between a supercell storm and other types is the presence of rotational energy. This causes the updraft to rotate (referred to as a 'mesocyclone') and helps to generate extreme weather in the supercell's surrounding vicinity. This can include immense rain showers, massive two-inch-wide hail and violent tornadoes.

Supercells are classified into two types, low-precipitation and high-precipitation. The former supercells tend to formulate in arid climates, such as the high plains of the United States, while the latter are often found in moist climates closer to the Earth's equator. Regardless of type, supercells form when winds coming in from various differing directions cause a rotational energy to be generated. This helps formulate an updraft and from that, precipitation is produced.

Interestingly, however – and the reason why this image is so amazing – precipitation tends not to fall back down through the supercell's updraft when generated, instead being carried many miles downwind. Here, though, the supercell is depositing a huge torrent of rainfall directly through the updraft. ✿

Supercells are incredibly rare, but their unique properties make them incredibly dangerous when they do occur

© Science Photo Library

Cold front conditions
As the warm air is forced upwards so quickly, when it cools and condenses it forms cumulonimbus clouds and therefore heavy rain or thunderstorms. Cumulus clouds follow on from this, with showery conditions and eventually clear skies.

In practice
The red curves of a warm front and blue triangles of a cold front are shown on a map to show where the fronts are, where they're heading and the weather they'll bring.

Warm front conditions
As the warm air slowly rises, it cools and condenses and clouds are formed. These are nimbostratus, causing steady rainfall, then altostratus accompanied by drizzle, and finally cirrus, when clearer skies can be seen.

Cold front
Heavy, cool air comes from the east behind a body of warm air, which is forced sharply upwards. The quick movement of air causes cool, windy conditions.

Warm front
This is where warm air from the south meets cold air from the north, and the warm air rises gradually above the cold air.

How do they predict the weather?

To take an umbrella or not?
How we get those all-important forecasts...

The simple fact of the matter is that weather is unpredictable. So how is it that we can gather information and make predictions about what conditions on Planet Earth will be like?

Most weather phenomena occur as a result of the movement of warm and cold air masses. The border between these bodies of air are known as 'fronts', and it's here that the most exciting weather, including precipitation and wind, occurs.

As a body of air passes across different types of terrain – such as over the oceans, low-lying areas or even mountainous regions – air temperature and moisture levels can change dramatically. When two air masses at different temperatures meet, the less dense, warmer of the two masses rises up and over the colder. Rising warm air creates an area of low pressure (a depression),

which is associated with unsettled conditions like wind and rain.

We know how a frontal weather system will behave and which conditions it will produce down on the ground. The man who first brought the idea of frontal weather systems to the fore in the early 20th Century was a Norwegian meteorologist called Vilhelm Bjerknes. Through his constant observation of the weather conditions at frontal boundaries, he discovered that numerical calculations could be used to predict the weather. This model of weather prediction is still used today.

Since the introduction of frontal system weather forecasting, the technology to crunch the numbers involved has advanced immeasurably, enabling far more detailed analysis and prediction. In order to forecast the weather with the greatest accuracy,

meteorologists require vast quantities of weather data – including temperature, precipitation, cloud coverage, wind speed and wind direction – collected from weather stations located all over the world. Readings are taken constantly and fed via computer to a central location.

Technology is essential to both gathering and processing the statistical data about the conditions down on Earth and in the upper atmosphere. The massive computational power inside a supercomputer, for example, is capable of predicting the path and actions of hurricanes and issuing life-saving warnings. After taking the information collected by various monitors and sensors, a supercomputer can complete billions of calculations per second to produce imagery that can reveal how the hurricane is expected to develop. ❋

What do the forecast symbols mean?

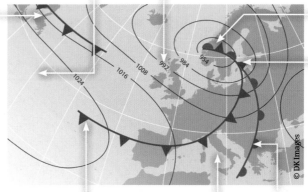

High pressure
Weather here will be clear and dry, due to the high pressure. If this high pressure occurs in summer weather will be warm, whereas in winter it will be cold and crisp.

Isobars
These indicate atmospheric pressure. Areas of equal atmospheric pressure are joined together with the lines shown and the numbers indicate pressure measured in millibars. Lower numbers indicate low pressure, while higher numbers indicate high pressure.

Wind
The conditions at this point will be windy. This is indicated by the position of the isobars; the closer together they are the windier the conditions.

Low pressure
At the centre of these circular patterns of isobars is where systems of high or low pressure lie. Where there is low pressure conditions will be rainy and windy.

Occluded front
This is where one front 'catches up' with another. In this example, the cold has caught up with the warm. Occluded fronts cause the weather to change quite quickly and, in this case, become similar to that of a cold front.

Cold front
As with any cold front, the weather here will be expected to be cool with heavy rainfall and possibly even thunderstorms. This will be followed by showers.

In between
After the passing of the warm front and before the arrival of the cold front conditions should be clear and dry, but normally only for a short period.

Warm front
The warm front will cause steady rainfall, followed by drizzle, accompanied by cloudy skies. These are typical conditions caused by any warm front.

How do golden eagles hunt?

Telescopic vision and terrifying talons – be glad you're not a Scottish rabbit

Golden eagles are apex predators, adapted to hunt in very harsh landscapes. With a wingspan of more than two metres, they are huge birds, capable of lifting prey weighing as much as five kilograms. There are documented cases of golden eagles attacking adult deer and even a bear cub but their usual targets are hares, foxes, grouse and, on the coast, seabirds.

Golden eagles nest in trees and on remote mountain crags. They can't hunt in thick forest so they have specialised to scour moors and uplands. Food is much scarcer here and the eagles have to patrol huge territories; sometimes as much as 160km2. To do this they operate like stealth bombers, flying very high above the ground to scan a wide area without alerting their prey. They need to be able to soar for hours at a time and strong enough to kill whatever animal presents an opportunity.

Flexible neck
Because the eyes are so large, they can barely move in their sockets. Instead the neck twists 270 degrees.

Large eyes
Facing forward to provide excellent binocular vision. They can spot a mountain hare from two miles away.

Primary feathers
The gaps between the 'fingers' of the primary feathers help to fine-tune the airflow over the wings.

Powerful wing muscles
Golden eagles can weigh up to 7kg but must be able to take off from the ground in a single bound.

Feathered legs
Unlike the long, bony legs of a swan, these are short and well muscled, with feathers to keep them warm.

Tail
The tail can act as a rudder, to compensate for crosswinds or be spread wide to increase lift.

Deadly talons
The curved claws restrain prey and kill it. Smaller animals are simply carried aloft, back to the nest.

What's inside a mosquito?

We take a look inside these miniature bloodsuckers

Mosquitoes are nectar-drinking insects, which – in the case of the females – also drink blood (haematophagy). This is undertaken as the female needs to obtain nutrients there within – such as iron and protein – to help develop her eggs. As such, the common mosquito has developed a highly complex form and system in order to extract these substances from their target host, including a saliva that negatively affects vascular constriction, blood clotting, platelet aggregation and angiogenesis, allowing it to drink freely. We take a look at the mechanisms it has evolved in order to do so. ✿

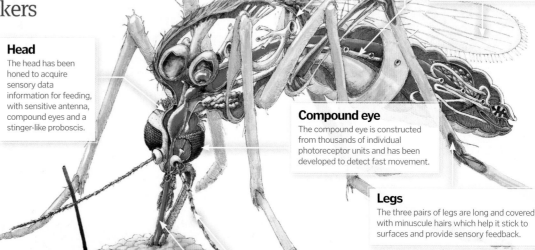

Thorax
This part of the mosquito is specialised for locomotion, with its three pairs of legs and single set of wings attached.

Abdomen
Comprised of seven segments, blood and nectar are directly sourced here. It is also the digestive area.

Wing
The wings consist of a series of longitudinal and cross veins through a lightweight outgrowth of the exoskeleton.

Head
The head has been honed to acquire sensory data information for feeding, with sensitive antenna, compound eyes and a stinger-like proboscis.

Compound eye
The compound eye is constructed from thousands of individual photoreceptor units and has been developed to detect fast movement.

Legs
The three pairs of legs are long and covered with minuscule hairs which help it stick to surfaces and provide sensory feedback.

Proboscis
The proboscis is used to inject the exploitative negative saliva needed to circumvent the target's vertebrate physiological responses, and also to extract blood from a target.

Antennae
The antenna is highly sensitive and plays a major role in detecting odours of potential targets.

© DK Images

How do ticks suck blood?

Discover how these little creatures make a tasty meal of their hosts

Ticks are extremely small parasites that feed on the protein-rich blood of other animals through the process of hematophagy. As they are arachnids they have eight legs, the first pair of which features a special sensory pit called the 'haller' organ, which can sniff out prey. After finding a suitable host, the tick anchors itself to the unwitting victim using its claws as well as its spiny legs and the special sucker pads on its feet. To puncture the skin and get to the blood, the tick uses its two fang-like chelicerae, and then extends a long serrated proboscis called a hypostome. The hypostome makes it difficult to remove an attached tick as, like a fishhook, it's covered with backwards-pointing barbs. The tick then sucks up blood until its body, also known as the idiosoma, is so bloated it can't take any more – this can take several days. ✿

© Science Photo Library

Ticks can swell to many times their size after feeding

Engorged
This image shows a tick filled with blood.

How does the Great White hunt its prey?

Exploring the great white shark's hunting habits

4. Touch-at-distance
A row of fluid-filled sensory canals on either side of the body respond to changes in pressure and movement, helping it feel the presence of objects in the water.

1. Smelly vision
A super sense of smell is the primary detector for the shark species when hunting prey. The great white can amazingly smell a single drop of blood in 100 litres of water.

3. Super hearing
Rapid, irregularly pulsed, broadband sounds at frequencies below 600 hertz, made by injured prey and spawning fish, can alert hunting sharks from over one mile away.

5. Swallow or spit
The great white shark has advanced taste receptors located on the swellings in the mouth and gums. These help determine the palatability of its food.

2. Electric impulse
Jelly-filled canals in the shark's head help detect electrical charges as small as 0.005 microvolts. Enough to detect the heartbeat of hiding fish.

Amazing!

WEIGHT: 5,000lbs
LENGTH: 13-23ft
SPEED: 15mph

The great white shark, or Carcharodon carcharias, can only be described as the largest predatory fish in the sea. But is this aquatic marauder as fearsome as the popular media would have us believe?

It's certainly a species long in the tooth, in more ways than one. Firstly each of its incisors is a perfect cutting implement, triangularly serrated on both sides. These can grow up to as long as three inches. Upon maturity an adult great white can have anywhere up to 3,000 teeth jam-packed within its gaping jawline.

The way in which this and its teeth operate accordingly is truly remarkable. The great white shark has a floating jaw, enabling it to hold onto its prey with the lower part, as the upper jaw clamps down, tearing away flesh. Couple this with great white sizes reported up to as big as 20 feet or more, carrying weight of up to 2,240 kilograms, or 4,938lb, and that's one killer bite.

The great white's anatomy almost contradicts itself. With a torpedo-shaped torso, it propels itself with its powerful tail, reaching speeds up to 15 miles per hour. These sharks move much like aircraft, less like conventional swimming fish species. Yet this momentum is used at an advantage, and the great white shark shows strategy in swiftly surprising prey from below. This usually consists of inflicting a fatal bite, which will sees its prey either die of shock or massive body trauma.

It's apparent that this species of shark has evolved into a remarkable hunting machine, the bloodhound of the sea. The great white has developed the most diverse array of sensors of any known predator.

How are caves formed?

Millions of years in the making, caves are wondrous and diverse natural phenomena, which have held humans in both awe and dread for thousands of years

Solutional caves, as found across the Yucatan peninsula, are the most commonly occurring Earth cavities found across the globe. They are formed when a soluble rock such as limestone or marble is dissolved slowly by natural acid in the resident groundwater that seeps through the planes, faults and joints which, over epochs, slowly become cracks, then gulleys and finally caves. This dissolving process produces a distinctive landform known as 'karst', which is characterised by subterranean drainage, sinkholes and extensive interlinked cave networks.

The other most notable feature of solutional caves are the striking calcium carbonate formations that are produced by the slow precipitation of acid-laced groundwater. These formations include: stalactites – from the Greek "that which drips", a type of secondary mineral that hangs from the ceiling of caves; stalagmites – from the Greek "drop", a secondary mineral material which drops from the ceiling to the floor where it forms a calcium carbonate deposit; and soda straws, which are thin mineral tubes that grow out of cracks and carry water in their interior.

While solutional caves are by far the most common caves found worldwide, other varieties also exist and can be formed in numerous different ways. Primary caves for example are formed at the same time as the surrounding rock, instead of afterwards like the solutional varieties that we've mentioned before. These caves are mostly formed by lava flowing downward and cooling and solidifying on top, while continuing to progress at the base, creating a lava tube once dissipated.

Another variety of cave formed in a similar manner to primary caves are glacial caves. Here, caves and tunnels are formed when embedded ice melts under glaciers and – as with the lava – flow downwards before eventually freezing again on top and solidifying once more. Finally, littoral caves (commonly referred to as sea caves) are formed when coastal rock is eroded away by the tidal action of the ocean waves, eating away at soluble rock along weakened points such as fault lines. ✿

A cave laced with stalactites, stalagmites and tube straws

© Semu

© Dave Bunnell

A cave explorer lowers himself over 600 feet into a sinkhole

> ❝ *Rock is dissolved slowly by groundwater so that faults and joints slowly become cracks, gulleys and caves* ❞

Soluble rock

This, a good cross-section diagram of a formation of solutional-formed caves, demonstrates how soft soluble rock is eroded over time by acidic groundwater. Water becomes acidic through a combination of climate effects (pollution) and by being absorbed by/passed over organic hydrocarbons.

Calcium carbonate

After the acidic groundwater penetrates the rock's planes, faults and joints, it can drip down from the ceiling of a preformed cave leaving mineral deposits either at its base, or on its roof, which then hardens into calcium carbonate formations such as stalactites and stalagmites.

© Dave Bunnell

New Mexico's Lechuguilla cave is an other-worldly example of an extremely deep cavern

Karst formation

As the soluble rock is eroded, a series of extensive tunnels, channels and holes is formed underground, culminating with many cave mouths often leading into valleys or rivers. In addition, if the erosion is severe then sinkholes may be formed (as can be seen here) when the roof of hollowed-out areas collapse in on itself. These are the characteristic features of karst topography.

© Science Photo Library

Subterranean drainage

Once formed, any drainage channels will continue to erode if the area is subjected to heavy rainfall, with the gulleys being carved out by underground streams and rivers.

> **"** *When drainage systems are overwhelmed by rainwater, the result can often be a torrent of water up to six metres high* **"**

1. Rainfall
A large amount of rainwater, possibly caused by a slow-moving thunderstorm or two in quick succession, falls onto the ground.

4. River overflows
A large amount of water running into a river or lake can eventually cause the water level to rise over the river banks.

2. Saturated soil
Soil with poor absorption, such as saturated or dry soil, is unable to take the water in. Instead, it flows along the surface as run-off water.

3. Steep incline
Flash floods are more likely to occur in hilly areas, where the water can move more quickly towards a lower point.

5. Rapid water
The rapidly expanding river bursts its banks and the water flows outwards, sweeping trees and debris with it, in a process that takes just several hours.

What causes flash floods?

Discover how these fast-moving walls of water become so dangerous

When natural or man-made drainage systems are overwhelmed by rainwater, the result can often be a torrent of water up to six metres (20 feet) high, known as a flash flood. Regular floods occur when, over time, a natural reservoir of water such as a river of lake gradually overflows and spills out into flood plains.

Flash floods, however, are the result of intense periods of rainfall that form into walls or waves of water surprisingly quickly, often in less than six hours.

Usually rainwater is absorbed and held by soil in the ground. This is why in the UK, despite experiencing a fairly large amount of rainfall, flash floods are rare. The danger occurs when one rainstorm quickly follows another or a slow-moving thunderstorm sits over a specific area. If the ground is already heavily saturated, frozen or covered in a material such as asphalt (used on roads), the water sits on top and moves as run-off to the lowest point it can reach, often a river or lake.

Flash floods are also relatively common in arid conditions, and a bigger danger than the risk of dehydration in a desert. Thunderstorms can form very quickly in these environments, and the water tends to flow over the surface rather than sinking underground, moving dangerously fast. ✿

How can you survive in the desert?

John 'Lofty' Wiseman's SAS desert survival techniques

John 'Lofty' Wiseman served in the SAS for 26 years, setting a record for the youngest person ever to pass selection when he was aged 18. In addition to extensive service worldwide in which John saw action in every theatre of operations and special operations required of the British Army, he ran the Survival Training School for 22 SAS Hereford, specialising in all aspects of survival training. We asked John to give us his top techniques for survival in a harsh desert environment.

Firstly, if your vehicle breaks down it is important to stay with it. A vehicle provides many things, including cover, a lengthy shadow for shade, a structure to attach an awning, a larger target for a rescue team to spot, as well as being a valuable source of fuel from its tanks (for fires) and water from its radiator (useful for soaking clothes and drinking if distilled).

Staying with your vehicle you should then prioritise constructing shelter, preferably an awning. Shelter is often discarded over water acquisition, as it's wrongly believed to be more important for survival. While maintaining hydration is crucial, without shelter a person will get heat stroke and die within hours. The best and easiest form of shelter to attain is to construct an awning, attaching it to the top of the vehicle. If the construction of an awning is not possible then utilise close rocky outcrops or the banks of a wadi.

Once shelter is acquired it is essential to cool down. To maintain hydration it is important to drink two and a half pints for every three and a half lost, or a minimum of half a pint per 24 hours, drunk at midday and lights down. On this point, when travelling or stranded with water supplies, always split it up over numerous containers or jerry cans instead of just storing it in one big tank. This way if you have an accident in the vehicle or on foot and

> ## *Without shelter a person will get heat stroke and die within hours*

the tank is punctured, broken or contaminated then you do not lose your entire water supply. Regardless if water supplies are high or low, it is important if possible to complement it with other sources. These can be attained through solar stills constructed by covering green plants under a plastic film or bag in a half metre deep and metre round hole. The condensation formed from the respiring plants at night – due to the drop in temperature – can be harvested.

In terms of food, snakes, spiders and scorpions may be eaten; however, with each it is important to discern whether poisonous. Snakes offer the best source of meat and can be ridden of stored poisons by cutting off their head. It is important to remember, however, that the digestion the body undertakes as a result of eating requires water to do so and therefore will contribute to dehydration. Remember, it takes three weeks for a human to die from lack of food, but only three days from lack of water.

In order to attract attention of search and rescue parties, signals should be made by launching flares, drawing SOS on the ground in stones, honking the vehicle's horn in six spaced blasts every five seconds and at night flashing its lights in the same way. Smoky fires should be constructed out of surrounding bush and scrub plants as well as any spare tyres the vehicle is carrying. A heliograph should also be used as much as possible, or if one is not available, a piece of foil, glass or mirror in order to reflect the Sun's light, causing a glint for searchers.

Other general advice would be to sleep as much as you can, eat only when necessary, keep your skin free of dirt and sand as this helps it sweat, treat all cuts and wounds immediately to prevent sores, when not on your feet put boots upside down on poles to prevent venomous creatures from crawling inside and keep the head covered when in direct sunlight.

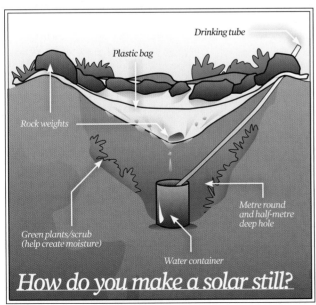

Drinking tube

Plastic bag

Rock weights

Green plants/scrub (help create moisture)

Metre round and half-metre deep hole

Water container

How do you make a solar still?

How can everyday items save your life?

Multiple flasks/containers
A flask gives you a secure, portable source of water, ideal if you are forced to take shelter far from your vehicle or reach higher ground in order to be spotted. If carrying water in a large container, split it up into many so you don't have all your eggs in one basket.

Razor
A razor (ideally with an open blade) can be utilised in various ways, including killing and skinning animals, reflecting the sun for attention, fashioning an awning or head-wrap and cutting branches and bushes for firewood.

Mirror
A mirror or other reflective object can be used to reflect the sun, thereby drawing attention to your position for rescue parties by its glint.

Plastic bag
A plastic bag can be used to create a solar still, perfect for collecting water from respiring plants.

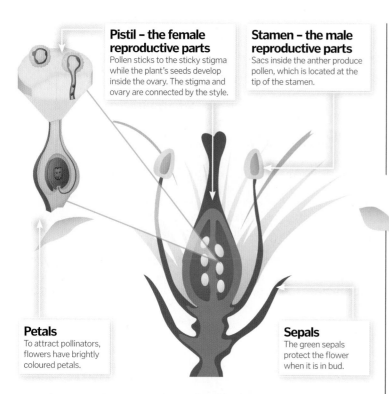

Pistil – the female reproductive parts
Pollen sticks to the sticky stigma while the plant's seeds develop inside the ovary. The stigma and ovary are connected by the style.

Stamen – the male reproductive parts
Sacs inside the anther produce pollen, which is located at the tip of the stamen.

Petals
To attract pollinators, flowers have brightly coloured petals.

Sepals
The green sepals protect the flower when it is in bud.

How do plants reproduce?

Plant pollination and beyond

Flowering plants propagate by way of pollination. Just as in human reproduction, there are male and female sex organs. This process, however, is much less strenuous than in animal intercourse; the male parts of the flower barely do anything.

The male parts of the flower, which produce pollen, are called stamens, and each one consists of a stalk, or filament, with what's known as an anther at the tip. The anther is full of tiny sacs in which the pollen grains develop and eventually break free.

The female reproductive organs are called pistils, and these consist of a sticky stigma at the tip, which the pollen sticks to, and an ovary, which is a bulbous structure full of ovules where seeds develop at the base of the pistil. The stigma and ovary are connected by a stalk called a style.

Pollen itself is produced by the male organs and is transferred to the female parts in order to form seeds. Self-pollination can occur when pollen sticks to the stigma of a flower of the same plant. Alternatively pollen can be transferred to another plant altogether, and this can either be as a result of the wind blowing the pollen through the air, or by the pollen getting stuck to industrious insects attracted by the blooms' colourful petals, who then roam from flower to flower unknowingly distributing pollen as they go.

When a male pollen grain lands on the female stigma of a plant of the same species, the grain develops a pollen tube that leads to an ovule within the ovary. The male cells then travel through the tube into the ovule, where it can proceed to fertilise the female egg inside. Once fertilisation has occurred, a seed forms in the ovary. Meanwhile, the ovary surrounding the seed becomes a fruit, which protects the seed and helps it develop into a plant itself. ✿

Why don't woodpeckers get headaches?

How a thick skull keeps it injury free

Woodpeckers whack their heads against wood up to 20 times a second, at 1,200 times the force of gravity, without suffering concussion, detached retinas or any other symptoms of head injury. But how?

Holes
Woodpeckers excavate small rectangular holes on the sides of tree trunks, prying off wood to expose tasty beetle larvae and carpenter ants.

Skull
Woodpeckers have a thicker skull than most other birds. It's made of extremely strong yet spongy compressible bone, to help cushion the blow. The beak and skull are linked by elastic connective tissue.

Brain
Unlike human brains, which are floating about in a pool of cushioning cerebrospinal fluid, woodpecker brains are tightly enclosed in the skull with practically no cerebrospinal fluid.

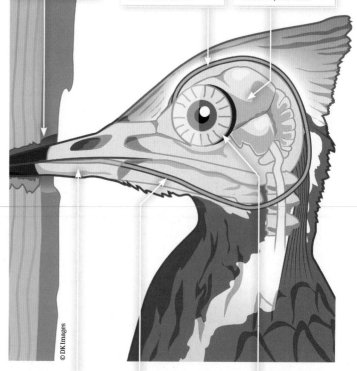

© DK Images

Beak
The strong bones that comprise the woodpecker's straight bill are strengthened by a horn-covered beak, which hammers into the wood and bark of a tree at something like 12,000 impacts per day in search of bugs and ants.

Hyoid apparatus
Within the long tongue is a skeletal structure called the 'hyoid apparatus'. This is a collection of small bones supported by cartilage and muscles, which fold up like an accordion and enable the woodpecker to stick its tongue out further.

Third eyelid
Woodpeckers have a thick inner eyelid, which acts as a seatbelt to ensure the bird's eyeballs don't pop out and also prevents tearing the retina. The eye is filled with blood to support the retina.

What's the deepest place on Earth?

Exploring the Mariana Trench, 11,034m below sea level

The Pacific Ring of Fire is a massive area around the edge of the Pacific Ocean where most of the world's volcanic and seismic activity occurs. Just south of Japan, at a maximum depth of 11,034m, lies the deepest point on the surface of the planet: the Challenger Deep.

This depression in the seabed is located at the southern end of the Mariana Trench, the geological product of the convergence of two tectonic plates – the Pacific Plate and the Mariana Plate – and a process called subduction whereby the larger and denser of the two converging plates (that being the Pacific Plate) gets subducted under the Earth's mantle, creating a deep depression in the Earth's crust. These trenches make up the deepest parts of the world's oceans – and for this reason such areas remain practically uncharted.

Less than five per cent of the world's oceans have been explored due to the inaccessible nature of deep sea (the lowest layer in the ocean) and the massive pressure (some 16,000psi)

exerted on objects at these depths. In 1960, however, intrepid oceanographers Jacques Piccard and Lt Don Walsh ventured to the bottom of the Mariana Trench in a bathyscaphe called the Trieste: the only manned submersible to reach the bottom and return in tact. Although the men could not collect photos, data, or samples from the seabed, their voyage provided a new vision of what could be achieved in deep-sea exploration.

More often these days, unmanned, remotely operated submarines and observation vessels are used for locating, mapping, collecting and photographing deep-sea geology and biology. In this pitch-black world it is extremely cold and the pressure of the seawater above makes for a very inhospitable environment for marine life let alone eager explorers. However, each new dive seems to uncover another species of aquatic life in this unique underwater ecosystem and with new developments in submersible vehicles we are drawing ever closer to uncovering more of this, the unfathomable deep. Right now, we've only scratched the surface. ✿

Sea level

Continental Shelf

Depth (1,000s of feet)

0

10

20

30

Continental slope

How was the Mariana Trench created?

1. Convergence
Due to the seismic activity where two oceanic plates meet, you will find an ocean trench and usually undersea volcanoes.

2. Trench
The deepest parts of the Earth's surface are created by the trench formed at the point of subduction.

3. Subduction
The larger, denser Pacific Plate is subducted under the Earth's crust beneath the Mariana Plate.

Mariana Plate

Pacific Plate

Abyssal plain

Trench

Has anyone been down there?

This is Lt Don Walsh (left) and Jacques Piccard (centre) in the pressure sphere on-board the Bathyscaphe Trieste. In 1960, these oceanographers embarked on the only successful manned expedition to the Challenger Deep.

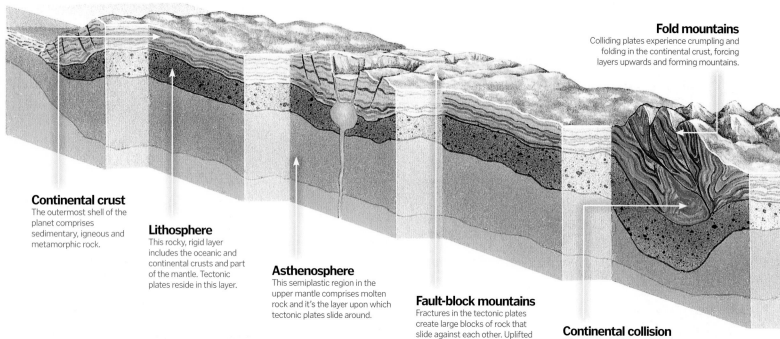

Fold mountains
Colliding plates experience crumpling and folding in the continental crust, forcing layers upwards and forming mountains.

Continental crust
The outermost shell of the planet comprises sedimentary, igneous and metamorphic rock.

Lithosphere
This rocky, rigid layer includes the oceanic and continental crusts and part of the mantle. Tectonic plates reside in this layer.

Asthenosphere
This semiplastic region in the upper mantle comprises molten rock and it's the layer upon which tectonic plates slide around.

Fault-block mountains
Fractures in the tectonic plates create large blocks of rock that slide against each other. Uplifted blocks form mountains.

Continental collision
When tectonic plates collide, the continental crust and lithosphere on one plate can be driven below the other plate, known as subduction.

How do you make a mountain?

All you need are a couple of tectonic plates and volcanoes

Mountains are massive landforms rising high above the Earth's surface, caused by one or more geological processes: plate tectonics, volcanic activity and/or erosion. Generally they fall into one of five categories – fold, fault-block, dome, volcanic and plateau – although there can be some overlap.

Mountains comprise about 25 per cent of our land mass, with Asia having more than 60 per cent of them. They are home to 12 per cent of the Earth's population, and they don't just provide beauty and recreation; more than half of the people on Earth rely on the fresh water that flows from the mountains to feed streams and rivers. Mountains are also incredibly biodiverse, with unique layers of ecosystems depending on their elevation and climate.

One of the most amazing things about mountains is that although they look solid and immovable to us, they're always changing. Mountains rising from activity associated with plate tectonics – fold and fault-block – form slowly over millions of years. The plates and rocks that initially interacted to form the mountains continue to move up to 2cm (0.7in) each year, meaning

that the mountains grow. The Himalayas, for example, grow about 1cm per year.

The volcanic activity that builds mountains can wax and wane over time. Mount Fuji, the tallest mountain in Japan, has erupted 16 times since 781AD. Mount Pinatubo in the Philippines erupted in the early-Nineties without any prior recorded eruptions, producing the second largest volcanic eruption of the 20th Century. Inactive volcanic mountains – and all other types of mountains, for that matter – are also subject to erosion, earthquakes and other activity that can dramatically alter their appearances as well as the landscape around us. There are even classifications for the different types of mountain peaks that have been affected by glacial periods in Earth's history. The bare, near-vertical mountaintop of the Matterhorn in the Alps, for example, is known as a pyramidal peak, or horn. ✿

© NASA

" One of the most amazing things about mountains is that although they look immovable to us, they're always changing "

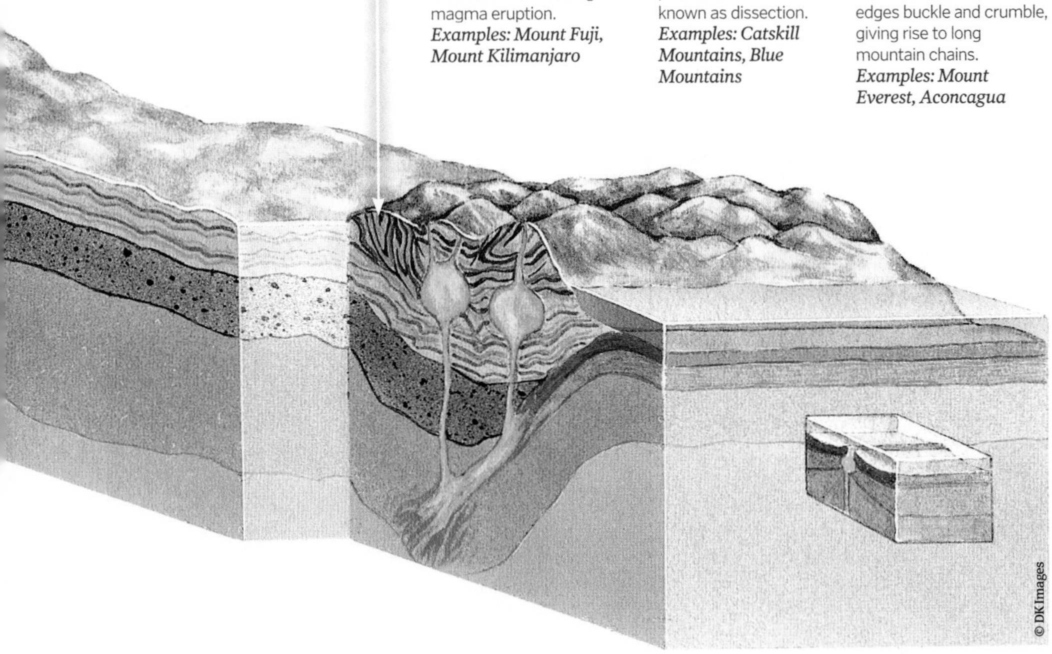

Volcanic mountains
These mountains form when molten rock explodes up through the Earth's crust and can still be volcanically active.

What are the different types of mountain?

Volcanic
These mountains are created by the buildup of lava, rock, ash and other volcanic matter during a magma eruption.
Examples: Mount Fuji, Mount Kilimanjaro

Plateau
Plateau mountains are revealed through erosion of uplifted plateaus. This is known as dissection.
Examples: Catskill Mountains, Blue Mountains

Fold
This most common type of mountain is formed when two tectonic plates smash into each other. The edges buckle and crumble, giving rise to long mountain chains.
Examples: Mount Everest, Aconcagua

Fault-block
Fault-block mountains form when cracked layers of crust slide against each other along faults in the Earth's crust. They can be lifted, with two steep sides; or lifted, with one gently sloping side and one steep side.
Examples: Sierra Nevada, Urals

Dome
These types of mountain also form from magma. Unlike with volcanoes, however, there is no eruption; the magma simply pushes up sedimentary layers of the Earth's crust and forms a round dome-shaped mountain.
Examples: Navajo Mountain, Ozark Dome

© DK Images

© Science Photo Library

Why do sinkholes appear?

Discover how limestone landscapes are riddled with hollows and holes

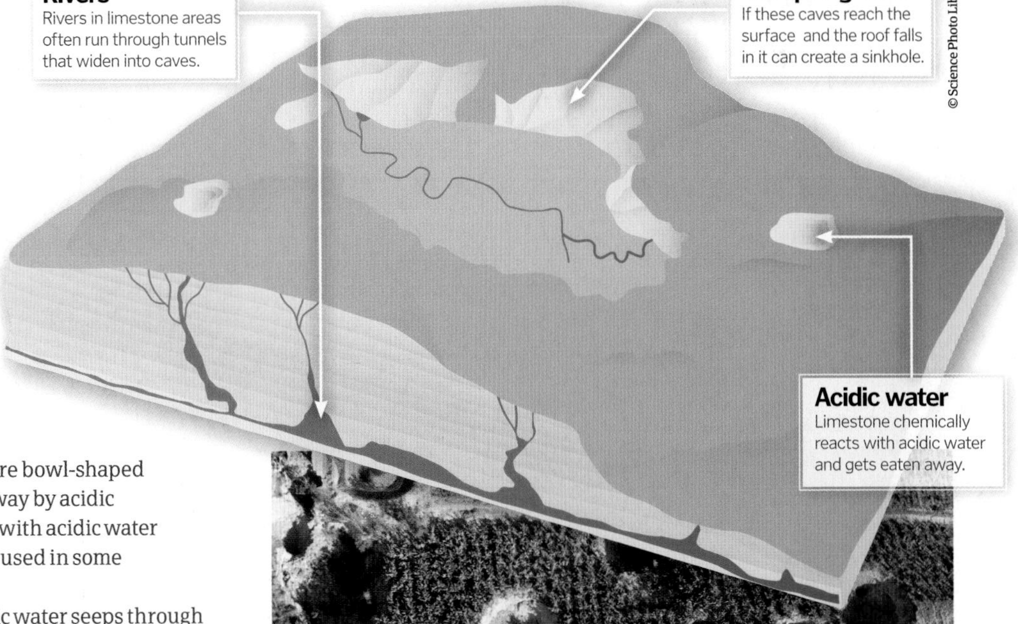

Rivers
Rivers in limestone areas often run through tunnels that widen into caves.

Collapsing cave
If these caves reach the surface and the roof falls in it can create a sinkhole.

Acidic water
Limestone chemically reacts with acidic water and gets eaten away.

Sinkholes, dolines, swallow or shake holes are bowl-shaped hollows created when limestone is eaten away by acidic groundwater. Limestone chemically reacts with acidic water because it's mostly calcium carbonate – the alkali used in some indigestion tablets to neutralise stomach acid.

Sinkholes form in two main ways. First, as acidic water seeps through and widens cracks in limestone. If the cracks are close together, a small hollow forms and grows bigger as rainwater flows into it.

Sinkholes also form when caves collapse. Rivers in limestone areas often run through underground tunnels that they widen into caves. If the cave reaches the surface and the roof falls in, it can create a sinkhole.

Holes in the ground in other rock types are sometimes called sinkholes. An enormous sinkhole that swallowed a Guatemala City clothing factory in May, for example, is in an area of volcanic rock and ash.

Do dogs see in black and white?

Contrary to popular belief, dogs do have some colour vision – though this is undoubtedly different to the vision of humans. In the human eye there are two types of photoreceptors called rods and cones. Rods help us to determine differences in brightness and darkness where cones are sensitive to colour. We have three types of cones: some are sensitive to red light, some are sensitive to green and some to blue. Dogs have more rods than humans and fewer cones. Rods need less light to work and this accounts for dogs having better night vision than humans. Humans rely more on cones and the differences in wavelength are harder to detect when there is less light, hence we don't see very well in the dark.

Dogs are said to have dichromatic vision; they can only see a part of the range of colours which are in our visible spectrum. It is thought that dogs can see different shades of yellow and blue as they have cones which correspond to being able to detect these wavelengths of light. Whether their yellow is the same as yours or mine is a different matter entirely.

> ❝ *Dogs do have some colour vision – though this is different to the vision of humans* ❞

Do fish really have a three-second memory?

This is a myth and there have been various studies disproving the commonly held belief. In January 2009, researchers from the Technion Institute of Technology in Israel taught fish to respond to a sound that meant feeding time in captivity. The fish remembered the sound months later having been returned to the wild, returning to a certain spot for feeding.

Why don't whales get the bends?

Any scuba diver is aware of the dangers of decompression. When you dive deep in high pressure water, the air which you breathe from your tank will have the same pressure that the water is exerting. If this were not the case then the air wouldn't come out of your tank. At a depth of 33 feet the air pressure is twice that of atmospheric air pressure on land.

High pressure nitrogen from this air dissolves in your bloodstream and water in your body. Anyone who had unscrewed a lid on a shaken fizzy drink bottle knows that bubbles start to fizz up due to the lessening of pressure. The same effect happens to the nitrogen in the bloodstream of a diver if they ascend too quickly.

So, how do whales and other marine mammals handle this tremendous pressure increase? They have adapted to collapse their thoracic cavity, lungs, and alveolar sacs. Whales have very weak and flexible rib cages. While diving, the thoracic cavity is collapsed so no air can get in. When this collapse occurs, there is still air with high nitrogen levels present, in the alveolar sac, which is the site of gas exchange. Marine mammals have adapted to this by creating a cartilage build up in the bronchioles. This allows for alveolar collapse and storage of the air in the bronchioles. This is important because nitrogen is no longer at the site of gas exchange and cannot be absorbed into the body. Therefore the nitrogen will not fizz in their bloodstream upon ascent, therefore making them effectively immune to the bends.

Why do bats insist on sleeping upside down?

This is partly because they can't grip with their 'hands' so use their feet instead, but the feet wouldn't support their weight if they stood on them. Also, bats can't launch themselves from the ground to take off like birds do, so from a hanging position they can use gravity to their advantage to get airborne, as well as being protected from predators.

How do Venus flytraps work?

Venus flytraps, like the rat-eating carnivorous plant, tend to grow in boggy soil that's low in nutrients, hence they need to find another source of food to sustain them, namely insects that happen to land on their leaves. These leaves are about eight to 15cm long and are 'hinged' along the midline with spiny teeth around the edges. The folding and trapping action is triggered by pressure on six sensitive hairs that, when stimulated will snap the leaf shut in about half a second, although the actual nature of the action is still debated. As well as these sensitive hairs, the leaf also has glands on its surface that secrete a sap which digests the insect's body. This process takes about ten days, after which the leaf reopens.

> ❝ *The folding and trapping action is triggered by pressure on six sensitive hairs* ❞

What is a stink plant and why does it stink?

The titan arum (or stink plant) is an odd plant however you look at it. Known as the 'Corpse Flower' in Indonesia, it's a colossal organism, the central column or 'spadix' growing up to three metres tall. The plant's corm – the underground root system where it stores its food – is the largest in the world, the one at Kew Gardens weighing in at an astonishing 91kg.

Once the flowers around it are ready for pollination, the spadix begins to generate the disgusting smell to attract sweat bees, beetles and other carcass-eating insects. Thinking they've found a meal, or somewhere to lay their eggs, the insects arrive, crawl over the flower and while they go away hungry, they also ensure pollination occurs. To make certain of this, the spadix's tip heats to near human body temperature while the red colouration and texture of the lower section completes the illusion.

If bees are too heavy to fly, how come they can?

The idea that bees shouldn't be able to fly has been around since the Thirties when a scientist attempted to calculate the lift generated by a bee based on their wing size with relation to body mass. The calculations were based on aircraft lift which describes lift for a fixed wing design. Bees wings are moving in a complex arrangement so trying to quantify this with calculations based on aircraft proved to be a big mistake.

High speed photography has shown us that the bee's ability to fly comes from the exotic way in which they flap their wings. The wings do not just go up and down, the root of the wing also moves the wing forwards and backwards so the tips of the wing move in an oval-type way. The incredible speed at which the wings perform this complicated movement creates air currents which are strong enough to allow for the bee to fly.

> " The bee's ability to fly comes from the exotic way in which they flap their wings "

Why is the sky blue and the grass green?

This is a good question as it's often quoted by folk in response to a question that they deem either unimportant or unanswerable or both, so it's good to have a scientific answer in your locker to fire back at them, so here goes. Grass is green because it contains a pigment known as chlorophyll, which is used in the process of photosynthesis where a plant produces sugar in the presence of sunlight. Now this leads to the question as to why chlorophyll is green? Well, this is because the arrangement of the atoms in chlorophyll means it absorbs every colour from the Sun except green, which it reflects. Our eyes see this green light and therefore grass is green!

The sky is blue because of the way light interacts with gasses in our atmosphere. Light from the Sun is made up of many different colours, these all travel as waves and each colour has an associated wavelength. Our atmosphere is filled with atoms and molecules of gas, mainly nitrogen and oxygen. When light hits these gas molecules some of it may get absorbed and then released again in a different direction. The colour which is radiated will be the same colour that was absorbed; however, some colours are more susceptible to this absorption and re-emission. It turns out that the wavelength of light corresponding to the colour blue is absorbed more often than any of the other colours. This process is called Rayleigh scattering (after the physicist Lord John Rayleigh). The reason we see a blue sky is because the shorter wavelength 'blue' light is scattered in all directions whereas the other colours are scattered much less. This blue light is travelling in more directions than the other colours and whichever direction you look, some of this blue light will be reaching you. Next time someone asks you, you'll know.

Why do sharks go into a tonic state?

Many animals are capable of entering a trance-like state called tonic immobility whereby they appear dead to their surroundings. In the case of sharks it has been observed on many different species such as the lemon shark, reef shark and tiger sharks upon simply placing them upside down. During tonic immobility the dorsal fin becomes straightened and the breathing and muscle contractions become more relaxed. It is such a reliable behaviour in certain sharks that it is used as a type of anaesthesia before minor surgery.

Some killer whales have learned to take advantage of this by using their tails to create currents in the water that can turn a shark over in order to eat it. The reason this happens to sharks is unclear, but it can be argued that tonic immobility has a role to play in survival, allowing the shark to blend into the surroundings by being completely motionless, but in this case it's obviously a disadvantage for the shark. It has also been speculated that it may be something to do with the mating ritual of certain shark species as in some cases it can be induced by massage.

What is an Indian summer?

The definition of an Indian summer is a period of mild sunny weather that is out of season. The term is commonly used to describe a sunny spell which can occur after the first frost. The first recorded usage of the term was in 1778, from a Frenchman who lived in America called John de Crevecoeur who mentioned it in a letter. The term had spread to Britain by the 19th Century.

Indian summers are caused by stalled high pressure. This high pressure pushes air towards areas of low pressure which makes wind. Due to the rotation of the Earth, these winds rotate counter-clockwise about the northern hemisphere and can sometimes curve south, picking up warmer air, bringing it further north and making it unseasonably warm.

How do you tell if a mushroom is poisonous?

There are many different types of mushroom so without getting a good grasp of individual kinds of mushroom it would be difficult to say whether it is poisonous or not. A general rule would be to never consume a mushroom unless you have a positive identification of that mushroom. Some deadly varieties of mushroom include the death cap, destroying angel, Galerina species, small Lepiota species and the deadly webcap – to be able to detect these you would need to have observed them all at different stages in their development. Also having knowledge of where the mushroom has come from can help as some mushrooms that are safe in Europe have deadly lookalikes in North America.

It is very wise to avoid old wives' tales such as 'a mushroom is poisonous if it tarnishes silverware or turns blue when bruised' as these are both completely false statements. The truth of the matter is that there are no external easy-to-identify characteristics that all poisonous mushrooms have in common. To be absolutely safe, unless you are an expert mushroom identifier then we would advise buying your mushrooms from a reliable source such as supermarkets or restaurants.

> **“ Some mushrooms that are safe in Europe have deadly lookalikes in North America ”**

Is eating fish good for your brain?

Yes, especially really oily fish which are rich in omega-3 fatty acids called Eicosapentaenoic acid (EPA) and Docosahexaenoic acid (DHA). Omega-3 is vital for brain growth/development, functioning and production of neurotransmitter – the chemicals which relay signals between the brain cells. The human body cannot easily synthesise these fatty acids and so a constant supply is very important. Just like a healthy machine your brain needs oil, and this comes in the form of omega-3.

How do Bonsai trees stay so small?

Bonsai is the Japanese art form, but the word is also used to cover any practice of growing very small trees in containers. Unlike dwarf plants, which are genetically small, Bonsai uses 'normal' trees and cultivates them to keep them small. The containers in which Bonsai trees are grown limit the expansion of their root system and place a cap on the amount of nutrients available to them, limiting their growth above the pot. Rigorous pruning and artificial shaping helps them mimic the shape of large trees, resulting in living scale miniatures.

What is St Elmo's fire?

St Elmo's fire can be described as a more or less continuous, luminous electrical discharge in the atmosphere, which emanates from elevated objects above the Earth's surface. These objects can include lightning conductors, wind vanes, or on the wings, tips or propellers of aircraft in flight. This electrical charge can also occur on an aircraft where a static charge has been produced by the frictional impact of ice, snow, rain, dust or sand. The phenomenon is usually of a bluish colour and has been seen as white or violet. When St Elmo's fire is present, it can be accompanied by a crackling sound which occurs when the electrical field close to the object becomes very strong. St Elmo's fire can also been termed 'corposant', which means 'holy body'. There are several other types of electrical phenomenon including sprites and elves.

Why do skunks smell bad?

Skunks are renowned for their ability to smell really bad. Not something you want to have associated with your species, but for skunks it's a massive advantage. Skunks do this by spraying a chemical called thiols which is made of sulphurous compounds and they have a very strong odour. Not only that but these thiols are very good at sticking to materials and mixing with chemicals to make the smell stick. If a skunk has sprayed this on any of your upholstery the smell can often last for weeks.

In fact scientists have successfully isolated the compounds that make the smell stick and applied it to perfumes and fragrances in order to give a longer lasting smell. A skunk will only spray if it is agitated or stressed and releases the spray from scent glands in the anus. In addition to smelling awful, the spray can cause vomiting and have effects similar to tear gas, which is a great defence mechanism. As an interesting side note, skunk spray is also phosphorescent, so it will glow in the dark.

History

" It was a vessel capable of blowing the largest enemy vessels out of the water with magnificent ferocity "

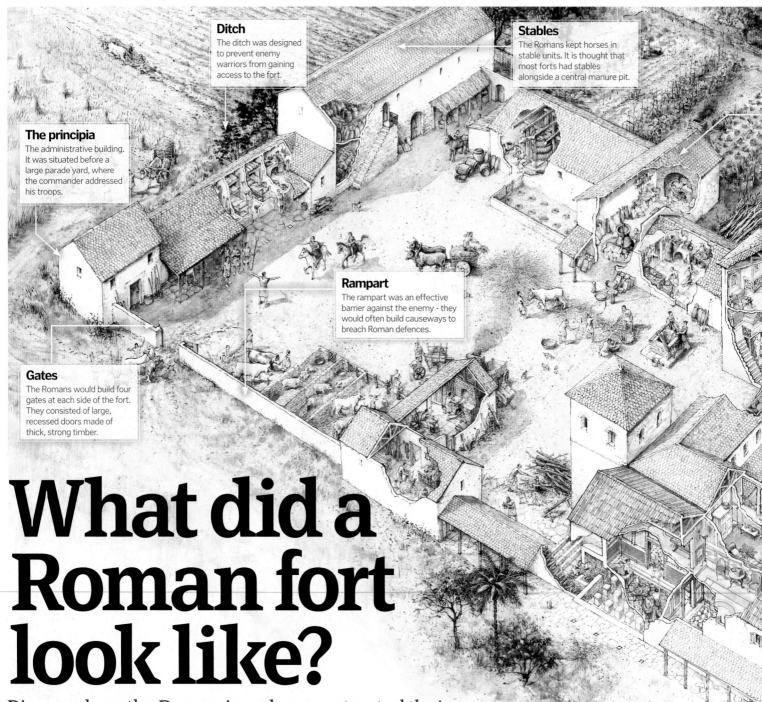

Ditch
The ditch was designed to prevent enemy warriors from gaining access to the fort.

Stables
The Romans kept horses in stable units. It is thought that most forts had stables alongside a central manure pit.

The principia
The administrative building. It was situated before a large parade yard, where the commander addressed his troops.

Rampart
The rampart was an effective barrier against the enemy - they would often build causeways to breach Roman defences.

Gates
The Romans would build four gates at each side of the fort. They consisted of large, recessed doors made of thick, strong timber.

What did a Roman fort look like?

Discover how the Roman invaders constructed their many strongholds around Britain

When the Romans invaded Britain, they monopolised native strongholds. As time passed, they built base camps that allowed their armies to travel safely through the country. At first they fortified these camps with timber, then from the 2nd Century AD they used stone. The Romans were expert builders and had perfected the art of masonry by creating a revolutionary new material that was known as 'opus caementicium' – a concrete made of rock, rubble or ceramic tiles. Walls were built by placing mortar and stone in large wooden frames, and the result was a facing that has endured centuries. Opus caementicium was regarded as an innovative discovery, enabling the Romans to create complex structures such as the arch and the dome.

Engineers built their forts on modified terrain – often choosing the summit or the side of a low hill, near a river or stream. Roman strongholds were built by a specialist corp that included a chief engineer; much of the manual work was undertaken by soldiers. Officers known as metatores were sent to mark out the ground for an encampment, using a graduated measuring rod known as a decempeda. Each fort was erected with a wide ditch, and also included a stockade or defensive barrier made of timber posts or stone. The Romans used the residue earth from the ditch to create a rampart. While tradition dictated that each fort had four stone gateways, it was equipped with watchtowers that could reach an impressive nine metres (30 feet) high.

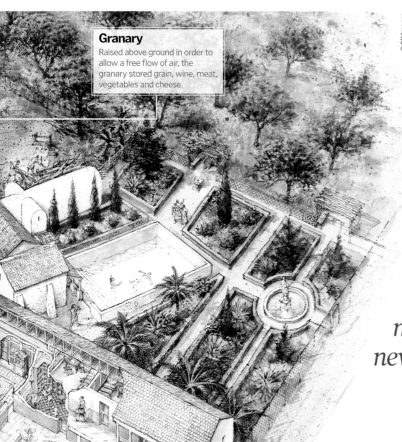

Granary
Raised above ground in order to allow a free flow of air, the granary stored grain, wine, meat, vegetables and cheese.

© DK Images

Barrack block
A series of long rectangular buildings. Each sleeping quarter had two rooms, one for the soldier's use and the second to store his equipment.

The fort worked on many levels – it served as a barracks, hospital, workshop, granary and stables. Every structure included a main street that ran unimpeded through the camp. In the centre was a parade yard and a commander's headquarters.

The Romans placed great emphasis on cleanliness, and so sanitary conditions were especially important. Forts had public baths and private latrines, consisting of rows of seats situated over a channel of running water. Drinking water, meanwhile, came from wells. ✿

What was life as a Roman soldier like?

The buccina (a type of trumpet) marked the start of every new day. The soldiers were highly disciplined – military aspirations and a strict code of honour dominated their lives. They practised sword fighting, hand-to-hand combat and military manoeuvres. Roman soldiers endured a gruelling regime that included running, swimming and marching over long distances. The day of a soldier could be divided into phases that revolved around 'the watch'.

There were a series of eight, three-hour watches, known as the 'vigilia', and each change of watch was signalled by the buccinator (buccina player). Sometimes soldiers were ill or sustained injuries, so the Romans instituted a permanent medical corps and hospital in the fort. The fort could also act as a trading station where vendors sold crafts, animals and food. It was here that liaisons, both romantic and political, were established.

> ❝ The Romans perfected the art of masonry by creating a revolutionary new material that was known as 'opus caementicium' – a concrete made of rock, rubble or ceramic tiles ❞

Are there any remains of Roman forts?

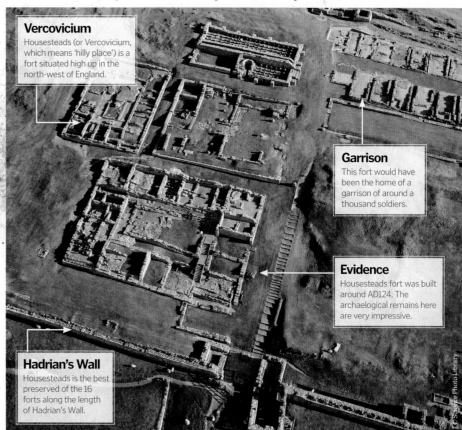

Vercovicium
Housesteads (or Vercovicium, which means 'hilly place') is a fort situated high up in the north-west of England.

Garrison
This fort would have been the home of a garrison of around a thousand soldiers.

Evidence
Housesteads fort was built around AD124. The archaelogical remains here are very impressive.

Hadrian's Wall
Housesteads is the best preserved of the 16 forts along the length of Hadrian's Wall.

© Science Photo Library

How did Romans like to relax?

Learn about bathing, Roman style

The Romans were expert builders; they knew that in order to make their cities thrive they must provide an excellent water system. Therefore great importance was placed on drainage, public fountains and baths. Roman baths were built not only in cities, but also in houses and even in forts. The baths were heated in one of two ways. The favoured method was natural hot springs, with thermae (bath houses) built around them. When the baths were supplied with water from rivers or aqueducts, however, it was heated by a fire before it passed through pipes to the bathing area. Both men and women could use the baths, but the females had to be separated from the males and used an adjoining complex that housed a smaller thermae. The bathing fees for women were much steeper than those required of men.

The bath building was entered through a passage that led into the room lined with seats and clothes pegs. This room, also known as the 'apodyterium', is where people undressed. Sometimes the visitors were accompanied by servants and slaves who helped them disrobe. The apodyterium was sometimes watched by an attendant. It's unlikely the Romans bathed naked; they were more likely to have worn a light covering known as the 'subligaculum' and sandals with thick soles to protect their feet from the heated floors.

Visitors to a Roman bath could enjoy three types of bath: the hot pool was known as the 'caldarium', the 'tepidarium' was kept at an intermediate temperature and the 'frigidarium' was used as a cold plunge pool. The building also had an atrium, which was employed as an exercise yard. The bath houses were equipped with large public latrines which consisted of marble seats placed over open channels, through which there was a constant flow of water.

Roman baths were frequented by the upper classes, who wished to network and conduct business affairs. While they bathed they were offered refreshments, and at an extra price the visitors could take massages. The treatments were undertaken by slaves known as 'aliptae'. The baths were also used for cultural purposes – they had libraries, eating areas and rooms for public speaking. ✿

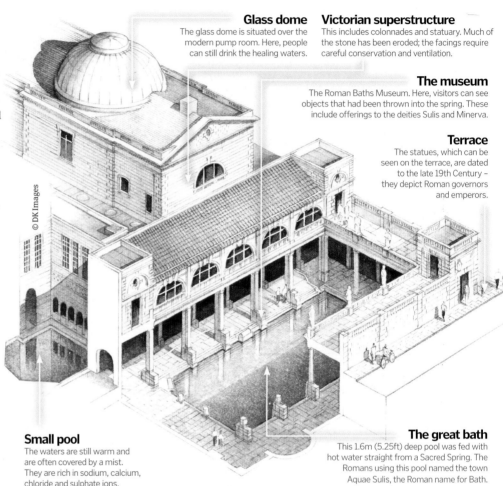

Glass dome
The glass dome is situated over the modern pump room. Here, people can still drink the healing waters.

Victorian superstructure
This includes colonnades and statuary. Much of the stone has been eroded; the facings require careful conservation and ventilation.

The museum
The Roman Baths Museum. Here, visitors can see objects that had been thrown into the spring. These include offerings to the deities Sulis and Minerva.

Terrace
The statues, which can be seen on the terrace, are dated to the late 19th Century – they depict Roman governors and emperors.

© DK Images

Small pool
The waters are still warm and are often covered by a mist. They are rich in sodium, calcium, chloride and sulphate ions.

The great bath
This 1.6m (5.25ft) deep pool was fed with hot water straight from a Sacred Spring. The Romans using this pool named the town Aquae Sulis, the Roman name for Bath.

How were Roman baths heated?

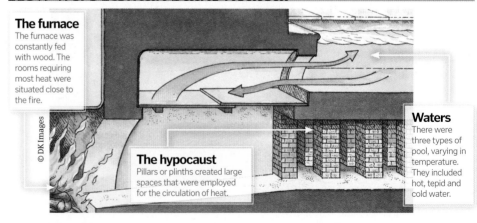

The furnace
The furnace was constantly fed with wood. The rooms requiring most heat were situated close to the fire.

© DK Images

The hypocaust
Pillars or plinths created large spaces that were employed for the circulation of heat.

Waters
There were three types of pool, varying in temperature. They included hot, tepid and cold water.

> ❝ *The baths were also used for cultural purposes – they had libraries, eating areas and rooms for public speaking* ❞

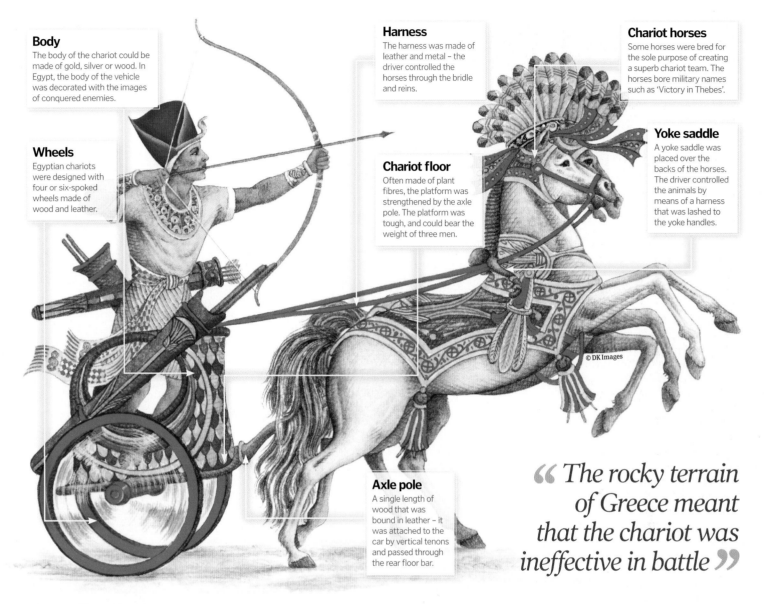

Body
The body of the chariot could be made of gold, silver or wood. In Egypt, the body of the vehicle was decorated with the images of conquered enemies.

Wheels
Egyptian chariots were designed with four or six-spoked wheels made of wood and leather.

Harness
The harness was made of leather and metal – the driver controlled the horses through the bridle and reins.

Chariot horses
Some horses were bred for the sole purpose of creating a superb chariot team. The horses bore military names such as 'Victory in Thebes'.

Chariot floor
Often made of plant fibres, the platform was strengthened by the axle pole. The platform was tough, and could bear the weight of three men.

Yoke saddle
A yoke saddle was placed over the backs of the horses. The driver controlled the animals by means of a harness that was lashed to the yoke handles.

© DK Images

Axle pole
A single length of wood that was bound in leather – it was attached to the car by vertical tenons and passed through the rear floor bar.

> *The rocky terrain of Greece meant that the chariot was ineffective in battle*

What were ancient chariots used for?

In the Ancient Near East, the chariot was as revolutionary as the modern fighter plane

The word chariot comes from the Latin 'carrus', which means wheeled vehicle. It had various uses, but in the Near East the chariot dominated the battlefield. These vehicles first appeared in Mesopotamia around 3,000-2,500 BCE. At first they were heavy and cumbersome, but as time passed they were designed with agility in mind, being made of light timber, plant fibres and leather. Design improvements were most noticeable during the Egyptian New Kingdom period, when the spoked wheel offered better control and turning.

The chariots of the Egyptians and Assyrians were designed to engage the enemy on wide, flat plains. They had semi-circular barriers that protected the driver while he controlled the vehicle, and were drawn by two horses attached to a central pole. The basket, which rested on a beam connected to the wheels, carried the driver, a shield bearer and a warrior, and was equipped with archery equipment, swords and auxiliary weapons.

From this elevated position, the bow became the soldier's principal weapon. From this platform, the warrior could easily decapitate enemy soldiers with his sword. The Egyptians included many magnificent chariots in their burials. While more simple military vehicles were made of wood and leather, others were cast in gold.

The rocky terrain of Greece meant that the chariot was ineffective in battle. Therefore, the ancient Greeks employed the chariot mainly as a ceremonial vehicle. Chariots were also used in racing tournaments, and in Rome they were drawn by magnificent horses. The Circus Maximus was an arena that held chariot races; this enormous track was so wide, it could support 12 competing chariots. Essentially, the chariot played a significant role in the development of these ancient empires in a number of social spheres. ✿

How did the first steam engines work?

For centuries the steam engine has been powering the British industry and even today steam plays a big part in the generation of electricity. We take a look at the men behind these major inventions

Until the start of the 18th Century, machines were powered by muscle, water or wind, but steam power provided the potential for growth and flexibility on a mass scale. Steam engines facilitated the birth of large factories as production moved from rural riverbanks to industrial towns, creating the formation of the cities we know today.

Steam power had been around for generations but it wasn't until 1698 that its application into industry was made. Military engineer Thomas Savery created a patent for raising of water by "the impellent force of fire", the first noted design of a steam pump. In 1712 Thomas Newcomen continued Savery's work and constructed the first successful steam engine, the atmospheric engine. Its purpose was to rid coalmines of floodwater, allowing miners to reach new depths. It was considered so efficient for its time the design wasn't altered for six decades and the template was copied up and down the country.

British engineer James Watt came to largely represent the face of the steam movement, because his many patents prevented other engineers from furthering the progression of steam-powered machinery until they expired in 1800, at which point a hungry new league of engineers took up the baton. Richard Trevithick pioneered 'strong steam' (steam at high pressure), meaning vapour could be 'compounded' and used repeatedly in a series of cylinders. Such a method was used in ships, railways and agriculture, inspiring new vehicles and machines, from self-propelled steam boats and

carriages to traction engines for the land and engine houses for grinding and processing grain.

By 1820 steam locomotives were commonplace and in 1830 'The Liverpool and Manchester Railway' opened as the world's first inter-city passenger railway, engineered by George Stephenson and utilising locomotives that were designed by his son Robert, including the magnificent Rocket.

Towards the end of the 19th Century inventors found new ways to maximise steam efficiency and in 1884 Charles Parson's steam turbines opened a whole new world of possibilities. Today steam-powered engines are no longer in widespread commercial use, but some of their applications can still be seen from the production of electricity to underwater jet engines. ✿

How old is steam power?

1698
Thomas Savery patents his machine for the raising of water by the "impellent force of fire", the first design of a steam pump.

1712
Thomas Newcomen builds the first practical steam engine. It is erected near Dudley Castle in Staffordshire.

1733
Savery's patent expires meaning more Newcomen engines could be built without infringement.

1769-1800
James Watt dominates steam-engine design and improvement. The Watt steam engine was the first to use steam at a pressure above atmospheric to drive the piston.

1804
Arthur Woolf builds a compound engine that matches the work of Watt's machines using half the fuel.

1806
Richard Trevithick becomes the first British engineer to use high-pressure 'strong' steam. The machine revolutionised transport.

1807
The first proficient commercial steam boat was launched; Robert Fulton's North River Steamboat.

1812
First commercial locomotive constructed by Matthew Murray. Eight years later there were 20 steam locomotives in service.

1827
Goldsworthy Gurney built a steam carriage to be used as a vehicle on the roads, motoring along at 15mph.

1884
The steam turbine replaced steam power in its previous form with Charles Parson's axial-flow turbine.

1918
The end of the longest working atmospheric engine. Built by Francis Thompson in 1791 it stood at Pentrich Colliery.

© Science Museum

Chimney
Smoke created in the firebox is passed to a smokebox beneath the chimney. This smoke is then released into the atmosphere.

Multi-tubular boiler
The Rocket's multi-tubular boiler improves the transfer of heat from the firebox gasses into the boiler water.

Cylinder
The Rocket's two cylinders contain rods, pistons and steam valves.

Blast pipe
A blast pipe inside the Rocket uses the steam exhaust to improve the air draught through the firebox where the coal's burned.

Couple
Any coaches attached to the Rocket were fastened by a couple at the back of the steam engine.

Direct coupling
One of the Rocket's main features is direct coupling, which uses connecting rods to link the pistons to the driving wheels.

What was medieval armour like?

Crafting, donning and utilising medieval armour were complex skills, requiring great expertise

Medieval armour worked by protecting its wearer in battle through a series of fashioned steel plates and chain mail links. To achieve this, armour was designed to absorb impacts from blunt weapons such as maces and flails and deflect slashing or piercing weapons that, despite the strength of the fashioned steel, could still pierce it at weak points with enough force. Despite their apparent appearance of massive weight, these suits of plate mail were actually rather light (on average around 25kg/55lb) and were individually crafted to fit their owner as well as possible, maximising movement and dynamism while also taking into account the fighting style of its wearer.

There were two centres of armour production during the middle ages, the south of Germany and the north of Italy. German sets of armour, such as the one featured here, were referred to as 'Gothic' in style and featured brutal, jagged lines and pointed tips. The Italian style was referred to as 'Milanese' – due to the armour smiths' proximity to Milan – and was more decorative and lighter than its German counterpart. Kings, princes, dignitaries and successful knights often commissioned armour personally, and these suits were often inlaid with personalised etchings or engravings. This trend became much more common after the style of wearing a cloth surcoat over suits of armour phased out at the end of the 14th Century, allowing knights to show-off their power and prowess in the form of ornate decoration.

Encased within plate armour such as this, a knight was only vulnerable to powerful steel crossbows and, due to the rapid increase in gunpowder technology during the 16th Century, handguns and muskets. In fact, as guns became more and more widespread, the plate mail armour was increasingly phased out due to its inability to stop fired rounds, ending up by the 17th Century reduced to purely ceremonial roles and historical re-enactments. ✿

> ❝ *Encased within plate armour such as this, a knight was only vulnerable to powerful steel crossbows* ❞

Helmet
Crucial for taking and deflecting critical blows to the head, helmets often only left a thin slit for the knight to see through. Protective visors were also common.

Breastplate
Ornate with elaborate designs common throughout the 15th Century, the breastplate was fashioned out of hardened steel to deflect blows.

Vambrace
These tubular parts of the suit of armour were lightweight and provided much-needed arm defence.

Besagew
To aid mobility in combat, full suits of armour left gaps around joints. To protect these around the armpit a knight would wear a pair of these mini shields.

Gauntlet
This was the armour to defend the hand, which evolved out of a chain mail mitten. However, by the 15th Century multi-plate gauntlets were being produced that allowed individual finger movement.

Chain mail
Underneath the plate mail knights would wear a body suit of chain mail in order to protect exposed areas between individual plates.

Greave
Similar in construction to the cuisse, the greave provided protection for the shin and lower leg.

Cuisse
Protecting the thigh of the knight, the tubular cuisse was connected to the greave through a knee plate and series of leather straps.

Sabaton
Sabatons were made from numerous articulated steel plates ending in a solid toecap.

© DK Images

What's inside HMS Victory?

One of the most famous ships of all time, HMS Victory was crucial to ensuring British naval supremacy during the late 18th and early 19th centuries

The only surviving warship to have fought in the American War of Independence, the French Revolutionary War and the Napoleonic wars, the HMS Victory is one of the most famous ships ever to be built. An imposing first rate ship of the line – line warfare is characterised by two lines of opposing vessels attempting to outmanoeuvre each other in order to bring their broadside cannons into best range and angle – the Victory was an oceanic behemoth, fitted with three massive gundecks, 104 multiple-ton cannons, a cavernous magazine and a crew of over 800. It was a vessel capable of blowing even the largest enemy vessels out of the water with magnificent ferocity and range, while also outrunning and outmanoeuvring other aggressors.

Historically, it was also to be Vice-Admiral Horatio Lord Nelson's flagship during the epic naval battle off the Cape of Trafalgar, where it partook in the last great line-based conflict of the age, one in which it helped to grant Nelson a decisive victory over the French and Spanish but at the cost of his own life. ✿

Turner's famous painting of the Battle of Trafalgar in which the HMS Victory is shown in the midst of battle

Sails

The HMS Victory is a fully rigged ship, with three sets of square sails covering 5,440m2. The breadth of the Victory's sails allowed it to sport a maximum top speed of nine knots when operational, which was for the time very impressive considering its size and weight. During the 18th and 19th centuries a fully rigged ship necessitated three or more masts each of which with square rigging. At full flight the Victory could spread a maximum of 37 sails at one time and could carry 23 spares.

Crew

There were over 800 people on board the HMS Victory, including gunners, marines, warrant officers and powder monkeys among many others. Life on board was hard for the sailors, who were paid very little for their services and received poor food and little water. Disease was rife too, and punishments for drunkenness, fighting, desertion and mutiny ranged from flogging to hanging.

© Alex Pang

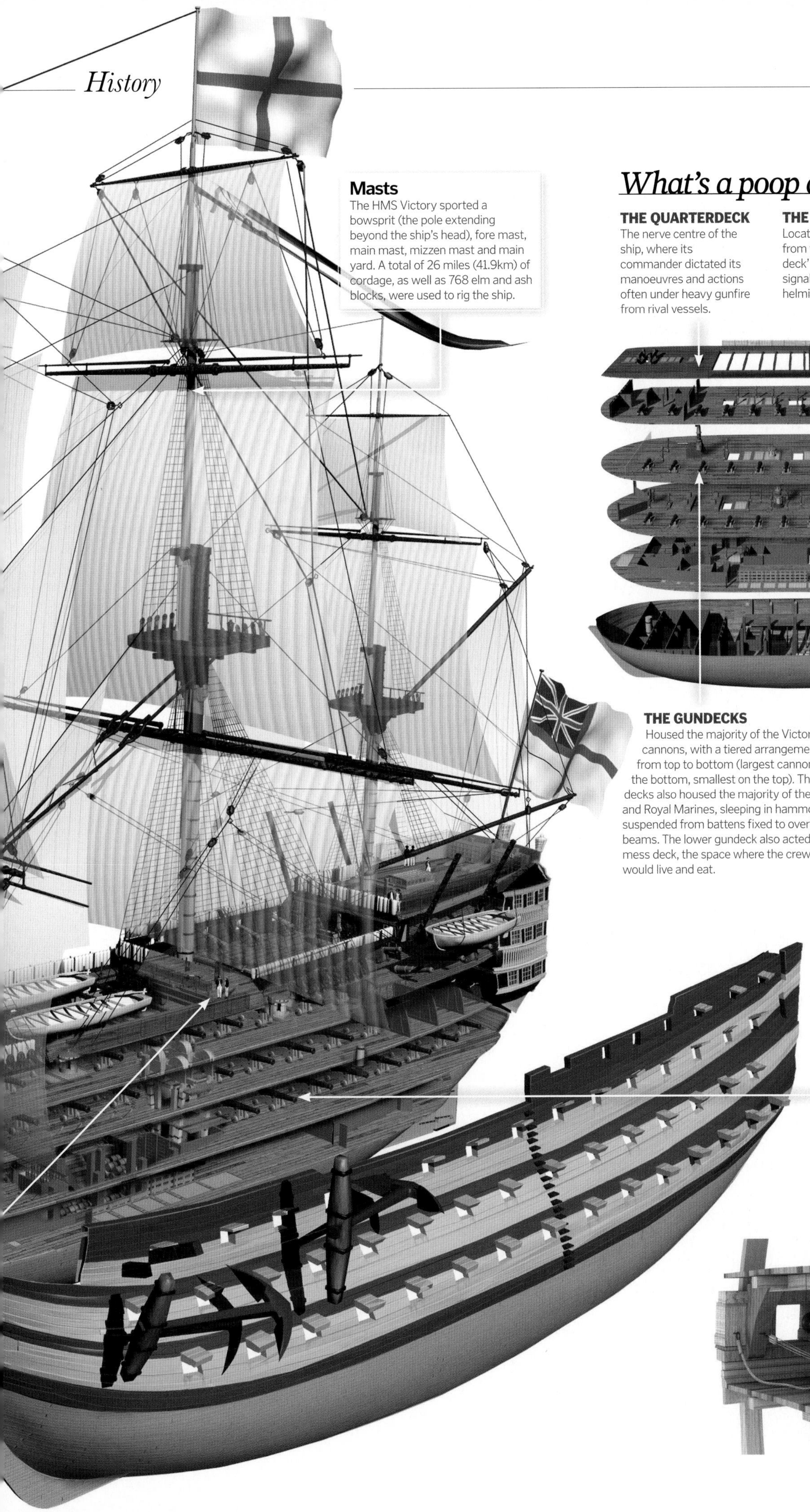

Masts
The HMS Victory sported a bowsprit (the pole extending beyond the ship's head), fore mast, main mast, mizzen mast and main yard. A total of 26 miles (41.9km) of cordage, as well as 768 elm and ash blocks, were used to rig the ship.

What's a poop deck?

THE QUARTERDECK
The nerve centre of the ship, where its commander dictated its manoeuvres and actions often under heavy gunfire from rival vessels.

THE POOP DECK
Located at the stern, this short deck takes its name from the Latin word puppis, which literally means 'after deck' or 'rear deck'. This deck was mainly used for signalling, but also gave some protection to the man helming the ship's wheel.

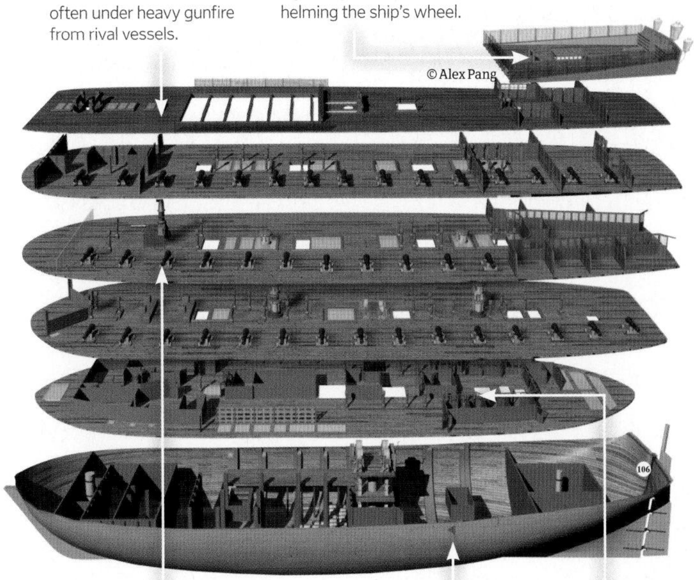

© Alex Pang

THE GUNDECKS
Housed the majority of the Victory's cannons, with a tiered arrangement from top to bottom (largest cannons on the bottom, smallest on the top). These decks also housed the majority of the crew and Royal Marines, sleeping in hammocks suspended from battens fixed to overhead beams. The lower gundeck also acted as mess deck, the space where the crew would live and eat.

THE HULL
The hull was the largest storage area on the ship where up to six months of food and drink could be stored, as well as any excess supplies.

THE ORLOP
The only other deck below the waterline, the orlop was another storage area and also habitation deck for certain crew members such as the purser.

Cannons
As a first rate ship of the line, the Victory was a three-gundeck warship with over 100 guns. In fact, the Victory was fitted with 104 cannons: 30 x 2.75 ton long pattern 32-pounders on the gundeck, 28 x 2.5 ton long 12-pounders on the middle gundeck, 30 x 1.7 ton short 12-pounders on the upper gundeck, 12 x 1.7 ton short 12-pounders on the quarterdeck, and 2 x medium 12-pounders and 2 x 68-pounder carronades on the forecastle.

© Alex Pang

How did the Samurai make their swords?

What makes samurai weapons so tough?

Samurai don't just see their swords as beautifully crafted weapons, they actually believe the sword embodies their soul. And so the process of creating such a treasured piece of kit is a measured and intricate one. The swords are made using a high-quality steel known as tamahagane, which is repeatedly heated, hammered flat and then folded. The sword-maker will repeat this technique until he is happy with the result.

There are several reasons behind this repetitive action. One is to eliminate any blade-weakening air bubbles that get into the steel during the heating process. Also, the process creates layers in the metal, which adds to the blade's strength. Not only this, but it also ensures that the natural strengthening property in the carbon is distributed evenly throughout the blade.

The blade cannot simply be thrust into cold water to harden as cooling it too quickly would make it brittle upon contact with an unfortunate combatant. Conversely, cooling it too slowly would make it soft and blunt. So samurai swordsmiths developed a method of optimum cooling for maximum strength. A thin layer of clay (made of ash, water and clay) was applied to the cutting edge of the sword keeping it hard and sharp, while a thicker layer was painted onto the back of the sword making it supple and shatterproof. With two edges cooling at different rates, the sword gets a distinctive curvature. A piece of art and an incredibly deadly weapon. ✿

How do zips unzip?

Discover the invention that took the textiles industry by storm

There are two main types of zip fastener – the coil and the metallic. Coil zippers are the more traditional variety found on garments worldwide, and make up the bulk of zipper sales. Coil zippers work by weaving two coils, one in spiral form and one in ladder form, to either side of two pieces of fabric. The twin coils are then interwoven by a slider – the small tab that you pull up and down – which forces the ladder side to hook to the coil side, interlocking them.

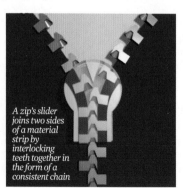

A zip's slider joins two sides of a material strip by interlocking teeth together in the form of a consistent chain

In contrast, metallic zippers, which are largely found on jeans, suitcases and heavy-duty overalls, do not have coiled teeth. Instead, they have individual pieces of metal made from aluminium and nickel, moulded into an interlocking shape and set on the fabric at regular intervals. The metallic zipper's slider then forces the individual teeth together to form a solid chain. Metallic zippers offer greater separation resistance than coil varieties, but cost more to make. ✿

What's in the Statue of Liberty?

The Statue of Liberty was officially titled 'Liberty Enlightening the World'. It was built as a monument commemorating the centenary of the Declaration of Independence

Constructed by the French, the Statue of Liberty was designed as a colossal copper statue. Gustave Eiffel, the designer of the Eiffel Tower, was asked to build a massive iron pylon and a skeletal framework to act as the support for the sculpture. While remaining fixed to its steel frame, the structure was able to move in the wind – subsequently, wind speeds of 50 miles per hour have been recorded, and the statue has been known to sway up to three inches under pressure.

The pedestal, crafted from Scottish sandstone, was built in the USA. Once this was erected, it was time to assemble the statue proper. Parts of the statue were shipped from France. They arrived in 350 pieces and were packed into 214 crates. It took four months to assemble the statue and secure it on the pedestal.

The pedestal is supported by two sets of iron girders which are connected by iron tie beams – these extend upwards into the framework of the statue creating a strong link from the ground. The Statue of Liberty was originally designed as a lighthouse and functioned as such from 1886 to 1902. It housed an electric light that could be seen several miles out to sea. ✿

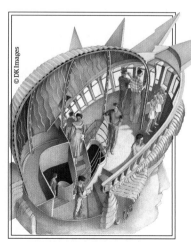

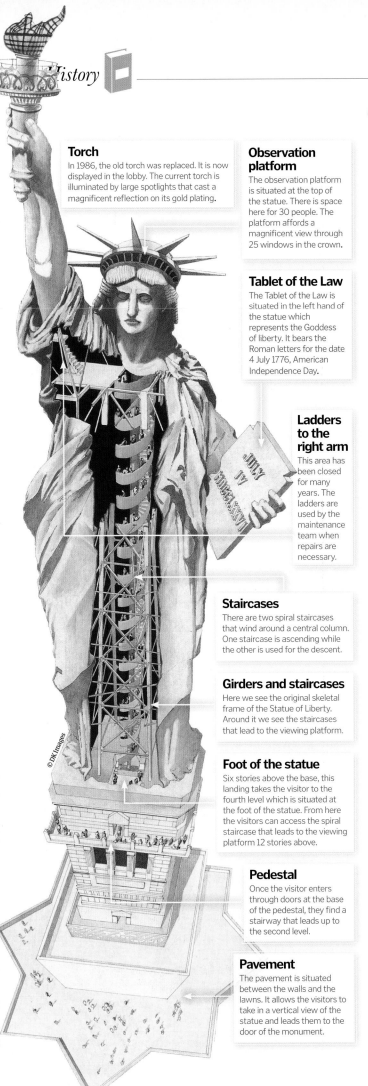

Torch
In 1986, the old torch was replaced. It is now displayed in the lobby. The current torch is illuminated by large spotlights that cast a magnificent reflection on its gold plating.

Observation platform
The observation platform is situated at the top of the statue. There is space here for 30 people. The platform affords a magnificent view through 25 windows in the crown.

Tablet of the Law
The Tablet of the Law is situated in the left hand of the statue which represents the Goddess of liberty. It bears the Roman letters for the date 4 July 1776, American Independence Day.

Ladders to the right arm
This area has been closed for many years. The ladders are used by the maintenance team when repairs are necessary.

Staircases
There are two spiral staircases that wind around a central column. One staircase is ascending while the other is used for the descent.

Girders and staircases
Here we see the original skeletal frame of the Statue of Liberty. Around it we see the staircases that lead to the viewing platform.

© DK Images

Foot of the statue
Six stories above the base, this landing takes the visitor to the fourth level which is situated at the foot of the statue. From here the visitors can access the spiral staircase that leads to the viewing platform 12 stories above.

Pedestal
Once the visitor enters through doors at the base of the pedestal, they find a stairway that leads up to the second level.

Pavement
The pavement is situated between the walls and the lawns. It allows the visitors to take in a vertical view of the statue and leads them to the door of the monument.

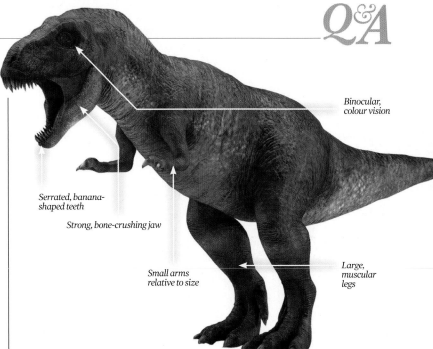

Binocular, colour vision

Serrated, banana-shaped teeth

Strong, bone-crushing jaw

Small arms relative to size

Large, muscular legs

How did T-rex hunt its prey?

The T-rex may have been one of the largest meat-eating dinosaurs, but it might not have been a predator at all

Tyrannosaurus rex – from Greek and Latin words meaning 'tyrant', 'lizard' and 'king' – was one of the largest carnivorous dinosaurs to walk the earth. It lived about 85 to 65 million years ago, in lightly forested North American river valleys and plains. The T-rex stood more than four metres tall and 12 metres long, weighing in at five to seven metric tons. Some fossil evidence shows that the female T-rex may have been the larger of the sexes, although there's no way to know for sure. Its banana-shaped, serrated teeth gripped flesh and its massive jaw crushed bones as it downed more than 200 kilos of meat in one gulp. Likely prey included the Triceratops horridus and the Torosaurus, each about the size of an elephant.

There have been several nearly complete Tyrannosaurus rex skeletons found since the first bones were discovered in 1894, some of which included soft tissue. From these, palaeontologists have learned that the T-rex had a lot of bird-like traits. It likely had a one-way air sac system that kept its lungs constantly full of fresh air, hollow bones to lighten its body weight, and binocular, colour sight. It also had a wishbone, or furcula. Some palaeontologists believe that our assumptions of scaly, lizard-like skin might not be entirely accurate and that T-rex could've even had feathers.

Controversy about the T-rex centres on whether it was a predator or a scavenger, as well as whether it moved slowly or quickly. Many palaeontologists believe that the Tyrannosaurus rex was strictly a predator, but those who question this assumption point to its short, weak arms with two-fingered hands, large legs suited for walking distances and a strongly developed sense of smell. These seem more in line with what we know of scavengers rather than predators. Others argue that muscle scars found on skeletons show that the T-rex had strong arms.

They also believe that their binocular sight and hollow bones indicate a faster-moving predator. However, predators today will sometimes scavenge if fresh prey isn't around, so T-rex could've actually been both. ✿

What happened at the Battle of Britain?

70 years ago an epic conflict took place between Allied and Axis powers. It was one of the defining moments of World War II and changed the nature of armed conflict forever

The Battle of Britain was an exclusively aerial campaign between Allied and Axis forces which began in the summer of 1940 and culminated in May of 1941. The objective of the German-led aerial assault on Britain was to completely destroy the Royal Air Force (RAF) and render Fighter Command useless, so a planned land invasion of Britain could begin. The Luftwaffe (Germany's air force) was ordered by Hitler to drive the RAF from the skies in 'the shortest possible time', and led by notable First World War veteran fighter pilot Hermann Wilhelm Göring, the then Reich Minister of Aviation, what was to follow was a costly – in terms of human life and financially – battle of attrition.

At the head of Britain's defence was Hugh Dowding, the then Air Chief Marshal of the RAF and Fighter Command, which had been set up in 1936 to oversee and manage Britain's emerging modern air force. Fighter Command led its RAF-based defence of Britain from Bentley Priory, London, communicating with airfields, radar stations, pilots and other communications headquarters over the south east (where the majority of the battle took place) and other regions of the country. At his disposal was a well-ordered yet numerically inferior air force to that of the Germans, with many pilots lacking valuable experience.

Contrary to Dowding, Göring inherited a Luftwaffe of great

Luftwaffe
Who led the German attack?

Name: *Hermann Wilhelm Göring*
Rank: *Reich Minister of Aviation*
Description: The last commander of legendary ace fighter pilot 'The Red Baron', Göring was responsible for German Luftwaffe. In his youth he had flown in the First World War and was respected by the Germans as a notable commander.

Name: *Hugo Sperrle*
Rank: *General Field Marshal*
Description: General Field Marshal of the Luftwaffe, Sperrle advised Hitler that the destruction of Britain's air force was key to winning the war. Air Fleet 3, which he commanded, played a major role in the battle but suffered heavy losses.

Name: *Albert Kesselring*
Rank: *General Field Marshal*
Description: Kesselring orchestrated combat in Poland, France and at the Battle of Britain. He is credited with the Coventry Blitz of November 1940 and won the respect of allied powers with his military accomplishments.

Who were 303 Squadron?

The Battle of Britain saw over a thousand enemy aircraft shot down by British RAF squadrons, and none more so than the famous Polish 303s. No. 303 Polish Fighter Squadron was one of 16 Polish squadrons in the Royal Air Force during the Second World War and won acclaim for their marksmanship and aerial ability during the conflict. Scoring higher than any other squadron, 303 competed with other RAF squadrons in a competition as to who could shoot down the most enemy aircraft. By the end of the Battle of Britain they had won unequivocally, recording an immense 808 hits. In fact, the top three places in this competition's leaderboard were taken by three of the 12 Polish squadrons, outgunning the best British squadron by far, who only racked up 150 hits.

Fighter Command
Who led Britain's resistance?

Name: *Hugh Dowding*
Rank: *Air Chief Marshal*
Description: An experienced officer, Dowding was set to retire shortly before WWII, only to be persuaded to stay on until the situation had stabilised. He is often credited as the mastermind behind Britain's success in the Battle of Britain.

Name: *Keith Park*
Rank: *Air Vice Marshal*
Description: In tactical command during the Battle of Britain, Park was in charge of protecting London from attack. Flying a personalised Hurricane, Park held a reputation as a shrewd tactician.

Name: *Trafford Leigh-Mallory*
Rank: *Air Officer Commanding*
Description: The commander of 11 Group RAF had open disagreements with Park and Dowding over the tactics to counter the German threat. He was credited as creating the 'Big Wing' fighter formation to hunt German bombers.

Battle map

Charting the key military bases, RAF and Luftwaffe headquarters, radar stations, and squadrons that partook in the Battle of Britain

Due to Germany's occupation of France, they could set up military bases at Calais and other coastal cities along the Channel. This put the German bombers in range of London and left the area to its south east (Kent) exposed to many attacks. Indeed, the majority of the Battle of Britain was fought over the south east of England and this led to the majority of Britain's air force bases being heavily used in the area. 11 Group RAF were responsible for protecting London and the south east, and they saw much action and suffered the bulk of the casualties during enemy attacks. As we see over the page, the careful and strategic use of the newly emerging technology of radar gave Britain valuable insight into the activities of approaching aircraft across the Channel, especially at night when countering German bombers in low-visibility situations.

A Spitfire flies over the south east of England

Key:

○	*Fighter command bases*
⊕	*Luftwaffe fighter bases*
+	*Luftwaffe bomber bases*
–·–·	*RAF group boundaries*
– – –	*Luftflotte boundaries*
⌒	*Range of Messerschmitt BF 109*
·–·–	*Range of low-level radar*
⌒	*Range of high-level radar*

13 GROUP

12 GROUP

10 GROUP

11 GROUP

LUFTFLOTTE 2

LUFTFLOTTE 3

Heinkel He 111's running aircraft bombing raids over Kent during the Battle of Britain

© Hohum

Hawker Hurricanes fly in a single line formation above Britain

RAF and WAAF staff plot bombing raids at RAF Uxbridge

How was the battle won?

Thanks to the emerging technology of radar, allied forces were equipped to counter German attacks

numbers and experience, with many of its pilots having gained valuable flight experience in WWI.

This allowed Göring and his commanders to launch large raids on Britain – one of the most notable being a 500-strong assault on 15 September 1940 – causing large damage to a wide variety of areas and military buildings as well as, by the end of the war, 43,000 civilian deaths. Despite Göring's leadership, his other commanders held differences of opinion in how the RAF

should be toppled – a factor that Dowding also had to deal with among Britain's commanders in how to defend the country.

Despite their experience and numbers, Germany failed to gain air superiority over Britain and by the end of the Battle they had lost 1,152 aircraft and 1,144 crew, compared to Britain's losses of 1,085 aircraft and 446 crew. Retrospectively, this result was caused by a single piece of state-of-the-art technology: radar.

The importance of radar in the Battle of Britain was massive, something that its then leader Hugh Dowding knew all too well. Britain was facing larger numbers of enemy aircraft, pilots with more flight experience and frequent bombing runs in the dead of night – the favoured time for German attacks. Radar then was key, allowing enemy airborne movement to be tracked from across the Channel and, crucially, allowing Britain's smaller air force to be managed more acutely.

The main advantage that radar gave was the ability to launch intercepting attack aircraft at the right time. Not too early – forcing planes to reland for refuelling, leaving them vulnerable to attack and costing cash-strapped Britain in fuel bills – and equally not too late – giving the German planes a crucial height advantage in the proceeding dogfight and allowing them to reach inland areas of Britain. Dowding, operating his stringent Fabian Strategy, used this to great effect, having information on approaching aircraft sent from coastal stations to Bentley Priory (Fighter Command headquarters) with great haste so that finessed tactical plans could be quickly drawn up and relayed to air force bases.

The system did have drawbacks however. While radar was excellent and highly accurate in detecting aircraft movement, it was quite poor in expressing the numbers of aircraft and their formations, two factors crucial in decision-making if an effective

resistance was to be mounted. Because of this, Dowding's system also incorporated RDF-based detection – which allowed formations to be determined as they formed over France – and the pre-existing Observer Corps, groups of mainly volunteer civilians dotted throughout Britain, visually relaying information on approaching aircraft numbers and formations to Fighter Command. Indeed, many historians argue that without the Observer Corps, no matter how refined Britain's radar-based systems became, the Battle of Britain would've been lost – an opinion vocalised by Dowding when he said that "they constituted the whole means of tracking enemy raids once they had crossed the coastline. Their works throughout [the war] was quite invaluable."

Importantly, despite the benefits radar was providing Britain's air force, Göring and his commanders underestimated its ability and importance in what was going to be the deciding factor in the Battle. While initially the Luftwaffe were ordered to attack RAF radar stations (an activity they completed with little success, knocking out only one radar station on the Isle of Wight for under 24 hours), their attention was soon turned to the towns and cities of Britain, as their grip on the conflict slackened. It is generally agreed by historians that if Göring had persisted with his targeting of Britain's radar stations, Germany would have had considerably more success than they historically achieved.

> **" At Dowding's disposal was a well-ordered yet numerically inferior air force to that of the Germans, with many pilots lacking valuable experience "**

A 303 captured Messerschmitt sporting anti-Hitler graffiti

A selection of pilots from 303 Squadron walk away from their aircraft

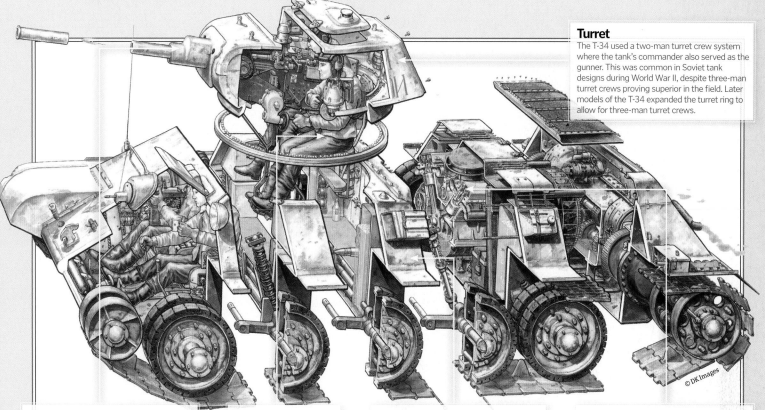

Turret
The T-34 used a two-man turret crew system where the tank's commander also served as the gunner. This was common in Soviet tank designs during World War II, despite three-man turret crews proving superior in the field. Later models of the T-34 expanded the turret ring to allow for three-man turret crews.

© DK Images

Cannon
The primary armament of choice for the T-34 was a 76.2mm F-34 tank gun, which was designed at the start of World War II. Unfortunately, by 1943 the power and range of the new German Tiger and Panther tanks rendered the F-34 obsolete and was replaced by the D-5T and ZiS-S-53 85mm guns.

Crew
The T-34 was controlled by a four-man team, with the gunner/commander and loader in the turret, and the driver and radio operator positioned in the frontal section of the hull.

Armour
The 1941 variant of the T-34 was equipped with 45mm front and side hull armour, 60mm turret armour and 63mm side armour plating. This provided superior protection for its crew than its predecessors – the BT-5, BT-7 and T-26 – however, heavy tanks such as the German Tiger could still easily breach it.

Engine
The T-34 used a 12-cylinder Gaz diesel V-2 engine, which was capable of churning out 500hp. Due to the tank's relatively light weight compared to its heavier contemporaries, this gave the T-34 a power to weight ratio of 17.5 horsepower per ton and, as a result, a good top speed of 33mph.

What made the T-34 so good?

Often credited as the most effective and influential tank of World War II, the T-34 brought a solid mix of speed, agility and stopping power to the theatre of war

One of the most numerous armoured vehicles during World War II, the Soviet Union's T-34 medium tank is considered by military historians to be one of the most important and influential tanks ever to be built.

Evolving out of the BT series of fast tanks (Soviet cavalry tanks with thin armour and high mobility), the T-34 at its introduction was the first tank to sport a complete balance between firepower, mobility, protection and longevity – something that modern tanks now take for granted. Further, it was an especially refined and simple design that allowed for costs (135,000 rubles) and production time frames to be kept low, meaning that many tanks could be produced in very little time and allow Russia to mitigate its higher-than-average losses quickly and cheaply. Indeed, this became a very important factor towards

the end of the war when the superior – but hard and expensive to manufacture – German Tiger and Panther tanks could not be replaced fast enough.

The T-34 was fitted with a good balance of weaponry, sporting a 76.2mm F-34 tank gun – ideal for taking down medium and light armoured enemy vehicles – and twin 7.62mm DT machine guns, perfect against unarmoured targets and to suppress advancing soldiers. Its armour also offered a great balance between protection and weight, with up to 63mm of armour plating standing between its crew and the shells and bullets of the enemy. This meant that only the largest of enemy cannons – such as the 88mm beast fitted to the German Tiger tank – could breach its hull or turret and, considering

its high top speed of 33mph, this was only possible if it became entrenched or caught unawares. By keeping the armour thickness to a medium level though, the total weight of the T-34 was kept down to 26 tons, under half that of the German Tiger and allowing the T-34 unrivalled dynamism in the field.

Historically, the T-34 will be remembered as the vehicle that swept German forces from Russia, advancing from Stalingrad all the way to Berlin in 1945. However, its usage continued right up to 1958, when it was finally replaced by its successor the T-54. Despite its official retirement however, the T-34 has continued to be used in Third World militaries right up to the present day and has also found itself bought and operated by both private collectors and military museums. ✿

© DK Images

An aerial view of the mountain as construction of Mount Rushmore neared completion

Gutzon Borglum inspects the work on the memorial from a bosun's chair. These were suspended from above with steel cables, while workers drilled into the granite with jackhammers.

Photo: Charles D'Emery

Photo: Rise Studio, Rapid City, South Dakota

How was Mount Rushmore made?

The explosive methods used to carve these stony-faced presidents into the granite

The ultimate symbol of American democracy, the Mount Rushmore National Memorial has presided over the Black Hills of South Dakota since its completion in 1941. The sculpture, depicting 60-foot effigies of presidents George Washington, Thomas Jefferson, Theodore Roosevelt and Abraham Lincoln, was designed by American sculptor Gutzon Borglum, who sadly passed away before the memorial was actually finished.

On a happier note, of the 400 workers involved in carving these iconic figureheads, none died during the mammoth undertaking – unusual for any construction of the time, let alone one involving dynamite and at such dangerous heights. In fact these workers even had to climb a mountain to get to work, but then this was during America's Great Depression, a time when a lot of people were just thankful to have jobs.

A massive 90 per cent of the rock removed from the mountain was blown away using dynamite. The powdermen in charge of the explosives set different-sized charges in specific locations in order to remove exact amounts of rock.

> **A massive 90 per cent of the rock removed from the mountain was blown away using dynamite**

So that's the main structural sculpting taken care of, now for the less explosive techniques. Men were lowered down in front of the 500-foot rock face in bosun's chairs, using thick steel cable. At the top of the mountain, men in winch houses controlled and lowered the cables by hand. If they winched too quickly, the workers in the bosun's chairs would be injured, and so call boys were employed to sit on the mountain edge and shout instructions to the winch men.

To sculpt the last six inches of stone, drillers and carving assistants used jackhammers and a technique called honeycombing, whereby they bored holes very close together. This weakened the hard granite so that it could be finished off by hand and then the presidents' faces were smoothed off using 'bumping' tools. ✿

What's the fastest steam train on Earth?

Beautiful, sleek, powerful, and capable of reaching speeds of 125mph. Introducing the Mallard steam locomotive...

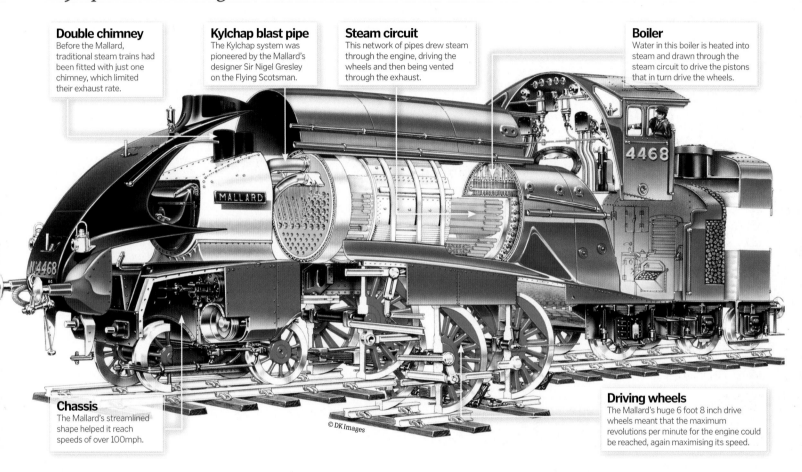

Double chimney
Before the Mallard, traditional steam trains had been fitted with just one chimney, which limited their exhaust rate.

Kylchap blast pipe
The Kylchap system was pioneered by the Mallard's designer Sir Nigel Gresley on the Flying Scotsman.

Steam circuit
This network of pipes drew steam through the engine, driving the wheels and then being vented through the exhaust.

Boiler
Water in this boiler is heated into steam and drawn through the steam circuit to drive the pistons that in turn drive the wheels.

Chassis
The Mallard's streamlined shape helped it reach speeds of over 100mph.

© DK Images

Driving wheels
The Mallard's huge 6 foot 8 inch drive wheels meant that the maximum revolutions per minute for the engine could be reached, again maximising its speed.

Steam engines use coal-powered boilers to generate steam, which is funnelled under pressure down a series of pipes, known as a steam circuit. This steam moves pistons that are attached to the train's wheels, and this is what drives them. The exhaust steam is then released via the funnel at the front of the train. The system is effective, but if the boiler is put under too much pressure it can explode, devastating the engine and killing or injuring the crew. Likewise, the exhaust has to be as efficient as possible, drawing steam and exhaust fumes out to both minimise pressure in the system and to allow more steam to be drawn through at a greater speed.

This is where the Mallard excelled; everything about this locomotive was designed for speed. The streamlined body, tested in a wind tunnel, meant it could run at over 100mph for extended periods of time. However, the secret of its success lay in its double chimney, which allowed for faster venting of exhaust gases at speed and its Kylchap blastpipe. Mallard was the first locomotive of her type to be fitted with this system from new. Its four linked exhaust pipes draw more exhaust gas through the system at a greater speed and with an even flow, minimising wear and ensuring that the boiler, steam circuit and pistons could work at maximum efficiency.

Mallard was literally built for speed, and on 3 July 1938 it reached 125.88mph on East Coast Main Line, south of Grantham. Mallard still holds this record, making it the fastest steam locomotive in the world, not to mention one of the most beautiful. ✿

What was the Kylchap blast pipe?

The Kylchap blast pipe used four stacked nozzles, the first taking exhaust steam, which fed into the second, where the exhaust steam was mixed with gas from the smokebox. This flowed into a third that added more exhaust gasses and this mixture, then into a fourth, which led to the engine's chimney. This meant that the flow of gas was more even through the engine and greatly increased its efficiency.

1

ȝ (`ahhh`)
Egyptian vulture. This ominous bird is associated with both battlefields and graveyards.

2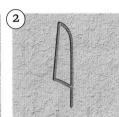

i
A flowering reed. The reed was used to make arrows and writing tools.

3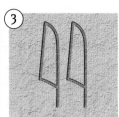

y (`eee`)
Two flowering reeds or strokes that may have represented the sound of the wind on rushes.

4

ꜥ (e)
The arm is often used in the Egyptian language to represent might or power.

5

w (`ooo`)
The quail chick adds a pleasant sound. It is often employed among signs that represent time.

6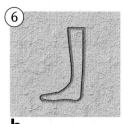

b
The foot and leg. Egyptians became familiar with human anatomy through mummification.

7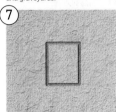

p
A seat, stool or throne. A sign in ancient Egyptian used frequently in royal titles.

8

f
The horned viper is one of many snakes used in ancient Egyptian, it is often attached to a verb.

9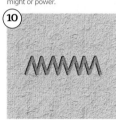

m
The owl is a common letter. It is rare to see the full face of any creature in imagery.

10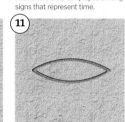

n
A water ripple is used to note transience, the words `to` and `towards` often contain this.

11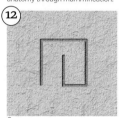

r
R is shown as a mouth. The letter is used in the words `recitation`, `to eat` or `to speak`.

12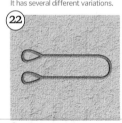

h
There are various `h` sounds in the alphabet. This sign shows a rural shelter or a house.

13

h (emphatic `h`)
A twisted piece of flax. Flax was a common material in ancient Egypt.

14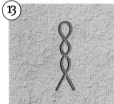

h (as in hock or lock)
The placenta can be found in many words including those that deal with fortune and smell.

15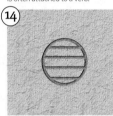

h (`ich`)
The belly of an animal; this letter is used in words that denote the physical form.

16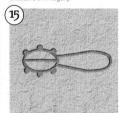

s - 2 symbols
A door bolt and a folded sheet of cloth. It sounds like the English `s`. It has several different variations.

17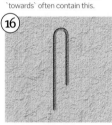

s (`sh`)
Water features were a symbol of affluence and upper class villas were designed with pools.

18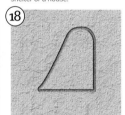

k (like `qu` in quaint)
The hill sign is used in the words `tall`, `high` and `exalted` as well as `high ground` or `summit`.

19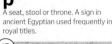

k
A reed basket with a handle. This can be used in many contexts and is employed as the pronoun `you.`

20

g
The Egyptians were fond of wine. The sign of this jar stand is transliterated with a hard `g`.

21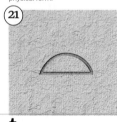

t
Bread was the most basic food in Egypt, here we see a small loaf of oven-baked bread.

22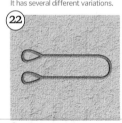

t (`tsh`)
Tethering rope. The Egyptians had 38 signs for ropes and baskets. `t` is also a pronoun.

23

d
Human hand. There are 63 signs for the human body. This sign was used for words of action.

24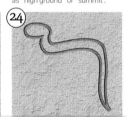

d (dj)
Snakes were feared creatures. This letter is often used in words of declaration or recitation.

What do Egyptian hieroglyphs mean?

Understanding the language of the gods

In order to learn the Egyptian script (known in ancient times as medu netcher or `words of the gods`), it is best to start with the alphabet, which is published here in full. As you start to recognise the words and names in the Egyptian script you begin to understand the excitement and adrenaline that historians must feel when deciphering an ancient text – by doing so, you gain a unique insight into this incredible and mysterious civilisation.

The language is elaborate but also very accessible; it employs a series of grammatical structures that include verbs, nouns, negatives and particles; the Egyptians also used onomatopoeic words, for example `cat` is written `meow.` The language also contains a series of pictograms and phonograms, and is interspersed by determinatives. These are placed at the end of words in order to clarify their meaning.

The script has an abundance of symbols that reflect the natural world; birds, mammals and trees often provide clues to the true meaning of the text. The language could be written left to right, or right to left, and executed vertically or horizontally. The script is continuous and you can learn to separate the words by identifying the determinative or the strokes at the ends of each section. ✿

Why does the Tower of Pisa lean?

Find out how the tower was made and how it went wrong...

The local architects and city officials designed the complex at Piazza dei Miracoli (the Square of Miracles) as a dedication to art, and as such it is thought the principles of science and engineering were not fully understood.

The tower was built in three stages over a period stretching nearly two centuries. The first part of the tower was built during a time of town prosperity and as such heavy white marble was used for the base and tower, with limestone used for the interior and exterior design features.

Disaster occurred just five years after work began, as the workers finalised the interior of the third floor. The tower was sinking because the weight of the marble building was too much for the extremely insufficient three-metre foundations which had been set in weak and unstable soil that contained a malleable mixture of clay, sand and rubble. The construction was halted for nearly a century to allow the soil to settle. In 1272 work recommenced as engineers began to build the tower's middle section. To compensate for the continuing problem of its lean, the workers built one side of the wall taller than the other. Subsequently the tower began to lean in the opposite direction and caused it to curve. War caused a break in construction and the seventh floor was not completed until 1319 and the eighth level, featuring the belfry, was finally added in 1372.

> ## "The tower was built over a period stretching nearly two centuries"

How does it not fall over?

In 1964 a desperate Italian Government requested aid to stop the tower from toppling. One of the first methods to be tested was to add 800 tons of lead counterweights to the raised end of the base, but this only added to its subsidence. With the problem worsening it was decided to close the tower in 1990 and remove the bells to relieve some of the weight.

Cables were cinched around the third level and grounded several hundred metres away to anchor the weight. Work began on removing some 38 cubic tons of soil from under the raised end of the base, which straightened the tower by 18 inches – regaining an angle last recorded in 1838. Ten years of corrective stabilisation followed and the tower reopened to the public in 2001. In 2008 another 70 tons of earth was excavated and for the first time the structure has officially stopped moving.

© DK Images

© DK Images

Bell tower
The Bell chamber was added in 1372. It features seven bells – one for each note of the musical scale. The largest of which was installed in 1655.

Shape
The tower has a cylindrical body encircled with arches and columns. The central body is a hollow shell which features an external wall of white and grey limestone.

Spiral staircase
The inner wall was fashioned from worked limestone and comprises a 296-step spiral staircase.

Curvature
In 1272 architects fashioned a corrective axial inclination where the walls on one side of the tower were taller than the other – giving the building its concave appearance.

Third floor
Upon reaching this level, engineers noticed the tower was starting to sink. The heavy white marble had become too heavy for the foundations set in soil.

First floor interior
Lining the inside the first floor is a series of arches in a typical Romanesque blind arcade style, intersected with columns displaying classical Corinthian capitals.

Foundations
Made of white marble, the construction began in 1173 during a time of prosperity in Pisa thanks to the success of its military.

What was it like inside a medieval castle?

The stereotypical fairy tale castle design was actually the result of centuries of improvement upon existing structures

Medieval castles were an important part of feudal society. They began to appear around 1066 AD with the invasion of William the Conqueror. As he moved through England, Scotland and Wales, William had more than 30 castles built to help maintain power over his newly conquered lands. These castles served as bases for lords who held land from king and pledged loyalty and military service to him in return. These lords leased parts of their land to lesser lords and barons, who had knights that served under them.

These imposing structures had multiple functions. Castles were bases of offensive operations, defensive strongholds, seats of government and private residences for land-holding barons, knights and lords and their families. Most were built in stages over long periods of time and modified as greater defences were needed. Although their structures varied, they generally consisted of a tall building in the centre, which could function as a residence, prison or storage area, surrounded by one or more walls. Some castles were built on a mountain or hilltop, or on the edges of cliffs, to make invasion that little bit more difficult. ☼

Master's lodgings
This room on the second floor of the keep is circular. Unlike many residential quarters in castles, it is elaborately and elegantly decorated.

Moat
This moat is at the south end between the outer and inner wall. Horses drank from it, and the water was used to fill baths.

Stone slope
Crusaders built this 24-metre thick stone slope to protect the castle's south side. Its smoothness made it difficult for invaders to scale.

The inner wall
Up to four metres thick, with seven guard towers, the inner wall can only be reached by going through a dark passageway and the great square tower, making it difficult for intruders to find their way to the keep.

> **❝** *Castles were bases of offensive operations, defensive strongholds, seats of government and private residences* **❞**

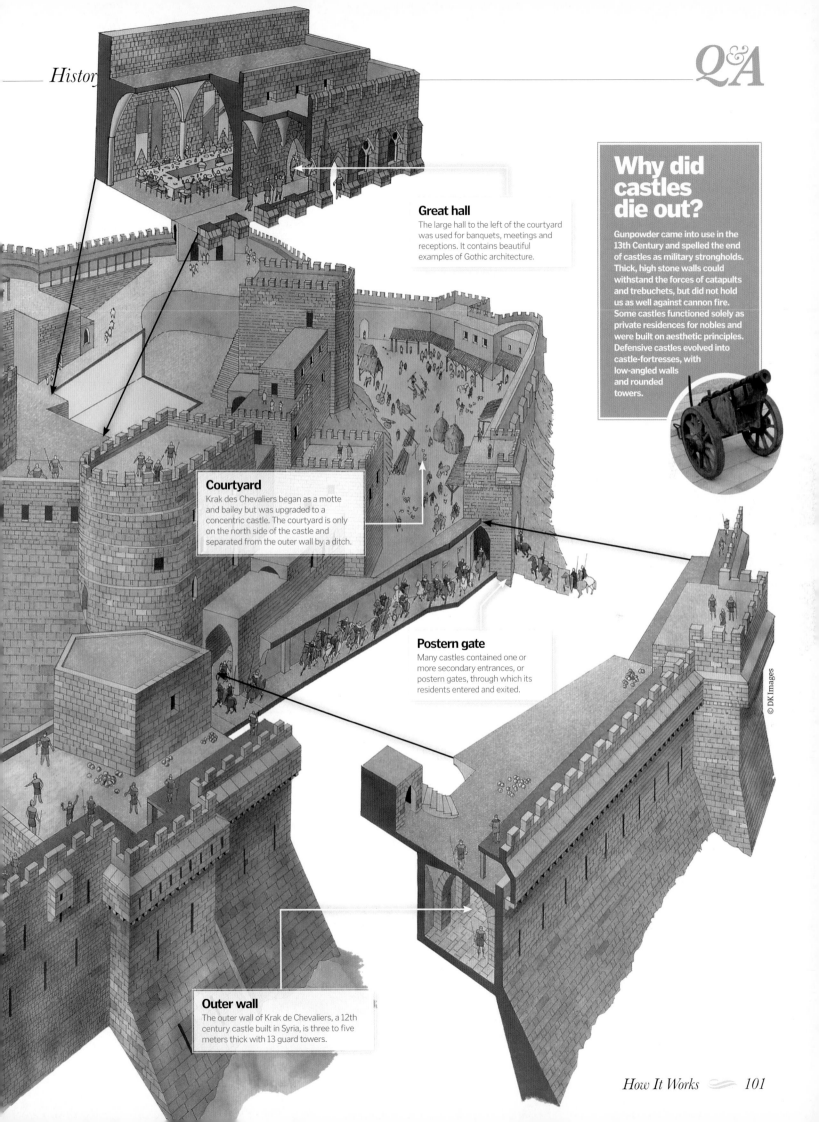

Great hall
The large hall to the left of the courtyard was used for banquets, meetings and receptions. It contains beautiful examples of Gothic architecture.

Why did castles die out?
Gunpowder came into use in the 13th Century and spelled the end of castles as military strongholds. Thick, high stone walls could withstand the forces of catapults and trebuchets, but did not hold us as well against cannon fire. Some castles functioned solely as private residences for nobles and were built on aesthetic principles. Defensive castles evolved into castle-fortresses, with low-angled walls and rounded towers.

Courtyard
Krak des Chevaliers began as a motte and bailey but was upgraded to a concentric castle. The courtyard is only on the north side of the castle and separated from the outer wall by a ditch.

Postern gate
Many castles contained one or more secondary entrances, or postern gates, through which its residents entered and exited.

Outer wall
The outer wall of Krak de Chevaliers, a 12th century castle built in Syria, is three to five meters thick with 13 guard towers.

© DK Images

How did the Great Fire of London start?

In 1666 London was the largest city in England. Home to 500,000, its congested design comprised an urban sprawl of over-crowded wooden homes inside a defensive city wall.

The Great Fire started on 2 September 1666 in the bakery of Thomas Farriner on Pudding Lane, Eastcheap. It's thought his maid forgot to ensure the ovens were put out, and just after midnight the fire took hold. The summer had dried the housing timber and a strong easterly wind fanned the blaze, ensuring it swept rapidly through the heart of the city on a three-day rampage.

The fire-fighting method of the time involved destroying the buildings in the path of the fire to isolate and control it. However, the Lord Mayor of London, Sir Thomas Bloodworth, delayed in giving the order to commence demolition.

Upon being woken by his servant in the early hours, MP Samuel Pepys who lived nearby decided to climb the Tower of London to survey the destruction. When he discovered the fire had begun to spread west, he took a boat along the Thames to Whitehall to inform King Charles II, who immediately ordered Bloodworth to start demolishing buildings and control the spread.

The Tower of London garrison used gunpowder to create breaks and halt the progression east, sparing the Tower and Charles II's court itself, but medieval London was already consumed. The fire was quenched when the strong winds dropped, but monuments including St Paul's Cathedral and London's centre of commerce the Royal Exchange had already succumbed. 87 churches were razed and 13,200 houses destroyed, rendering 90 per cent of the population homeless. The city was rebuilt on roughly the same street plan and Londoners were encouraged to relocate by the sovereign who feared a rebellion by dispossessed refugees.

> ❝ The Great Fire started on 2 September 1666 in the bakery of Thomas Farriner on Pudding Lane ❞

How did the mouldboard plough work?

The first plough, the mouldboard's ancestor, was no more than a stick dragged in the ground. The ancient Egyptians developed the use of animals like oxen or cows to pull a plough, and the Greeks added wheels to this design for greater control and manoeuvrability.

Ploughs simply moved aside the soil to break it up and create a furrow to plant seeds into. But in the 1600s, the Dutch improved ploughs using a mouldboard that turns over the top soil and deposits it over the previous furrow. This design was more efficient, allowing more land to be cultivated.

What was the first printing press like?

Before 1440 only a few thousand handwritten texts existed across Europe. Inspired by the growing demand for lower cost books, Johannes Gutenberg, a German goldsmith, created the printing press – a faster form of semi-mechanical production that revolutionised the world.

Based on the same principles of the screw-type presses used to squash grapes in the Rhine Valley, Gutenberg fathomed a machine that applied pressure to an inked surface on text that rested upon a medium such as paper, thereby transferring an image or text. The machine first featured moveable wooden letters carved by hand, but the plucky inventor later developed an alloy from lead, tin and antimony that could be moulded precisely and quickly into long-lasting printing blocks. Handwritten tomes used water-based ink, but Gutenberg devised the creation of oil-based inks which stuck better to the metal types. These inky-surfaced type blocks were arranged into words and sentences and held by a wooden form, pressure was applied and the letters were pressed onto the surface of paper.

It is thought that the German produced hundreds of texts during his life, but his magnum opus is regarded as the Gutenberg Bible, the very first book to be published as a volume.

How did early calculators work?

Blaise Pascal invented his shoebox-sized calculator to assist his father with his business. The Pascal calculator consists of numbered setting wheels that are linked through gears to numbered drums. From the left each wheel represents units of 1, 10, 100, 1,000, 10,000 and 100,000. To add 4 and 9, you dial 4 on the first wheel, and then dial 9. After reaching 9, the gearing mechanism turns the drum in the second window representing units of 10 to 1. The machine then displays 13 as the answer. For use with French currency, the first two wheels are fitted with 12 and 20 spokes to represent deniers and sols, with the remaining wheels counting livres.

It is possible to use the device to subtract numbers (using the nines complement method), multiply by using repeated addition, or divide numbers by using repeated subtraction. Unfortunately, its complexity and cost hampered its widespread use.

How did Galileo's telescope work?

Galileo's telescope employed the same mechanics as modern-day refractor telescopes. It consisted of a tube containing a simple arrangement of a convex objective lens (which changes the path of incoming light waves) and a concave eyepiece lens. Light passing through the objective lens is bent to a focus near the eyepiece, magnifying the image. The main downside to the telescope was its narrow field of view, which diminished with magnification, so only a portion of the moon can be viewed at one time.

Why was Hadrian's Wall built?

An enduring sight on the rural landscape of northern England, Hadrian's Wall stands as a symbol of Roman engineering. Commissioned by Emperor Hadrian in 122AD, for around six years three legions of the Roman army worked on its construction. At 73 miles the fortification is northern Europe's largest ancient monument, extending across the north of England from Bowness-on-Solway in the west to Wallsend near Newcastle-upon-Tyne in the east.

45 miles of the eastern portion was constructed from local stone with an inner core of rubble. The area to the west, meanwhile, consisted of a turf barrier made with a cobbled base. Hadrian's Wall was mistakenly thought to have been built to keep the Scots out, but historians believe it was likely built as a form of border control to monitor population flow between England and Scotland.

How did the Romans go to the toilet?

Originally installed in the homes of the rich as a status symbol, and in army barracks to prevent diseases spreading, the 'flushing toilet' was intended to rid the city of Rome of human waste and maintain good sanitation. By AD 315 the capital had 144 public toilets, predominantly housed within the confines of the public baths.

The toilets were communal and featured a marble bench with a succession of holes. The bench was built over a channel of flowing water which would 'flush' the human waste away. Seven rivers were forced to run through the city's man-made sewers which served as a way of flushing the sewage out of Rome.

A shallower, narrower channel of water ran in front of the seats and was created as an off-shot from the main source. Placed within this stream were sticks holding a sponge, ready for the Roman to wipe themselves clean after using the facilities.

How did the medieval sextant work?

To measure the angle between the horizon and a star, the Sun, the moon or a planet, the user has to peer through the telescope and locate the horizon.

The tool features two mirrors that are parallel but are offset from one another; a horizon mirror and an index mirror. The telescope must be fixed to look at the horizon and the radial arm is moved along the arc scaled in degrees. The arm is moved to manoeuvre the mirrors into position so that the reflection of the targeted star, for example, comes into view – first reflected in the index mirror and then off the horizon mirror down through the telescope until it lines perfectly with the horizon in a dual-like view.

Practitioners claim the angle between the first and last direction of the ray of light is twice the angle between the mirrors – which is measured on the arc to decipher the angle of the star.

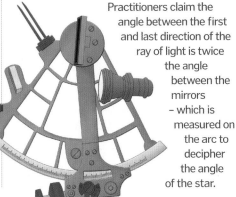

How did battering rams break down city walls?

Pioneered by the ancient Assyrians, battering rams broke the restrictions of hoplite warfare dramatically, making formerly impregnable city walls vulnerable to attack. Rams worked by suspending a large, iron-capped wooden trunk under a wooden frame, which was often covered by wooden plates and damp animal skins for protection from enemy missiles (arrows were often lit in an attempt to burn the ram's frame).

The ram – with an iron cap that was often forged to resemble a ram's head – was then swung by soldiers within the frame backwards and forwards (generating momentum within a restricted plane) against the stone wall, eventually leading to its resistance being broken.

Battering rams were not only used as a siege weapon used for over 1,500 years until gunpowder superseded it as the primary method of breaching fortifications, but also in industry. Roman historian Pliny the Elder describes battering rams being used for mining purposes, where tough, hardened rock needed to be broken to make valuable ores accessible. Today, though, battering rams are usually restricted to handheld devices, used by emergency services to breach doors to gain entry to a compromised building complex.

How do dynamo generators work?

A dynamo electric generator converts mechanical energy into electrical energy. It rotates coils of metal wire (the mechanical energy) within a magnetic field to force the field to push on the electrons in the metal and vary its flux (amount of field passing through the coils). This, as according to Faraday's law – the induced electromotive force in any closed circuit is equal to the time rate of change of the magnetic flux through the circuit – causes the induction of electric current (electrical energy).

Therefore, dynamos have three main components – the stator, armature and commutator. The stator is a stationary structural frame that provides the dynamo's constant magnetic field, while the armature is the dynamo's central set of wire windings that are rotated by mechanical energy. The commutator is a rotary electric switch that is mounted to the armature's central shaft and reverses the electrical potential within the wire with each half turn of the armature, to convert alternating current into direct current.

Today, direct current dynamos are rarely used, due to the worldwide dominance of alternating current and its ease of conversion using solid-state materials.

What was the Leyden Jar?

The Leyden Jar was independently invented by the Dutch physicist Pieter van Musschenbroek and Ewald Georg von Kleist, Dean of the Kamin Cathedral in Pomeranian, in 1745. Musschenbroek, based at the University of Leiden (Leyden), kept better records and it became known as the Leyden Jar.

The Leyden Jar enables you to store static electricity for several minutes or even days. To discharge it you merely complete the circuit between the outer foil and the top of the rod. If, for example, you touch them you will receive a very powerful electric shock that can cause serious injury.

In the 19th Century they were used to experiment with electricity and promoted as 'cure all' devices. These were the first capacitors, and the same principles are used for capacitors used today in amplifiers and radio equipment.

What were the first antiseptics?

The theory that germs, in the form of microscopic organisms, are responsible for infection encouraged the use of antiseptics in conjunction with better standards of hygiene.

The widespread use of antiseptics in hospitals was heralded by the work of British surgeon Joseph Lister, who was the professor of surgery at the University of Glasgow in the late 1860s. He was inspired by French chemist Louis Pasteur, who claimed that gangrene is caused by micro-organisms that can be killed off by heat, filtration or the application of chemicals.

Lister experimented with various forms of chemical antiseptic. He discovered that a solution of carbolic acid (phenol) applied to dressings, wounds and his surgical instruments greatly improved recovery from surgical procedures.

Phenol kills germs by disrupting their cell walls, which causes their cellular contents to leak out. If the solution is too strong it can also be damaging to skin. German bacteriologist Heinrich Koch proved that tuberculosis was caused by bacterium in 1882. This helped bring about the acceptance of antiseptic procedures throughout the world.

What's inside a naval mine?

Naval mines are a contact-initiated type of explosive that can either be moored to the ocean floor by steel cables or left free to drift around unimpeded. Modern contact mines work by encasing a large quantity of an explosive substance – such as trinitrotoluene (TNT) – in a spherical metal shell covered with hollow lead protuberances, each containing a glass vial filled with sulphuric acid. When crushed by the hull of a ship or submarine, these protuberances, known as Hertz Horns, cause the vial inside to break and the acid to run down into a lead-acid battery stripped of acid electrolyte. The mixing of the freed acid with the battery energises it, triggering the electronic detonator, causing the mine's substance to ignite and explode.

Damage rendered to vessels by contact mines is three-fold. First, the explosive substance will cause direct damage – ie a hole in the hull will be blown open. This will cause severe damage to multiple watertight compartments and expose nearby crew to severe shrapnel debris. If the vessel is of small dimensions, an explosion of this type will likely sink it; if of large dimensions, it will cause it to become immobile. Second, when the mine explodes it will cause a bubble within the water, which – due to the difference in localised pressure – will collapse from the bottom. If this collapse occurs onto the ship's hull its force can puncture a metre-wide hole straight through the ship, killing all crew in its path instantly. Finally, contact mine explosions produce a shock wave that can cause any nearby vessel to resonate violently, causing engines to rip from their housing cases of large ships and breaking smaller ones apart entirely.

How did early music boxes work?

The music or musical box consists of a cylinder that is rotated by a small clockwork mechanism.

Pins placed on the cylinder pluck the teeth of a stationary steel comb to create a tune (or 'air' as it is sometimes called). The movement works best in a wooden box as it acts as an ideal medium for transmitting and amplifying the sound.

Music boxes quickly came into vogue in the 19th Century when they were first made by watchmakers in Switzerland. These devices could become quite elaborate and employed multiple cylinders or discs to play complex tunes. Today, they are still popular as jewellery boxes and as novelties, and can be highly sought after by collectors.

Why is Ben so Big?

Though synonymous with the clock tower, 'Big Ben' is the nickname of the 13-ton bell at the heart of the building. Big Ben was cast by Warners of Norton near Stockton-on-Tees in August 1856 and taken to London by rail and sea, and crossed Westminster Bridge on a carriage pulled by 16 white horses.

Before being winched up the tower, it was tested daily until in October 1857 a huge crack appeared. Warners blamed the clockmaker for upping the hammer's weight from 355kg to 660kg and demanded a fortune to start over. So it was decided the new bell would be cast by George Mears at the Whitechapel Bell Foundry. Mears' bell was 2.5 tons lighter but had to ascend the tower on its side – a task that took 30 hours. Then, in September 1859 the new bell also cracked and didn't ring for four years until Sir George Airy, the Astronomer Royal, suggested turning the bell and cutting a square into the metal to halt the crack, plus using a lighter hammer. And this is the bell we hear today.

Lister

" *Cyberspace is massive and it's expanding just about as fast as the universe itself* **"**

Technology

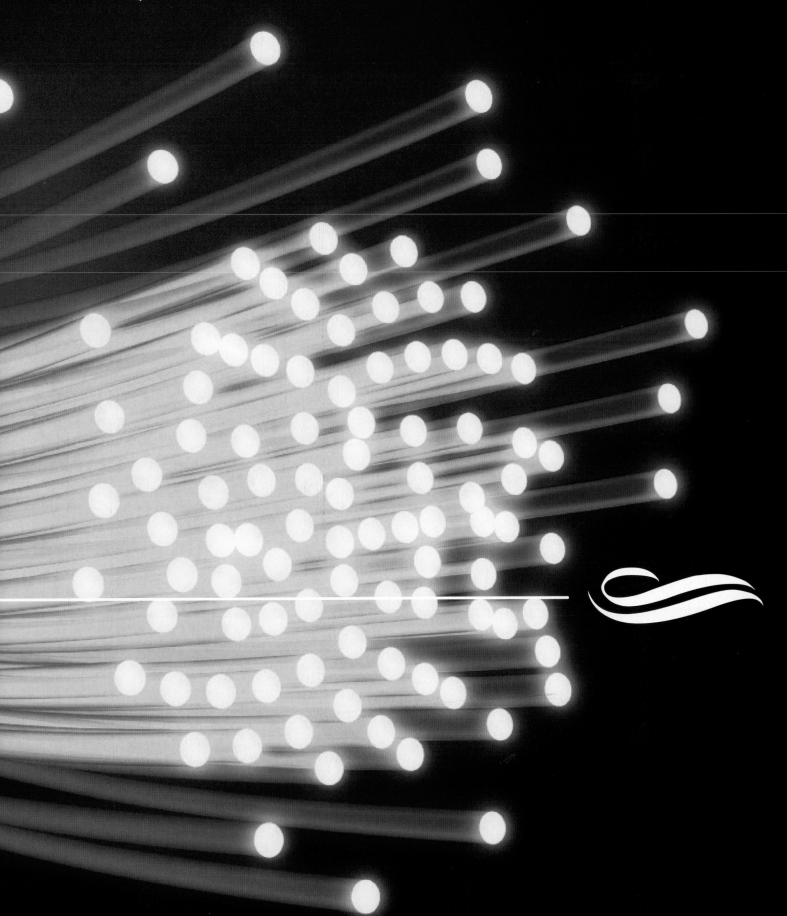

What is nuclear power?

Is it an ecological saviour or a looming catastrophe?

After the Three Mile Island meltdown in 1979 and the Chernobyl disaster in 1986, nuclear power shot to the top of the environmental villains list. But in the face of mounting global warming concerns, it might be poised for a comeback. Since nuclear power produces no greenhouse gasses, proponents are touting it as a greener alternative to fossil fuels. They argue that one pound of enriched uranium (the chief nuclear fuel) can provide the same energy as 3 million pounds of coal or 1 million gallons of gasoline.

But there's quite a catch. Nuclear fuel produces radioactive waste, which can cause cancer, trigger birth defects, and spawn mutants. The technology is both fascinating and ominous and we'll be explaining just how it works over the next few pages.

Nuclear power plants are complexes that span many square miles, but the real action happens on a subatomic level. The sole purpose of a plant is to harness the energy of nuclear fission – a reaction where an atom's nucleus splits into two smaller nuclei.

Specifically, nuclear plants typically derive power from inducing nuclear fission in enriched uranium oxide, comprising 96-97 per cent uranium-238 and three to four per cent uranium-235. Uranium is the heaviest of all natural elements and one of the easiest to break apart. When a relatively slow-moving free neutron runs into a uranium-235 atom, the atom will absorb the neutron, and the extra energy will make the atom unstable. The atom immediately splits apart into two smaller atoms and two to three free neutrons. A fraction of the atom's original mass becomes energy, in the form of heat and high-energy photons called gamma rays.

With the right mix of uranium-235, you get a chain reaction. Some of the free neutrons generated in the fission reaction encounter other uranium-235 atoms, causing those atoms to split apart, producing more free neutrons. Collectively, the splitting atoms generate a substantial heat. All the equipment in a nuclear plant has one core function: safely harnessing this heat to generate electricity.

The heart of a nuclear power plant is the reactor, which contains the uranium fuel and the equipment that controls the nuclear fission reaction. The central elements in the reactor are 150-200 bundles of 12-foot-long fuel rods. Each bundle includes 200-300 individual rods, which are made from small uranium oxide pellets. The rods are immersed in a coolant and housed in a steel pressure vessel.

The fission reaction continues indefinitely when, on average, more than one neutron from each fission reaction encounters another uranium atom. This state is called supercriticality. In order to safely heat the water, the reactor must keep the fuel slightly supercritical, without allowing a runaway fission reaction.

The key mechanism for controlling the reaction rate are a series of control rods, made from neutron-absorbing material such as cadmium. Operators can move the control rods in and out of the bundles of uranium rods. To slow down the fission reaction, operators lower the rods into the bundles. The rods absorb neutrons from the fission reactions, preventing them from splitting additional nuclei. Operators can stop the fission reaction by lowering the control rods all the way into the uranium rod bundle. To accelerate the fission reactions, operators partially raise the rods out

How does a pressurised water reactor turn subatomic particle activity into usable power?

1. Fuel rods
Hundreds of 12-foot uranium rods undergo a fission reaction, releasing substantial heat.

2. Reactor
A steel pressure vessel contains the uranium rods, surrounding water and other reactor components.

3. Control rods
Operators can speed up or slow down the fission reaction by raising and lowering neutron-absorbing rods between the fuel rods.

4. Pump
A water pump keeps water circulating, which transfers heat away from the reactor core.

5. Pressuriser
The pressuriser contains water, air, and steam. By adding or releasing air in the pressuriser, operators can control the pressure of the coolant water around the reactor.

6. Heat exchanger
A pipe carries hot water from the reactor to a separate reservoir of water.

7. Steam generator
The hot pipe leading from the reactor heats a separate reservoir of water to the boiling point, generating steam.

8. Steam line
Steam travels from the steam generator to the turbine.

9. Turbine
Rushing steam spins the turbine.

10. Generator
The turbine spins a rotor that sits in a magnetic field in a generator, inducing an electric current.

11. Transformer
The generator transmits electricity to a transformer connected to the power grid.

12. Condenser
A pipe carrying a steady supply of cold water, typically from a cooling tower, cools the steam, causing it to change back to liquid water.

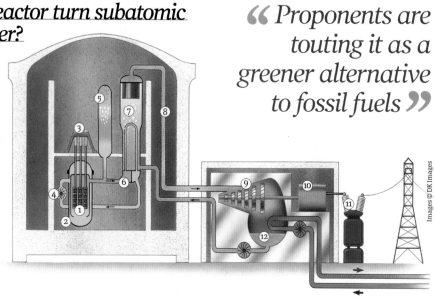

Images © DK Images

> ❝ *Proponents are touting it as a greener alternative to fossil fuels* ❞

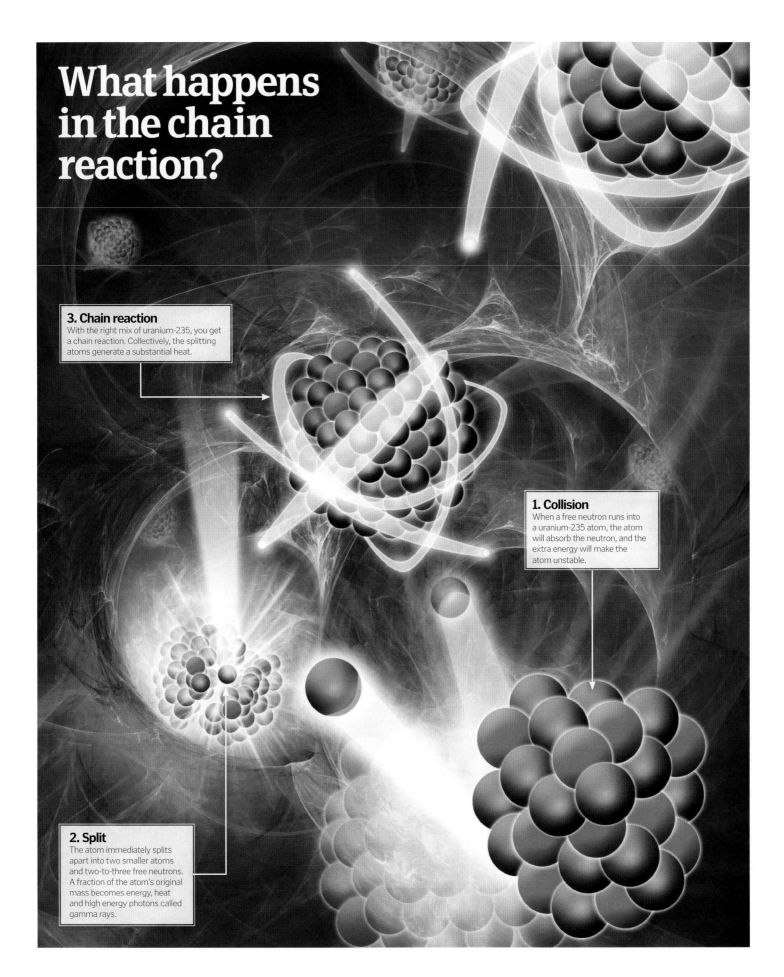

What happens in the chain reaction?

3. Chain reaction
With the right mix of uranium-235, you get a chain reaction. Collectively, the splitting atoms generate a substantial heat.

1. Collision
When a free neutron runs into a uranium-235 atom, the atom will absorb the neutron, and the extra energy will make the atom unstable.

2. Split
The atom immediately splits apart into two smaller atoms and two-to-three free neutrons. A fraction of the atom's original mass becomes energy, heat and high energy photons called gamma rays.

What does a nuclear power plant look like?

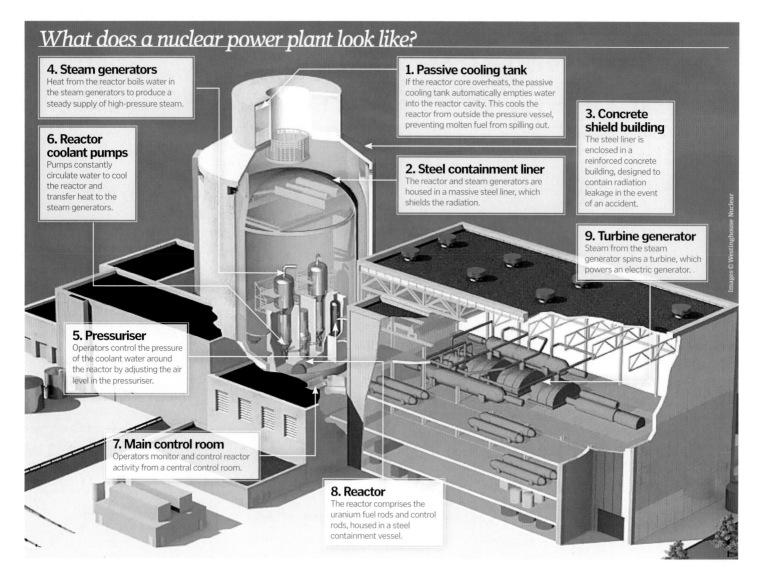

4. Steam generators
Heat from the reactor boils water in the steam generators to produce a steady supply of high-pressure steam.

6. Reactor coolant pumps
Pumps constantly circulate water to cool the reactor and transfer heat to the steam generators.

5. Pressuriser
Operators control the pressure of the coolant water around the reactor by adjusting the air level in the pressuriser.

7. Main control room
Operators monitor and control reactor activity from a central control room.

1. Passive cooling tank
If the reactor core overheats, the passive cooling tank automatically empties water into the reactor cavity. This cools the reactor from outside the pressure vessel, preventing molten fuel from spilling out.

2. Steel containment liner
The reactor and steam generators are housed in a massive steel liner, which shields the radiation.

3. Concrete shield building
The steel liner is enclosed in a reinforced concrete building, designed to contain radiation leakage in the event of an accident.

9. Turbine generator
Steam from the steam generator spins a turbine, which powers an electric generator.

8. Reactor
The reactor comprises the uranium fuel rods and control rods, housed in a steel containment vessel.

Images © Westinghouse Nuclear

of the bundle. This increases the rate of free neutrons colliding with uranium atoms to keep the fission reaction going.

Apart from the fission reaction, a nuclear plant works the same basic way as a coal-burning plant: the fuel generates heat, which boils water, which produces steam, which turns a turbine, which drives an electric generator.

In a pressurised water reactor, the heat from fission doesn't produce steam directly. The fission reaction heats the water inside the pressure vessel to about 325 degrees Celsius, but the water is kept under high pressure to keep it from boiling. A pumping system drives this hot water through a pipe that runs to a separate water reservoir, in the steam generator. The pipe heats the water in the steam generator to the boiling point, and it produces steam. The rushing steam turns a turbine and then reaches a cooling system. As the steam cools, it condenses back into a liquid. The liquid water returns to the reservoir, and boils again, repeating the cycle. As the turbine spins, it

powers a generator, which produces an electric current. And voilà: usable electric power.

Nuclear fission produces high levels of gamma and beta radiation, which can mutate cells, causing cancer and birth defects, among other things. Naturally, the most important concern when designing a nuclear power plant is containing this dangerous radiation.

A modern nuclear power plant has many layers of protection. The pressure vessel that contains the uranium rods is encased in a thick concrete liner, which blocks gamma radiation. The entire reactor and the steam generator system are housed in a giant steel liner,

providing additional radioactive shielding. The steel liner is surrounded by an outer concrete structure, designed to contain the radiation, even in the event of an earthquake. Modern nuclear power plants also include advanced automatic cooling systems, which kick into action in the event of the reactor or other equipment overheating.

The spent uranium rods are also highly radioactive, which means power plants can't just throw them away. The best solutions anyone has come up with so far is to encase the nuclear waste in massive concrete and steel structures or bury it underground.

What are the pros and cons of nuclear power?

The remarkable advantage of nuclear power plants is that they generate electricity without emitting any air pollution. The clouds billowing from cooling towers are nothing but harmless steam.

Nuclear power does take a toll on the environment, however. Mining uranium destroys natural habitats, and the activity

involved in both mining and processing uranium produces greenhouse gasses.

The bigger problem is fuel radioactivity. As Chernobyl demonstrated, accidents can cause widespread disease. Nuclear waste remains highly radioactive for thousands of years, and there's already more than 60,000 metric tons of it to deal with.

Nobody wants it in their backyard. Another concern is waste falling into the wrong hands, giving terrorists material for weapons.

In recent years, dozens of nations have decided the benefits are worth the risks and are forging ahead. They're touting nuclear power as the way of the future – just as it was 60 years ago.

Control rods are positioned in between fuel rods to slow or speed up the reaction

Are there different types of nuclear reactor?

The most common design is the pressurised water reactor (PWR). PWRs use pressurised water both as a moderator (the material that slows down free neutrons, increasing the rate of fission reactions) and as a coolant (the substance that transfers heat away from the reactor core to the steam generator). Another common design, the advanced gas-cooled reactor, uses graphite as a moderator and carbon dioxide as a coolant. The chief advantage of this design is that it's possible to heat carbon dioxide to higher temperatures than water (about 650°C vs 325°C). The greater heat capacity greatly improves plant efficiency.

Advanced gas-cooled reactor (AGR)

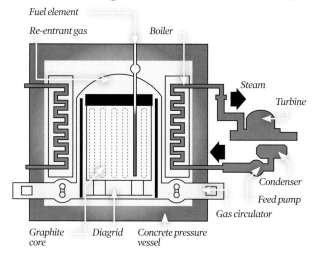

Fuel element
Re-entrant gas
Boiler
Steam
Turbine
Condenser
Feed pump
Gas circulator
Graphite core
Diagrid
Concrete pressure vessel

Pressurised water reactor (PWR)

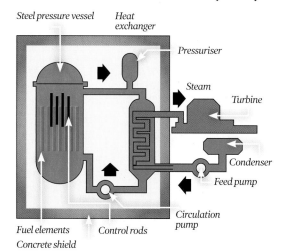

Steel pressure vessel
Heat exchanger
Pressuriser
Steam
Turbine
Condenser
Feed pump
Circulation pump
Fuel elements
Control rods
Concrete shield

How do they make whisky?

Discover the complex, multi-stage process involved in making this age-old alcoholic drink

The first main stage of whisky production is malting, a process of soaking barley in water for days. This increases the moisture content of the grains and causes germination, which converts the starch in the grains into fermentable sugars. The grains are then separated from the heated water and dried.

Next, the dried malt is crushed into grist and added to water, heated to 60°C in a mashing process. This step creates a sugar solution (wort), which is then separated from the grains. The grains are disposed of and the wort is sent for fermentation in a series of wooden containers called 'washbacks'. After two to three days in a washback, the wort generates a low-alcohol liquid, know as the 'wash'.

Distillation follows, a complex process of evaporation and condensing of the wash in stills. This enriches the alcohol content of the wash and produces a high-alcohol liquid that can then be matured into drinkable whisky. Finally, maturation is achieved by depositing the young whisky into oak casks. ✿

2. Vapour
Vapour is carried to a second column, the 'rectifier'. Deposited into the cool top of the column, it condenses and falls through perforated copper plates, re-heating as it gets to the heated bottom.

4. Impure
Low-alcohol content vapour and impurities are evaporated at the top of the rectifier, before being dumped back into the analyser. These go up through the column and condense back into liquid form. This waste is then siphoned off.

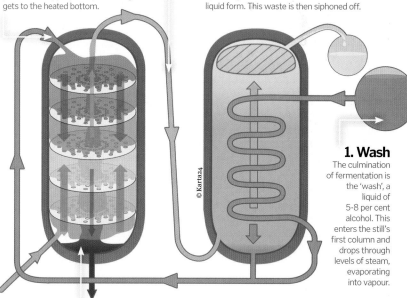

© Karta24

1. Wash
The culmination of fermentation is the 'wash', a liquid of 5-8 per cent alcohol. This enters the still's first column and drops through levels of steam, evaporating into vapour.

3. Enriched
At each plate, parts of the condensing liquid reach their transition stage, returning to vapour, while others with lower boiling points progress downwards. Turned vapour is enriched by the higher alcohol content liquid.

5. Liquid
The remaining alcohol-rich liquid is drawn out through the bottom of the rectifier. Only the 'middle cut' of this spirit goes on to filling and maturation, with the initial 'foreshot' and 'tail cuts' diverted back into the stills. The middle cut has an alcohol content of about 75 per cent.

❝ Maturation is achieved by depositing the young whisky into oak casks ❞

How does a crane assemble itself?

One of the most remarkable engineering feats of tower cranes is that they can literally build themselves. With help from a large mobile crane, construction workers secure the base sections of the tower and assemble the top unit of the crane – the slewing unit, jib and machinery arm.

But before the top section of the crane is attached, workers slide a hydraulic climbing unit around the base of the tower. Once everything is in place, the hydraulic climbing unit lifts the entire top section of the crane (including the horizontal jib and operator's cab) just enough to slide in a new section of tower beneath. Once the new section is secured, the hydraulic unit continues to climb up, section by section, as the crane slowly builds itself higher.

Jib arm
The horizontal arm of a tower crane can extend outward 85m. The arm has three sides forming an isosceles triangle with a trolley track running along the bottom section.

Trolley
The trolley and hook are connected by cables to a trolley motor mounted on the upper side of the jib arm. The operator can roll the trolley back and forth with hand controls.

Cat head tower
On hammerhead tower cranes, the cat head tower reinforces the jib arm and counterweight jib using thick steel cables called pendants.

Operator's cab
It's a long climb to the cab, where the crane operator has a bird's-eye view of the construction site through floor-to-ceiling windows.

Machinery arm
The power to raise and lower the load line is supplied by a huge winch located along the counterweight jib or machinery arm.

The tower
Also known as the mast, each 2.8-metre tower section has four sides, each with vertical, horizontal and diagonal trusses that give them full structural integrity.

Counterweights
Multiple concrete slabs – each weighing several tons – are hung or piled on the very back end of the counterweight jib to overcompensate for the crane's lifting capacity.

How do cranes get so high?

These colossal constructions are engineering marvels

Tower cranes flock to money. During the economic boom years, high-rise construction cranes migrated from Beijing to Shanghai to Dubai, where it was estimated in 2006 that there was one tower crane for every 44 residents of the desert boom-opolis.

Tower cranes are feats of structural engineering that often outshine their creations. They are designed to stand 80 metres tall and reach 80 metres out supported only by a narrow steel-frame mast, a concrete foundation and several counterweights.

The engineering principle that keeps the twiggy tower crane from tipping over is something called a 'moment'. If you hang a weight from the crane's jib arm, it exerts a rotational force or torque where the arm connects to the top of the mast. The magnitude and direction of this force (clockwise or anti-clockwise) is called the moment. If the weight is hung close to the mast, the magnitude of the moment is lower than if the weight is hung far out on the jib. To keep the crane upright, counterweights are used to create a moment of equal magnitude in the opposite direction, balancing out the rotational forces.

Once a tower crane meets its maximum unsupported height, it can be tethered to the building itself and continue to grow with the rising skyscraper. The tower cranes that rose with the construction of the record-breaking Burj Khalifa skyscraper in Dubai reached a truly dizzying height of 750 metres. ❁

Slewing unit
This motorised pivot allows the jib arm to rotate nearly 360 degrees to lift and drop materials all across the construction site.

Hydraulic climbing section
The hydraulic unit attaches to the outside of the tower. A powerful hydraulic arm lifts the entire top section of the crane just enough for the crane to insert a new section beneath.

Concrete foundation
Large tower cranes get their core stability by burying the bottom of the tower in several metres of concrete weighing 185 tons.

How does a Yale-style lock work?

Pin tumbler locks, as made famous by the Yale lock manufacturer, use a simple yet ingenious manner to form a secure locking mechanism that has evolved over thousands of years

A pin tumbler lock is a lock mechanism that uses pins of varying lengths to prevent the lock from opening without the correct key. The pin tumbler design is based on a main barrel that is drilled with five to six cylinder slots that are set close together in a line. Inside each cylinder a metal pin (tumbler) is fitted, with a second pin (driver) on top of it, pushed down by a tiny coil spring. This means that when no key – or indeed the wrong key – is inserted the pins are pushed down across the plug's shear line (the line where the plug is inserted into the outer casing) and it cannot rotate and open. Only when the correct key is inserted are the pins elevated into alignment with the shear line and the lock allowed to open. ✲

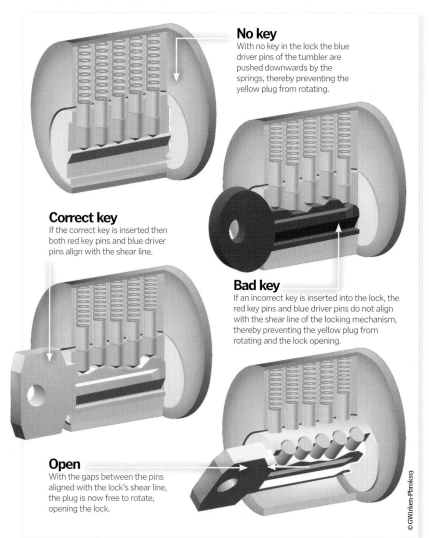

No key
With no key in the lock the blue driver pins of the tumbler are pushed downwards by the springs, thereby preventing the yellow plug from rotating.

Correct key
If the correct key is inserted then both red key pins and blue driver pins align with the shear line.

Bad key
If an incorrect key is inserted into the lock, the red key pins and blue driver pins do not align with the shear line of the locking mechanism, thereby preventing the yellow plug from rotating and the lock opening.

Open
With the gaps between the pins aligned with the lock's shear line, the plug is now free to rotate, opening the lock.

© GWirken-Pbrokst3

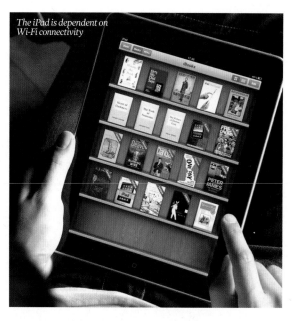

The iPad is dependent on Wi-Fi connectivity

What is Wi-Fi?

How data gets transferred wirelessly to your laptop

M any electronic devices such as laptops, games consoles and mobile phones can be connected to the internet – or to each other – securely, quickly and wirelessly, using radio frequencies instead of cables to transmit data.

Wireless signals can be transmitted to many devices

A wireless network comprises a source computer connected to the internet using an Ethernet cable, a router to translate data (1s and 0s) into a radio signal and an antenna inside the wireless device to pick up the signal. Like using a walkie talkie, sending information via radio waves requires the frequency bands to be broken down into channels to avoid outside interference.

To enable, say, a laptop to connect to a wireless network, the laptop requires a wireless adaptor, which can both send and receive data to and from the network router, which can also send and receive data. Both devices are fitted with decoders, which convert radio signals into digital form. When you want to connect your laptop to the internet, the adaptor communicates with the router via radio signals. The router decodes the signals and, via the Ethernet connection, fetches the relevant data from the internet. This info is converted into radio signals and sent to the laptop's wireless adaptor where it is decoded, giving you the internet page you requested. ✲

What on earth is that?

Guitar string
Magnification: x75
Here, you can see the inside of a 'super-wound' guitar string under a scanning electron microscope.

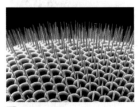

Fly eye
Magnification: x180
This is a scanning electron microscope image of the drosophilidae compound eye of a fruit fly.

Snowflake
Magnification: x100
Computer-generated colours have been used on this snowflake to highlight its crystalline structure.

Moth
Magnification: x75
In this close-up view of a pyralidae moth you can see the side of its head, including its compound eye and its proboscis.

Peacock mite
Magnification: x260
Here's a pest commonly found in the tropics known as a peacock mite, imaged here on a tea stem.

How do electron microscopes operate?

We put these marvellous magnification machines under the microscope

When the scanning electron microscope (SEM) was unveiled in 1935, its reception was lukewarm at best. Despite the potential to magnify objects up to 300,000 times, scientists struggled to see a commercial use for the bulky and expensive machines. However, their application was vastly underestimated, and today more than 50,000 are in use worldwide, largely for industrial purposes. SEMs have a variety of modern-day uses, from forensics to microchip production and insect observation.

SEMs have many advantages over other methods of magnification such as optical microscopes. For example, they do not rely on light for their images, which is a major drawback of their optical counterparts. Light is unpredictable as it can diffract and bend around objects, potentially making observations very difficult. As their name suggests, scanning electron microscopes instead rely on the release of electrons to make observations.

Inside a scanning electron microscope's casing are an electron gun, several coils, and condensing lenses that work together to observe a target sample in super-fine detail.

The core principle of an SEM is that it uses a 'tracing' technique to produce a replicated 3D image of the original sample being studied. It does this by scanning its electron beam over an object and measuring the electrons given off at a particular point. Using this process it can create a 'trace' of the object, and output an amplified image to a display. This is made possible by scanning coils, which create a magnetic field that moves the beam across the surface of the sample. The smaller the area the beam sweeps across the larger the magnification will be, and vice versa.

One of the most important aspects of using an SEM is preparing a sample for observation and ensuring that there is nothing that could hinder the final image. Samples must be thoroughly cleaned to get rid of any dust, debris or alien material not native to the sample that could skew results. The sample must also be able to conduct electricity. If it can't, electrons will not leave its surface when struck by the beam. Objects that aren't already conductive will be coated in a fine layer of gold or platinum in a process known as 'sputter coating'. This also prevents the sample becoming damaged by the beam during observation. ✻

> **" SEMs have a variety of modern-day uses, from forensics to microchip production and insect observation "**

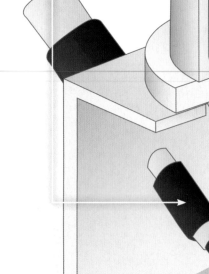

Electron gun
A steady beam of high-energy electrons is fired into the machine, created either by thermal energy (thermionic guns) or electrical fields (field-emission guns).

Lenses
A series of magnetic lenses bend and focus the beam into a precise spot to ensure only a specific part of the sample is hit by the beam at any one time.

Sweep
Scanning electromagnetic coils move the focused beam across the sample in rows, so that the whole sample is subjected to the beam.

Bad vibrations
The sample is placed on a stage inside a chamber of the machine. This must be kept extremely still as SEMs are very sensitive to vibrations.

Q&A

Vacuum

The inside of the microscope is a vacuum. For a sample to survive it must sometimes be specially prepared, often being coated in gold, which also enables it to conduct electricity and release detectable electrons.

Anode

The negatively charged electrons are accelerated and confined into a beam by a positively charged electrode, called an anode.

Objective lens

This magnetic lens focuses the beam further onto a specific area of the sample.

Backscattered electron detector

Additional electrons are counted by another detector that determines the composition of the sample and also deduces the elements present.

Secondary electron detector

As the beam strikes the surface of the sample it knocks the electrons loose. By counting the number of electrons released, a detector can produce a magnified image of the sample.

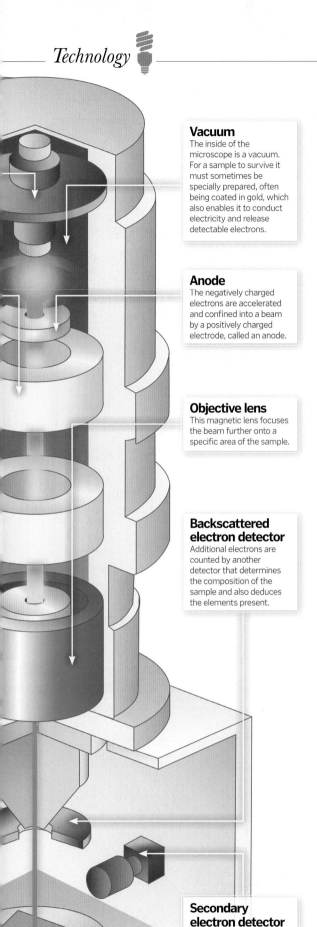

LCD display

User directional commands and transaction information, as well as machine advertisements, are displayed here.

Coin tray

A depositing tray for the user's coinage. Small perforations in the tray filter detritus from the collection.

Waste filter

A slanted chute with a porous, grooved bottom plate. Liquids fall through the plate and an internal fan blows lint away.

Escrow tray

A tray that holds sorted and tabulated coins prior to the affirmation or rejection of the transaction by the user.

Storage container

Affirmed transactions are deposited from the escrow tray into a storage container ready for removal by staff.

Maintenance printer

A secondary printer utilised by operating staff to receive statistical/operational read-outs from the machine.

Voucher dispenser

The total transaction – minus the processing fee – is calculated and printed here on a redeemable voucher.

Coin sorter

A mechanical hopper-based system that filters coins by size. Coins fall onto a circular tray that agitates coins into preset holes.

Rejection chute

Rejected transactions lead to coinage being returned to the user via a rejection chute. Foreign coinage is also rejected here.

Computer system

Currency calculation, processing fees and the operating software are controlled from a computer system.

What's inside a coin counter?

The science of sorting and technology of tabulation explained

Currency-counting machines – such as those proliferated by American company Coinstar – work in a two-stage process, firstly separating coins by type and secondly tabulating the partial or total coinage.

Individual coin types are separated by a hopper-based filtering system, which usually involves coins being deposited onto a circular tray via a top-mounted chute, and then mechanically agitated into preset coin slots via the force of gravity. At this stage the hopper mechanism also filters out illegal or non-coinage, rejecting it via a front-mounted return chute. As the legal coins are filtered from the tray, they drop through individual funnels into a holding container, where they are mechanically weighed.

The overall weight of an individual stack of coins is then assessed by a central computer system. This has preset weight-to-value ratios logged within its tabulation software that – after the coins have been mechanical weighed and converted into a binary format – it can draw upon to calculate the coins' total value. This method of calculation, when combined with all other stacks of coin types, allows the total value of inserted coins to be determined. This information is then presented to the user via a front-mounted LCD display.

Before transactions are completed, however – affirmed by the user manually – the machine's computational software deducts a processing fee from the total coinage tabulated if the user wishes to collect/transfer the funds. This is usually around ten per cent of the total value of the inserted coins. Once completed, the coin counter generates a redeemable voucher from a front-mounted printer, which can then be cashed by store staff. ✿

Does AI exist?

From autonomous vehicles to data mining, we are living in the age of intelligent machines

What is artifacial inteligance?" you ask Google. To which it replies, "Did you mean artificial intelligence?" Of course you did. Meanwhile, in the 0.15 seconds it took you to realise your own stupidity, an intelligent machine has assembled 17,900,000 results for your consideration – including video, audio, historical records and the latest headlines – ordered by relevance and reliability. 20 years ago, this type of artificial intelligence would have been the stuff of science fiction, but now we simply call it 'technology'.

Artificial intelligence began over 60 years ago as a philosophical question posed by the brilliant English mathematician Alan Turing: "Can machines think?" In 1955, the words 'artificial intelligence' first appeared in print in a proposal for a summer academic conference to study the hypothesis that "every aspect of learning or other feature of intelligence can in principle be so precisely described that a machine can be made to simulate it".

At its core, the science of AI is the quest to understand the very mechanisms of intelligence. Intelligence in humans or machines can be defined as the ability to solve problems and achieve goals. Computers, it turns out, are the ideal machines for the study of AI, because they are highly 'teachable'. For half a century, researchers have studied cognitive psychology – how humans think – and attempted to write distinct mathematical formulas, or algorithms, that mimic the logical mechanisms of human intelligence.

Machines have proven extraordinarily intelligent, with highly logical problems requiring huge numbers of calculations. Consider Deep Blue, the chess-playing computer from IBM that beat grandmaster Gary Kasparov using its brute processing strength to calculate a nearly infinite number of possible moves and countermoves.

Alternatively, consider the everyday examples of astonishing AI, like the GPS navigation systems that come standard in many new cars. Speak the address of your destination and the on-board computer will interpret your voice, locate your precise location on the globe and give you detailed directions from Moscow to Madrid. Or even something as 'simple' as the spell check on your word processor, casually fixing your typos as you go.

And then there are AI machines that go far beyond the everyday, like robots. Today's most extraordinary robotic machines are much more than logically intelligent; they're also physically intelligent. Consider Stanley, the 100% autonomous vehicle that barrelled

> ## *We're teaching machines to rely less on pure logic and more on probabilities and experience, what we might call 'intuition'*

through the Mojave Desert to win the 2005 DARPA Grand Challenge. Stanley used GPS data to pinpoint its location, as well as laser-guided radar and video cameras to scan the distance for obstacles in real-time. Internal gyroscopes and inertial sensors feed constant streams of data into the on-board computer to control steering and acceleration.

The Honda ASIMO (Advanced Step in Innovative MObility) robot grabbed the world's attention with its human-like walk, a feat of intelligent engineering. ASIMO uses infrared and ultrasonic sensors to gauge distances from floors, walls and moving objects, and constantly adjusts its balance and motion with 34 high-precision servo motors. ASIMO's processors are so lightning-fast, you can shove the robot sideways in mid-stride and it will 'instinctively' throw its weight onto an outside foot to right itself.

Perhaps the greatest achievements of artificial intelligence over the past half-century have been illustrated by the way that machines can intelligently process information. Google is just one example of intelligent information technology that can parse obscene amounts of data into useful information. Intelligent cell phone networks bounce packets of voice data along the most efficient path. Logistics software is the engine of global business, calculating the most efficient and profitable way to procure supplies, manufacturer and ship products around the world. Credit card companies use intelligent software to analyse the buying patterns of millions of cardholders and identify the subtle red flags that signal fraud or theft. In the information age, we rely on these intelligent machines to make sense of streams of seemingly random data.

As processing power continues to multiply, we are coming closer to answering Turing's original question: "Can machines think?" We are teaching machines to rely less on pure logic and more on probabilities and experience, what we might call 'intuition'. And they are fast learners... ✿

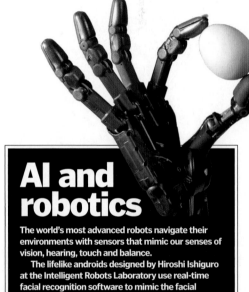

AI and robotics

The world's most advanced robots navigate their environments with sensors that mimic our senses of vision, hearing, touch and balance.

The lifelike androids designed by Hiroshi Ishiguro at the Intelligent Robots Laboratory use real-time facial recognition software to mimic the facial movements of the 'controller'.

Walking robots like ASIMO are equipped with an internal gyroscope and speed sensor to help it maintain balance, even when shoved. Infrared and ultrasonic sensors are used to gauge the distance of the floor and the speed and path of approaching objects. Sensors in hands and feet help it 'feel' the six axes of force – up/down, left/right, forwards/backwards – and the degree of force applied.

Where did artificial intelligence begin?

5th Century BCE
Aristotle's logic
Aristotle defines syllogistic logic – how a single conclusion is drawn from two premises.

400 BCE
Mechanical dove
Archytas of Tarentum constructs a wooden dove that can flap its wings and even fly.

13th Century
Lullian machine
A Spanish monk creates a machine that draws conclusions from different paired symbols.

15th Century
Spring-driven clocks
These clocks and watches are the world's first mechanical measuring machines.

1642
Pascal's calculating machine
The wooden box with a metal crank can handle both addition and subtraction.

1801
Punch cards
A French silk weaver automatically controls a loom using a series of punch cards.

1821
Difference Engine No 1
Charles Babbage envisages a complex calculating machine.

1850s
Boolean algebras
George Boole uses syllogistic logic to reduce maths functions to two symbols: 0 and 1.

1889
Electric tabulating system
Herman Hollerith devises a way to mechanically record data.

1910
Principia Mathematica
A three-volume work to derive mathematical truths from a set of axioms using symbolic logic is produced.

The IBM Watson supercomputer

What's IBM's Watson?

In February 2011, an IBM supercomputer named Watson trounced two previous champions of the US trivia quiz show *Jeopardy!*. Watson parsed natural language questions fast enough to beat the quickest human minds. IBM researchers preloaded the computer with hundreds of millions of pages of data, then armed it with algorithms for searching and 'reading' text – separating subjects, verbs and objects. But this was much more than a super-powered Google search. Watson used advanced algorithms to 'reason' which of its millions of hypothetical answers was most likely to be true. The 'face' behind the *Jeopardy!* podium was backed by a roomful of servers, comparing results in fractions of a second until the computer had enough statistical confidence to buzz in. Watson technology is already being considered as the brains behind an automated physician's assistant.

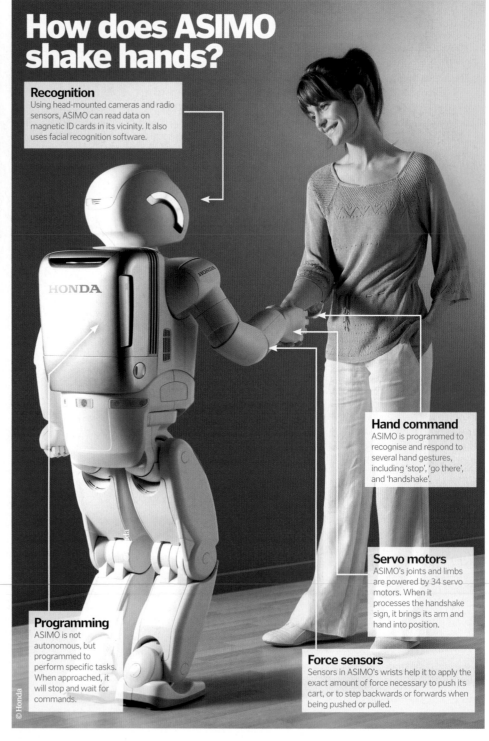

How does ASIMO shake hands?

Recognition
Using head-mounted cameras and radio sensors, ASIMO can read data on magnetic ID cards in its vicinity. It also uses facial recognition software.

Hand command
ASIMO is programmed to recognise and respond to several hand gestures, including 'stop', 'go there', and 'handshake'.

Servo motors
ASIMO's joints and limbs are powered by 34 servo motors. When it processes the handshake sign, it brings its arm and hand into position.

Programming
ASIMO is not autonomous, but programmed to perform specific tasks. When approached, it will stop and wait for commands.

Force sensors
Sensors in ASIMO's wrists help it to apply the exact amount of force necessary to push its cart, or to step backwards or forwards when being pushed or pulled.

Where did artificial intelligence begin?

1921
'Robot' coined
A science fiction play is the first to call automatons 'roboti', Czech for 'forced labourers'.

1936
Turing machine
Polymath Turing describes his 'machine', a theoretical device that establishes the logical foundation for computer science.

1943
Cybernetics
Studies help to understand machine learning.

1949
Computer chess
Claude Shannon proposes the functions for programming a computer to play chess.

1955
'Artificial intelligence' invented
John McCarthy uses the phrase in a proposal for a conference on machine learning.

1956
First AI program
The Logic Theorist is the first program written to mimic the human thought process.

1979
Autonomous robot
The Stanford Cart successfully navigates a room full of obstacles using sensors and software.

1997
Deep Blue
World chess champion Gary Kasparov loses to the IBM supercomputer.

1997
Google
The web's most influential piece of AI programming is launched.

2011
IBM Watson
The DeepQA supercomputer uses language analysis algorithms to beat two former *Jeopardy!* champions.

What do machines think?

The human brain is a profoundly complex machine. What we regard as simple common sense is actually a combination of stored knowledge, logical reasoning, probability and language interpretation. In the last 50 years, AI researchers have made strides towards building a machine that can truly 'think'

Probability

Humans are likely to base decisions on the probability of something being true, given past experiences and the current conditions. AI machines can be programmed to reason in similar ways. Computers are excellent statisticians, and with the right algorithms, they can quickly make billions of calculations to decide which answer/action is most likely to produce the desired result. As new evidence is presented, AI machines use Bayesian probability to overlap the new set of probabilities over existing calculations.

Algorithms

Algorithms are the bits of programming logic that instruct the computer how to do something. A good example is the minimax algorithm that helps a chess-playing computer like IBM's Deep Blue decide its next move. Minimax algorithms assign a value to each position and piece on the board and search through all possible moves to decide which delivers the best results. To optimise the search, Deep Blue only considered the next 12 moves instead of every possible move and countermove, until checkmate.

Logic

Dating back to the days of Aristotle, philosophers have attempted to map and define the logical processes by which we make decisions. Rather than living life on a whim, the 'rational actor' makes choices and takes action based on evidence and inference, cause and effect. If a machine is to become a rational actor, it must be programmed to recognise that if A and B are true, then the only logical conclusion is C. The challenge of AI is to create mathematical models for logical processes that the machine can use to make reasonable decisions based on evidence and probability.

Language

Human beings have many ways of learning, such as listening, watching, reading and feeling. The only way for a machine to learn is through language. Computer programming languages are grounded in logic. Consider the most basic if/then statement: If X is greater than 1, then go to Y. With greater processing power, computers are being taught to interpret natural language – the way humans communicate. IBM's Watson computer can read natural text because it was programmed to parse sentences for subject, verb and object and compare those entries with its vast database of knowledge.

Search and optimisation

Google is an example of artificial intelligence – if it was only a search engine, it would randomly assemble a list of every webpage that included your term. But Google programmers have armed the engine with algorithms that help it optimise searches to retrieve the most relevant matches first. AI machines use the same methods to search for the most logical response to environmental data (don't run into that table) or direct queries (what's the balance on my bank account?). They're programmed to use heuristics – short cuts – to eliminate the least-probable search paths.

Reasoning

It was once believed that the AI brain could only reason according to strict rules of logic. Question-answering computers like IBM's Watson are proof that machines can be taught to reason on higher levels. Watson begins with straight logic: searching its vast database of knowledge for keywords in the question. But then it uses much more complex algorithms to identify related concepts and make the kind of intuitive connections we call 'experience'. Probability is a huge component of higher-level machine reasoning, using unprecedented processing power to give the most likely answer from a nearly limitless range of knowledge.

> **"** *Roller coasters incorporate solutions that are at the leading edge of scientific development* **"**

Corkscrew
Among the most famous roller coaster elements – trains enter the corkscrew and are twisted through 360 degrees to emerge travelling in a different direction.

Zero gravity roll
Riders experience 0g – gravity is cancelled out by opposing forces so there is a feeling of weightlessness. It is often felt on uphill 360-degree twists.

Train
Two or more cars linked up are called a train. The position of the car in a train dictates the effects on the riders.

Brake run
These are sections of track, usually at the end, that incorporate a braking device to slow the roller coaster. These can be skids, a fin on the car or, more recently, magnetic eddy current brakes.

Dive loop
A dive loop is a type of roller coaster inversion where the track twists upwards and to the side, and then dives toward the ground in a half-vertical loop.

How safe are roller coasters?

They strike fear into many, but we still love them! Here, we detail the engineering achievement that is the roller coaster

Believe it or not, some of the world's most forward-looking engineering is actually in operation right now, in the unexpected setting of the world's theme parks.

From the pioneering 18th Century 'Russian Mountains', people have been hooked on the frightful thrill of a roller coaster – and ever since, the challenge has been to make an even bigger, even better, even more terrifying one.

Today, they incorporate solutions that are at the leading edge of scientific development. This means they are able to accelerate as fast as a drag racer and let passengers experience G-forces way in excess of a Formula 1 race car.

They do all this in complete safety, having passed the very strictest engineering standards. People travel for miles to ride on the latest roller coaster – they'll even cross continents just to experience the thrill. ✿

Lift hill
The lift hill is the first rising section of track containing the drive mechanism to raise the roller coaster to the summit.

© Alex Pang

Headchopper
Designers build the layout tightly so they 'appear' to risk chopping passengers' heads off as they approach! The reality is there's ample clearance, but it's a big part of the thrill.

How do roller coasters roll?

Roller coaster trains are unpowered. They rely on an initial application of acceleration force, then combine stored potential energy and gravitational forces to continue along the track. This is why they rise and fall as they twist and turn.

There are various methods of launching a roller coaster. Traditionally, a lift hill is used – the train is pulled up a steep section of track. It is released at the top, where gravity transfers potential energy into kinetic energy, accelerating the train. Launches can be via a chain lift that locks onto the underneath of the train, or a motorised drive tyre system, or a simple cable lift.

There is also the catapult launch lift: the train is accelerated very fast by an engine or a dropped weight.

Newer roller coasters use motors for launching. These generate intense acceleration on a flat section of track. Linear induction motors use electromagnetic force to pull the train along the track. They are very controllable with modern electronics. Some rides now have induction motors at points along the track, negating the need to store all the energy at the lift hill – giving designers more opportunities to create new sensations. Hydraulic launch systems are also starting to become more popular.

Careful calculation means a roller coaster releases roughly enough energy to complete the course. At the end, a brake run halts the train – this compensates for different velocities caused by varying forces due to changing passenger loads.

© 2010 Merlin Entertainments Group

How are roller coasters designed?

Roller coasters comprise many elements, each with its own specific physical characteristics. Designers give a ride character by applying an understanding of physics to build up a sequence of thrills. These are all interrelated and mean the experience of every ride is exciting and unique.

Computer models can analyse the forces that will be produced by each twist and turn, ensuring they are kept within specific boundaries. Roller coasters may look like a random snake of track, but the reality is years of scientific calculations to provide just the right effects.

The Stealth ride at Thorpe Park isn't for the faint-hearted

© 2010 Merlin Entertainments Group

How do coasters create G-force?

The aim of a roller coaster is to subject forces on the body people do not normally experience. These have to be within safe medical limits, and to do this designers consider physiology. The body is more able to tolerate vertical forces rather than horizontal ones. This is particularly the case for compression forces. Many roller coasters therefore compress passengers firmly into their seats, with forces up to +6g, but won't let them 'float' out too severely – the effects of a negative 2g force will still be strongly felt!

An intolerance of side forces is why many roller coaster corners are banked. This reduces the G-forces on passengers to around 1.5g, helping protect necks. It is unable to deal with high side forces so careful consideration must be given here to not injure people.

Overall, though, a roller coaster is the only thing this side of a race car or space shuttle where you can feel what such incredible forces are like. Are your body and your constitution up to it? ✿

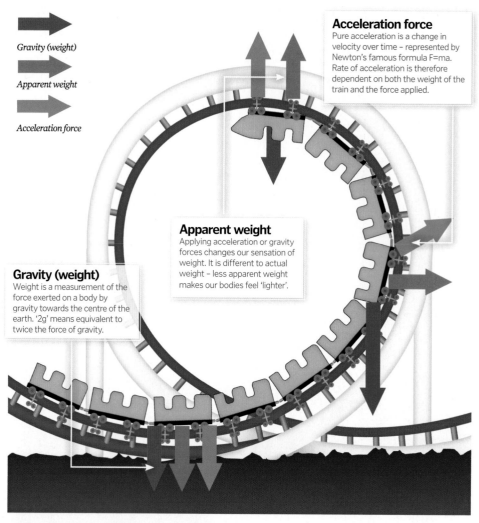

→ Gravity (weight)

→ Apparent weight

→ Acceleration force

Acceleration force
Pure acceleration is a change in velocity over time – represented by Newton's famous formula F=ma. Rate of acceleration is therefore dependent on both the weight of the train and the force applied.

Apparent weight
Applying acceleration or gravity forces changes our sensation of weight. It is different to actual weight – less apparent weight makes our bodies feel 'lighter'.

Gravity (weight)
Weight is a measurement of the force exerted on a body by gravity towards the centre of the earth. '2g' means equivalent to twice the force of gravity.

Summit approach
The approach to a summit appears to be about to launch you into the air as no track is visible in front!

Loop
Serious G-force is felt during the loop, along with disorientation as the track disappears over your head.

Need for speed
The roller coaster is accelerated to the ground faster than gravity – this causes negative G-force that presses you back into the seat.

What is bulletproof glass?

Shattering the science behind what makes the breakable unbreakable

Bullet-resistant glass works by absorbing a bullet's kinetic (movement) energy and dissipating it across a larger area. Multiple layers of toughened glass are reinforced with alternated layers of polycarbonate – a tough but flexible transparent plastic which retains the see-through properties of glass. As a bullet strikes the first glass layer, the polycarbonate layer behind it forces the glass to shatter internally rather than outwards.

This process absorbs some of the bullet's kinetic energy. The high velocity impact also flattens the bullet's head. Imagine trying to pierce through a sheet of cotton with the top end of a pencil. It would be very difficult compared to using the sharp pointed end. The same principle applies here. The flat-headed bullet struggles to penetrate the layer of polycarbonate. As the bullet travels through each layer of glass and polycarbonate, the process is repeated until it no longer has the speed and shape to exit the final layer. ❈

What makes bulletproof glass bulletproof?

- Anti-scratch coating
- Polyester
- Polyvinyl butyral
- Glass
- Polyurethane
- Polycarbonate
- Polyurethane
- Glass
- Polyvinyl butyral
- Ceramic paint (dot matrix)
- Glass

❝ *Imagine trying to pierce through a sheet of cotton with the top end of a pencil* ❞

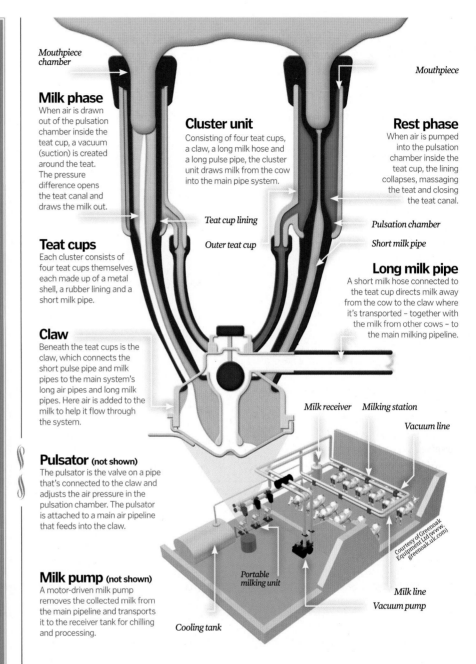

Mouthpiece chamber

Mouthpiece

Milk phase
When air is drawn out of the pulsation chamber inside the teat cup, a vacuum (suction) is created around the teat. The pressure difference opens the teat canal and draws the milk out.

Cluster unit
Consisting of four teat cups, a claw, a long milk hose and a long pulse pipe, the cluster unit draws milk from the cow into the main pipe system.

Rest phase
When air is pumped into the pulsation chamber inside the teat cup, the lining collapses, massaging the teat and closing the teat canal.

Teat cup lining

Outer teat cup

Pulsation chamber

Short milk pipe

Teat cups
Each cluster consists of four teat cups themselves each made up of a metal shell, a rubber lining and a short milk pipe.

Long milk pipe
A short milk hose connected to the teat cup directs milk away from the cow to the claw where it's transported – together with the milk from other cows – to the main milking pipeline.

Claw
Beneath the teat cups is the claw, which connects the short pulse pipe and milk pipes to the main system's long air pipes and long milk pipes. Here air is added to the milk to help it flow through the system.

Milk receiver   *Milking station*

Vacuum line

Pulsator (not shown)
The pulsator is the valve on a pipe that's connected to the claw and adjusts the air pressure in the pulsation chamber. The pulsator is attached to a main air pipeline that feeds into the claw.

Courtesy of Greenoak Equipment Ltd (www.greenoakuk.com)

Portable milking unit

Milk line

Vacuum pump

Milk pump (not shown)
A motor-driven milk pump removes the collected milk from the main pipeline and transports it to the receiver tank for chilling and processing.

Cooling tank

How do you milk a cow?
You'll need a mechanism unlike any udder

The milk is extracted using a vacuum applied to the cow's teats. Milk stored in the udder is drawn into a system of pipes leading to a receiver tank where the milk is collected before being passed to the cooling tank.

A 'cluster' of four teat cups – each consisting of a stainless steel shell, a flexible rubber lining and a short pulse pipe – are attached to the teats. Between the outer shell and lining is a pulsation chamber that collapses with the addition of air from a pulsator. When the chamber is devoid of air

(milk phase) a vacuum is created, which gently draws milk from the teat. When the chamber is filled with air (rest phase) the lining of the teat cup collapses and massages the teat. Continued repetition of these phases not only aids milk production by mimicking the action of a suckling calf, it also promotes blood circulation.

To help the milk flow away through the pipeline, once out of the cow the milk is mixed with air added by a claw – the claw connects the teat cups to the milk and pulse tubes. ❈

How thin can TVs get?

OLED displays are changing the face of our TVs, monitors and mobile phones

1. Cathode
Current passes through the cathode layer to the anode.

Cathode

Emissive layer (organic molecules or polymers)

Conductive layer (organic molecules or polymers)

Anode

Substrate

2. Electrons
As the current passes through the structure, electrons are added to the emissive layer.

3. Emissive layer
Electrons are removed from the conductive layer, leaving holes filled by the electrons from the emissive layer.

4. Creating light
As the electrons enter the holes they produce extra energy, which is emitted as light. The amount of light produced depends on the amount of power required.

© Sony

TVs have come a long way since the massive boxes hogging the corner of your living room. Yet even your current flat-screen LCD TV will soon look unwieldy compared to the next generation of products. With OLED (organic light-emitting diode) technology televisions, computer monitors, mobile phones and pretty much anything else with a screen are set to become thinner than ever before.

OLED is a major step on from the LCD technology that is currently used. In simple terms, it is created from organic materials that emit light when power is passed through it. An OLED display contains thin films of organic materials placed between two conductors; as the current passes through, the display lights up. This self-illuminating function removes the need for the backlight that is an essential requirement of a traditional LCD screen. There

are two kinds of OLED display, of which AMOLED (active matrix) is the most important. Designed for larger displays (of over about three inches), it allows for each individual pixel on the screen to be controlled separately.

The three key benefits to OLED displays all stem from that lack of a backlight. The immediate consequence is that devices can be made thinner – a 40-inch LCD TV needs a backlight large enough to span and light the entire surface of the screen evenly. Without this problem, the same sized OLED-based TV could be little more than an inch thick, and as miniaturisation of the other components powering devices develops further, they will only continue to get thinner.

The next benefit is that without that backlight, the screens draw far less power. While a black image on an LCD display is backlit to the same degree as a white screen,

the light on an AMOLED display directly corresponds to the brightness of each individual pixel. For devices that run on battery power, like mobile phones, this is a massive boon. The final benefit comes in the form of a massive improvement in image quality, with greater contrast between light and dark colours thanks to the absence of the backlight that turns blacks into dark greys on a traditional LCD.

Of course, thinner hardware is only the first step in what OLED technology will bring us. Through nanotechnology companies like Sony and Toshiba have created screens that measure less than half a millimetre thick, making them extremely flexible. Imagine a mobile phone with a large screen that can be folded to keep it pocketable, or even wearable computers built into clothing – this is no longer just the stuff of science fiction. ✿

How do satnavs know where you are?

It's all made possible by satellites orbiting the Earth at over 8,000mph...

Orbiting the planet 11,000 miles above us, satellites are constantly sending signals down to Earth. These satellites and GPS technology started out as part of the USA's military attempt to improve missile accuracy.

The satellites send a constant stream of signals broadcasting their exact position to Earth, where a GPS or satnav system can receive it. The signal sent to your receiver will tell it how far away the satellite is and its direction. Once the receiver has this information from three different satellites it can start calculating your position, using triangulation. There are 12 satellites on each side of the Earth at any one time, as they have to cover the whole planet. These will be at different positions in the sky. Once you have four satellite signals, your receiver can start to calculate altitude as well as position. The more signals you receive, the more accurate the results will be during the journey.

New systems will become available over the next few years that improve on the average 15m accuracy. These systems rely on new satellites that orbit to stay in exactly the same position, and ground stations to relay the signals. In Europe the system in development is called EGNOS and promises accuracy to 2m. ✿

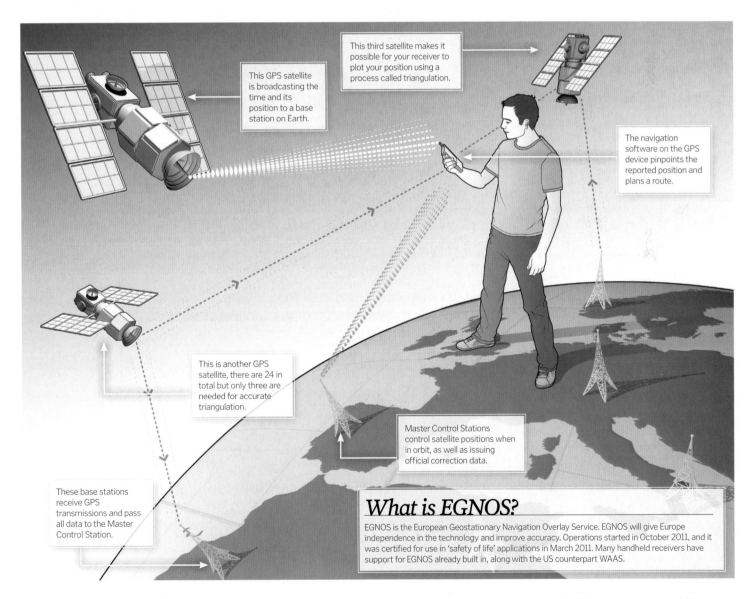

This GPS satellite is broadcasting the time and its position to a base station on Earth.

This third satellite makes it possible for your receiver to plot your position using a process called triangulation.

The navigation software on the GPS device pinpoints the reported position and plans a route.

This is another GPS satellite, there are 24 in total but only three are needed for accurate triangulation.

Master Control Stations control satellite positions when in orbit, as well as issuing official correction data.

These base stations receive GPS transmissions and pass all data to the Master Control Station.

What is EGNOS?

EGNOS is the European Geostationary Navigation Overlay Service. EGNOS will give Europe independence in the technology and improve accuracy. Operations started in October 2011, and it was certified for use in 'safety of life' applications in March 2011. Many handheld receivers have support for EGNOS already built in, along with the US counterpart WAAS.

> ❝ *Once the receiver has this information from three different satellites it can start calculating your position using triangulation* ❞

What happens when a pistol is fired?

The colourful profile of the semi-automatic weapon continues to shape public opinion, but there is more to its substance than style alone

PISTOL KEY:

1	Single action (SA) trigger/double action (DA) trigger	8	Firing pin
2	Disconnector (engaged in semi-automatics)	9	Breech
3	Sear	10	Extractor
4	Safety grip (must be depressed or gun will not fire)	11	Chamber
5	Magazine/Magazine spring (holds upwards of 15 rounds or more)	12	Barrel rifling
6	Centerfire cartridge	13	Slide
7	Hammer	14	Top locking lugs
		15	Recoil spring
		16	Link
		17	Muzzle

The semi-automatic pistol is a functionally different animal to the romanticised revolver of the Wild West. The motivation for semi – and for that matter, full – automatics derive from energy generated by the firing process to self-load and prime a new round. This comes in a variety of flavours, including recoil, blowback and gas.

Recoil is the gun's kick-back, balancing the bullet's forward momentum – or as Newton says, with every action must come an equal and opposite reaction. Here, the opposing recoil force drives the gun backwards, initiating momentum in the 'slide' and barrel that are mechanically engaged. Separation of the two typically allows the breech to open as the slide carries on, self-loading and cocking the gun in the process.

With blowback the barrel and slide are not wed. The barrel is typically fixed to the frame with the shunting force of the exploding cartridge operating against the breech face itself and forcing the slide to the rear. The infamous AK-47 is a further example of a system that siphons gas drawn from the fired cartridge explosion to cycle the self-loading process.

Despite these distinctions, the term automatic is often clouded with reference to loading and firing. Though its function is distinct from its ancestors, the triggering mechanism of semi-automatics such as the US Army's M1911 mean they can only discharge one round for every reciprocal pull of the trigger. This differentiates them from full automatics which utilise a trigger mechanism that actuates a continuous self-loading/firing cycle until a gun's clip is spent or trigger released.

Due to the unwieldy nature of full automatic pistols, semi-automatic variants are now common throughout the military and the police. ✿

What is the firing cycle?

1. Cock
The weapon is first primed by manually racking the slide, which cocks the hammer and chambers the round.

6. Up and out
The breech opens; the extractor and ejector take turns to draw and kick out the spent chambered cartridge. The slide continues passing over and recocking the hammer.

3. ...fire!
The primer explodes the gunpowder, sheaving the bullet from its case. Expanding gasses force the bullet down the barrel past helical grooves that impart spin to improve accuracy in flight.

2. Squeeze
The hammer is held by a small notch or 'sear'. Upon pulling the trigger the sear moves and spring-loaded hammer slips free, striking the firing pin which in turn hits the primer.

Auto fire stage 1

4. Shots away!
Combustion gasses provide muzzle velocity upwards of 250m/s; in turn the slide recoil is locked to the barrel by 'lugs'. As the bullet exits, bore pressure falls.

5. On the slide
At this point the 'link' pivots the barrel out of lock and the lugs disengage; the slide continues to retreat under conserved momentum, compressing the recoil spring.

Auto fire stage 2

Semi vs fully automatic

While both loading mechanisms are automated, the advantage of going full automatic means there is no trigger disconnect and no mechanical delay in the cycling of fire representative of semi-automatic weapons.

Therefore, while they are great in a tight spot and satisfy a penchant for wanton carnage, such continuous fire – allied to a typically low weight and no shoulder stock – makes them tough to control; and a tendency to kick up during firing make them prone to vertical spray.

'Cook-off' is also a factor in full automatics, where a round may dispense prematurely from the over-heated chamber. Full automatics often benefit from an open bolt policy, where the slide is held back at the end of the cycle to allow cooling air to filter the barrel.

Another issue is slam fire. This occurs when the slide is released and the force of it closing is powerful enough to detonate the primer. They are also subject to jamming, where the cartridge can stick while entering, or ejecting from, the chamber.

2. Reconnecting the disconnect
Linked to the trigger, this acts as a second sear, which catches the hammer or striker if the trigger is held. The disconnector is active until the trigger is released, and the hammer falls back on the regular sear.

4. Closed-bolt design
Commonly seen in semi-automatics that are less prone to 'cook-off', but also found on full automatics. Once cocked, the slide is forward and breech closed, with the chamber housing a fully loaded round.

1. Safety first
With frame-mounted safety locking the hammer and slide allow the gun to be carried in a "cocked and locked" state.

5. First shot accuracy
The single-action trigger (unlike double-action) doesn't cock the hammer, so requiring a shallow press; minimising mechanical disturbance and enhancing the aim.

3. The round house
The magazine is a distinct separation from classic cylindrical multi-chambered revolvers, housing upwards of 15 rounds or more. Note the chambered centerfire round: unlike rimfire, whose primer is built into the rim of the base; therefore when struck the case is not deformed and can be re-used.

> **“ Semi-automatic variants are now common throughout the military ”**

7. Relock...
The slide is propelled forward by the unwinding recoil spring; the returning breech closes and the slide locks into place with the barrel.

9. Trigger happy
In a full automatic the disconnector is not engaged in events. Therefore, keeping the trigger pulled results in a continuous cycling of fire until it's released or all ammo is spent.

Auto fire stage 3

8. ...and reload
The slide returns over the hammer (now cocked) and strips a round from the magazine, which is then thrust forward into the chamber.

How does a Google search work?

How exactly does Google return all those search results?

G oogle's name is synonymous with internet search and browsing. The Google homepage has become the gateway into the world wide web and its plainly presented, mostly blank starting screen is no accident – it is meant to represent an open page just waiting to be filled with search results based on your area of query.

Google understands that cyberspace is massive and it is expanding just about as fast as the universe itself. Just like our own cosmos there are chunks of matter out there in the form of huge planets of data (let's call them web portals in this instance) with their own ecosystems inside of which users interact.

The problem is, no one has been able to create an accurate and definitive map of the universe, or cyberspace for that matter, due to the constantly changing dynamic shape of both worlds. But Google is there to guide us with some clever technologies and more than a couple of nifty tricks, which you may not even be aware of as you surf the web.

What's really clever about Google's search function is that when most of us use it we think that we're searching the internet itself. In fact we're not. We're searching Google's index of the web. Google doesn't have connections to

every single corner of the internet, but the company's indexes are pretty darn good. In fact, they are among the biggest databases on the planet. We're talking about many billions of webpages stored on thousands of machines around the world.

But how does Google build this index – and how does it 'populate' it with accurate and meaningful results data that will be useful to users? Even Google has to start somewhere, so it uses software programs known as spiders, also commonly referred to as crawlers or Googlebots. These useful little crawlers are sent out initially to the most logical places on the web. If you search for 'Marmite', most likely the first site the

> **" Google understands that cyberspace is massive and it is expanding just about as fast as the universe itself "**

spider will have compiled your search results by visiting will be www.marmite.com, so no rocket science as yet. This first stage of website search is known as the 'seed' level.

After we pass the seed level we start to branch out. The spiders will then crawl outwards further and follow links from the initial pages that it finds and start to weave a web of interconnected websites that share relevance in terms of content. The spider builds up a pattern of pages linked to pages, which must be recursively revisited in order to ensure they still contain content relating to the original search. Pages are revisited based on frequency 'policies' that are set by software that resides on Google's servers. But what we need to remember is that the web is so vast and changeable that no spider will ever capture all the information out there.

So let's start with a search. Say we want to look up 'toasted cheese sandwiches'. We type in those three words and press Return. Google's query processor software then gets to work filtering through its indexes to decide which links to present. But hang on – what's to stop us getting results on cheese making, results on toaster-buying advice and results on the Earl of Sandwich? Well, Google asks questions. More than 200 questions in fact. You could say that

What does Google actually do to get search results?

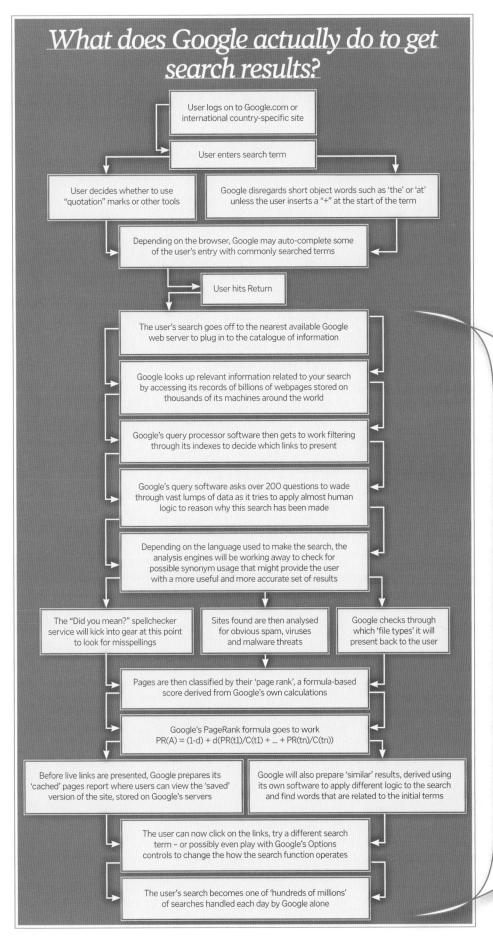

- User logs on to Google.com or international country-specific site
- User enters search term
- User decides whether to use "quotation" marks or other tools
- Google disregards short object words such as 'the' or 'at' unless the user inserts a "+" at the start of the term
- Depending on the browser, Google may auto-complete some of the user's entry with commonly searched terms
- User hits Return
- The user's search goes off to the nearest available Google web server to plug in to the catalogue of information
- Google looks up relevant information related to your search by accessing its records of billions of webpages stored on thousands of its machines around the world
- Google's query processor software then gets to work filtering through its indexes to decide which links to present
- Google's query software asks over 200 questions to wade through vast lumps of data as it tries to apply almost human logic to reason why this search has been made
- Depending on the language used to make the search, the analysis engines will be working away to check for possible synonym usage that might provide the user with a more useful and more accurate set of results
- The "Did you mean?" spellchecker service will kick into gear at this point to look for misspellings
- Sites found are then analysed for obvious spam, viruses and malware threats
- Google checks through which 'file types' it will present back to the user
- Pages are then classified by their 'page rank', a formula-based score derived from Google's own calculations
- Google's PageRank formula goes to work
  $$PR(A) = (1-d) + d(PR(t1)/C(t1) + ... + PR(tn)/C(tn))$$
- Before live links are presented, Google prepares its 'cached' pages report where users can view the 'saved' version of the site, stored on Google's servers
- Google will also prepare 'similar' results, derived using its own software to apply different logic to the search and find words that are related to the initial terms
- The user can now click on the links, try a different search term – or possibly even play with Google's Options controls to change the how the search function operates
- The user's search becomes one of 'hundreds of millions' of searches handled each day by Google alone

Time taken for search: **0.5 seconds**

Search preferences can be tweaked to provide greater accuracy in results

Did you mean...?

As we've said, we've been searching for a "Toasted Cheese Sandwich". However, if you type "taosyed cheeese samdwhich" the Did you mean... feature will offer suggestions based on the correct spelling. So how does it work?

Google engineer Noam Shazeer developed a spelling correction system that would form part of Google's core search software to perform this trick. He developed a system that would collate the most frequently misspelled words relating to real words. Consistently within the top ten search terms globally, "Britney Spears" has been searched for and misspelled so many times that there are now hundreds of listed misappropriations of her name – view them at www.google.com/jobs/britney.html.

Google's software uses a little artificial intelligence here because it tries to apply human logic to the vast lumps of raw data that it has to wade through.

To decide which 'toasted cheese sandwich' website to present to us, Google asks whether the words appear in the website's title or URL. Google asks how many times the words appear in the correct order on any given website. Does the page include synonyms for 'toasted cheese sandwich' such as 'grilled cheddar buttie' or 'hot cheesy panini'. Discussing the mechanics of how to describe a toasted cheese sandwich might sound silly, but it's all logical to the guys who run Google's data centre.

As well as checking for poor design or poor content quality, Google will also check for the presence of obvious spam, viruses and malware. Our search process will then start to classify pages by their 'page rank', which is a formula-based score derived from Google's own calculations. A page rank score is obtained by analysing how many external pages point to a particular website or cite it as a reference or authority on a subject. All this is done in roughly half a second and your search term results will, depending on your web-connection speed, come back to you nearly instantaneously.

Now, of course Google could be on the pay roll of the international cheese sandwich society (for example) and so therefore be quite keen to present you with certain pages relating to that organisation's own interests. But it's not. Google's results are impartial and the company will not take payments from companies who want to push up their page-ranking results. Although there will be 'Google Ads' down the

> ## *Part of the concept of web search is that we often don't really know what we're looking for until we find it*

What does a search result look like?

Google's search results have evolved. Now we get relevant advertising slots at the top and down the right-hand side of our search page. As well as standard results (below) we'll also get location-based results that are tied in with Google Maps

Statistics bar
Displays the results returned and the time it took to search.

Page title
The name of the websites returned.

Snippets
A short description/preview of the contents of the website.

More results
Click to access more results via other search tools.

URL
A pointer to a 'resource' on the world wide web.

Cached – similar results
Click on the cached link to see the site as it was when first indexed.

Sponsored results
Paid for by advertisers in return for this placement.

right-hand side of the page and sometimes on top, which have been classified as 'relevant' and 'supporting' to your search term.

So, just how should you read a Google search result? Is it as simple as just clicking the top result on the page? Have you actually read down below the headline to look at some of the other information that the search engine is presenting to you? Right underneath your highlighted blue link you will see a short description of the website's content. This is part of the metadata of the website itself – or to put it another way, it is information about information. Either way you look at it, it's your fastest route to getting a handle on what you're likely to find if you decide to click onwards.

Right underneath the website description is the site's cached results, which can be displayed

if you want to be able to cross-reference exactly when the last time the Googlebots dipped onto the site in question for an update.

This version of the page will also give you colour-coded highlighted mark-ups of your search terms showing you exactly where they have been used. The cached version of the page is actually stored on Google's own servers and it is this content that the company uses to calculate and establish the site's page ranking. If the web server that hosts the 'live' version of the site you want to visit is acting up or working too slowly, you might like to remember that Google's servers are generally set to run pretty fast, so you could always use this version of the page instead.

Beside the 'Cached' link you'll see the 'Similar' link and this is pretty self explanatory. Part of

What is a page rank formula?

$$PR(A) = (1-d) + d(PR(t1)/C(t1) + ...$$

This looks complicated, but it's really very simple: PR(A) stands for the Google page rank of our arbitrary example page A. t1 – tn are the pages that link to page A. C is the number of outbound links that a page has and in this case our C variable is examining pages t1 to tn. d is a damping factor, which is usually set to 0.85 – this is a standard function used when working with numerical algorithms. It is likely that Google has progressed the form of this equation, but that it is still largely based on this initial form.

Where are the Google data centres?

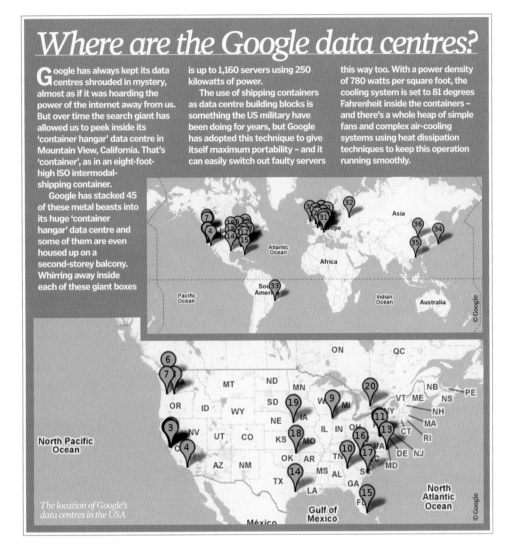

Google has always kept its data centres shrouded in mystery, almost as if it was hoarding the power of the internet away from us. But over time the search giant has allowed us to peek inside its 'container hangar' data centre in Mountain View, California. That's 'container', as in an eight-foot-high ISO intermodal-shipping container.

Google has stacked 45 of these metal beasts into its huge 'container hangar' data centre and some of them are even housed up on a second-storey balcony. Whirring away inside each of these giant boxes

is up to 1,160 servers using 250 kilowatts of power.

The use of shipping containers as data centre building blocks is something the US military have been doing for years, but Google has adopted this technique to give itself maximum portability – and it can easily switch out faulty servers

this way too. With a power density of 780 watts per square foot, the cooling system is set to 81 degrees Fahrenheit inside the containers – and there's a whole heap of simple fans and complex air-cooling systems using heat dissipation techniques to keep this operation running smoothly.

The location of Google's data centres in the USA

---

the concept of web search is that we often don't really know what we're looking for until we find it. Google can help here with some tangential results that you may not have considered searching for. Google uses its own server-based software to apply different logic to the initial search and find words that are related to the initial terms. You can play with this function more extensively if you use Google's Advanced search function or if you type 'related: URL' where URL is the full website address that you want to examine, as in 'related: http://www.howitworksdaily.com'.

Once you really dig into Google search you can start playing around with the user options, which are accessible right from the Google homepage. Not only can you change the language interface that is presented to you, but you can also change the native language that you are searching in and that you want results delivered back to you in.

You can also set the SafeSearch option to block pages with sexually explicit content and you can even change your search format to display preferences more suited to a mobile smartphone or PDA. ✿

$$+ \; PR(tn)/C(tn))$$

How do you get to the top of the list?

Search engine optimisation (or SEO) is all about how a website owner tries to optimise and improve the visibility of their pages so that they feature among Google's (or another search engine's) search results. SEO is based upon the website's ability to be found organically and algorithmically without any paid-for marketing support.

Content is king!

It's all down to content on the internet, so if you 'populate' your website with words that are frequently used in search requests then your SEO score will improve.

Egg recall **Facebook** YouTube
Britney Spears Floods
eBay **Edward Cullen**
President Obama Craigslist
Weather **Glee spoilers**

Metadata matters

If you edit your website's metadata information to also include popularly searched-for terms then you become more prominent on the web as a whole.

Meta-tagging and release

Technologies such as a the 'Canonical meta tag' and the '301 redirects' URL redirect tools can improve your page ranking as they ensure that internal website pages (ie inside of and beyond your homepage) all go to add towards your score.

Don't get cross, get cross-linked

You can cross-link less prominent pages within your total website's data stash to point to the most important pages with the most highly searched-for words and phrases to increase your overall ranking.

Use common sense

There are just certain words and phrases that you or anyone else would naturally associate with websites pertaining to every subject under the sun. So use your common sense, look at what other successful sites have done and rework a few popular ideas in your own style.

How do oil rigs work?

The world produces over 82 million barrels of oil every day, much of it in harsh conditions, miles from shore and safety if an emergency happens. So how is it done?

O il has been around for millions of years, located deep below the land or sea where it became trapped under layers of permeable rocks or slowly seeping to the surface. Although examples of oil drilling were documented in 4th Century China, the first modern oil gathering structure was built in 1897 and by 1928 mobile rigs consisting of a simple barge with a drill mounted on top had set the scene for a revolution that fuelled Western industrial dominance for the next century.

Over 82 million barrels of oil are produced every single day, a process that usually starts with a range of surveys; from geographical and geomagnetic surveys to the deep echo sounding or seismic reflection surveys that pinpoint the likely location of a substantial deposit. Only then, and after the necessary permits have all been obtained of course, can the rigs move in – multi-million pound structures and teams of professionals that locate, make the well safe and finally drill down to its precious commodity.

Today, there are over 40,000 oil fields around the world, with most offshore drilling undertaken in the Continental shelf – the sunken perimeter of a continent's original glacial shape. From the $100 million monsters that plumb the deepest waters in the Gulf of Mexico, to the smaller North Sea structures that nevertheless have to withstand 90-knot winds and 60-foot waves. Mobile rigs are usually reserved for exploratory work, owned by private contractors and leased to the oil companies who then have limited time to find, tap and process their precious bounty. Larger manned platforms and spars can service up to 30 wellheads, tapping into multiple wells up to five miles from the platform itself. ✿

Derrick
The derrick usually towers over the rest of the rig and is used to house the drill machinery and feed in new pipe as the drill descends.

Cranes
Offshore rigs have multiple cranes that are continually used for lifting containers, drill equipment and sections of piping to the top of the derrick.

Legs
Platforms required to drill thousands of feet below sea level rest on concrete or steel legs, securely anchored to the seabed and particularly hard to remove after use.

Deck
The working space aboard an offshore platform where drilling rigs, production facilities and crew quarters are located. Larger platforms may use nearby 'flotels' for crew quarters.

Jacket
Jackets are usually vertical steel sections piled into the seabed, protecting the central drill shaft against damage or interference.

Wells
With each platform needing to service up to 30 wells at different depths and positions, flow lines and umbilical connections are required to connect them all to the main rig.

© DK Images

What's life like on an oil rig?

Required to work for up to six months a year, oil workers are well compensated for the undeniably hazardous conditions they work in. Wages are typically higher than in similar engineering disciplines and the larger platforms and spars come complete with facilities more appropriate to a cruise ship than a floating factory.

These facilities can include private rooms for the 100+ crew, cinemas, 24-hour restaurants and even gyms. Supplies are usually brought in by helicopter or ship, making oil platforms better stocked than most workplaces and significantly more important to the local economies they reside in. It is estimated that every offshore worker supports up to ten more in local industries such as food, transport or maintenance.

However, the dangers are constant and largely unpredictable. Offshore drilling involves not just dealing with highly flammable oil and gas, with the added danger of this being pumped out at exceptionally high pressures, but also extreme wind and sea conditions. When danger strikes, support is often miles away by helicopter or ship, and despite the high levels of training and increasingly safe equipment, offshore fatality rates have been on the rise in recent years. In addition to this, workers are often prone to alcoholism or drug abuse to overcome the isolation and gruelling 12-hour shifts.

What are the different types of rig?

Drill Ships

Designed for speculative or deep water mining, these vessels are converted to include a drilling platform in the centre. Drill ships use sophisticated sensors and satellite tracking to keep them moving while lined up to the well.

Semi-submersibles

Made up of floating pontoons and columns able to sink in the water where they are anchored to the sea floor or kept in place by steerable thrusters. Effective at drill depths of up to 6,000 feet, they're designed for quick deployment.

Jack-up

Mobile platforms can be raised above the sea on extendable steel legs. Designed for depths of 500 metres or less, they are useful for small to mid-sized deposits and typically only support smaller crews.

Rig

An immovable structure of concrete and steel that rests on the seabed with deck space for multiple rigs, crew quarters and production facilities. Their design and expense makes them appropriate for larger offshore deposits.

Spar

Perfect for major oil fields such as the North Sea, spars are drilling platforms fixed to giant, hollow hulls that can descend up to 250 metres, still above the ocean floor and secured by cables.

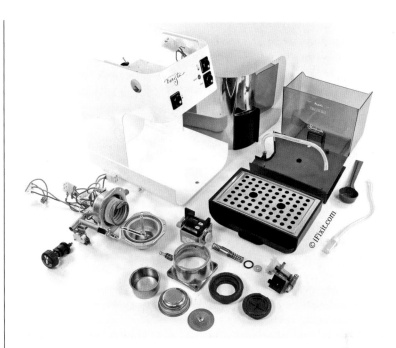

© iFixit.com

How can a machine make an espresso?

The science and technology behind a silky smooth dose of caffeine

Espresso is a brewing method for coffee that, through the filtering of ground coffee through highly pressurised water, generates an intense, deep and syrupy caffeinated beverage. Standard filter coffee is brewed using a drip method – heated water is simply poured over coffee grinds and allowed to filter through them under gravity alone, absorbing their oils and essences. However, espresso is a considerably more complex brewing method that involves many stages of preparation and production. These variables, which can have a dramatic impact on the finished product, include water temperature, pressure level, filter type, tamp level (how much the ground coffee is compacted before brewing), fineness of the bean grind, type of grinder, freshness of the beans and type of bean roast.

For the espresso machine brewing process, the beans, which have been grown and roasted, are first ground into incredibly fine, uniform grains using a grinder. Next the grains are compacted by a tamper (a weighted device used to compress the grains) into the coffee machine's portafilter, a basket device used to control the flow of water filtered through the grains. On home espresso makers, this filter is usually the pressurised variety, which is designed to automatically compensate for poor/uneven grind and tamps. The espresso machine's pump then draws water from its tank into its boiler for heating to the correct temperature. Advanced machines use a 'roller coaster' technique, where the ideal temperature is maintained in a constant process of water heating, temperature checking, boiler disconnection, temperature checking and water reheating. This means that the water temperature constantly fluctuates either side of the ideal, resulting in a faster ideal temperature pick-up time when water is required for an espresso.

Finally, the water is pressurised and forced through the filter and coffee grains. The heat and pressure of the water extracts and emulsifies the essences of the ground coffee, producing a thick, syrupy liquid topped with a layer of crema – a fine-celled foam imbued with the taste and aromatic properties of the bean. ✿

What makes Paypal secure?

The technology behind these protected online payments

PayPal works by utilising thousands of separate servers running the Linux operating system, literal 'blocks' of servers that can be redistributed to perform different tasks in tandem with one another. These thousands of servers connect with an offline database of customer information to transfer data back and forth between payee and recipient. However, the servers don't share information with each other, so anyone trying to break into the system would have to scour the heavily encrypted servers one by one to piece together the relevant data. This separation of the servers allows PayPal to remain secure while quickly processing the millions of payments it receives, as it would be almost impossible to obtain access to the different servers simultaneously to gather data.

The process is best shown through a step-by-step transaction. When a product is bought, the buyer – who has supplied PayPal with their bank details – authorises a transaction via credit card or cheque to debit their account for the purchase price.

This transaction is handled directly by PayPal, who contact the seller's bank, credit card association and card issuer, paying the various interchange fees necessary to process it. The seller's money is then deposited into a dedicated PayPal account. This process is mirrored for the merchant, but is processed on a completely separate server for security reasons.

Finally, after a set period of time, the money is transferred to the buyer's account in another completely separate transaction across another server. ✿

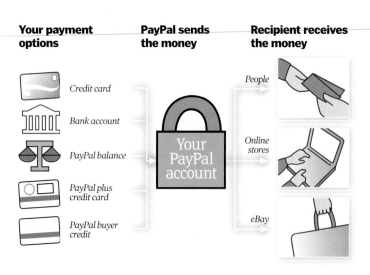

Your payment options — **PayPal sends the money** — **Recipient receives the money**

Credit card
Bank account
PayPal balance
PayPal plus credit card
PayPal buyer credit

Your PayPal account

People
Online stores
eBay

1. Method
PayPal accepts many different types of payment method, from cheque to credit card. The type of payment affects the amount of interchange fees that are paid and processing time.

2. Interest
PayPal makes money by accruing interest on banked payments, as well as direct fees charged according to an item's value.

3. Exchange
PayPal payments are not restricted just to online stores and auction houses, with people able to directly wire funds to any other person with an email address.

How do metal detectors work?

Find out how to locate buried treasure using magnetism

The most common metal detector uses a Very Low Frequency (VLF) technology to search for hidden objects. It employs one of the basic laws of electromagnetism, that an object in an alternating magnetic field (switching from north to south polarity) will create an oscillating field of its own in opposition.

A transmitter coil emits this field, switching at a frequency of thousands of times per second. A device known as a magnetometer within a receiver coil can detect magnetic pulses pushed upwards from the object underground in response, and alert the user of the metal detector via a beep or on screen.

By cleverly employing a process known as phase shifting, the VLF detector can deduce what sort of object is beneath the surface. This method works by calculating the time difference between the frequency of the transmitter's field and the corresponding response from underground. This all depends on how easily the object conducts electricity, and once this is known its composition can then be approximated. ✿

Control box
Here the circuitry and controls for the user to operate the detector are located, as well as a jack to connect headphones.

Stabiliser
Constantly swinging the detector can be hard work, so a stabiliser often wraps around the arm to help keep it steady.

Shaft
The shaft allows the detector to be adjusted to an optimum height, while also connecting the controls to the coil.

Transmitter coil
An alternating magnetic field that is emitted from the transmitter coil causes metallic objects to emit their own detectable field.

Receiver coil
The receiver detects an object's magnetic field. The stronger the field received, the closer the object is to the surface, and vice versa.

What makes a phone vibrate?

How does this setting on a mobile phone let the user know they have a call without alerting everyone around them?

It works via a three-stage process that begins with an incoming call, text or whatever you've set your phone to alert you to. When the phone picks up this incoming information, it closes a circuit, activating a small motor built into the body of the phone. This motor then vibrates until you answer the call or 'wake' the phone up, which in turn tells the phone you're aware of the incoming call or message.

On its own this motor wouldn't vibrate (instead it would simply make noise), so a weight is built onto the drive shaft of the motor. This is deliberately off-centre, meaning that when the phone rings, the motor activates and the weight spins, jostling the phone a fraction and making it reverberate. ✿

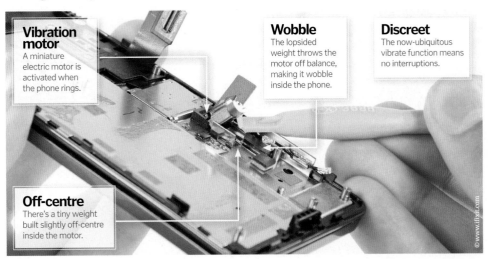

Vibration motor
A miniature electric motor is activated when the phone rings.

Wobble
The lopsided weight throws the motor off balance, making it wobble inside the phone.

Discreet
The now-ubiquitous vibrate function means no interruptions.

Off-centre
There's a tiny weight built slightly off-centre inside the motor.

How do toilets flush?

Ever wonder about water closets?
Here are the facts about flushing...

Modern flush toilets work in two main stages. First, in order to empty waste from the bowl, a complex flush mechanism is activated. This section is contained within the toilet's tank – the part of the toilet positioned above the bowl – and is initiated when a user presses the toilet's handle. Once pushed, the handle pulls up a chain connected to a flush valve – a rubber stopper that acts as a gateway to the bowl, siphon and trapway. The water in the tank, which has been filled via a filler tube from the mains supply, then exits the tank and descends into the bowl. It follows a rim shelf perforated with equidistant holes, as well as a smaller secondary passage directly into the toilet's siphon – the kinked pipe that sits between the trapway and the bowl.

The release of the tank's water occurs in roughly three seconds, which creates a vacuum effect that depressurises the trapway, generating a large suction force that drags the contents of the bowl down into the sewerage system.

Once flushed, the toilet's tank needs to refill itself for further use. First, now the tank is devoid of water, the flush valve falls back down onto the gateway to the bowl. This reseals the tank. Next, the tank filler valve is switched on either electronically or by a traditional ball cock (a float mechanism that pivots on an axle to open the filler valve when the water falls). This allows water to re-enter the tank through the filler tube, filling it to a preset level, as well as down the overflow tube to refill the bowl.

The filler valve is then shut once more, either by the rising of the float or by another control system. Finally, the refilling of the tank re-pressurises the siphon and trapway, blocking any gasses and waste from re-entering. It re-creates a large water surface area in the main bowl, ready for reuse. ✿

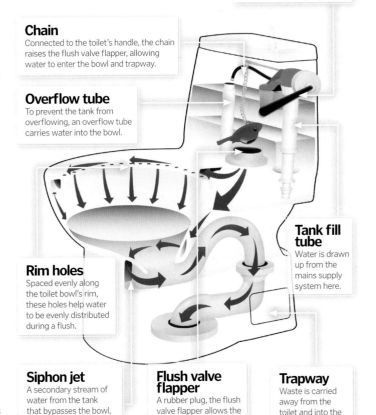

Handle
When the handle is pushed the fill valve opens, allowing water to refill the tank.

Chain
Connected to the toilet's handle, the chain raises the flush valve flapper, allowing water to enter the bowl and trapway.

Overflow tube
To prevent the tank from overflowing, an overflow tube carries water into the bowl.

Tank fill tube
Water is drawn up from the mains supply system here.

Rim holes
Spaced evenly along the toilet bowl's rim, these holes help water to be evenly distributed during a flush.

Siphon jet
A secondary stream of water from the tank that bypasses the bowl, the siphon jet adds power to the flush.

Flush valve flapper
A rubber plug, the flush valve flapper allows the tank to refill with water between flushes.

Trapway
Waste is carried away from the toilet and into the sewer system via the trapway.

What's inside the server rooms?

The 11 server rooms at Data Centre IV accommodate 660 racks of servers, each capable of holding up to 80 servers all connected to the internet. The temperature in a room containing thousands of constantly running processors is therefore controlled by six air conditioners to prevent overheating. As well as getting too hot, there are also numerous outside factors to consider when protecting these valuable servers. Every room is equipped with sensitive smoke, fire and water detectors that use laser particle detectors to check the air. In the event of a fire, the data centre is capable of dealing with the flames safely. Of course the use of water in a room full of electrics would be catastrophic; instead, 1&1 uses argon gas. Unlike carbon dioxide, which is denser than air (and sinks), or nitrogen, which is lighter than air (and rises), argon spreads out evenly across a room and chokes the fire because it is inert and doesn't react with other substances. It also leaves just enough oxygen present for people to breathe. Meanwhile, to protect against electronic threats, 1&1 Internet has a team of 40 dedicated experts who seek out and block fraudsters, such as phishing websites attempting to obtain sensitive information from web users. Data centres are also obliged to work with the authorities and have to retain emails and data for several months, in case it's needed for criminal investigations.

© 1&1 Internet

Where does the internet live?

Discover the giant databanks that store and protect the world wide web

When you visit a website, content is sent over the internet to your browser from a web server: a computer that stores the website data. Although any computer can act as a web server, to remain operational it must be managed under regulated conditions. This is costly, and while some of the world's major online corporations support their own server rooms, most websites and companies take advantage of the convenient web hosting hospitality of a data centre. A business may have a dedicated server, or multiple users may share one.

These state-of-the-art facilities power tens of thousands of servers, each capable of hosting hundreds of sites. And because data centres hold sensitive information and are relied upon by businesses, they have strict security regulations and environmental controls to ensure the security of the data by staying operational 24 hours a day.

For an idea of just how much information passes through a data centre, one of the world's largest web hosting companies, 1&1, currently manages a third of all the home pages in Germany and over half the country's email inboxes. With all this sensitive data knocking about, data centres go to extreme lengths to avoid system failure. Failsafe emergency power supplies kick in so that even if the main grid suffers a power outage, service is uninterrupted.

First to the rescue in the event of a power cut are four huge battery blocks. These are each capable of supporting the servers for 17 minutes, after which a fifth reserve battery block comes into action. If power still isn't returned after that time, five large 16-cylinder diesel generators on the roof of the centre kick into action and supply power to the site for as long as diesel fuel is available. During a power cut, the Karlsruhe 1&1 facility is the only light in the city. ⚙

How safe is the data?

Considering the quantity of highly sensitive information within the walls of a data centre, no unauthorised access is permitted. Before an employee can even set foot into 1&1's state-of-the-art Data Centre IV in Germany, they must pass through an airlock to ensure no unauthorised entry. Any employee entering the centre must carry a valid chip card, which contains their identifying information to be confirmed by passing a series of protocols, including entering a PIN code and passing weight and biometric checks to determine the identity of the employee. Once authorised, the inner airlock door is opened and access to the facility is granted. Meanwhile, over 150 CCTV cameras watch and record the employee's every move throughout their time at the centre.

> ❝ *Within a data centre are hundreds of rows of servers in dedicated server rooms* ❞

How does a camera take a picture?

Many camera owners are content to shout "Cheese" and push the shutter button to get an image, but we go under the hood to find out how it happens

Main dial
All the shooting modes are positioned on this dial including; Auto, Program (P), Aperture priority (A), Shutter priority (S/Tv) and Manual (M). Some shortcut scene modes such as portrait, landscape and macro are also available here.

Built-in flash
Most DSLRs will accommodate a 'built-in' or 'pop up' flash tucked into the top ledge. In some shooting modes the flash will pop up automatically and in other scenarios photographers can activate the flash themselves. Behind this sits the flash hotshoe where external flash units can be slid into position.

Top dial
This dial enables users to alter values such as the f-stop (aperture) and shutter speed when in the appropriate modes (AP or S) or when shooting in manual.

Flash button
Depending on the shooting mode or creative purpose users may need to activate the flash manually, in which case this button should be pressed.

Lens mount
When the markers are aligned correctly, photographers can slot a lens on to the mount and twist it into a locked position.

Shutter button
Depressing this button halfway will focus the lens on the scene in front of the lens when set to Auto Focus. Pressing this button completely will take the shot.

Focus Assist beam
When shooting in low light levels a light will emit from this area, illuminating the subject to help the autofocus find its focus point. In many cameras this also doubles up as the self timer indicator, where it will flash during the countdown.

Lens
The larger ring on the lens body operates the lens's focal length and the front, the smaller ring controls the focus when in manual.

Mirror system and image sensor
The mirror flips up out of the way when the shutter is released to reveal the image sensor behind it, this then electronically captures and records the picture.

Lens switches
On the side of the lens there is a switch marked AF and MF – these refer to auto and manual focus. Some lenses will also include a stabilisation switch, which can be activated or deactivated. It is recommended to have this on when shooting handheld and off when resting on a tripod.

There's no doubt that the digital format has revolutionised the imaging industry and in turn the way we work our cameras. Furthermore the internal DNA of the camera has been entirely restructured to make way for the new electrical system... or has it?

In fact film and digital cameras operate in a similar manner. Varying the size of the lens's diaphragm (aperture) in tandem with the amount of time the shutter is open, focusing light onto the image detection material... the only difference is that now received in an electrical rather than chemical form.

A DSLR (digital single-lens reflex) camera employs a mechanical mirror system that directs the light travelling through the attached lens upwards at a 90-degree angle allowing the photographer to compose the shot through the viewfinder. As the shutter button is pressed the exposure takes place: the mirror swings out of the way and the shutter opens allowing the lens to project the light onto the image sensor. In low light scenarios the shutter will need to stay open for a longer period of time for the image to be recorded, which is why photographers support their cameras with tripods as the smallest degree of camera shake will disturb the quality.

The sensor is formed of millions of pixels laid out in thousands of rows and columns: the more pixels or dots of light, the higher the megapixel count and in theory the higher the resolution. The light travels through a colour filter above the sensors and is converted from light waves into an analogue signal which is then processed through a digital convertor. Next the conversion is fine tuned through a series of filters that adjust aspects such as white balance and colour. The resulting image can be made into a JPEG by compressing the file size and discarding unnecessary pixels. The final image is shown on the LCD. ✿

What makes the cork pop?

Bottle
A bottle of bubbly typically holds nine grams of CO_2, equating to five litres of gas once the cork is released.

Cork
As the bubbles build up pressure within the bottle, releasing the cork will allow the CO2 to escape as a gas.

Spray
Slowly turning the bottle can prevent the gas suddenly escaping and producing the 'bang' associated with champagne... but where's the fun in that?

Why is champagne bubbly?

Discover how this popular celebratory drink is made

Champagne begins life as a basic wine, created from a variety of grapes to provide a mix of juices that give it a smoother taste. By converting the natural sugar of the grapes into alcohol through fermentation and pressing, the carbon dioxide is initially removed. Champagne grapes tend to be more acidic but contain less sugar than those used in regular wines, simply due to the fact that they are harvested earlier.

Yeast and sugar are then added to the wine. When yeast comes into contact with sugar molecules it undergoes a chemical reaction that produces CO2, giving the champagne its fizz, a process that usually takes a few weeks or months.

Next, the wine is bottled and slowly rotated to allow the residue yeast and sugar to collect at the neck, known as riddling. The finest champagnes are often allowed to ferment in this manner for more than seven years, but more commonly the process is left for about two years. Finally, an automated method called dégorgement freezes and removes this sediment before sweet wine or sugar is added according to the type of champagne required. It's then corked. ✿

What's inside a piano?

How does one of the most popular instruments on the planet get its distinctive sound?

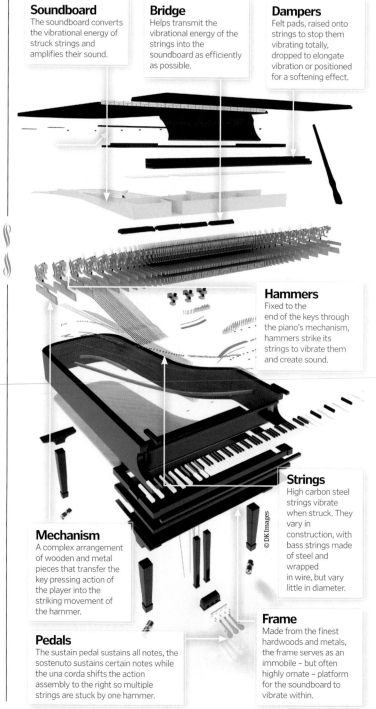

Soundboard
The soundboard converts the vibrational energy of struck strings and amplifies their sound.

Bridge
Helps transmit the vibrational energy of the strings into the soundboard as efficiently as possible.

Dampers
Felt pads, raised onto strings to stop them vibrating totally, dropped to elongate vibration or positioned for a softening effect.

Hammers
Fixed to the end of the keys through the piano's mechanism, hammers strike its strings to vibrate them and create sound.

Strings
High carbon steel strings vibrate when struck. They vary in construction, with bass strings made of steel and wrapped in wire, but vary little in diameter.

Mechanism
A complex arrangement of wooden and metal pieces that transfer the key pressing action of the player into the striking movement of the hammer.

Pedals
The sustain pedal sustains all notes, the sostenuto sustains certain notes while the una corda shifts the action assembly to the right so multiple strings are stuck by one hammer.

Frame
Made from the finest hardwoods and metals, the frame serves as an immobile – but often highly ornate – platform for the soundboard to vibrate within.

© DK Images

How do kettles boil water?

1920's technology that makes tea-making a piece of cake

The electric kettle works thanks to two key design breakthroughs achieved in Britain in the Twenties and Thirties. The first is the immersed heating resistor, the piece of technology responsible for actually heating the water in the kettle. Resistors, which take the form of the heating element in the bottom of the kettle, work by resisting the flow of electric current passed through them, creating resistance and consequently heat. This heat is then passed into the water, which is subsequently heated up. The second of these advances allowed for an automatic cut-off point, preventing the kettle from perpetually heating up the water. A bimetallic strip was introduced to the electric kettle by Russell Hobbs in 1955 which when heated by steam expanded, triggering a shut-off switch.

Although some kettles have fancier and more complex heating and shut-off designs, it is through these two basic principles that the electric kettle evolved into the appliance we have in our kitchens and workplaces today. ✿

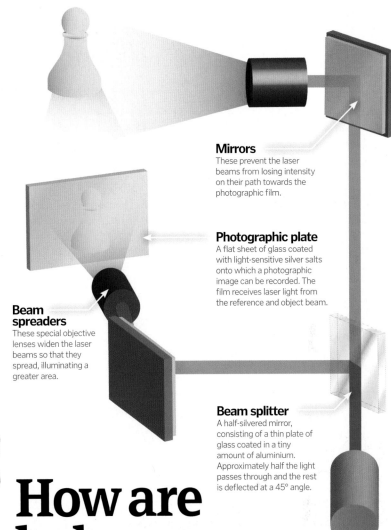

Mirrors
These prevent the laser beams from losing intensity on their path towards the photographic film.

Photographic plate
A flat sheet of glass coated with light-sensitive silver salts onto which a photographic image can be recorded. The film receives laser light from the reference and object beam.

Beam spreaders
These special objective lenses widen the laser beams so that they spread, illuminating a greater area.

Beam splitter
A half-silvered mirror, consisting of a thin plate of glass coated in a tiny amount of aluminium. Approximately half the light passes through and the rest is deflected at a 45° angle.

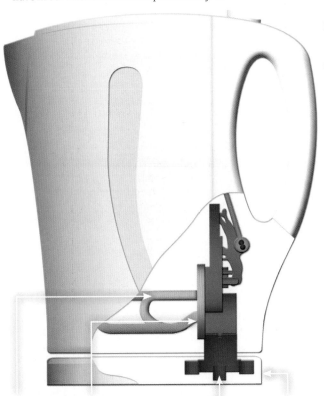

Heating element
This works by resisting the flow of electrical current, which creates the heat that heats the water.

Bimetallic strip
When the water heats up it causes the bimetallic strip to bend which triggers the switch that cuts off the power.

Power adaptor
Connecting the heating element to the power supply allowing the flow of current through the element.

Detachable base
A feature on all modern kettles, the base contains contacts that allow the flow of electricity to the element.

How are holograms projected?

Mirrors and laser beams help produce these illusive images

A hologram is a 2D image that seems to have real three-dimensional depth. Although Hungarian physicist Dennis Gabor invented holography in 1947, he could not put his theory into action until the invention of the laser in 1960. You see, to create a hologram you require the monochromatic light – that being light of a single wavelength – produced by a laser. The process relates to how the light is reflected onto a sheet of photographic film. A single laser beam is split into two – an object beam and a reference beam – by an appropriately named beam splitter, which allows part of the beam to pass through it and deflects the rest at a 90-degree angle towards the photographic film.

As the object beam heads towards the object, it passes through a beam spreader that diffuses the light, illuminating more of the object. En route to the photographic film, the reference beam also passes through a beam spreader to widen the beam and light up the holographic image. The two beams meet at the same point on the photographic film, creating an interference pattern that's preserved in the layers of silver in the film and gives contours to the hologram. ✿

How do barcodes work?

Barcodes are a machine-readable way of writing letters and numbers. A laser is shone onto the barcode and the reflected light can be interpreted by the barcode reader. There are many types of barcodes, but the ones most commonly found in supermarkets use a row of lines of different widths. The different widths represent different numbers. In the UK many items are coded with a GTIN – Global Trade Item Number. This allows the manufacturer to print the barcode on the packages which can then be read in many different shops. The numbers are unique to that item. The barcode only has a number, but no product information. That is held in a database which the retailer can access at the point of sale. It also means that shops can set their own prices and change them easily without re-labelling every item on the shelves.

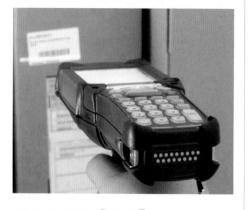

How do fans make you feel cooler?

Switching on a fan and feeling a nice breeze can feel very refreshing on a hot day, but what is going on? Is the fan taking some of the heat energy away? In a small, perfectly insulated room, switching on a fan can increase the temperature in the room as fans usually have a motor which gives out heat. The reason why fans make you feel cool is due to something called the wind-chill effect. Blowing air over your skin causes quicker evaporation of sweat which allows your heat energy to escape much quicker than normal, making you feel cooler. Let's hope we'll be needing them in the summer!

What's the difference between hi-def and normal TV?

Recently, TV took the biggest leap in picture quality since the arrival of colour back in the Sixties. High definition TVs offer images up to four times as detailed than those by standard TVs. Standard definition (SDTV) televisions display the picture in a series of interlaced lines. Interlacing is showing alternate lines every other frame. This saves bandwidth but reduces quality. Analogue TV has 625 interlaced lines of which 576 contain picture information.

Broadcasters experimented with analogue HDTV but found it used too much bandwidth to be viable. With the introduction of digital television broadcasting, digital compression can be used to shrink the HDTV signal to a reasonable size. The output of modern TVs is described using numbers. For example, 720p means 720 progressively scanned lines. That's much more detail than 576i or SDTV and even better pictures can be had with TVs that can display 1080i (i for interlaced) or even 1080p (p standing for progressive).

> **❝** _Recently, TV took the biggest leap in picture quality since the arrival of colour back in the Sixties_ **❞**

What is distributed computing?

Distributed computing is a term used to describe any process conducted by many separate computers connected by a network, all working towards the same goal but not necessarily doing the same job. A famous example was SETI@home which used idle time on home computers to process large amounts of radio telescope information one chunk at a time.

What is jailbreaking an iPhone?

Apple ensures the quality of software available for the iPhone by screening before release through the built-in App Store. There are other applications that will run on an iPhone but haven't made it into the App Store. There are several ways you can get round the restrictions and install third-party software. The phone is then said to be jailbroken.

How do microwaves cook food?

Microwaves are a form of electromagnetic wave like any other radio wave. Microwave ovens heat the water molecules inside foods, which gives off heat energy that can be used by other molecules in the food to warm them up as well. This is why pasta and rice often need water added in order to heat them up.

What are pixels?

Pixel is short for Picture Element. When we see graphic images on digital devices the display divides the screen into thousands or millions of pixels, arranged in rows and columns. Each pixel has its own address in this grid and is represented by dots or squares. Pixels build up a sample of an original image and are the smallest component of a digital image. The more pixels used to represent an image, the closer it will resemble the original. The number of pixels used to create an image is often referred to as the 'resolution'. The best digital cameras have the highest pixel count because they produce a higher-quality image. In colour images a pixel typically comprises three or four colour dots – a red, a blue and green. When these colour dots converge, they build coloured pixels.

Why don't mobile phones get viruses?

A computer virus is a little program written especially to do a certain task on a computer with a known operating system and known weaknesses. If you tried to run the virus program on a mobile phone, it probably will not work, as most viruses are written for just one OS. Computer viruses don't evolve by themselves so it's unlikely that viruses will be able to infect operating systems other than that which they are written for. As many newer phones are actually tiny computers, running a variant of UNIX, they benefit from the robust security that the OS is famed for. There are viruses especially for mobile phones, but these do not spread rapidly because we do not all have the same software on our phones. Soon enough crackers will try to write more viruses for mobile phones and the manufacturers will have to ensure they create software to protect the users.

How do cigarette filters work?

Filters were added to cigarettes in the Fifties when it was discovered that smoking causes lung cancer, leaving cigarette manufacturers under pressure to convince people that smoking was safe. The filters are made of a synthetic fibrous mass called cellulose acetate, which is a kind of fine plastic packed tightly so that it looks like cotton wool. The material is designed to accumulate the vapours and tar in the fibres before they reach the smoker's mouth. However, filters in no way lessen the unhealthy smoke being inhaled. In fact, chemicals are added to make cigarettes taste better and to increase the speed at which nicotine is delivered to the brain, thereby keeping users hooked.

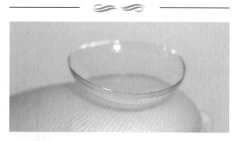

How do lenses magnify or minimise things?

A lens is a transparent piece of glass or plastic with at least one curved surface. Light moves faster in air than it does through glass or plastic. So, when a beam hits a lens, it slows down. And when a beam enters glass at an angle, the part of the beam that hits the glass first slows down sooner making the beam turn. Once the beam hits the air again, it speeds up and completes the trajectory. In this way, a lens can focus the light from an object into an image of the object on the other side.

Convex lenses (sometimes called positive lenses) which are thick in the middle and curve out on one or both sides, take the light beams and redirect them towards the centre. Convex lenses are also called converging lenses. Concave, or diverging lenses, are thick at the edges and curve inward on one or both sides. Concave lenses take light beams and redirect them away from the centre. Concave lenses are used in things like TV projectors to make light rays spread out into the distance.

How do fibre optics transfer data?

Fibre optics represents an evolutionary leap in the speed and bandwidth capacity of telecommunications systems. Copper cable, once the standard for phone lines, can transmit a few million electrical signals per second, while fibre can handle 20 billion light pulses per second. To understand how fibre optic cables work, think of them as long tubes with mirrored walls. If you were to shine a laser pointer into the tube at a slight angle, the laser beam would bounce its way down the tube, reflecting off the mirrored walls until it reached the end.

Instead of using mirrors, the walls of fibre optic cable are made of two concentric layers of silica glass called the core and cladding.

Cladding has a lower refractive index than the core, causing a phenomenon called total internal reflection. When light strikes the cladding at a low enough angle, it is reflected back into the core without losing any energy.

There are two major types of fibre optic cables: single-mode and multi-mode. Single mode fibre has the narrowest core – a tenth of the diameter of a human hair – and uses a powerful laser to send data long distances. Multi-mode fibre has a wider core with room to bounce around many simultaneous signals. Multi-mode fibre uses weaker (and much less expensive) LED lights and is better suited for short runs like local computer networks.

> " *Copper cable can transmit a few million electrical signals per second, while fibre can handle 20 billion light pulses per second* "

Just what is 3G?

3G or 3rd Generation is a set of standards for mobile phones and other mobile devices. Services include mobile voice telephone, video calls, and wireless data connections. 3G allows simultaneous use of speech and data services and higher data rates up to 14.0 Mbit/s downloads on some systems. 3G networks offer users more advanced services than numerous previous phone standards. When a Wi-Fi connection cannot be found by the smartphone, it will likely connect to a 3G network.

Why do I need an electrical adaptor abroad?

If you travel to a different country, one of the first things you might look for in your hotel room is a plug socket. Only there is a good chance it will look different, maybe bigger, smaller or have a different number of holes. This is because back when electricity grids were first being introduced, many countries decided to develop plugs and sockets of their own rather than adopting a world standard.

As well as the shapes and sizes of the plug sockets changing depending on the country, the voltage and frequency of the AC current varies too. For example Europe and most other countries in the world use a voltage which is twice that in the US. Plug an appliance from the US into a power supply in Europe without an adaptor and you will probably see a spectacular yet highly dangerous firework display as the voltage will be too high. It is worthwhile to check the power outlets of the country you are visiting before you travel, then you can make sure you take the correct adaptor.

Who invented the mobile phone?

The invention of the first handheld mobile phone is credited to Dr Martin Cooper and his team at Motorola in April 1973. The first call he made was to his rival inventor, Joel Engel at Bell Laboratories, who had also been racing to invent the first mobile phone. Before this time, radiophones on-board ships and in cars were available; however, Dr Cooper's phone was the first truly handheld modern mobile phone. It weighed in at around two kilograms and had a battery life of only 20 minutes. According to Cooper, this didn't matter as you couldn't really hold the phone up for that long!

How can I keep my PC safe when using Spotify?

The most reliable way is to have up-to-date anti-virus software on your computer. You could try to operate by trust alone, but many viruses are – as you know – hidden and the person who sent it to you may not know the virus is there, or even that they are sending anything.

Anti-virus software can work in two separate ways. One is to look for suspicious behaviour, such as a file that copies itself. The other is to check any files being received, created or saved against what is known as a virus dictionary. This is a list of all known viruses and needs to be kept up-to-date with the latest definitions of viruses. Spotify, which shares music between users, doesn't let the users upload anything manually, so no one can add a virus into the mix. It also controls and encrypts what is being transferred, presumably running them through its own virus protection too.

Why do the fuses sometimes blow in my house?

When a certain amount of current being drawn from a plug socket is exceeded, the fuse is designed to 'blow' to protect the wiring in the house and the appliances connected to that specific circuit. Electricians install fuses as a safety feature so that a large surge in power does not cause an electrical fire. A fuse is simply a small wire running from one electrode to another electrode and encapsulated in some kind of fire-proof casing.

An appliance that needs more power than a fuse can supply will ultimately blow the fuse. Most houses use circuit breakers that operate by similar means, although these differ from fuses in that they can be reset. If too many appliances try to draw power from a wiring system at once, switching on a new appliance can 'trip' the circuit breaker and cut power, which is why switching on an appliance such as a light can cut the power in a house.

How do the streetlights turn on automatically?

The most commonly used component in streetlights is called a cadmium sulphide photoresistor, or a CdS cell for short. The CdS cell changes the resistance of a circuit depending on the amount of light shining on it. When lots of light falls on a CdS cell, then the resistance is very low, which means it conducts electricity well. When there is not much light, the photo-resistor has a high resistance which means not much current can flow.

This change in current can then be used to control a relay. A relay is basically an electromagnetic switch; when the electromagnet has a high current (lots of light falling on the photo-resistor – daytime) then it pushes the switch open so no current can flow to the streetlight. When it gets dark, then not much current can flow to the electromagnet so the switch closes and allows electricity to flow to the streetlight, turning it on.

> **❝** *The cadmium sulphide photoresistor cell changes the resistance of a circuit depending on the amount of light shining on it* **❞**

Transport

" Each B-2 costs $737 million and must be kept in a climate-controlled hangar "

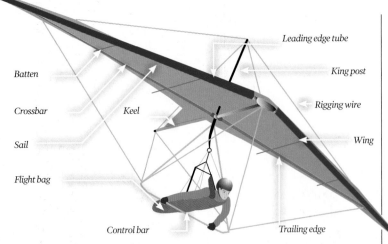

Leading edge tube

Batten

King post

Crossbar

Keel

Rigging wire

Sail

Wing

Flight bag

Control bar

Trailing edge

How do hang gliders fly?

Propelled upwards solely by hot air, hang gliders make engineless flight possible

Hang gliders work by generating lift through both their body and wing shape, as well as exploiting the natural meteorological updrafts created in Earth's atmosphere. Through these factors, hang gliders can use gravity as a source of propulsion, yet stay airborne for lengthy periods of time, extending their lift-to-drag ratio considerably. This relationship between the amount of lift the glider is capable of and the amount of drag inflicted on it by the atmosphere's air molecules is key to its sustained flight, with the more metres of forward glide to every one metre of descent, the better.

When hang gliders were first invented, their heavy construction materials (wood and heavy metals) prevented pilots from achieving a good ratio. Today, however, super-lightweight carbon composite materials allow gliders to have significant glide ratios, usually over 15:1.

Construction consists of two main parts, the control frame and the wings. The wings (usually made from composite-framed fabric) are designed to generate as much lift as possible as air passes over them, as well as maintain pitch and yaw equilibrium when gliding. The control frame is attached to the centre of the wings and is triangular in shape; it provides a fixed platform for the pilot to be strapped to and shift within to alter course and altitude. Control is achieved by the pilot moving his weight fore or aft in opposition to the frame. Modern control frames feature docking points for navigation instrumentation such as GPS, as well as for other electronics such as radios and variometers (rate of climb/descent indicators). ✿

> ❝ *Carbon composite materials allow gliders to have significant glide ratios* ❞

How do jet skis work?

Isaac Newton has no idea how much fun he's responsible for

Jet skis work off Newton's third principle, that each action has an equal and opposite reaction. Here, the action is pushing a large volume of water out of the back of the jet ski and the reaction is pushing the jet ski forward through the water at speed. It's a remarkably simple principle which is achieved by using an equally simple device – an impeller drive.

The impeller sits inside a shaft that runs the length of the craft and is driven by the ski's engine. It's designed like a propeller and when the engine spins it, the blades of the impeller turn at speed, forcing water through the shaft and out through the nozzle at the rear of the ski, pushing it along.

Of course, everyone falls off every now and then, so modern jet skis all have a 'starter pin' or key that's placed in a slot near the ignition and is attached to the driver. If they fall overboard, the pin is yanked out and the ski coasts to a halt, preventing collisions and meaning the driver never has to swim too far to get back to it. ✿

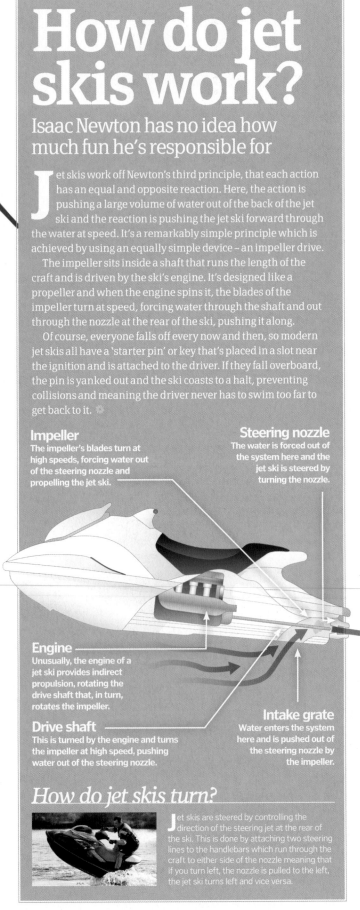

Impeller
The impeller's blades turn at high speeds, forcing water out of the steering nozzle and propelling the jet ski.

Steering nozzle
The water is forced out of the system here and the jet ski is steered by turning the nozzle.

Engine
Unusually, the engine of a jet ski provides indirect propulsion, rotating the drive shaft that, in turn, rotates the impeller.

Drive shaft
This is turned by the engine and turns the impeller at high speed, pushing water out of the steering nozzle.

Intake grate
Water enters the system here and is pushed out of the steering nozzle by the impeller.

How do jet skis turn?

Jet skis are steered by controlling the direction of the steering jet at the rear of the ski. This is done by attaching two steering lines to the handlebars which run through the craft to either side of the nozzle meaning that if you turn left, the nozzle is pulled to the left, the jet ski turns left and vice versa.

What do anti-lock brakes do?

ABS is standard on nearly every new car; behind the little
yellow light lies a highly advanced system

It is very easy to lock a wheel under braking in a car, particularly when it is raining. A locked wheel provides minimal braking force, though – peak brake efficiency is found at the point just before the wheel locks. Anti-lock braking systems (ABS) avoid the pitfalls of locked wheels while maximising the benefits of being able to get near this point.

ABS applies a computer algorithm to the mechanical action of braking. The system uses feeds from wheel speed sensors. A locked wheel decelerates fast compared to the other three – such an incident instructs the computer to release brake pressure on that wheel. The wheel accelerates again; once it is in sync with the other three, brake pressure is regained until the wheel just starts to lock again – and once more it is released.

High-tech valves can run this cycle many times a second, maintaining the wheel just on the point of locking (that's the characteristic 'judder' of ABS operation). This maximises braking effect while avoiding dangerous lock-ups where the driver's control is lessened. ✿

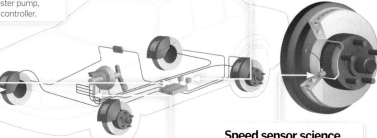

Fast communication
CANbus allows fast communications between the engine control unit and sensors. A microprocessor processes this data and converts the signals. The hydraulic control unit and ECU are positioned close together, so the valves are controlled by the ECU.

Advanced braking components
ABS is made up of four key components – wheel speed sensors, booster pump, valves and a controller.

Sensing the lock
Inputs for ABS come from wheel speed sensors. These read inputs from toothed wheels mounted to the driveshaft.

Valves
These solenoid valves modulate the pressure from the brake master cylinder to ensure 'too much' cannot be sent to the brake, locking it.

Speed sensor science
Speed sensors comprise a magnet enclosed within a coil. They give off a magnetic field that interacts with contact on the toothed ring, creating a signal. The controller converts the number of pulses into a digital signal, and processes this.

© Florian Linder

How do traffic jams start?

Ever wondered why traffic grinds to
a halt for seemingly no reason?

5. Ghost
By the time the traffic at the back of the shock wave reaches the point of the original incident, the causes of the jam are long gone.

4. Acceleration
The offending vehicle A has now completed its manoeuvre and left the motorway. However, acceleration is still hindered and slowed by traffic density and vehicle limitations.

3. Domino
This braking effect is then transferred to each following vehicle, the total speed of the cars decreasing the further back in the chain they are, until standstill is reached. Often the shock wave travels over 2km (1mi) to the rear, leaving drivers completely unaware of the cause of their deceleration.

2. Impact
The immediate impact of the error is that the vehicles behind cars A and B must break suddenly to 72km/h (45mph) to avoid crashing into them from the rear as they brake. This applies to vehicles in all three lanes, as car A crosses each of them to exit the motorway.

1. Error
The traffic shock wave begins when a vehicle, travelling at the road's stated speed of 96km/h (60mph), manoeuvres at the last minute. In this example, car A swerves across car B, causing the latter to brake to 80km/h (50mph) in order to remain at a safe distance.

What's inside the Euro

The fighter plane that is so advanced it can't be flown by a human without the help of a computer

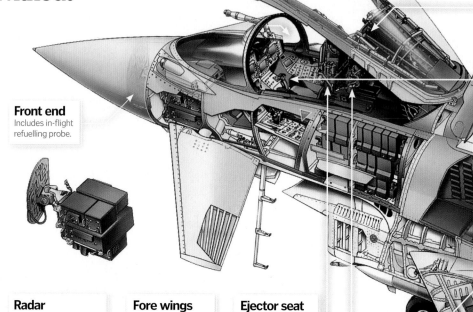

The Eurofighter Typhoon may be the world's most advanced killing machine, but it is also an extraordinary symbol of peace and co-operation. After centuries of fighting, a handful of European countries came together to produce this incredible aircraft.

From a plan that started way back as 1979, the Eurofighter was developed by Germany, Italy, Spain and the UK (France was involved for a while but then snuck off to do its own thing), and production is split between the four countries. At present there are plans to produce no fewer than 707 examples of the fighter jet. As well as the four core countries, the plane is also being used by other air forces around the world, including those of Austria, Saudi Arabia and Greece.

Why? Because it's quite simply the most technologically advanced fighter jet on the planet, and also the most capable.

It's what's known as a swing-role weapon system, which means that it is capable of different operational tasks and can even switch from one duty to another on a single mission. For instance, it can be used as an air-to-air (short and medium range) fighter to gain all-important air superiority, while at the same time carrying large, long-range ground-attack weapons for taking out an enemy's air defence systems.

This flexibility is further enhanced by the plane's incredible flying prowess. It boasts STOL (short take-off and landing) which means that it needs just 700 metres

Front end
Includes in-flight refuelling probe.

Radar
Advanced ECR-90 radar can track multiple targets at long range.

Fore wings
Made from titanium, these aid agility and responsiveness.

Ejector seat
Pilot can eject from the plane at speeds of up to 600 knots.

Twin seat
A special twin-seater Eurofighter is used for training.

Stealth fuselage
A low frontal cross-section and the use of carbon fibre (70 per cent) and glass reinforced plastics (12 per cent) help ensure the Eurofighter can avoid detection by enemy radar. Metals, mostly aluminium and titanium, make up just 15 per cent of the body.

Weapons
There are 13 external weapon stations on the underside.

A stunning machine with awesome firepower

to take-off or land (the 747 you go on holiday in requires over 3,000 metres).

More impressively, the Eurofighter is incredibly manoeuvrable. This is thanks in part to its 'relaxed stability' design, which is a reassuring way of saying that the aircraft is inherently unstable, especially at subsonic speeds. Put simply, the plane's delta wings and small fore fins create a pressure (lift) point which is forward of the centre of gravity during subsonic flight. And that means it is impossible for a human to fly the plane without the aid of a complex computer system that makes constant adjustments to the wings' flaps quicker than the pilot could. Once the speed of sound is broken, though, the pressure point moves back and the aircraft becomes much more stable (although the computer aids remain).

The same flight control systems also make the Eurofighter surprisingly easy to fly, therefore freeing up the pilot to concentrate on tactical tasks.

No wonder the Eurofighter Typhoon is changing the way the world's air forces think about fighter planes. ✿

" It is impossible for a human to fly the plane without the aid of a complex computer system that makes constant adjustments to the wings' flaps "

fighter Typhoon?

Cockpit
The high-tech cockpit is designed to make life easy for the pilot. Many functions are controlled by voice, while a heads-up display puts essential data right in front of the pilot.

Joystick
The Hands on Throttle and Stick (HOTAS) is a single joystick that gives fingertip control of up to 24 functions, including throttle, manoeuvring, target manipulation and weapon control.

Wings
Delta wings have a span of 10.95 metres and hold the fuel tanks.

Tail fin
Made from carbon fibre, it provides lateral stability and houses communication systems.

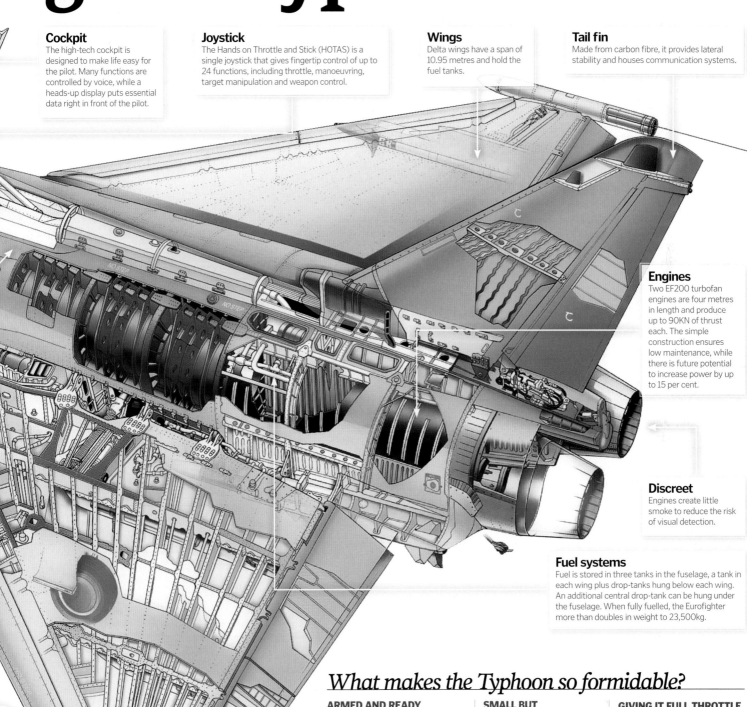

Engines
Two EF200 turbofan engines are four metres in length and produce up to 90KN of thrust each. The simple construction ensures low maintenance, while there is future potential to increase power by up to 15 per cent.

Discreet
Engines create little smoke to reduce the risk of visual detection.

Fuel systems
Fuel is stored in three tanks in the fuselage, a tank in each wing plus drop-tanks hung below each wing. An additional central drop-tank can be hung under the fuselage. When fully fuelled, the Eurofighter more than doubles in weight to 23,500kg.

All pictures courtesy of Geoffrey Lee from planefocus

What makes the Typhoon so formidable?

ARMED AND READY FOR ACTION
The Eurofighter's formidable arsenal. The large items are, in fact, fuel tanks, although long-distance missiles can be fitted. The yellow devices are laser-powered bombs, while the smaller grey items are short-range air-to-air missiles. The thin armaments visible at the back of the fuselage are beyond-visual-range air-to-air missiles. There is also a Mauser BK-27 automatic cannon.

SMALL BUT PERFECTLY FORMED
The Eurofighter is remarkably compact – look at the size of the pilot in the cockpit to get an idea. The wingspan is 10.95 metres (less than that of a WWII Spitfire) and the length is 15.96 metres. This helps the aircraft to be incredibly agile, allowing it to change direction fast, as well as accelerate at an astonishing rate.

GIVING IT FULL THROTTLE
The Eurofighter's twin Eurojet turbofan engines combine a jet nozzle with a ducted fan. This allows efficiency at low speeds combined with relatively quiet operation. They are equipped with afterburners (shown in operation here) which inject neat fuel into the jet stream to give a short increase in power. However, the Eurofighter can cruise at supersonic speeds without afterburner help.

What's in a submarine?

Take a look beneath the hull of the world's most advanced sub, HMS Astute

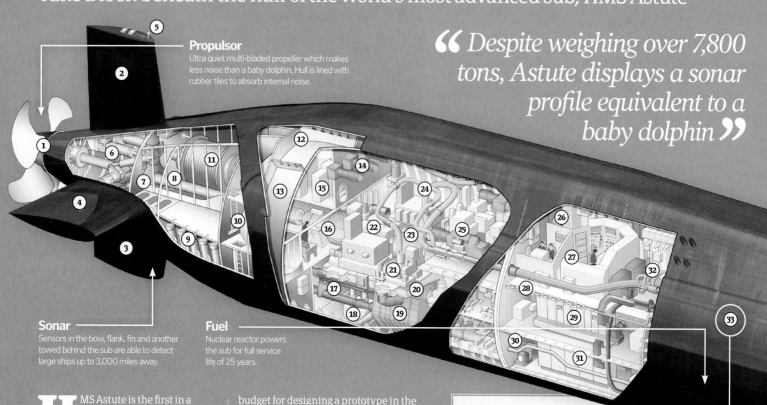

Propulsor
Ultra quiet multi-bladed propeller which makes less noise than a baby dolphin. Hull is lined with rubber tiles to absorb internal noise.

❝ Despite weighing over 7,800 tons, Astute displays a sonar profile equivalent to a baby dolphin ❞

Sonar
Sensors in the bow, flank, fin and another towed behind the sub are able to detect large ships up to 3,000 miles away.

Fuel
Nuclear reactor powers the sub for full service life of 25 years.

HMS Astute is the first in a program to design seven Astute-class subs to replace the Royal Navy's aging Swiftsure and Trafalgar-class. Three similar subs (Ambush, Artful and Audacious) have already been approved to follow.

Around 6,000 people were involved in Astute's construction at BAE's Devonshire Dock Hall in Barrow-in-Furness, the largest shipbuilding construction complex of its kind in Europe, covering an area of 25,000 square metres. Astute's construction required over 1 million components including 7,000 design drawings., 10,000 separate engineering requirements and 100km of pipework.

A number of technical challenges had to be overcome during the 17-year cycle from concept design to nuclear-powered vessel. Not least of these was the fact that with space at an absolute premium, Astute's machinery and equipment is three times more densely packed than that of a surface warship.

Astute was the first nuclear submarine to be designed entirely in a 3D Computer Aided Design environment. With very little time or budget for designing a prototype in the usual manner, this system of 'virtual' prototyping harnessed the power of computer test and visualisation, along with continuous design and careful systems analysis. Some areas of the Astute, such as the command deck and forward engine room, were manufactured in modules, assembled in the workshop. They were then shipped to the Devonshire dock hall and carefully placed within the hull; an example of 'plug and play' construction that not only saved time but also minimised rework.

The structure of the sub is made up of a pressure hull – a perfect cylinder with rounded dome ends demonstrating that circularity is one of the keys to surviving deep ocean pressures. There are six sections between the end domes each containing different packages of equipment, and the hull sections are meticulously welded together in a process involving more than two kilometres of welding, all completed without a single defect and exhaustively examined for flaws using x-ray and ultra-sonic technology.

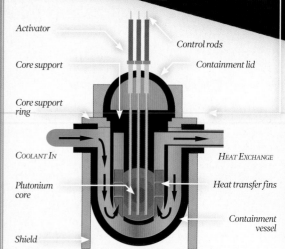

Activator

Control rods

Core support

Containment lid

Core support ring

COOLANT IN

HEAT EXCHANGE

Plutonium core

Heat transfer fins

Containment vessel

Shield

How does a reactor power a submarine?

Astute's Rolls Royce PWR2 (Pressurised Water Reactor) contains enough nuclear fuel to power the submarine for its entire 25-year service. This energy is generated by nuclear fission that takes place inside a heavy shielded reactor compartment that protects the crew and environment from radiation.

Water is pumped around a circuit where it is heated by the fission process, maintaining enough pressure to prevent the water from boiling. This heat is then used to generate steam, via steam generators, to drive the main turbine engines. A system of clutches and gearing drive a propulsor that transmits the power to propel the submarine. Steam is also used to drive the turbo-generators that supply the submarine with electricity.

YOU ARE WHAT YOU EAT

1 On a ten-week patrol, the crew of Astute would get through an average 18,000 sausages and 4,200 Weetabix for breakfast.

FIRST IN CLASS

2 Since 1945, Barrow has built the first of class for every Royal Navy submarine as well as every submarine currently in service with the Navy.

NO EASY TASK

3 One of the most challenging engineering projects in the UK, building Astute has been described as "more complex than the space shuttle".

What is it like to pilot the Astute?

Andy Coles, OBE is 47 and commanding Astute will mark the pinnacle of a 30-year Navy career that began as a radar operator. He told us what he's most looking forward to from the experience.

"HMS Astute is a keenly awaited and extremely capable submarine which will prove to be a very potent weapon for the Royal Navy for the next 25 years. She represents a massive increase in capability over previous classes and I am really looking forward to putting the submarine through her paces during sea trials. Her offensive capability has been greatly enhanced; while she carries the same Spearfish torpedoes and Tomahawk Cruise missiles as previous classes, Astute's payload is significantly increased and a return to six torpedo tubes greatly enhances the flexibility. Astute is also the first submarine to have non-hull-penetrating optronics masts, making it much easier for me to see what is happening on the surface as the picture is displayed on several large screens in the Control Room, the submarine's operations centre. One of the significant design changes is to enable the submarine to operate with Special Forces and I am looking forward to proving that part of the sea trials.

"Of course, none of this would work if it wasn't for the people. Astute has been designed to reduce the manning at sea. I have a highly trained crew; from the officers, senior ratings and junior ratings who operate the submarine, to marine engineers, weapon engineers to ensure the weapon and electrical systems are at maximum readiness and warfare specialists to operate them. Finally, I have a team of logisticians who look after everything from storing the submarine to providing three meals a day for 100 submariners."

ROYAL NAVY

Air and water

These units convert sea water into fresh water and oxygen. Air is purified to remove waste and carbon dioxide, hydrogen and carbon monoxide

Masts

Two masts carrying thermal imaging and low light cameras replace the periscope. Breaking the surface for less than three seconds is enough for a 360° view of the surroundings. Six other masts service satellite, radar and navigation systems

Galley

Five chefs provide a 24-hour service to the crew

Washing and sleeping

One bunk for each crew member and 11 extra bunks for passengers, most likely special forces soldiers. The 98-man crew share five showers, five toilets, two urinals and eight hand basins

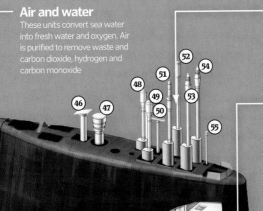

Is it packing weapons?

When it comes to offensive capability, Astute marks a significant leap over the submarine classes it replaces. With a total of 38 Spearfish torpedoes and Tomahawk missiles – more than any previous RN submarine – and six 21-inch torpedo tubes, Astute has the capability to accurately engage targets over 1,000 miles away while remaining undetected.

Powered by a high-performance thermal engine, Spearfish has an analogue homing system and communicates with the launch submarine through a wire-guidance link.

Meanwhile the Tomahawk Block IV Land Attack Missile (LAM) is the latest version of McDonnell Douglas's medium-to-long range cruise missiles, designed to operate at low altitude and launch while the Astute is submerged. It can deliver pin-point strikes 2,000km from the coast.

Weighing nearly two tons, the Spearfish is a serious weapon

Mini-Guide Key

Each part of the submarine explained in this key guide

1	Propeller
2	Upper rudder segment
3	Lower rudder segment
4	Starboard hydroplane
5	Aft anchor light
6	Rudder and hydroplane hydraulic actuators
7	No. 4 main ballast tank
8	Propeller shaft
9	High pressure bottles
10	No. 3 main ballast tank
11	Towed array cable drum and winch
12	Main ballast vent system
13	Aft pressure dome
14	Air treatment units
15	Naval stores
16	Propeller shaft thrust block and bearing
17	Circulating water transfer pipes
18	Lubricating oil tank
19	Starboard condenser
20	Main machinery mounting raft
21	Turbo generators, port and starboard
22	Combining gearbox
23	Main turbines
24	Steam delivery ducting
25	Engine room
26	Watertight bulkhead
27	Manoeuvring room
28	Manoeuvring room isolated deck mounting
29	Switchboard room
30	Diesel generator room
31	Static converters
32	Main steam valve
33	Reactor section
34	Part of pressure hull
35	Forward airlock
36	Air handling compartment
37	Waste management equipment
38	Conditioned air ducting
39	Galley
40	Fwd section isolated deck mountings
41	Batteries
42	Junior ratings' mess
43	RESM office
44	Commanding officer's cabin
45	Port side communications office
46	Diesel exhaust mast
47	Snort induction mast
48	SHF/EHF (NEST) mast
49	CESM mast
50	AZL radar mast
51	Satcom mast
52	Integrated comms mast
53	Visual mast – starboard
54	Visual mast – port
55	Navigation mast
56	Bridge fin access
57	Junior ratings' bathroom
58	Senior ratings' bathroom
59	Battery switchroom
60	Control room consoles
61	Sonar operators' consoles
62	Senior ratings' bunks
63	Medical berth
64	Weapons stowage and handling compartment
65	Sonar array
66	Maintenance workshop
67	Sonar equipment room
68	Forward hydroplane
69	Hydroplane hydraulic actuator
70	Hydroplane hinge mounting
71	Ship's office
72	Junior ratings' berths
73	Torpedo tubes
74	Water transfer tank
75	Torpedo tube bow caps
76	Air turbine pump
77	No. 2 main ballast tank
78	High pressure air bottles
79	Forward pressure dome
80	Weapons embarkation hatch
81	Gemini craft stowage
82	Hinged fairlead
83	Anchor windlass
84	No. 1 main ballast tank
85	Anchor cable locker
86	Bow sonar

How big is an aircraft carrier?

Living on an aircraft carrier can be a stimulating, equally exhausting experience. Learn why, despite its massive size, there can be no room for passengers...

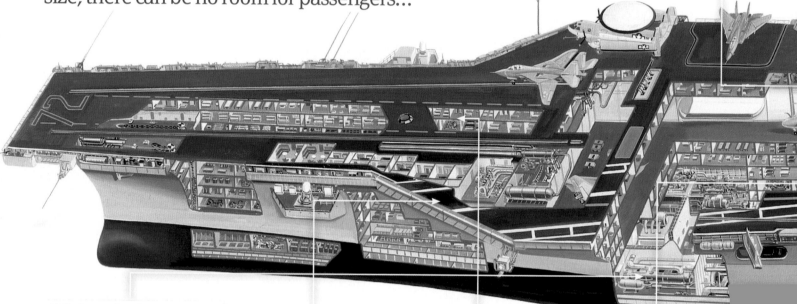

The captain's log
The captain's quarters double as office space and afford comparative luxury with a 30x30-foot living space. The captain, bar admiral, is the only crew member to enjoy the luxury of his own private bathroom.

Full steam ahead
Two nuclear fission reactors heat water which passes under pressure driving four steam turbines that turn four bronze propellers – each measuring 20ft and weighing 30 tons apiece – to achieve a maximum speed of 35 knots (equivalent to 40mph). The protruding bulbous bow adds buoyancy, reducing drag for enhanced handling and propulsion. It adds extra lift to the flight deck that aids in an aircraft's launch.

Hitting the deck
Two angled flight-decks support the CATOBAR (Catapult Assisted Take Off But Arrested Recovery) system. This speeds up flight-deck operations allowing for simultaneous landing and launch of aircraft.

Crew quarters
Crew typically endure cramped living quarters with triple-stacked bunks, often sharing compartments and toilet facilities with upwards of 60 people while navigating near-vertical stairwells and a warren of tight corridors.

Is there a doctor on board?
Yes. The medical department is located under the hangar deck to ease patient access, offer stability during surgical procedures and protection from damage under fire. On Nimitz-class carriers it operates a spacious surgical suite and intensive care unit.

Landing on a postage stamp

Despite its 4.5 acres, the carrier has limited space and planes require mechanised support to take off and land. Aircraft are spotted by tractors, readied with fuel pumped from tanks below deck and primed with missiles. During a take off the carrier speeds into the wind, causing air to flow over the deck. This acts in conjunction with powerful steam-driven 'Fat Cat' catapults that propel 30-ton jets with the necessary speed and lift to launch at a rate of up to four every minute.

Hitting a 'postage stamp' on open water, aircraft rely on 1.375-inch-thick arrest cables, suspended five inches off the flight deck, separated at 35-40-foot intervals. These cables connect to hydraulic cylinders that act as giant shock absorbers. When the tail hook connects with a cable it pulls a piston within a fluid-filled chamber of the cylinder; as it's drawn down energy is absorbed, bringing aircraft to a halt. Smaller carriers forgo the CATOBAR system for short take-off and vertical landing (STOVL). The Royal Navy developed a 'ski jump' ramp at the end of the deck to help launch aircraft that require little or no forward movement to take off or land.

The island
Approaching 50m tall the tower is one tenth as wide at the flight deck where space is at a premium. It bristles with radar and communication antenna that can sense the proximity of the fleet, target encroaching threats and receive TV/satellite reception.

The 'yellow gear'
The 'yellow gear' supports air operations and includes: the mobile crash crane or 'tilley' that removes flight-deck obstructions, the forklift, tow tractors for spotting of aircraft, and jet engine starting units.

Aircraft carriers of the world don't come much larger than the US Navy's nuclear-powered Nimitz-class. At 4.5 acres and stretching 1,092 feet, the flight deck of USS Abraham Lincoln dwarfs the Chrysler Building – and it's not even the biggest around. Despite its awesome profile, however, its role is more than symbolic. The carrier can balance and mobilise a seagoing airbase of multiple strike and combat support aircraft, with a ship's company of over 5,000 souls. It can deploy anywhere within international waters while retaining the sovereign territory of its home place of berth. Therefore, unlike an airbase stationed on foreign soil, no permission for landing or overflight rights is required.

Despite its loner appearance, however, the aircraft carrier is not without friends; it is often flanked by a more nimble carrier 'battle' group that can offer added protection, tactical options and extra supplies to the fleet. ✿

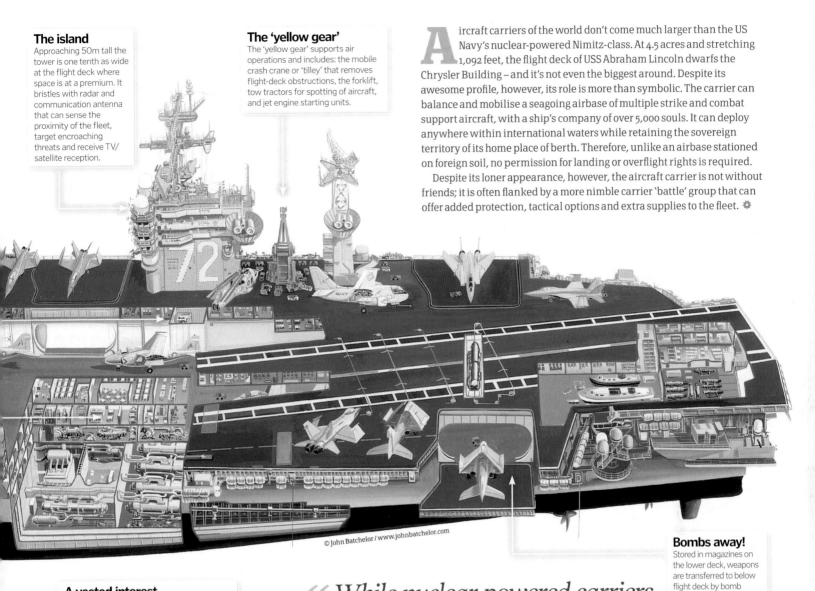

© John Batchelor / www.johnbatchelor.com

A vested interest
Coloured vests signify flight-deck function. The whites represent safety officer and crew; blue are the aircraft handling and chock crewmen; green is the catapult and arrest crews; yellow includes the catapult/flight-deck officers; and brown, the plane captains.

Bombs away!
Stored in magazines on the lower deck, weapons are transferred to below flight deck by bomb elevators; once assembled they are transferred to carts and the flight deck elevators where they can be manually fitted by flight deck crew.

> ❝ *While nuclear-powered carriers have unlimited range, non-nuclear ones make do with 17ft to the gallon* ❞

No man is an 'island'

The primary flight control (or 'Pri-Fly') is home to the Air Boss. With a crow's nest view of proceedings and an array of GPS receivers and radar screens to hand, he choreographs the well-oiled ritual of take-off and landings, flight-deck manoeuvres and those in-flight aircraft in proximity to the ship.

Below, the Bridge is home to the Officer of the Deck (OOD) – appointed on four-hourly rotations by the Commanding Officer (Captain). He stays at his station while 'under sail' and is responsible for all safety and operational decisions from navigation through to communications. With its computer-enhanced air detection systems, the nearby CDC (Combat Direction Centre) provides the Tactical Action Officer with real-time data to assist his role in supporting the CO in defensive/offensive operations.

No hanging about below deck

Hangars serve as dual-purpose maintenance and storage facilities for half the carrier's aircraft contingent

at any one time, with the remainder in flight or housed on the flight deck.

Typically each bay is separated by a steel dividing door; a throwback to Kamikaze raids of WWII to confine and limit the incendiary threat of fire. The hangar and flight deck are connected by lifts. With its increased capacity, the Nimitz-class carriers like the USS Abraham Lincoln operate four deck edge high-speed elevators, each capable of lifting two F/A-18 jets; in so doing it can relocate eight aircraft simultaneously from hangar to flight deck in a matter of seconds.

What powers the USS Nimitz?

America's Nimitz-class aircraft carriers are powered by two small on-board pressurised water reactors (PWR), which drive the ship's four steam turbines that not only power four five-bladed propellers, but also generate electricity to power everything on the ship. The nuclear reactions taking place in the PWRs can generate enough power to reach a top speed of 30 knots. Inside the reactor cores a huge amount of energy is given off due to fission – the splitting of large atoms (uranium) into smaller ones and releasing kinetic energy in the process.

There are two separate loops inside each aircraft carrier's nuclear power station. The primary loop contains superheated water, or coolant (in liquid form). This coolant is pumped through the uranium-fuelled reactor – where it reaches up to 900°F – under high pressure so it

doesn't boil inside the core. This superhot water is then passed through a steam generator. The heated water in the primary loop doesn't get converted to steam itself (because it's under high pressure), rather the intense heat of it is used to convert the cooler water in the separate secondary loop into turbine-driving steam to power the generator. And because the loops are separate and the water never mixes, the radioactivity is safely contained in the reactor of the primary loop. The steam from the turbine is then cooled and condensed, converting it back into liquid water ready to run the cycle again.

The reactors rarely require refuelling – maybe once every 25 years – offering carriers practically unlimited range. Refuelling involves removing the used core and replacing it with a shiny new one replenished with enriched uranium nuclear fuel.

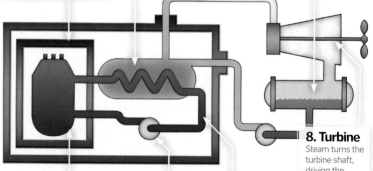

5. Steam generator
The steam generator uses heat from the coolant in the primary loop to turn the water in the secondary loop to steam ready to turn the turbine. Once the coolant's heat is released at the steam generator, the colder coolant returns to the reactor to go round again.

4. Radiation shield
Concrete surrounds the radioactive materials, confining the dangerous radioactivity.

6. Steam
The steam created in the secondary loop turns the turbine, driving a generator that produces electricity.

7. Condenser
This device turns the steam into liquid by cooling it. The condensed water is then piped back into the steam generator to be reheated again.

3. Reactor
Nuclear fission of uranium fuel takes place inside the tightly sealed reactor, releasing huge amounts of heat (between 500°F and 900°F), which is transferred to the coolant.

1. Primary coolant pump
Circulates coolant around the reactor and through the steam generator.

2. Pressurised water (coolant)
Natural water is superheated but doesn't boil because it is kept under high pressure.

8. Turbine
Steam turns the turbine shaft, driving the generator and producing electricity. A Nimitz's two PWRs generate enough electrical power to supply a population of 100,000.

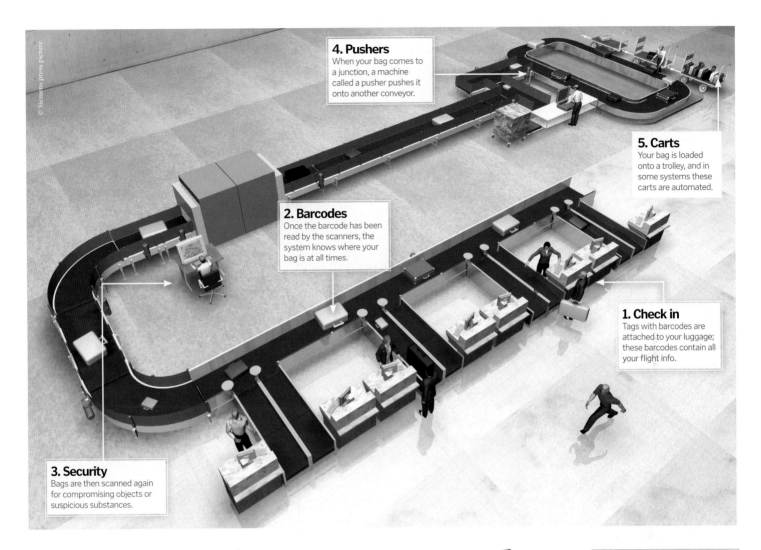

© Siemens press picture

4. Pushers
When your bag comes to a junction, a machine called a pusher pushes it onto another conveyor.

5. Carts
Your bag is loaded onto a trolley, and in some systems these carts are automated.

2. Barcodes
Once the barcode has been read by the scanners, the system knows where your bag is at all times.

1. Check in
Tags with barcodes are attached to your luggage; these barcodes contain all your flight info.

3. Security
Bags are then scanned again for compromising objects or suspicious substances.

How does baggage travel from plane to passenger?

The long journey your luggage has to take

A baggage handling system consists of a series of automated conveyor belts, destination-coded vehicles (DCVs) – unmanned carts mounted on tracks and powered by linear induction motors – label scanners, sorting machines and security checkpoints that serve three main tasks. The first is to move bags from an airport's check-in area to the departure gate, to transfer luggage from one gate to another, and to move baggage from arrival gates back to the baggage claim area safely.

To understand how the system works, it is best to follow a single bag from check-in to an aircraft. From check-in a bag has a label attached to it that acts as a tag, containing all necessary information on its target destination and delivery time frame, before being carried off on a conveyor belt to an automated barcode scanner. Here its tag is read and loaded onto the system's computer database, allowing it to track the individual piece of luggage throughout the rest of its journey.

After this initial scan the luggage is then carried by further conveyor belts to a security checkpoint and x-ray machine, where it is scanned automatically again for compromising objects or suspicious substances. Once it has been cleared by security the baggage is then loaded onto a DCV and carried through underground tunnels (sometimes up to a mile away from the initial check-in desk) to its target destination gate. At the junction for the requested gate, the DCV then dumps the luggage onto a parallel-running conveyor that takes it to the gate's sorting station.

At this point the automation in the baggage handling system ends and human baggage handlers then sort and load the luggage into containers ready to be wheeled to the plane's hold. Luggage is separated depending on size, end destination (ie is the passenger going to be transferred at the next airport or is that their end destination) and type – skis and other odd-shaped objects for example. ✿

What is the longest conveyor belt?

Running from the coastal town of El Aaiún up to the phosphate mines of Bu Craa, lies a conveyor belt of over 100km in length. Staffed by the mine's Moroccan work force, all resources excavated from the mine are transported along the conveyor belt to the coast in order that they may be directly loaded onto cargo ships. Recently, as part of the National Geographic Megaflyover project, the conveyor belt had a portion of it imaged in super high resolution, allowing its epic scale to be better appreciated. The belt dwarfs the longest airport system of conveyor belts yet built, a record currently held by Dubai International Airport with its amazing 92 kilometres of baggage handling machinery.

How do planes fly?

Take to the skies and discover how hundreds of tons of metal can remain airborne

When we finally made the pivotal breakthrough, man-made flight took off in a hurry. In 45 years, we went from the Wright Brothers' beach hops to businessmen harassing stewardesses at 20,000 feet and test pilots moving faster than sound. Each leap forward came from ever-greater feats of engineering.

For millennia, would-be aviators knew bird flight had something to do with wing structure, but were clueless regarding the details. As it turns out, the shape of a wing is optimised to generate lift, an upward force caused by manipulating airflow. A wing has a rounded leading edge with a slight upward tilt, a curved topside, and a tapered trailing edge pointing downward. This shape alters the flow of air molecules into a downward trajectory. This results in – as Newton put it in his Third Law of Motion – "an equal and opposite reaction." When the wing pushes the air molecules down, the molecules push the wing up with equal force. The airflow also creates a lower pressure area above the wing, which essentially sucks the wing up.

Constructing wings is the easy part. To fly, you need to generate enough forward force – or thrust – to produce the necessary lift to counteract gravity. The Wright Brothers finally accomplished this by linking a piston engine to twin propellers. A plane propeller is simply a group of rotating wings shifted 90 degrees, so the direction of lift is forwards rather than upwards. In 1944, engineers upgraded to jet engines, which produce much greater thrust by igniting a mixture of air and fuel, and expelling hot gasses backward.

A pilot controls a plane by adjusting movable surfaces on the main wings, as well as smaller surfaces and a wing-like rudder on the tail. By changing the shape and position of these structures, the pilot varies the lift force, acting on the different ends of the plane to essentially pivot the plane along three axes: its pitch (up or down tilt of the nose), roll (side to side rotation), and yaw (turn to the left or right).

For the sake of efficiency, engineers keep planes as light and aerodynamic as possible. The first planes – sparse wooden frames covered in fabric – were lightweight and open, which minimised drag, the backwards force of air resistance.

But the structure was only strong enough to handle low speeds. 'Hot-rod' a Wright Brothers' plane with a jet engine, and the extra thrust would tear it apart. Along with more powerful engines, engineers had to develop stronger metal frameworks and streamlined aluminium alloy surfaces.

Modern fighter jets are manufactured from super-strong, lightweight composite material, applied in layers to form precise, aerodynamic shapes. This helps them get up to more than twice the speed of sound. ✿

Drag
The mass of molecules in the air creates resistance to the forward-moving plane, causing backward drag that works against the thrust. As the plane speeds up and encounters more air particles per second, drag increases.

Yaw
Planes have a vertical tail rudder, which is similar to the rudder on a boat. When you tilt the rudder to the left, rushing air will pivot the tail to the right. To turn successfully, it's necessary to adjust the yaw and roll simultaneously.

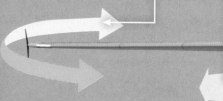

> ❝ *Many fighter jets are aerodynamically unstable. Flying requires a computer to make constant adjustments* ❞

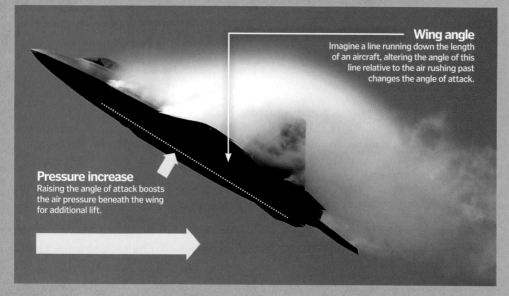

Wing angle
Imagine a line running down the length of an aircraft, altering the angle of this line relative to the air rushing past changes the angle of attack.

Pressure increase
Raising the angle of attack boosts the air pressure beneath the wing for additional lift.

How does the pilot make a plane climb?

Imagine a straight line going through the middle of a wing. The angle of attack is the angle of this line relative to the direction of rushing air. As you increase this angle, you boost the air pressure under the wing, resulting in greater lift. Pilots increase the angle of attack in order to climb, and decrease it to level out or dive.

Channel your inner seven-year-old, and try it yourself. Carefully, stick your hand out the window of a moving car with your palm down, and your thumb side tilted slightly up. Tilt the thumb side up, and your hand directs even more air downward, and you feel a greater upward push. If you keep pivoting your hand, however, you'll reach a point where air can't flow easily around it. The lift drops suddenly, and your hand flies straight back. In aeroplanes, this is called the stall point, and it's usually bad news for pilots.

What forces act on an aeroplane in flight?

There are a number of important forces affecting an aircraft in flight. Find out what they are...

Lift

The relative pressure of air rushing over and under the wings generates the upward lift force that keeps the plane aloft. In a typical small plane, the force of lift equals about ten times the force of thrust. Lift increases with the wings' surface area.

Pitch

Tail wings called stabilisers include adjustable flaps called elevators. When the elevators are tilted up, they generate lift that forces the tail downward. The nose tilts up, increasing the wing's angle of attack, causing the plane to climb. Tilting the elevators down lifts the tail, pitching the plane forward into a dive.

Gravity

Planes need sufficient lift to overcome the continual downward force of gravity. The heavier the plane, the more lift is needed – either from larger wings, greater thrust, or both.

Thrust

The forward thrust of the plane, generated by propellers, jet engines or rockets, counteracts drag and moves the wings through the air to generate lift.

Roll

To roll the plane, the hinged wing surfaces, called ailerons, have to be adjusted. To roll right, the aileron on the right wing has to be raised, which reduces lift, while simultaneously lowering the aileron on the left wing, which increases lift. The left wing rises and the right wing drops, rolling the plane to the right.

What forces act on the airfoil?

Lift
The air flowing over the top has further to go, so must travel quicker to keep up with the air below.

Airfoil
The airfoil is thin at the front, thicker in the middle and thinner again at the rear end.

Drag
Air resistance pulls the aircraft in the opposite direction.

More than a century after the Wright Brothers, physicists are still debating exactly how wings work. Accessible explanations for the rest of us can't help but leave things out, and some common answers are flat-out wrong.

The crucial thing to understand is that air is a fluid, and that wings alter the flow of that fluid. The top and bottom of the wing both deflect air molecules downwards, which results in an opposite upward force. In the typical airfoil design, the top of the wing is curved. Flowing air follows this curve, causing it to leave the wing at a significant downward angle. This also generates a low-pressure area above the wing, which helps pull it up.

Long, skinny wings are more efficient because they produce minimal drag proportional to lift. But they're also fragile and slow to manoeuvre. In contrast, stubby wings offer high agility and strength, but require more thrust to produce lift.

What happens during takeoff and landing?

1. Acceleration
To generate adequate lift from the ground, the pilot increases the size and camber (top curvature) of the wings by extending flaps at the back, and slats in the front.

2. Take-off
The pilot raises the tail elevators, and rushing air pushes the tail down. This raises the nose up, and increases the wings' angle of attack, producing enough lift for takeoff.

3. Flight
In flight, the pilot retracts the flaps and slats, and continually adjusts the ailerons, rudder and elevators to manoeuvre the plane.

4. Landing
The pilot reduces thrust to slow the plane and extends the landing gear, flaps and slats. When it touches down, the pilot extends spoilers on top of the wing to quickly decrease the lift.

What makes the Stealth Bomber so stealthy?

The B-2 is extraordinary, both in terms of appearance and design

Fly-by-wire
The B-2's unique shape makes it unstable, and it relies on a computer to stabilise it and keep it flying.

Windows
The B-2's windows have a fine wire mesh built into them, designed to scatter radar.

Crew compartment
The B-2 carries two crew, a pilot and a mission commander with room for a third if needed.

Air intakes
To further reduce the B-2's signature, the engine intakes are sunk into the main body

Rotary launch assembly (RLA)
The RLA allows the B-2 to deploy different weapons in quick succession.

Landing gear doors
The landing gear doors are hexagonal to further break up the B-2's radar profile.

The 'flying wing' shaped Stealth Bomber is a unique aircraft that's designed to make it as invisible as possible. Its shape means there are very few leading edges for radar to reflect from, reducing its signature dramatically. This is further enhanced by the composite materials from which the aircraft is constructed and the coatings on its surface. These are so successful that despite having a 172-foot wingspan, the B-2's radar signature is an astounding $0.1m^2$.

The B-2's stealth capabilities, and aerodynamic shape, are further enhanced by the fact its engines are buried inside the wing. This means the induction fans at the front of the engines are concealed while the engine exhaust is minimised. As a result, the B-2's thermal signature is kept to the bare minimum, making it harder for thermal sensors to detect the bomber as well as lowering the aircraft's acoustic footprint.

The design also means the B-2 is both highly aerodynamic and fuel efficient. The B-2's maximum range is 6,000 nautical miles and as a result the aircraft has often been used for long-range missions, some lasting 30 hours and in one case, 50. The B-2 is so highly automated that it's possible for a single crew member to fly while the other sleeps, uses the lavatory or prepares a hot meal, and this combination of range and versatility has meant the aircraft has been used to research sleep cycles to improve crew performance on long-range missions.

Despite this, the aircraft's success comes with a hefty price tag. Each B-2 costs $737 million and must be kept in a climate-controlled hangar to make sure the stealth materials remain intact. These problems aside though, the Spirit is an astonishing aircraft, although chances are, you won't see one unless the pilots want you to... ✿

> *The B-2 is so automated that a single crew member can fly while the other sleeps, uses the lavatory or prepares a hot meal*

Flying wing
The B-2's shape means it has very few leading edges, making it harder to detect on radar.

Composite materials
Any radar returns are reduced by the composite materials used, which further deflect any signals.

© John Batchelor / www.johnbatchelor.com

Carbon-reinforced plastic
Special heat-resistant material near the exhausts mean the airframe absorbs very little heat.

Bomb rack assembly (BRA)
The bomb rack assembly can hold up to 80 500lb bombs.

Engines
The B-2's four General Electric F118s don't have afterburners as the heat these generate would make the aircraft easier to detect.

Not one you're likely to find in an I-Spy book...

© Northrop Grumman

Main control
Dictating orders, the elements of the fin system are enacted and disseminated here.

Bridge control
The position and equipment used by the officers to issue commands.

Local control
This unit controls the movement of individual fins and their machinery.

Oil header tank

Stabiliser unit
This helps to maintain fin positioning and ship stability while moving.

Pump motor starter

Hydraulic unit
The power to move the massive fins and bring them in and out of the ship comes from hydraulics.

Fin
The part of the system that can be extended out of the body, used to prevent roll and achieve an accurate and efficient tracking course.

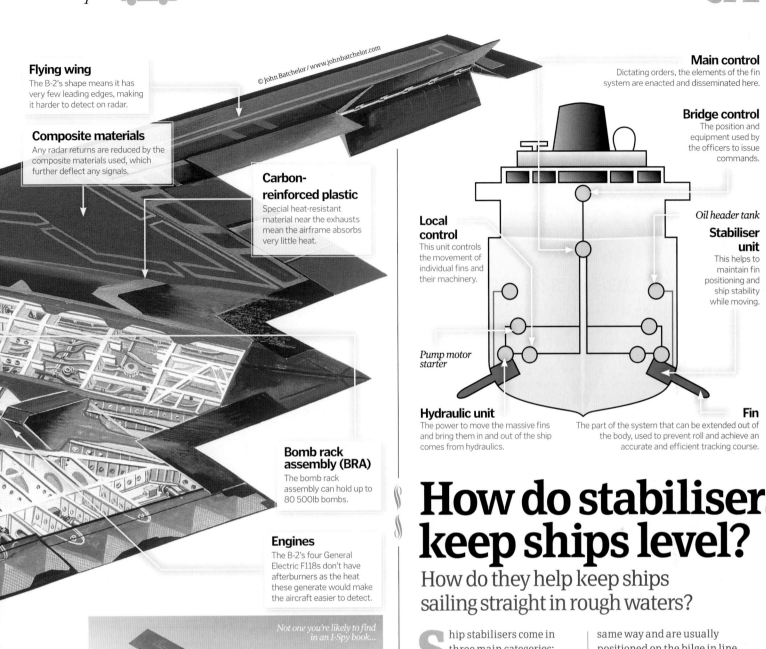

How do stabilisers keep ships level?

How do they help keep ships sailing straight in rough waters?

Ship stabilisers come in three main categories: bilge keels, ship stabilisers and gyroscopic ship stabilisers. Bilge keels are long thin strips of metal that run in a 'V' shape along the length of a ship at the turn of the bilge (the area on the outer surface of a ship's hull where the bottom curves meet the vertical sides). Bilge keels work by dampening a ship's roll capability by counteracting roll pressure with physical hydrodynamic resistance. Bilge keels are one of the simplest and cheapest ways to stabilise a ship and mitigate roll.

Ship stabilisers differ to bilge keels in shape and positioning, resembling fins rather than gills and are often positioned in pairs at the stern and bow of a ship. They do, however, work in the same way and are usually positioned on the bilge in line with the ship's bilge keel. Due to their larger size and protrusion, ship stabilisers offer greater resistance to ship roll but negatively affect its manoeuvrability and increase its hull clearances when docking.

Finally, gyroscopic ship stabilisers – which are the stabiliser of choice on most modern, large-scale vessels – are complex fin systems that cannot only be incrementally adjusted in their angle of attack (a vector representing the relative motion between lifting body and the fluid through which it is moving) to counteract roll, but also brought in and out of the hull at will thanks to specially tailored hydraulic mechanisms. ✿

How does a hovercraft hover?

Why do these incredible machines traverse both land and sea with ease?

The ability of hovercraft to cross dry land as well as water has seen them employed in the military and tourism sectors for many years. Although once billed as the next generation of transportation, they have somewhat decreased in popularity over the last decade. Despite this, their usefulness is still readily apparent.

The core principle of a hovercraft is that the hull of the vehicle is suspended on top of a giant cushion of air, held in place by flexible rubber that allows it to traverse difficult terrain or choppy waves without being torn apart. At the centre of a hovercraft is a huge fan that fires air downwards, pushing the hull off the ground as high as two metres (6.5 feet). Smaller fans on top of the hull push air backwards, giving the hovercraft forward momentum. Rudders direct this flow of horizontal air to allow a hovercraft to change its direction.

Traditional hovercraft have an entirely rubber base that allows for travel on land or sea, but others have rigid sides that, while suited only to water, can have propellers or water-jet engines attached for a quieter craft. ✿

Cargo
Most modern hovercraft are used for military purposes, like this Landing Craft Air Cushion (LCAC), which can transport vehicles and troops with ease.

© Alex Pang

How does the air cushion work?

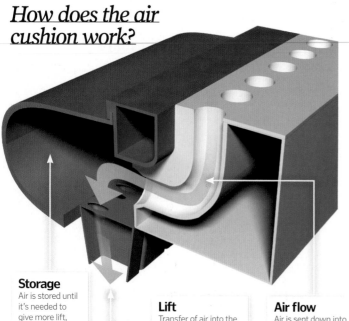

Skirt
This flexible and inflatable barrier traps the cushion of pressurised air beneath the hull, in addition to increasing the height of the hull to allow it to move over obstacles.

Storage
Air is stored until it's needed to give more lift, when air escapes through the hovergap.

Lift
Transfer of air into the plenum chamber increases pressure and allows the craft to rise.

Air flow
Air is sent down into the plenum chamber of the hovercraft from the main fan.

Plenum chamber
The region of trapped air underneath the craft is known as the 'plenum chamber', which controls the escape of air to create a high-pressure environment and thus a circulation of controllable air.

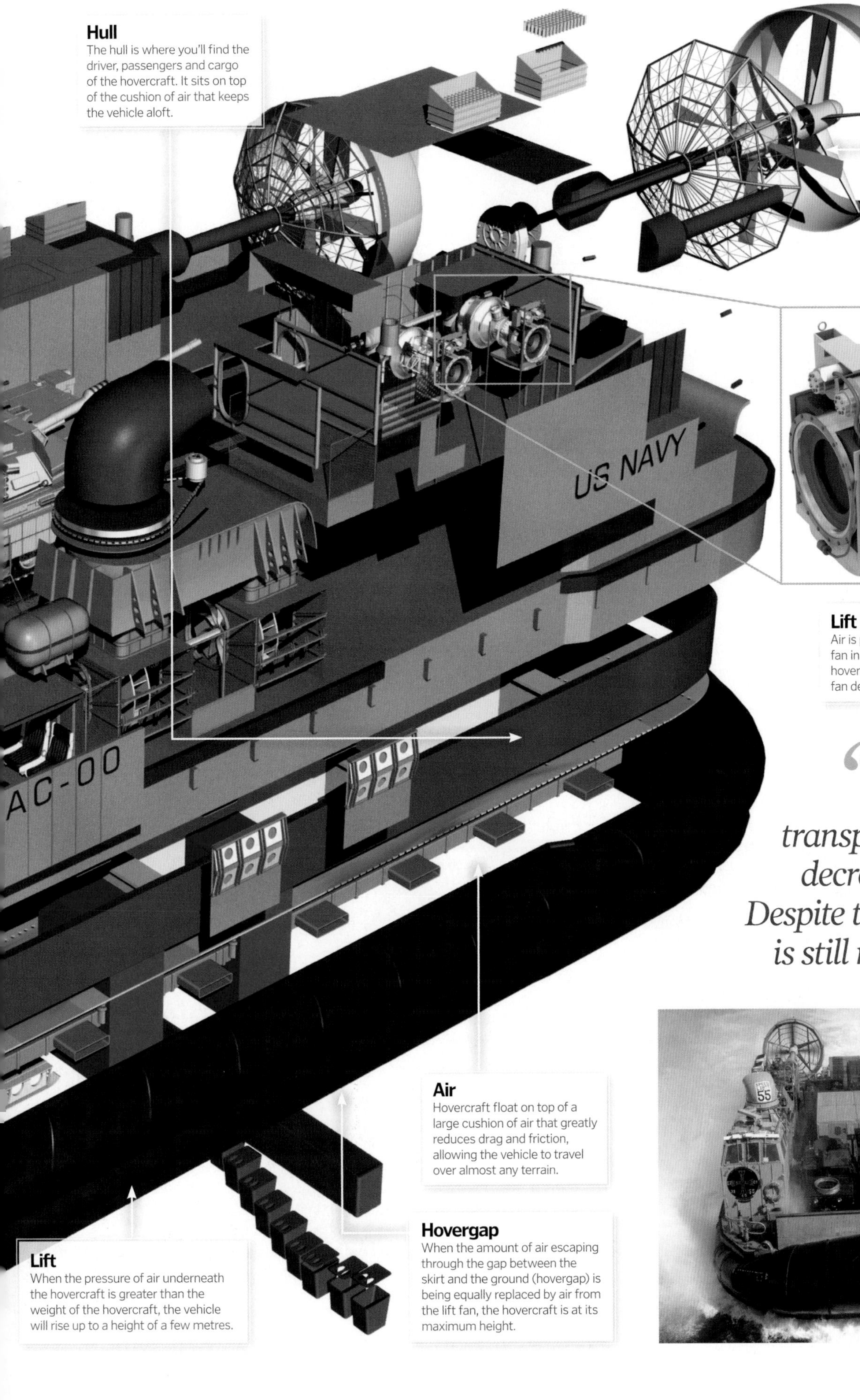

Hull

The hull is where you'll find the driver, passengers and cargo of the hovercraft. It sits on top of the cushion of air that keeps the vehicle aloft.

Rudders

Flaps at the back control the hovercraft like an aircraft, directing airflow in certain directions to allow it to be steered.

Thrust fans

The hovercraft gains its propulsion from these backwards-facing fans, normally mounted on the back of the vehicle. Some use ducted fans while others favour naked propellers.

Lift fan

Air is pumped into the plenum chamber by the main fan in the centre of a hovercraft. Although some hovercraft divert air from the thrust fans instead, lift fan designs are much easier to construct.

US NAVY

AC-00

Air

Hovercraft float on top of a large cushion of air that greatly reduces drag and friction, allowing the vehicle to travel over almost any terrain.

Hovergap

When the amount of air escaping through the gap between the skirt and the ground (hovergap) is being equally replaced by air from the lift fan, the hovercraft is at its maximum height.

Lift

When the pressure of air underneath the hovercraft is greater than the weight of the hovercraft, the vehicle will rise up to a height of a few metres.

> **❝** *Once billed as the next generation of transportation, they have decreased in popularity. Despite this, their usefulness is still readily apparent* **❞**

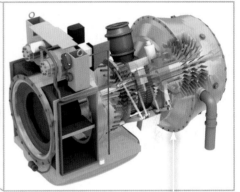

Worldwide military forces have many different uses for hovercraft

Who was Sir Frank Whittle?

Sir Frank Whittle is credited with inventing the modern jet engine, along with German Hans von Ohain, who independently came up with a similar idea at the same time.

Born in Coventry in 1907, Whittle trained as an RAF officer and wrote a thesis on future aircraft which considered the idea of using a piston engine to create compressed air for thrust. He abandoned that plan but later thought of using a turbine in place of a conventional engine. He passed his idea to the Air Ministry but was told that it would never work.

Undeterred, Whittle raised finance to set up his own company, Power Jets Limited. He struggled to keep it going until, with the Second World War looming, the Air Ministry finally realised the project's potential and began to fund it.

Finally, in 1939, the Air Ministry commissioned the Gloster Whittle – the first British jet plane, soon after the Germans trialled their Heinkel He 178 – the world's very first jet aircraft.

Whittle later moved to the United States, where he died in 1996 but is still remembered for changing the face of aviation forever.

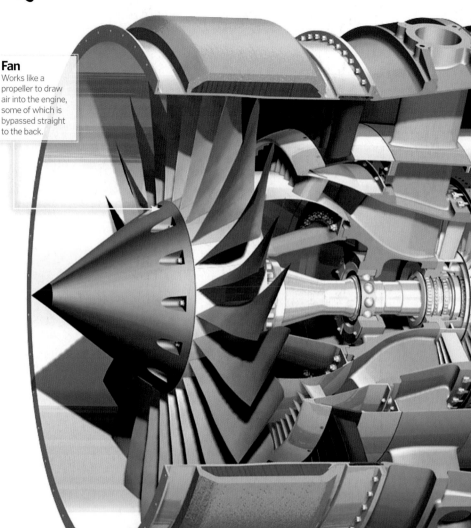

Fan
Works like a propeller to draw air into the engine, some of which is bypassed straight to the back.

© Rolls-Royce

How complex is a jet engine?

It may be simpler than the engine in your car...

The very first aircraft used engine-driven propellers to drive them through the air and, of course, many planes still use propellers today. However, if you want to achieve serious speed in the air then you're going to need an awful lot of thrust, and for that you need a jet engine.

To demonstrate how a jet works, hold a high-pressure hosepipe up to the palm of your hand – the pressure of the water squirting out the end will try to push your hand back. In fact, the engine on a jet ski works by firing water out of a nozzle to drive the vessel forward.

The simplest form of jet is the firework rocket, which dates back to the 13th Century. An explosive is ignited and the resultant gasses are propelled out of a nozzle which creates thrust to push the rocket forwards. Rocket engines in spacecraft work in the same way; they're simple but use a huge amount of fuel in a short time, and aren't practical for everyday use. Most so-called jet planes actually have turbofan gas-turbine engines. Near the front of the engine is a compressor, which is essentially a larger number of vanes that suck air in, compress it, and then force it at high-pressure into a combustion chamber. At this point the air is moving at hundreds of miles an hour.

Fuel is injected into the combustion chamber, where it mixes with the fast-moving compressed air and is ignited. The hot gasses then pass back where they drive a turbine which, in turn, provides propulsion for the aforementioned

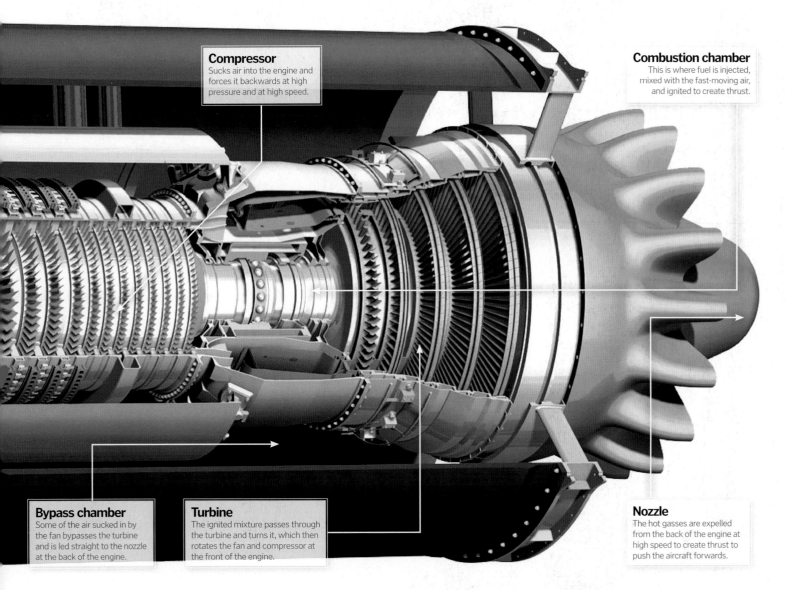

Compressor
Sucks air into the engine and forces it backwards at high pressure and at high speed.

Combustion chamber
This is where fuel is injected, mixed with the fast-moving air, and ignited to create thrust.

Bypass chamber
Some of the air sucked in by the fan bypasses the turbine and is led straight to the nozzle at the back of the engine.

Turbine
The ignited mixture passes through the turbine and turns it, which then rotates the fan and compressor at the front of the engine.

Nozzle
The hot gasses are expelled from the back of the engine at high speed to create thrust to push the aircraft forwards.

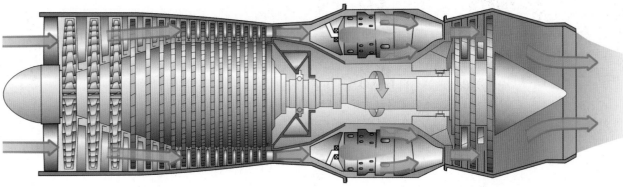

> *The simplest form of jet is the firework rocket, which dates back to the 13th Century*

compressor. The remaining energy is expelled from a nozzle at the back of the engine to create forward thrust.

At the very front of a turbofan engine is a large fan that also sucks air in. Some of this air is picked up by the compressor but the rest bypasses the main turbine and is led around to the back of the engine where it supplies additional thrust.

Because a turbofan relies on the rotating turbine to drive the compressor and fan, and the turbine can't turn without air from the

compressor, it needs help to get started. This is done with compressed air that spins the compressor and fan at such a speed that, when the fuel is ignited, there is enough airflow to ensure the hot gasses are thrust backwards and don't explode.

Compared to the internal combustion engines used in cars and propeller-driven aircraft, a turbofan is reassuringly free of complex parts and so is extremely reliable. Which in the case of an aeroplane is reassuringly good news! ✿

What's the sound barrier?

Breaking the sound barrier means exceeding the speed of sound at 40,000 feet – that's about 660 miles per hour

When Chuck Yeager broke the sound barrier with the Bell X-1 rocket plane in 1947, his mum wasn't mad. This was one case where breaking something was a good thing. The sound barrier is simply the point an object exceeds the speed of sound – a speed many scientists once considered impossible.

Sound is a travelling wave of pressure. A moving object pushes nearby air molecules, which push the molecules next to them, and so on. As a plane approaches the speed of sound, its pressure waves 'stack up' ahead of it to form a massive area of pressurised air, called a shock wave. Shock waves would shake old planes violently, creating an apparent 'barrier' to higher speeds.

You can hear shock waves as sonic booms. Sometimes they're even visible: the high pressure area can cause water vapour to condensate into liquid droplets, briefly forming a cloud around the plane. ✲

How do combines work?

More than an overgrown lawn mower, combines are mobile multitaskers

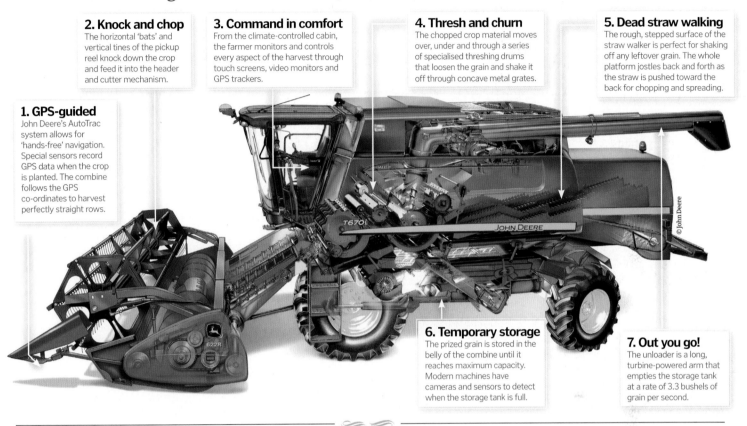

2. Knock and chop
The horizontal 'bats' and vertical tines of the pickup reel knock down the crop and feed it into the header and cutter mechanism.

3. Command in comfort
From the climate-controlled cabin, the farmer monitors and controls every aspect of the harvest through touch screens, video monitors and GPS trackers.

4. Thresh and churn
The chopped crop material moves over, under and through a series of specialised threshing drums that loosen the grain and shake it off through concave metal grates.

5. Dead straw walking
The rough, stepped surface of the straw walker is perfect for shaking off any leftover grain. The whole platform jostles back and forth as the straw is pushed toward the back for chopping and spreading.

1. GPS-guided
John Deere's AutoTrac system allows for 'hands-free' navigation. Special sensors record GPS data when the crop is planted. The combine follows the GPS co-ordinates to harvest perfectly straight rows.

© John Deere

6. Temporary storage
The prized grain is stored in the belly of the combine until it reaches maximum capacity. Modern machines have cameras and sensors to detect when the storage tank is full.

7. Out you go!
The unloader is a long, turbine-powered arm that empties the storage tank at a rate of 3.3 bushels of grain per second.

How do submarines dive?

What enables them to dive and ascend on command?

Like ships, submarines can float because the weight of water that they displace is equal to their weight, creating a buoyant force that counteracts gravity. However, the main competency of the submarine is its ability to exist and travel while totally submerged, diving to incredible depths. So how does it vary the buoyant force acting upon it in order to do so?

To control buoyancy, modern submarines utilise a system of ballast tanks positioned between a double hull. The ballast tanks can be filled either with pressurised air, which reduces the submarine's overall density, or water from the ocean, which increases it. This is achieved by a series of vents and hydraulic panels that move in sync depending on the submarine's manoeuvre. If diving, air from the ballast tanks is vented out of the vessel and replaced with water, and if ascending, vice versa. To maintain a set depth, the submarine then merely balances the load in the ballast accordingly to generate equilibrium.

In addition to the ballast system, submarines are also fitted with sets of short, wing-shaped hydroplanes that can be adjusted dependent on the angle of the dive needed. These hydroplanes work by forcing passing water over the submarine's stern, which forces it downwards. ✿

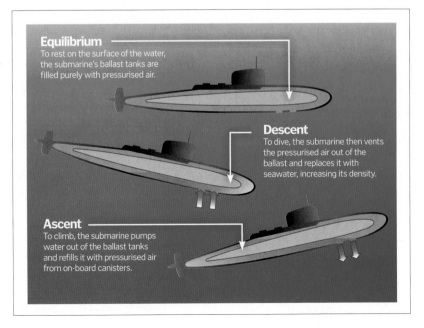

Equilibrium
To rest on the surface of the water, the submarine's ballast tanks are filled purely with pressurised air.

Descent
To dive, the submarine then vents the pressurised air out of the ballast and replaces it with seawater, increasing its density.

Ascent
To climb, the submarine pumps water out of the ballast tanks and refills it with pressurised air from on-board canisters.

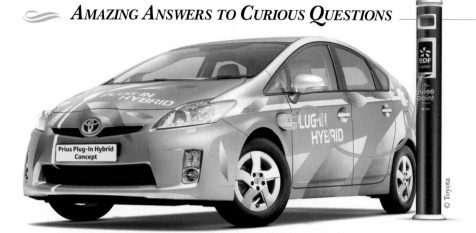
© Toyota

Why don't forklift trucks tip over?

Unfortunately they do. Used mainly in warehouses to lift and move heavy loads, forklifts are very dangerous; every year there are over 8,000 accidents involving them. The average weight of a forklift is about three times that of an average car, and this weight is mainly distributed at the rear to counterbalance the load on the forks at the front. The front wheels, meanwhile, act as a fulcrum.

© Toyota

Are hybrid cars really environmentally friendly?

It depends on how they are used. They're great for city drivers, when a hybrid can rely almost fully on its electric motor, which is quiet, doesn't create any emissions, will turn off completely when the car is stationary and, crucially, gives superb fuel economy.

Get driving your car on the open road, though, and the hybrid will have to fall back onto its petrol engine, because the electric motor simply doesn't have the power to drive the car at higher speeds, nor the energy to run for long distances. In such cases, then, the hybrid will act just like a comparable conventional petrol-powered car, and offer similar fuel economy and the same emissions.

Indeed, some small modern diesel-engined cars produce lower emissions and give better economy than hybrids when driven in this way. They are usually cheaper to buy, too. You should also take into account that the manufacturing of batteries for a hybrid car requires a lot of energy. And then, after they have reached the end of their life (which may be after just two years), more energy is required to decommission and recycle them. This and the development impact actually makes hybrid cars less environmentally friendly than you may think.

> ❝ Some small modern diesel-engined cars produce lower emissions and give better economy than hybrids ❞

How do railway lines not buckle?

Expansion joints are structures placed at points along a railway track in order to cope with expansion and contraction of the rails due to changes in the temperature. When it gets hot the rails get longer as the metal expands. If this was just one long track then it would create a problem, so the track is divided up into sections separated by these expansion joints.

These joints pose another problem, however, in that they become areas of weakness along the track and require lots of maintenance and can eventually lead to deformations in the track. Not good news in times of rising ticket prices for passengers. The most common type of track now in use is called continuous welded rail. In this type of rail, the rails are welded together to form one long continuous rail which may be up to several kilometres in length. They are bolted into place using a series of sleepers that are made from concrete or timber.

So how does this type of rail cope with the expansion and contraction problem? Well, because there are fewer joints, the track is stronger and gives a smoother journey. This allows for less friction and trains can consequently go faster. When the tracks have just been laid down, they are heated up to a high temperature which causes expansion. They are then fastened to their sleepers in their expanded form and upon attempting to contract as they cool down they simply can't. In essence they are like a piece of stretched elastic which is fixed down firmly.

What's the highest a hot air balloon has been?

The record for a hot air balloon is 21,027 metres. This was set in Bombay in 2005 by Indian businessman Vijaypat Singhania, who was 67 years old, in a Cameron Z-type balloon. In 1960, US Air Force Captain Joseph Kittinger reached a height of 31,090 metres but that was in a helium balloon. Oh, and he then jumped out and parachuted back to earth, therefore breaking another record!

© Wally

How do boats brake?

Different types of boat use different ways to propel themselves through the water. For boats with propellers, like motorboats and pedalos, the spinning propeller pushes water back and this pushes the boat forwards. You can slow them by stopping the propeller spinning. If you spin the propeller backwards, the boat will push water forwards and this will start to push the boat backwards and it will slow down a bit faster. Sail boats are different. If you want to completely stop your boat then don't forget an anchor or you'll drift away with the wind and currents.

How does the speedometer in a plane work?

The official name for an aircraft speedometer is an Airspeed Indicator or ASI. Airspeed is a measurement of the plane's speed relative to the air around it. On the aircraft there is a tube called the pitot tube. The open end of the pitot tube is usually mounted on a wing and faces toward the flow of air. The airspeed indicator actually measures the difference between a static sensor inside the plane (not in the air stream) and a sensor (the pitot) in the air stream.

When the aircraft is standing still, the pressure in each tube is equal and the airspeed indicator shows zero. The rush of air in flight causes a pressure differential between the static tube and the pitot tube. The pressure differential makes the pointer on the airspeed indicator move. An increase of airspeed leads to the pressure at the end of the pitot tube raising.

In turn, the air pressure pushes against a diaphragm that moves a connected mechanical pointer on the face of the indicator (the gauge in the cockpit). The indicator is calibrated to compensate for winds in the air using electronic read-outs from the air and the ground. This system also compensates for altitude and air temperature to make the airspeed measurement accurate.

❝ The airspeed indicator actually measures the difference between a static sensor inside the plane and a sensor in the air stream ❞

How do propellers drive boats and ships?

A propeller doesn't push a ship through the water – it 'lifts' it. Take a close look at the shape of a propeller. With its thicker leading edge, concave underside and precise pitch (or angle), it looks like an aeroplane wing. That's because both aeroplane wings and propellers are types of aerofoils.

When an aerofoil passes through a fluid, the fluid is forced to move faster along the curved top surface, creating a drop in pressure. With less pressure on top of the aerofoil and more pressure below, it lifts. That's exactly what happens when a boat propeller cuts through the water. As it slices vertically in a circular motion, it creates horizontal 'lift' at right angles to the motion, pushing the boat or ship along.

Choosing the right size of propeller for the boat is very important – get the size wrong (eg too high a pitch for the engine power/ boat speed) and the risk of cavitation is increased. Cavitation is caused when the surface of the blades become covered in tiny vacuum bubbles.

A smaller degree of cavitation will cause vibration and if left in this condition for long periods will cause 'cavitation burns', which is where the vacuum bubbles implode with enough force to start sucking metal off the blade surface.

Severe cavitation can cause the propeller to break away completely, leaving the boat stranded and offering the possibility of a long row home.

What is a nautical mile?

A nautical mile is based on the circumference of the Earth. If you cut the Earth in half at the equator, pick up one of the halves and look at the equator as a circle. Divide that circle into 360 degrees. Then divide a degree into 60 minutes. A minute of arc on the planet Earth is one nautical mile. Because this takes into account the arc of the Earth, it is used in air and sea travel. A nautical mile is 1,852 metres, 1.852 kilometres, 1.1508 miles, or 6,076 feet.

The nautical mile is used by sea and air navigators because of its convenience when working with charts and maps. Most nautical charts are constructed on a scale that varies from the equator to 80° north or south latitude. This means it is difficult to show a single linear scale for use on charts (realistically on scales smaller than about 1/80,000). This isn't practical for more accurate navigation using lower scale charts.

Since a nautical mile equals a minute of latitude, it is easy to measure a distance on a chart with dividers, using the latitude scale on the side of the chart directly to the east or west of the distance being measured. Being used to working with miles and kilometres means that this sounds complicated, but for the purpose of working with charts and maps it is far easier for the navigators to use.

What does a car handbrake actually do?

A car's handbrake is the lever to a completely mechanical braking system, which will bypass the primary hydraulic system if it fails. When the handbrake is applied, the brake cable passes through an intermediate lever, to increase the force of your pull; this force is then split evenly between your brakes by an equaliser. Typically, a mechanical lever is added to the existing disc or drum brakes on the car. In drum brakes, the handbrake cable runs directly to a lever on the brake shoes. In disc brakes an additional lever and corkscrew is added to the existing calliper piston. When the handbrake is pulled, the lever forces the corkscrew against the piston, which would normally be activated by the hydraulic foot pedal system.

Although it is reassuring to have a secondary braking system for emergencies, the primary use of the handbrake tends to be when parking as they remain engaged until a release button is pressed, stopping your car potentially rolling away. This is good practice, as it keeps your brake cable from seizing up, ready for when you really need it. In fact, using your handbrake to stop a moving car can actually damage the brake system, so it is best to save this for real emergencies!

What keeps submarines underwater?

In order to understand what allows submarines to stay underwater, it is important to first look into why things float on water in the first place. Archimedes showed that an object will float if the weight of that object is less than the weight of the water it displaces. As you may be aware, when you get in a bath you are displacing the water – this causes the water level to rise. The effect is known as buoyancy and accounts for why big steel ships don't sink.

Submarines fall into two different categories: static divers and dynamic divers. Static diving uses differences in weight to affect the buoyancy, whereas dynamic diving uses speed and power to submerge, a little bit like how aeroplanes fly. Static diving submarines can submerge by taking on more water through the use of ballast tanks. To return to the surface they can dump this extra weight to regain their buoyancy. The mechanism by which these ballast tanks work may involve an electric motor or compressed gas. Dynamic divers use fins or hydroplanes along with speed to force themselves underwater. This means if they slow down they return to the surface. The important thing to remember is that a submarine isn't just air inside; yes it has some, but it's the overall weight with respect to the amount of displaced water which causes something to float or sink.

Why do wheels look like they spin backwards?

This is due to an effect that is known as 'aliasing' and is most likely to be observed on TV due to the 'frame rate' of the camera filming it. Video cameras work by capturing lots of still images in a very short space of time. For example, television cameras capture roughly 50 frames a second. This is quite sufficient to fool our eyes and brain into thinking we are seeing a continuous moving image.

Now imagine a wheel with four spokes at right angles to each other and focus on the spoke in the 12 o'clock position. If, by the time the next frame captures an image, that spoke has moved clockwise almost one whole revolution to 11 o'clock then your brain will interpret the spoke as having moved anti-clockwise from the 12 o'clock position to the 11 o'clock position, making the wheel appear like it is rotating backwards.

This effect can also be seen quite well under a fast-moving strobe light, as essentially the strobe is doing the same thing as the camera and giving you lots of snapshots of an image. Under certain conditions, street lights can highlight this effect as they are constantly flickering on and off about 50 times a second due to the alternating current.

Space

" *The farther you look into space, the farther back in time you'll see* **"**

What happened at the Big Bang?

As an elegant explanation of the origins of both atoms and galaxies, the Big Bang is the ultimate theory of everything

Time: Zero to 10^{-43} seconds

The Planck era

The Planck era describes the impossibly short passage of time between the absolute beginning of the universe (zero) and 10^{-43} seconds (10 trillionths of a yoctosecond, if you're counting!). In this fraction of an instant, the universe went from infinite density to something called Planck density ($10^{93}g/cm^3$), the equivalent of 100 billion galaxies squeezed into the nucleus of an atom. Beyond the Planck density, rules of General Relativity don't apply, so the very dawn of time is still a complete and utter mystery.

Inflation era

In the Eighties, cosmologists theorised a period of spontaneous expansion in the very early moments of time. Instantaneously, every point in the universe expanded by a factor of 1,027. The universe didn't get bigger, it just was bigger. Because the universe got so big, so fast, its naturally spherical shape appeared flat to objects on the surface, solving one of the early problems with the Big Bang theory.

Quark era

After the explosive inflation period, the universe was a dense cauldron of pure energy. Under these conditions, gamma rays of energy collided to briefly form quarks and anti-quarks, the fundamental building blocks of matter. Just as quickly, though, the quarks and anti-quarks collided in a process called annihilation, converting their mass back to pure energy.

TIME → 10^{-36} to 10^{-32} after Big Bang → 10^{-32} to 10^{-12}

Quark · Antiquark · Quark - antiquark pair · X-boson

The Big Bang theory begins with a simple assumption: if the universe is expanding and cooling – something Edwin Hubble and company proved at the beginning of the 20th Century – then it must have once been very small and very hot. From then on, the simple becomes infinitely complex. Big bang theory is nothing less than the summation of everything we've learned about the very big (astrophysics) and the very small (quantum physics) in the history of human thought.

Cosmologists – people who study the origin and evolution of the universe – theorise that 13.7 billion years ago, a bubble formed out of the void. The bubble, many times smaller than a single proton, contained all matter and radiation in our current universe. Propelled by a mysterious outward force, the bubble instantaneously expanded (it didn't explode) by a factor of 1,027, triggering a cosmic domino effect that created the stars, the galaxies and life as we know it. ✿

❝ *The bubble, many times smaller than a single proton, contained all matter in our current universe* ❞

Particle soup

If you turn the heat up high enough, everything melts. When the universe was 10-32 seconds old, it burned at a magnificent 1,000 trillion trillion degrees Celsius. At this remarkable temperature, the tiniest building blocks of matter – quarks and anti-quarks, leptons and anti-leptons – swirled freely in a particle soup called the quark-gluon plasma. Gluon is the invisible 'glue' that carries the strong force, binding quarks into protons and neutrons.

Let there be light

The primordial soup of the early universe was composed of pairs of particles and anti-particles (mostly quarks, anti-quarks, leptons and anti-leptons). Picture this ultra-hot, supercharged environment as the original super collider. Particles and anti-particles smashed together in a process called annihilation, producing beams of photons (light radiation). As more particles collided, more light was generated. Some of those photons reformed into particles, but when the universe finally cooled enough to form stable atoms, the spare photons were set free. The net result: the universe contains a billion times more light than matter.

X-bosons

A funny thing happened at 10-39 seconds after the beginning of time. The universe produced huge particles called X-bosons (1,015 times more massive than protons). X-bosons are neither matter nor anti-matter and exist only to carry the Grand Unified Force, a combination of the electromagnetic, weak and strong forces that exist today.

The Grand Unified Force drove the early expansion of the universe, but rapid cooling caused X-bosons to decay into protons and anti-protons. For reasons that aren't clear, a billion and one protons were created for every billion anti-protons, creating a tiny net gain of matter. This imbalance, forged during a short blip in time, is the reason for our matter-dominated universe.

Recreating the Big Bang

CERN's Large Hadron Collider (LHC) is the world's largest particle accelerator. At full power, trillions of protons will travel at near light speed through super-cooled vacuum tubes buried 100 metres below the surface. As the protons smash into each other – at a rate of 600 million collisions per second – they will generate energy 100,000 times hotter than the Sun, a faithful re-creation of the cosmic conditions milliseconds after the Big Bang. Using ultra-sensitive detectors, scientists will scour the debris trails for traces of quarks, leptons and even the Higgs boson, a highly theoretical particle believed to give mass to matter.

A computer simulation of the decay path of a Higgs boson after two protons collide in the LHC

Separation of the Electroweak force

During the Planck era, the four forces of nature were briefly unified: gravity, the strong force, electromagnetism and the weak force. As the Planck era ended as the universe cooled, gravity separated out, then the strong force separated during the inflation. But it wasn't until the end of the Quark era that the universe was cool enough to separate the electromagnetic and weak forces, establishing the physical laws we follow today.

110^{-9} to 10^{-62}

Higgs boson (hypothetical)

Photon

Quark–anti-quark forming and annihilating

Higgs boson (hypothetical)

W-boson

Decaying X-boson

Graviton (hypothetical)

X-boson decay products (particles and antiparticles)

Antiquark pair

Antineutrino

The origins of matter

Everything in the universe – the galaxies, the stars, the planets, even your big toe – is made of matter. In the beginning (roughly 13.7 billion years ago), matter and radiation were bound together in a superheated, super-dense fog. As the universe cooled and expanded, the first elemental particles emerged: quarks and anti-quarks. As things cooled further, the strong force separated, pulling together clumps of quarks into protons and neutrons, building the first atomic nuclei. Half a million years later, conditions were finally cool enough for nuclei to pull in free electrons, forming the first stable atoms. Small fluctuations in the density of matter distribution led to clusters and clouds of matter that coalesced, over hundreds of millions of years, into the stars and galaxies we explore today.

Dark forces

So what is the universe made of? Well, there is more to the universe than meets the eye. Cosmologists have proven that the visible or 'luminous' portions of the cosmos – the stars, galaxies, quasars and planets – are only a small fraction of the total mass and composition of the universe. Using super-accurate measurements of cosmic microwave background radiation fluctuations, scientists estimate that only 4.6 per cent of the universe is composed of atoms (baryonic matter), 23 per cent is dark matter (invisible and undetectable, but with a gravitational effect on baryonic matter), and 72 per cent is dark energy, a bizarre form of matter that works in opposition to gravity. Many cosmologists believe that dark energy is responsible for the accelerating expansion of the universe, which should be contracting under its own gravitational pull.

Hadron era

When the expanding universe cooled to 1,013K (ten quadrillion degrees Celsius), quarks became stable enough to bond together through the strong force. When three quarks clump together in the right formation, they form hadrons, a type of particle that includes protons and neutrons. Miraculously, every single proton and neutron in the known universe was created during this millisecond of time.

Lepton era

During this comparatively 'long' era, the rapidly expanding universe cools to 109K, allowing for the formation of a new kind of particle called a lepton. Leptons, like quarks, are the near mass-less building blocks of matter. Electrons are a 'flavour' of lepton, as are neutrinos.

Nucleosynthesis era

For 17 glorious minutes, the universe reached the ideal temperature to support nuclear fusion, the process by which protons and neutrons bond together to form atomic nuclei. Only the lightest elements have time to form – 75 per cent hydrogen, 25 per cent helium – before fusion winds down.

10^{-6} to 1 second

1 second to 3 minutes

3 minutes to 20 minutes

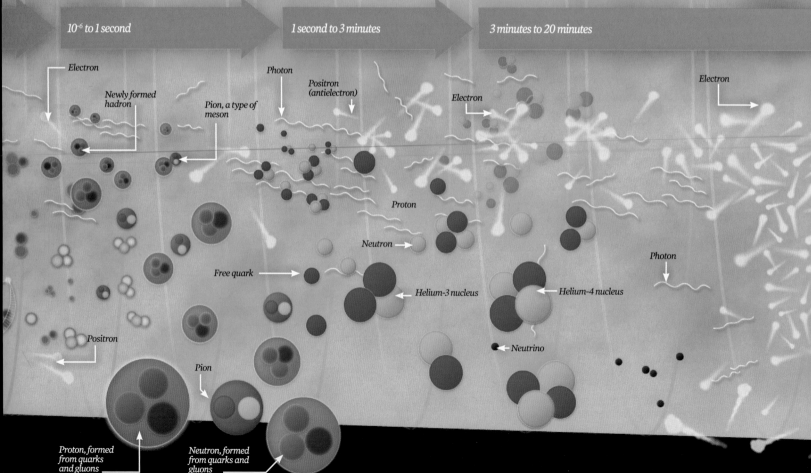

Electron

Newly formed hadron

Pion, a type of meson

Photon

Positron (antielectron)

Electron

Electron

Proton

Neutron

Photon

Free quark

Helium-3 nucleus

Helium-4 nucleus

Positron

Neutrino

Pion

Proton, formed from quarks and gluons

Neutron, formed from quarks and gluons

What does cosmic microwave background radiation mean?

As the universe expands, it also cools. The inconceivable heat released during the Big Bang has been slowly dissipating as the universe continues its 14 billion-year expansion. Using sensitive satellite equipment, cosmologists can measure the residual heat from the Big Bang, which exists as cosmic microwave background radiation (CMBR). CMBR is everywhere in the known universe and its temperature is nearly constant (a nippy 2.725K over absolute zero), further proof that the radiation emanated from a single, ancient source.

Minute differences in microwave background radiation levels (+/- 0.0002K) reveal fluctuations in the density of matter in the primitive universe

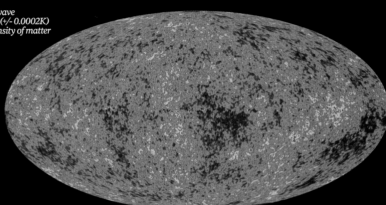

Opaque era

These are the 'dark ages' of the universe, when light and matter were intertwined in a dense cosmic fog. Photons of light collided constantly with free protons (hydrogen ions), neutrons, electrons and helium nuclei, trapping the light in a thick plasma of particles. It is impossible for cosmologists to 'see' beyond this era, since there is no visible light.

Balance of elements

When the temperature dropped to 10,000K, electrons slowed down enough to be pulled into orbit around atomic nuclei, forming the first stable, neutral atoms of hydrogen, helium and other trace elements. As atoms started to form, photons were freed from the cosmic fog, creating a transparent universe. All cosmic background radiation originated with this 'last scattering' of photons.

Matter era

During the Opaque era, matter and light were stuck together as plasma. Photons of light applied radiation pressure on matter, preventing it from bonding together to form atoms and larger particles. When light and matter 'decoupled', the radiation pressure was released as light, freeing matter to clump and collect in the first clouds of interstellar gas. From there, the first stars were born around 400 million years after the Big Bang.

20 minutes to 377,000 years

500,000 to the present

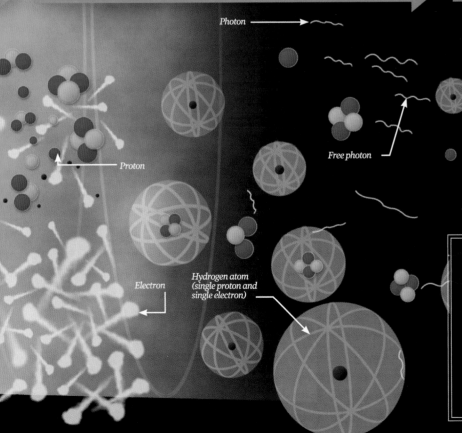

Photon ⟶

Helium atom (two protons and two electrons)

Free photon

Proton

Electron

Hydrogen atom (single proton and single electron)

The 'God' particle

We take for granted the idea that if something is made of protons, neutrons and electrons, then it inherently has mass. But cosmologists now believe that no particle has mass simply by merit of its existence. Instead, mass is bestowed on particles as they pass through a Higgs field, a theoretical quantum field named after British physicist Peter Higgs. Imagine the Higgs field as a bowl of honey and quantum particles as a string of pearls. As you drag the pearls through the honey, they are imbued with mass. Every quantum field has a fundamental particle, and the particle associated with Higgs field is the Higgs boson. One of the goals of the Large Hadron Collider at CERN is to prove the existence of the elusive Higgs boson once and for all.

How is a

There may be as many as 10 billion trillion stars in the 100 billion galaxies throughout the universe, but 'only' about 100 billion in our galaxy, the Milky Way. Most stars comprise plasma, helium and hydrogen. They form when giant molecular clouds (GMCs), also known as star nurseries, experience a gravitational collapse. This increase in pressure and temperature forces fragments into a body known as a protostar. Over the course of its life, a typical star goes through continuous nuclear fusion in its core. The energy released by this fusion makes the star glow.

Stars are classified according to the Hertzsprung-Russell Diagram, which lists their colour, temperature, mass, radius, luminosity and spectra (which elements they absorb). There are three main types of star: those above, below and on the main sequence. Within these types, there are seven different classifications. We're most familiar with the main sequence star that we call the Sun, a type G yellow-white star with a radius of 700,000 kilometres and a temperature of 6,000 kelvin. However, some stars above the main sequence are more than a thousand times larger than the Sun, while those below the main sequence can have a radius of just a few kilometres.

LOW-MASS STARS

Red dwarf

The cool star
Red dwarfs are small and relatively cool stars, which while being large in number tend to have a mass of less than one-half that of our Sun. The heat generated by a red dwarf occurs at a slow rate through the nuclear fusion of hydrogen into helium within its core, before being transported via convection to its surface. In addition, due to their low mass red dwarfs tend to have elongated life spans, exceeding that of stars like our Sun by billions of years.

Giant molecular cloud *Proto-stars*

SUN-LIKE STARS

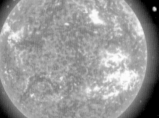

Red giant

Almost a star
A protostar is a ball-shaped mass in the early stages of becoming a star. It's irregularly shaped and contains dust as well as gas, formed during the collapse of a giant molecular cloud. The protostar stage in a star's life cycle can last for a hundred thousand years as it continues to heat and become denser.

Star or planet?
A brown dwarf is sometimes not even considered a star at all, but instead a sub-stellar body. They are incredibly small in relation to other types of stars, and never attained a high enough temperature, mass or enough pressure at its core for nuclear fusion to actually occur. It is below the main sequence on the Hertzsprung-Russell Diagram. Brown dwarfs have a radius a few times the size of Jupiter, and are sometimes difficult to distinguish from gaseous planets because of their size and make-up (helium and hydrogen).

A star explodes
If a star has enough mass to become a supergiant, it will supernova instead of becoming a white dwarf. As nuclear fusion ends in the core of a supergiant, the loss of energy can trigger a sudden gravitational collapse. Dust and gas from the star's outer layers hurtle through space at up to 30,000 kilometres per second.

Brown dwarf

HIGH-MASS STARS

The rarest star
Supergiants are among the rarest types of stars, and can be as large as our entire solar system. Supergiants can also be tens of thousands of times brighter than the Sun and have radii of up to a thousand times that of the Sun. Supergiants are above the main sequence on the Hertzsprung-Russell Diagram, occurring when the hydrogen of main sequence stars like the Sun has been depleted.

> ❝ There may be as many as 10 billion trillion stars in the 100 billion galaxies throughout the universe ❞

star born?

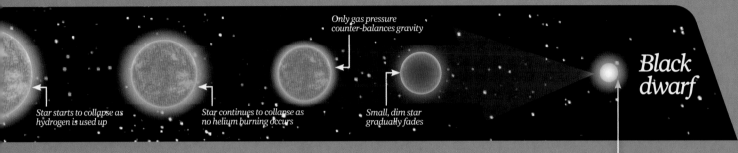

Only gas pressure counter-balances gravity

Star starts to collapse as hydrogen is used up

Star continues to collapse as no helium burning occurs

Small, dim star gradually fades

Black dwarf

Catch a dying star

White dwarfs are considered the final phase in a star's life cycle unless it attained enough mass to supernova (and more than 95 percent of stars don't). The cores of white dwarfs typically comprise carbon and oxygen, left over after the gas is used up during nuclear fusion and occurring after a main sequence star has gone through its giant phase. A white dwarf is small, with a volume comparable to that of Earth's, but incredibly dense, with a mass about that of the Sun's. With no energy left, a white dwarf is dim and cool in comparison to larger types of stars.

The stellar remnant

Black dwarfs are the hypothetical next stage of star degeneration after the white dwarf stage, when they become sufficiently cool to no longer emit any heat or light. Because the time required for a white dwarf to reach this state is postulated to be longer than the current age of the universe, none are expected to exist yet. If one were to exist it would be, by its own definition, difficult to locate and image due to the lack of emitted radiation.

White dwarf

Black dwarf

Beyond the supernova

A hypernova is a supernova taken to an even larger degree. Supergiant stars with masses that are more than 100 times that of the Sun are thought to have these massive explosions. If a supergiant were close to Earth and exploded into a hypernova, the resulting radiation could lead to a mass extinction.

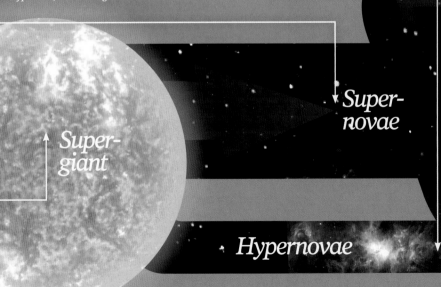

Neutron star

Super-giant

Super-novae

Hypernovae

The neutron dance

Neutron stars are a potential next stage in the life cycle of a star. If the mass that remains after a supernova is up to three times that of the Sun, it becomes a neutron star. This means that the star only consists of neutrons, particles that don't carry an electrical charge.

The absence of light

Stellar black holes are thought to be the end of the life cycle for supergiant stars with masses more than three times that of our Sun. After supernova, some of these stars leave remnants so heavy that they continue to remain gravitationally unstable.

Black hole

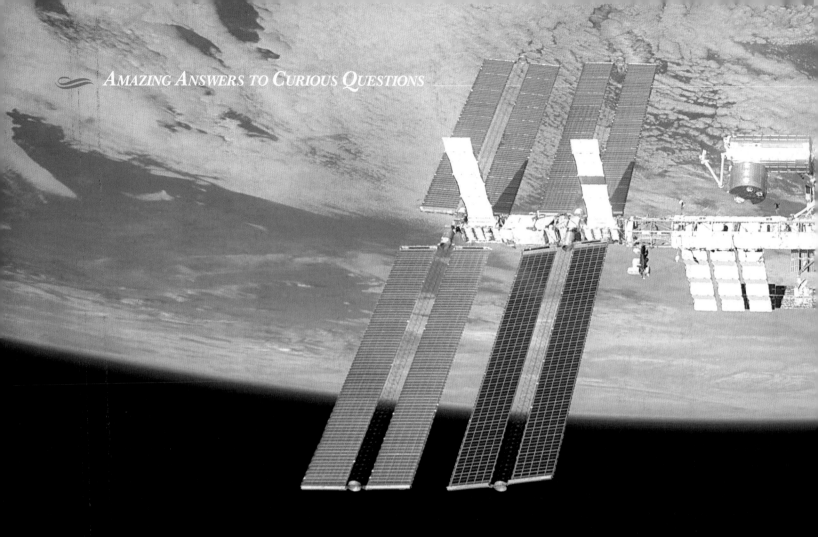

What's it like to

How astronauts and cosmonauts live on the ISS

Man has had a continuous presence in space since 2000 on the International Space Station. In 1998, the Zarya module was launched into orbit by the Russian Federal Space Agency. This was the first piece of the ISS. Now that it is complete but for one more module, the ISS is the largest satellite to ever orbit the Earth. Due to be finished in 2012, the ISS is the most expensive object to ever be constructed.

The ISS wasn't the first space station, however; in 1971 the Soviet Union launched the Salyut, which was the first in a series of space stations. Two years later, NASA launched Skylab. However, both of these programmes were single modules with limited life spans. In 1986, the Soviet Union launched the Mir, which was intended to be built upon and added to over time. The United States planned to launch its own space station, Freedom, but budgetary restraints ended the project. After the fall of the Soviet Union, the United States began negotiating with Russia, and several other countries, to build a multinational space station.

Until Expedition 20 in May 2009, crews on the International Space Station consisted of two-to-three astronauts and cosmonauts, who stayed for six months. Now the ISS is large enough to support a six-man crew, the stay has been reduced to just three months. The current ISS crew is a crew of five: ESA commander Frank De Winne, NASA flight engineer Jeffrey N Williams, CSA flight engineer Robert Thirsk and cosmonauts Maxim Suraev and Roman Romanenko.

The crew typically works for ten hours a day during the week and five hours on Saturdays. During their eight scheduled night hours, the crew sleeps in cabins while attached to bunk beds, or in sleeping bags that are secured to the wall. They also have to wear sleep masks, as it would be difficult to sleep otherwise with a sunrise occurring every 90 minutes.

All food is processed so it is easy to reheat in a special oven, usually with the addition of water. This includes beverages, which the crew drinks with straws from plastic bags. Exercise is a very important part of daily life for the crew of the ISS

because of microgravity's adverse effects on the body. The astronauts and cosmonauts may experience muscle atrophy, bone loss, a weakened immune system and a slowed cardiovascular system, among various other problems. To help counteract this, the crew exercises while strapped to treadmills and exercise bicycles.

Research is the main reason for the station's existence in low Earth orbit (about 330 kilometres above the planet's surface). Several scientific experiments spanning fields including astronomy, physics, materials science, earth science and biology take place on the station simultaneously. For example, US astronauts are currently conducting about ten different experiments, with an additional five automated experiments. They are also partnering on more than 20 manned and automated experiments with astronauts and cosmonauts from other countries.

Since 1998, more than 130 experiments have been conducted on the ISS, and each month brings more published research too.

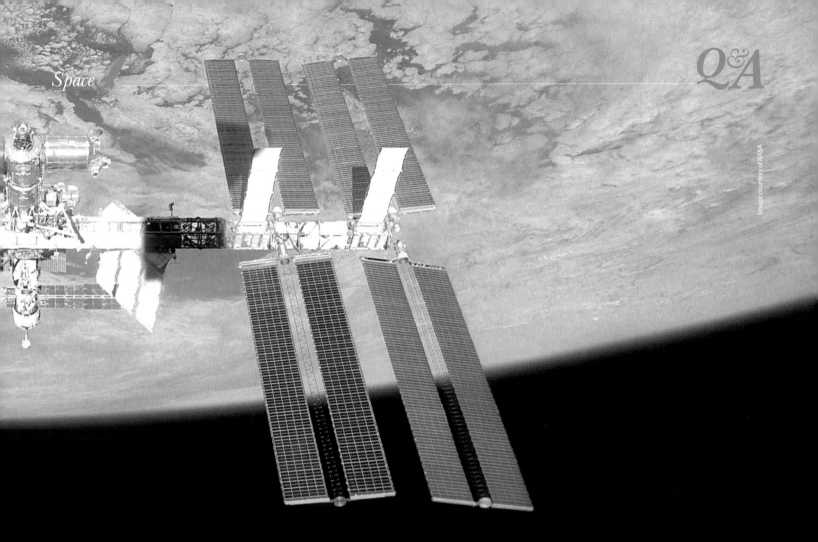

Image courtesy of NASA

live in space?

One of the overarching research goals for the station is to learn about the long-term effects of space on the human body. Many of the experiments also study the different ways things react in a low gravity, low temperature environment. There is also an experiment involving the use of ultrasounds so that remote doctors can diagnose medical problems (there is no doctor on the ISS), with the hopes that the technology can also be used on Earth.

The ISS is now all but complete. The only component yet to be added is Russia's Nauka module, planned to launch in mid-2012. With funding and interest remaining high, it is expected that the ISS will continue operation until at least 2020. ✿

What is the Zvezda Service Module?

Transfer compartment
The transfer compartment contains three docking ports. Currently it is docked with the Pirs and the Poisk.

Transfer chamber
This chamber contains computers and docking equipment. It can be used to dock with spacecrafts.

External handrails
The handrails are used during spacewalks, or extra-vehicular activity (EVA).

© ESA, D. Ducros

Facilities
The Zvezda contains a toilet and hygiene facilities, as well as a kitchen with freezer and refrigerator.

Work compartment
Two crew members live, sleep, work and exercise in this compartment.

> *"One of the overarching research goals for the station is to learn about the long-term effects of space on the human body "*

What's in the Columbus Module?

The Columbus is a research laboratory designed by the ESA – its largest contribution to the ISS

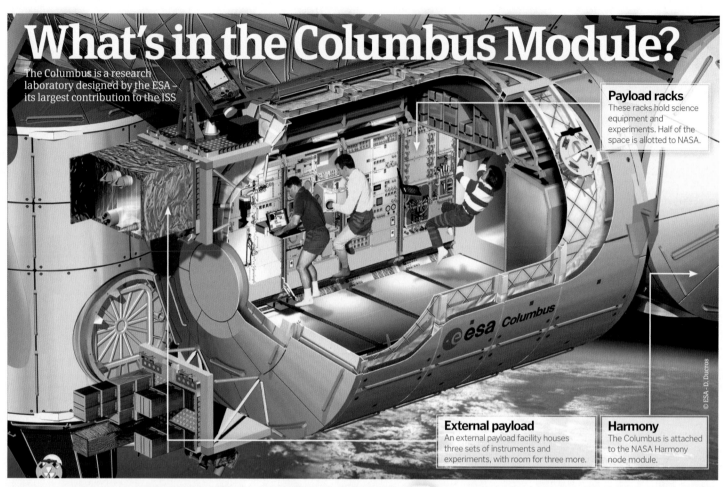

Payload racks
These racks hold science equipment and experiments. Half of the space is allotted to NASA.

External payload
An external payload facility houses three sets of instruments and experiments, with room for three more.

Harmony
The Columbus is attached to the NASA Harmony node module.

© ESA - D. Ducros

What's the ATV Dock?

The Automated Transfer Vehicle (ATV) is an expendable unmanned resupply vehicle developed by the ESA

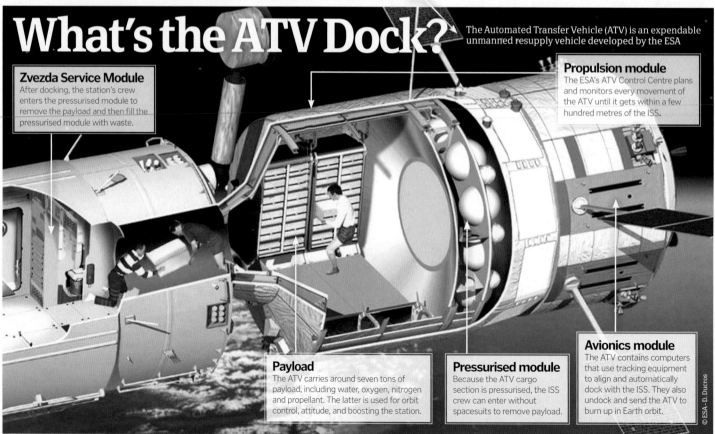

Zvezda Service Module
After docking, the station's crew enters the pressurised module to remove the payload and then fill the pressurised module with waste.

Propulsion module
The ESA's ATV Control Centre plans and monitors every movement of the ATV until it gets within a few hundred metres of the ISS.

Payload
The ATV carries around seven tons of payload, including water, oxygen, nitrogen and propellant. The latter is used for orbit control, attitude, and boosting the station.

Pressurised module
Because the ATV cargo section is pressurised, the ISS crew can enter without spacesuits to remove payload.

Avionics module
The ATV contains computers that use tracking equipment to align and automatically dock with the ISS. They also undock and send the ATV to burn up in Earth orbit.

© ESA - D. Ducros

What's what on the ISS?

The ISS in early construction while in orbit in 1999

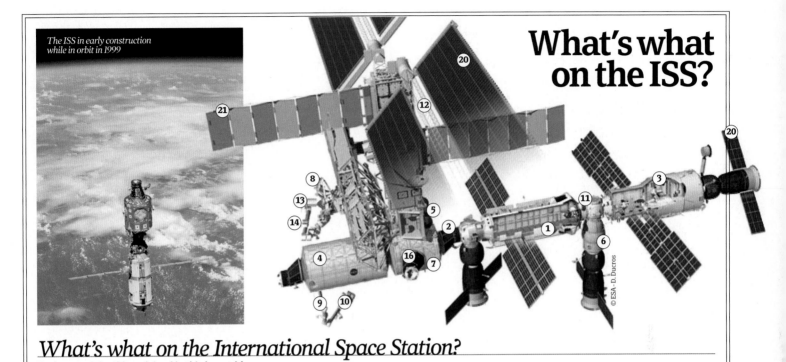

© ESA - D. Ducros

What's what on the International Space Station?

Each part of the ISS explained in this key guide

1. Zarya
The Zarya, launched in 1998 and built by the RKA, is now a storage component. As the first module it provided storage, power and propulsion.

2. Unity
Built by NASA and launched in 1998, Unity was the first node module to connect to the Zarya. It provides a docking station for other modules.

3. Zvezda
The RKA-built Zvezda launched in 2000. It made the ISS habitable by providing crew cabins and environmental control as well as other systems.

4. Destiny
The Destiny is a NASA laboratory. Launched back in 2001, it also contains environmental controls and works as a mounting point for the Integrated Truss Structure.

5. Quest
The 2001 NASA-built Quest is an airlock used to host spacewalks. The equipment lock is used for storing the spacesuits, while the crew lock allows exit to space.

6. Pirs
A mini-research module called Pirs was launched in 2001 by the RKA. It can dock spacecraft and also host spacewalks by cosmonauts.

7. Harmony
Harmony, built by NASA in 2007, is a node module. It serves as a berthing point and docking station for modules and spacecraft.

8. Columbus
The Columbus, launched in 2008, is an ESA laboratory specifically designed for experiments in biology and physics. It provides power to experiments mounted to its exterior.

9. Kibo Experiment Logistics Module
This JAXA module (also known as JEM-ELM) is part of the Japanese Experiment Module laboratory and was launched in 2008. It contains transportation and storage.

10. Kibo Pressurised Module
Also launched in 2008, the JEM-PM is a research facility and the largest module on the ISS. It has an external platform and robotic arm for experiments.

11. Poisk
The RKA-built Poisk (MRM2) launched in November 2009. In addition to housing components for experiments, it serves as a dock for spacecraft and a spacewalk airlock.

12. Integrated Truss Structure
The ISS's solar arrays and thermal radiators are mounted to this structure, which is more than 100 metres long and has ten separate parts.

13. Mobile Servicing System
Also known as the Canadarm2, this CSA-built robotic system used to move supplies, service equipment and assist astronauts on spacewalks.

14. Special Purpose Dexterous Manipulator
The SPDM, or Dextre, is a robot built by the CSA and is extremely dextrous. It can perform functions outside the ISS that had previously required spacewalks to happen.

15. Tranquillity
The Tranquillity is NASA's third node module, launched in February 2010. It contains the ECLSS as well as berthing stations for other modules.

16. Cupola
The seven windows of this observatory module, launched with Tranquility in February 2010, make it the largest window ever used in space.

17. Rassvet
Launched in May 2010, this second RKA mini-research module also serves as storage.

18. Leonardo
A pressurised multipurpose module, the Leonardo will launch in September 2010. It will serve as a storage unit and free up space in the Columbus.

19. Nauka (MLM)
Scheduled to be launched by the RKA in May 2012, this multipurpose research module will be a rest area for the crew as well as doubling up as a research laboratory too.

20. Solar Arrays
These arrays convert sunlight into electricity. There are four pairs on the ISS.

21. Thermal Radiators
The Active Thermal Control System (ATCS) removes excess heat from the ISS and vents it out into space via these radiators.

> ## "A series of complex treaties and agreements govern the ownership, use and maintenance of the station"

Who built the ISS?

The ISS currently comprises ten different modules and an Integrated Truss Structure. The modules are contributions from the Russian Federal Space Agency (RKA), NASA, the Japanese Aerospace Exploration Agency (JAXA), the Canadian Space Agency (CSA) and the European Space Agency (ESA), which includes 18 member countries. A series of complex treaties and agreements govern the ownership, use and maintenance of the station. When completed, there will be 16 different modules.

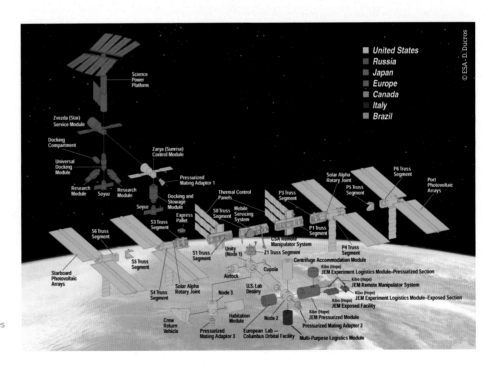

© ESA - D. Ducros

- United States
- Russia
- Japan
- Europe
- Canada
- Italy
- Brazil

What's inside the Sun?

The giant star that keeps us all alive...

A celestial wonder, the Sun is a huge star formed from a massive gravitational collapse when space dust and gas from a nebula collided, It became an orb 100 times bigger and weighing over 300,000 times that of Earth. Made up of 70 per cent hydrogen and about 28 per cent helium (plus other gasses), the Sun is the centre of our solar system and the largest celestial body anywhere near us.

"The surface of the Sun is a dense layer of plasma at a temperature of 5,800 degrees kelvin that is continually moving due to the action of convective motions driven by heating from below," says David Alexander, a professor of physics and astronomy at Rice University. "These convective motions show up as a distribution of what are called granulation cells about 1,000 kilometres across and which appear across the whole solar surface."

At its core, the Sun's temperature and pressure are so high and the hydrogen atoms are moving so fast that it causes fusion, turning hydrogen atoms into helium. Electromagnetic radiation travels out from the Sun's core to its surface, escaping into space as electromagnetic radiation, a blinding light, and incredible levels of solar heat. In fact, the core of the Sun is actually hotter than the surface, but when heat escapes from the surface, the temperature rises to over 1-2 million degrees. Alexander explained that astronomers do not fully understand why the Sun's atmosphere is so hot, but think it has something to do with magnetic fields. ✿

Radiative zone
The first 500,000k of the Sun is a radioactive layer that transfers energy from the core, mostly toward the outer layers, passed from atom to atom.

> « *When heat escapes from the surface, the temperature rises to over 1-2 million degrees* »

Sun's core
The core of the Sun is an extremely hot region – about 15 million degrees – that produces a nuclear fusion and emits heat through the layers of the Sun to the surface.

Convective zone
The top 30 per cent of the Sun is a layer of hot plasma that is constantly in motion, heated from below.

All images courtesy of NASA

Right conditions
The core of the Sun, which acts like a nuclear reactor, is just the right size and temperature to produce light.

Engine room
The centre of a star is like an engine room that produces the nuclear fusion required for radiation and light.

How does the Sun affect the Earth's magnetic field?

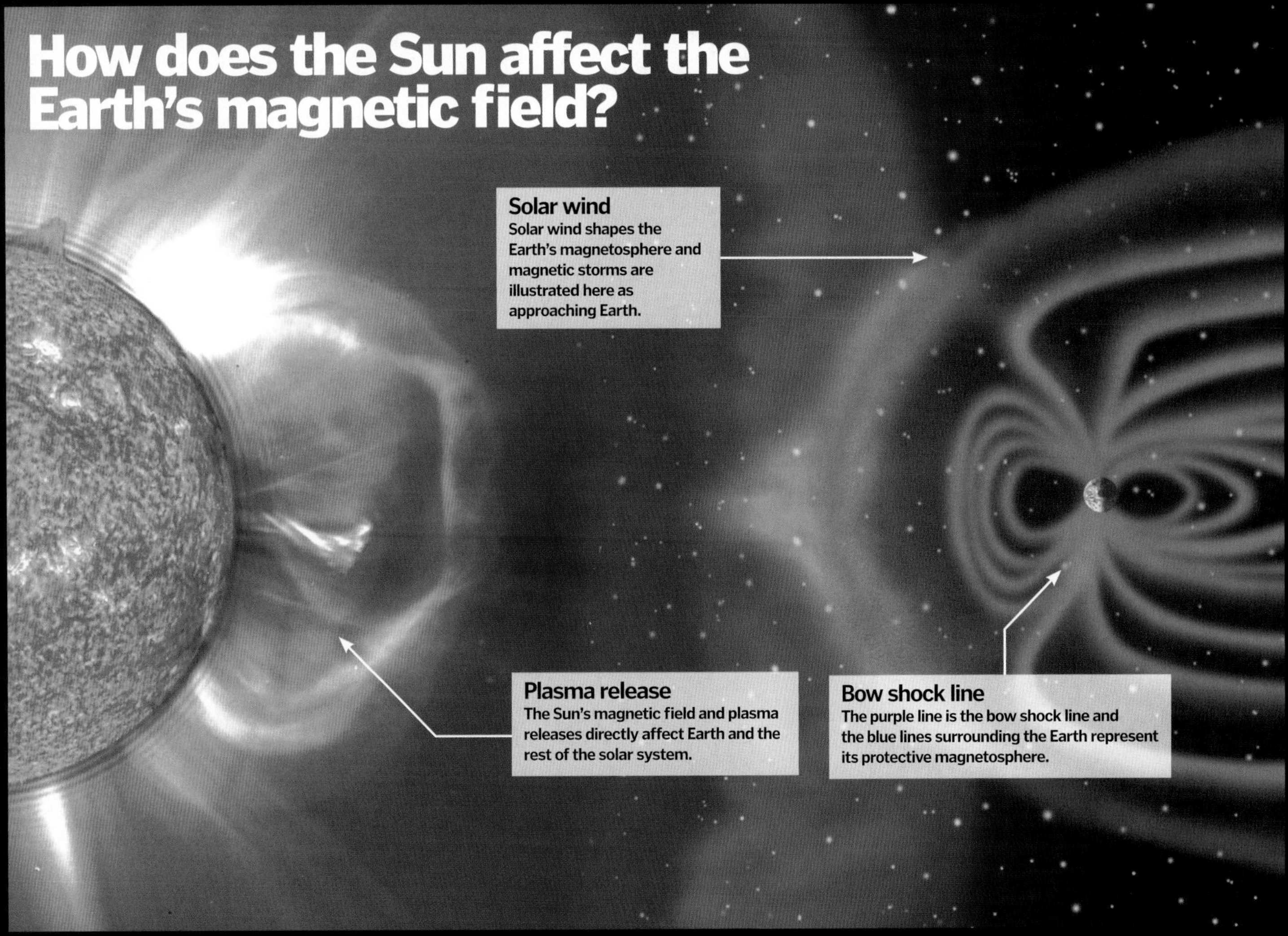

Solar wind
Solar wind shapes the Earth's magnetosphere and magnetic storms are illustrated here as approaching Earth.

Plasma release
The Sun's magnetic field and plasma releases directly affect Earth and the rest of the solar system.

Bow shock line
The purple line is the bow shock line and the blue lines surrounding the Earth represent its protective magnetosphere.

What is a sunspot?

Signifying cooler areas, sunspots show up as dark dots on the photosphere (the visible layer of plasma across the Sun's surface). These 'cool' regions – about 1,000 degrees cooler than the surface temperature – are associated with strong magnetic fields. Criss-crossing magnetic-field lines can disturb the flow of heat from the core, creating pockets of intense activity. The build up of heat around a sunspot can be released as a solar flare or coronal mass ejection, which is separate to but often accompanies larger flares. Plasma from a CME ejects from the Sun at over 1 million miles per hour.

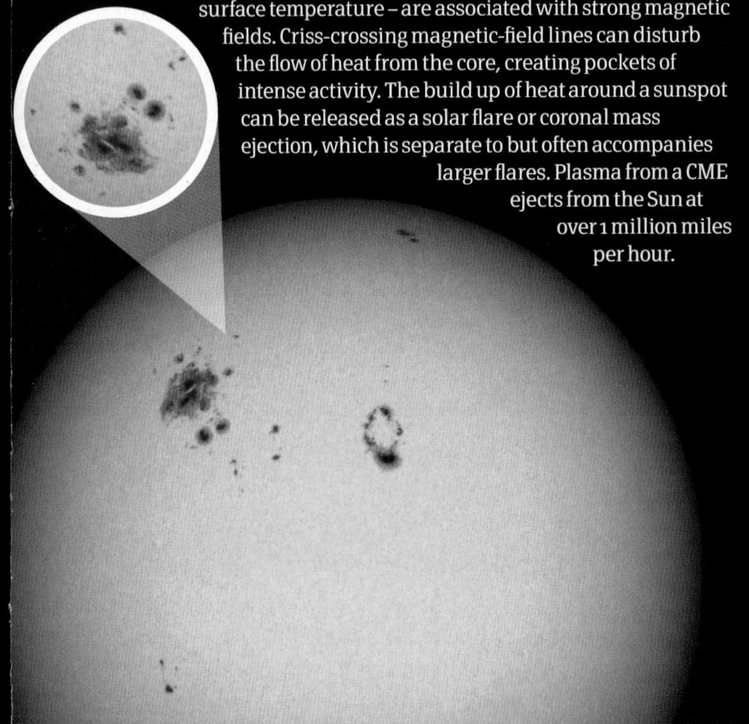

What is a solar flare?

A massive explosion, but one that happens to be several million degrees in temperature...

"A solar flare is a rapid release of energy in the solar atmosphere (mostly the chromosphere and corona) resulting in localised heating of plasma to tens of millions of degrees, acceleration of electrons and protons to high energies, some to near the speed of light, and expulsion of material into space," says Alexander. "These electromagnetic disturbances here on Earth pose potential dangers for Earth-orbiting satellites, space-walking astronauts, crews on high-altitude spacecraft, and power grids on Earth."

Solar flares can cause geomagnetic storms on the Sun, including shock waves and plasma expulsions

What makes a failed star?

These 'sub-stellar' objects are barely bigger than planets, so what makes brown dwarfs stellar at all?

It's a conundrum that's racked the field of astronomy for the last 30 years – is a brown dwarf star really a star at all? Since they don't have the mass to initiate nuclear fusion like a normal star during its formation, they're often referred to as 'failed stars'. With masses that range from just a few times larger than our solar system's gas giant Jupiter, to around 75 times its size, brown dwarfs are often considered to be the missing link between gas giant planets and red dwarf stars – the smallest known 'true stars'.

Measuring or even discovering the presence of a brown dwarf star is notoriously difficult because they're so cool and small, so scientists use the presence of lithium as a determining factor. The presence of lithium is actually common in all young stars, but is usually burnt up in the first 100 million years of its life. Since the core of a brown dwarf isn't hot enough to get rid of the lithium it's a very useful indicator in labelling low-mass stellar objects 'brown dwarf stars'. ✿

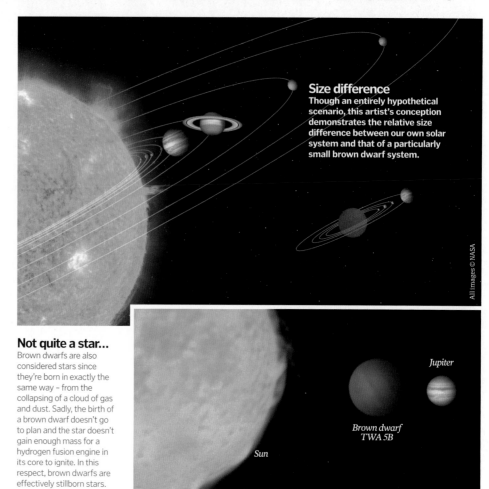

All images © NASA

Size difference
Though an entirely hypothetical scenario, this artist's conception demonstrates the relative size difference between our own solar system and that of a particularly small brown dwarf system.

Not quite a star…
Brown dwarfs are also considered stars since they're born in exactly the same way – from the collapsing of a cloud of gas and dust. Sadly, the birth of a brown dwarf doesn't go to plan and the star doesn't gain enough mass for a hydrogen fusion engine in its core to ignite. In this respect, brown dwarfs are effectively stillborn stars.

Jupiter

Brown dwarf TWA 5B

Sun

What is the Goldilocks Zone?

Life-sustaining planets require such exacting standards that scientists call the area they occupy 'the Goldilocks Zone'

Solar systems must be in the right place in the galaxy to sustain the formation of terrestrial planets, but not receive high doses of radiation

If the Earth had formed just a few percentage points closer or further from the Sun, it would be either covered in ice or have no oceans

The Goldilocks Zone is an area 'just right' for a life-sustaining planet – the perfect distance from a star with a surface neither too hot nor too cold. It is an intersection of life-sustaining regions within both a solar system and a galaxy. Astronomers believe that the Goldilocks Zone ranges from 0.725 to three astronomical units (each about 150 million kilometres, or the mean distance between the Earth and the Sun).

Recently some planetary bodies have come close to fitting the bill. The April 2007 discovery of Gliese 581c in the Libra constellation, for example, seemed promising until further research proved it was too hot. However, a nearby planet, Gliese 581d, may turn out to be just right. At the same time, the definition of the Goldilocks Zone is expanding as scientists discover life on Earth in places previously thought too extreme to sustain it. ✿

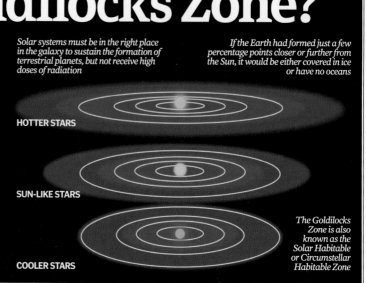

HOTTER STARS

SUN-LIKE STARS

COOLER STARS

The Goldilocks Zone is also known as the Solar Habitable or Circumstellar Habitable Zone

Inside a 100-foot diameter vacuum chamber, NASA researchers successfully deploy ten-metre solar sails along delicate, but rigid extendible booms

Image courtesy of NASA

How do solar sails work?

A cosmic kite blown by photons is our greatest hope for interstellar travel

When the Space Shuttle fuels up for a short commute to the International Space Station, 95 per cent of its weight is in the gas tank. The sheer weight of rocket fuel is one of the greatest obstacles to interstellar space travel. That's why space futurists are so excited about solar sails, a 'fuel-free' craft powered by beams of sunlight.

Sunlight travels in packets of energy called photons. When a photon reflects off a mirrored surface, it imparts two minuscule taps of energy: once during the initial impact and once as it's reflected. For decades, scientists theorised that if you could make a reflective surface big enough and light enough, it could be nudged through space by a constant barrage of photons. That theory was tested in 2010, when the Planetary Society, co-founded by the late Carl Sagan, launched a 350-square-foot solar sail made of aluminised Mylar (1/5,000 of an inch thick) into space.

Solar sails don't have dramatic blast-offs, but rely on a more patient form of power: constant acceleration. A massive solar sail of 600,000 square metres would accelerate at an underwhelming one millimetre per second. After a day, however, the sail would be moving at a rate of 310kps (195mph). After 12 days, it would reach 3,700kps (2,300mph).

Imagine its velocity after six months – enough, scientists hope, to sail out of our solar system into the great beyond. ✲

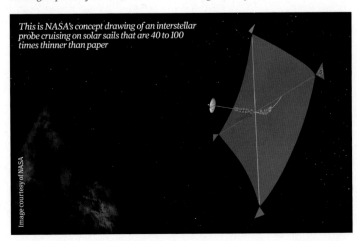
This is NASA's concept drawing of an interstellar probe cruising on solar sails that are 40 to 100 times thinner than paper

Image courtesy of NASA

When will we see Halley's Comet again?

Closest approach to Sun: 88 million km (55 million miles)
Furthest distance from Sun: 5.3 billion km (3.3 billion miles)
Orbital period: About 76 years
First recorded: 240 BC
Last recorded: 1986
Next appearance: 2061
Diameter: 16 x 8 x 7km
Mass: 2.2 x 10^14 kilograms

What is Halley's Comet?

The details on this fiery ball and why it returns to the night sky

Comets are dirty snowballs made of dust and ice left behind when our solar system formed. Halley's Comet is the best-known short period comet – a comet that has orbited around the Sun more than once in recorded history.

Comets' orbits can be tilted at a large angle relative to the orbits of the planets. Halley's Comet's orbit is so tilted it looks to orbit backwards compared to the planets. Its orbit is also very elongated so the distance between Halley's Comet and the Sun changes dramatically as it travels.

When the comet is far from the Sun, it's a frozen ball called a nucleus. As it comes closer, it heats up and spews out dust and gas to form a glowing cloud – the coma – and long tail. Each time Halley's Comet returns towards the Sun, it loses more ice until, eventually, there will be too little to form a tail. ✲

> ❝ *Halley's Comet's orbit is so tilted it looks to orbit backwards compared to the planets* ❞

How do the sea

Get out your torch and a beach ball – it's time to talk about tilt

The Earth is a wonky planet. Every year we make a complete near-circular revolution around the Sun, but every day our planet spins around a lopsided axis. This imaginary line that runs through the centre of the planet from the North Pole to the South Pole is tilted at a 23.5° angle, and this wonky tilt is the reason for the seasons.

During June and July in the northern hemisphere, the North Pole is tilted toward the Sun and South Pole tilted away. This means that solar radiation hits the northern hemisphere "head on" and is absorbed in a more concentrated area. Because the southern hemisphere is angled away from the Sun, the same amount of solar radiation is spread across a much larger surface area.

But differences in solar intensity aren't enough to create summer and winter. The tilt of the axis also creates radical differences in the length of solar exposure, what we define as daylight. If we go back to our June and July example, the northern hemisphere is directly facing the Sun, which means the Sun carves a high path across the sky, creating longer daylight hours. In the southern hemisphere, the Sun travels much closer to the horizon, which limits daylight hours significantly.

The combination of longer days and concentrated sunlight gives us summer. Shorter days and dispersed solar energy gives us winter. Autumn and spring mark the transitional periods when days are getting longer or shorter and temperature variations tend to be less extreme. ✿

3. Summer solstice
On roughly 21 June, the North Pole tilts the closest to the Sun, bathing the northern hemisphere in summer and the southern hemisphere in winter.

2. Tilted axis
The seasons are powered by the angle of the Earth's axis, which tilts 23.5 degrees away from being perfectly perpendicular with its orbital plane.

1. Revolution
The Earth travels in an elliptical orbit around the Sun, but the path is nearly circular, meaning our distance from the Sun is relatively constant year-round.

1. The tropics
All year long, the region within the tropics of Cancer and Capricorn receives the most direct and intense sunlight.

2. Concentrated surface area
Since the Sun's rays strike the region around the equator at nearly a 90˚ angle, the intensity of the radiation is concentrated on a relatively small surface area.

3. Scattered surface area
Near the poles, the Sun's angle of incidence is much lower, meaning solar radiation scatters across a much larger surface area, losing its intensity.

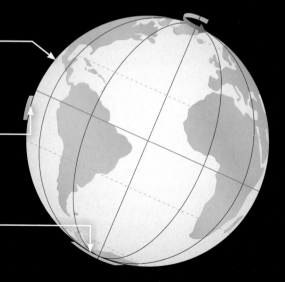

sons work?

5. Vernal equinox
At this point in the orbit, the Sun shines evenly across the entire face of the Earth, neutralising the effect of the tilted axis.

4. Winter solstice
At the opposite end of the Earth's orbit, it's the southern hemisphere's turn to receive the most direct sunlight while Europe and the United States enter winter.

The cycle of seasons

The seasons correspond not only to the Earth's position in orbit around the Sun, but your physical location on the Earth. At different times of the year, different parts of the planet receive more direct sunlight and longer days (spring and summer), while others receive less direct sunlight and shorter days (fall and winter).

6. Autumnal equinox
As with the vernal equinox, the first day of autumn has exactly 12 hours of daylight and 12 hours of darkness.

> *« The planet is tilted at a 23.5-degree angle, and this wonky tilt is the reason for the seasons »*

Why is it hotter at the Equator?

It gets hotter as you move closer to the equator because the region between the tropic of Cancer and the tropic of Capricorn receives more direct and concentrated solar radiation.

The reason for this is not because the tropics are 'closer' to the Sun than other parts of the planet. It has to do

with something called the 'angle of incidence'. During the vernal and autumnal equinoxes, the Sun's rays strike the equator at a precise 90º angle. Since the solar radiation rains down on the Earth so directly, its intensity is concentrated in a relatively small area. Compare this with the solar

exposure of Iceland, which sits right on the Arctic circle at roughly 66 degrees north of the equator. During the autumnal equinox, the Sun's rays hit Iceland on a much shallower angle of 70 degrees, spreading their radiation across a much larger surface area, thereby decreasing their intensity.

Solstice vs equinox

The winter solstice is commonly referred to as the "shortest day of the year". Although 21 December is still 24 hours long, it has the fewest hours of sunlight. On this day, the North Pole is tilted the furthest from the Sun, causing the Sun to trace a low path in the sky. As the months pass, the Sun's course drifts upward until we reach the vernal equinox, a day with exactly 12 hours of light and 12 hours of darkness. Around 21 June, the North Pole tilts closest to the Sun, the Sun rides high in the sky and we have the summer solstice, the longest day of the year. As the Sun's path sinks back toward the horizon, we reach the autumnal equinox, the second time all year when day and night are perfectly equal.

Seasons at the top of the world

For people living at the equator, seasons are virtually meaningless. The closer you are to the equator, the less your weather is affected by the tilt of the Earth. If you tilt a globe back and forth, the top and bottom appear to move further away from you, while the middle will remain relatively central.

In high-latitude regions the differences between seasons are extreme. In the dead of winter in northern Norway, the northern hemisphere is tilted so far away from the Sun that it doesn't peak over the horizon for two months. In the middle of summer, the Sun travels directly overhead, tracing a loop through the sky that holds back the night for 2.5 months.

Are all galaxies the same?

They might be grouped like a galactic tuning fork, but galaxy types don't always sing from the same hymn sheet

There are several galaxy classification systems, but the most widely used is the Hubble Sequence, devised by the great Edwin Hubble in 1926 and later expanded upon by Allan Sandage among others. It's more commonly known as the Hubble tuning fork due to the shape the system represents in diagrammatic form.

Hubble's system was designed to demonstrate the various classifications of three main classes of galaxy broken down into elliptical, spiral and lenticular shapes. The latter is essentially an intermediate of the other two types. The tuning fork was erroneously thought that each galaxy type represented snapshots of the entire life span of galaxies, but it has since been demonstrated that this is not the case.

The most recent version of Hubble's tuning fork comes courtesy of the Spitzer Space Telescope's infrared galaxy survey made up of 75 colour images of different galaxies and includes a new sub-section of irregular galaxy types. You can find a full resolution image of this remarkable accomplishment at **sings.stsci.edu/ Publications/sings_poster. html**. Thanks to the internet, anyone can try their hand at galaxy classification and further the science – simply go to **www.galaxyzoo.org** and join in alongside 150,000 other volunteers. ✿

All images © NASA

How are galaxies classified?

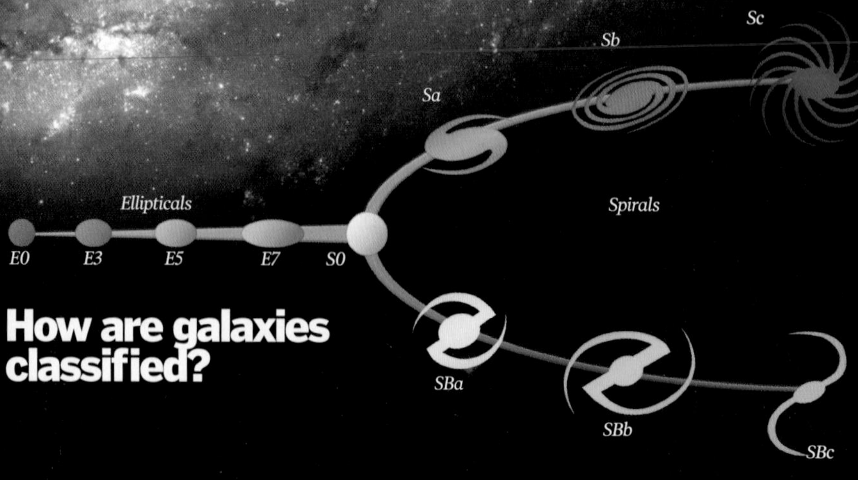

Ellipticals

E0   E3   E5   E7   S0

Sa

Sb

Sc

Spirals

SBa

SBb

SBc

Types of galaxies
Galaxies can be categorised into these types...

Elliptical galaxies
On the far left of the Hubble Sequence lies the elliptical galaxy types. They show no defined features like the intricate dust lanes seen in classic spiral galaxy types, besides a bright core. Ellipticals are represented by the letter E, followed by a number that represents the ellipticity of its shape.

Spiral types
Appearing flatter on the sky than an elliptical galaxy, spiral galaxies feature two or more spiral 'arms' that wrap around the galaxy core and are made up of vast lanes of stars. The upper half is populated with the standard spiral type, while the lower half contains 'bar' spirals. The twist of the spiral begins at the end of an extended bar.

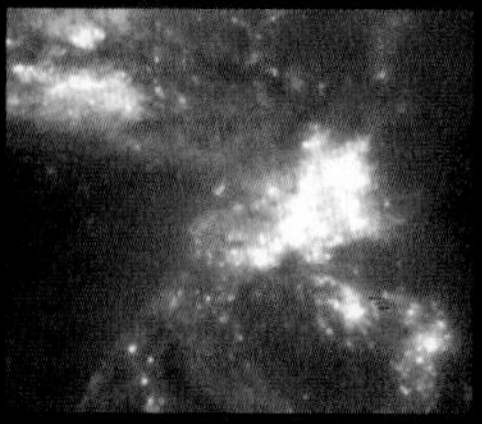

Lenticular galaxies
Where the handle of the tuning fork and the two spiral arms meet lie the lenticular galaxies. These galaxies feature aspects of both spiral and elliptical galaxies and didn't actually feature on Hubble's original sequence. They have a bright central bulge like an elliptical galaxy, but are surrounded by a structure not unlike a disc.

Who was Edwin Hubble?

No person in history has had a greater impact in determining the extent of our universe than Edwin Hubble. From proving that other galaxies existed to giving evidence that galaxies move apart from one another, Hubble's work defined our place in the cosmos. Shown here posing with the 48-inch telescope on Palomar Mountain, the Orbiting Space Telescope was named in memory of his great work.

Today a great controversy rages on about the rate of the universe's expansion, parameterised by a quantity known as Hubble's Constant.

Why does night follow day?

The seemingly straightforward phenomenon that we call night and day is anything but simple

What we term 'night and day' is a phenomenon known as rotation. The Earth rotates around its axis, an imaginary line that extends from its North Pole to its South Pole, once every 24 hours. This axis of our planet is tipped at an angle of about 23.5 degrees from the vertical.

As the Earth rotates, the part of it illuminated by the Sun experiences daytime, while the dark part experiences night. When the Sun appears above the horizon in the east and sinks below it in west, we call this sunrise and sunset. But this is an illusion created by the Earth's counter-clockwise rotation – because of course the Sun isn't actually rising or sinking at all.

True solar time is based on the apparent motion of the Sun as we observe it, as with a sundial. This measurement varies from day to day because of the Earth's elliptical orbit – it rotates faster when closer to the Sun and slower when further away from it. The tilt of Earth's axis also means that true solar days are shorter at some times of the year and longer at others. A mean solar day is an average so that all of our days are of equal length. This is the time we use to set our clocks. Sidereal time takes into account how long it takes the Earth to rotate with respect to the apparent movement of the stars instead of the Sun. A sidereal day is about four minutes shorter than a mean solar day. Astronomers use sidereal time to determine the placement of the stars in the sky at any given time.

Although a rotation of the Earth takes 24 hours, that doesn't mean that daytime and nighttime are each 12 hours long. On average, nights are shorter than days. This is due to the Sun's apparent size in our sky as well as the way that our atmosphere refracts sunlight. The lengths of our days and nights depend on our location on the Earth's surface as well as the time of year. ✿

How do you weigh planets?

It seems like an impossible task, but how can scientists use an orbiting moon to work out the weight of a planet?

Newton's Law of Gravitation states that every planetary body has its own gravitational field that pulls on nearby objects – such as moons or spacecraft – with a force proportional to its mass and inversely proportional to the square of the distance between the two objects. Newton also discovered that an object – a moon, for instance – will move at a constant speed and in a straight line unless acted upon by a force such as gravity that will keep the moon in orbit.

By observing the effect of a planet's gravitational attraction on an orbiting moon, scientists can measure the planet's mass. The gravitational attraction between the moon and the planet depends on their mass and the distance between their centres. The heavier the planet, the stronger its attraction to the moon and the faster the moon will travel. Measuring the distance from the planet to the moon and calculating how long it takes to orbit enables astronomers to calculate the weight of a planet. ✿

How is day and night explained

This image shows the Earth's axis is tilted towards the Sun during the summer, or northern solstice. This occurs around 21 June and changes the lengths of nights and days depending on where you live. The five major circles of latitude mark the shifts in length.

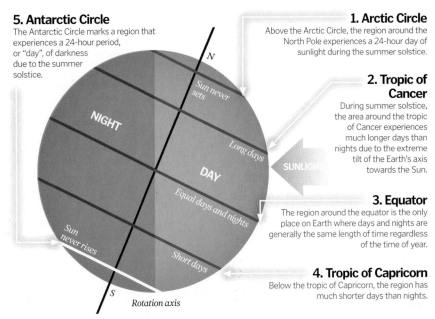

5. Antarctic Circle
The Antarctic Circle marks a region that experiences a 24-hour period, or "day", of darkness due to the summer solstice.

1. Arctic Circle
Above the Arctic Circle, the region around the North Pole experiences a 24-hour day of sunlight during the summer solstice.

2. Tropic of Cancer
During summer solstice, the area around the tropic of Cancer experiences much longer days than nights due to the extreme tilt of the Earth's axis towards the Sun.

3. Equator
The region around the equator is the only place on Earth where days and nights are generally the same length of time regardless of the time of year.

4. Tropic of Capricorn
Below the tropic of Capricorn, the region has much shorter days than nights.

N

Sun never sets

NIGHT

Long days

DAY

SUNLIGHT

Equal days and nights

Sun never rises

Short days

S

Rotation axis

What's inside a black hole?

Almost incomprehensible in size, black holes are hauntingly beautiful phenomena where the laws of space and time are rewritten

A black hole is a region of space containing, at its centre, matter compressed into a point of infinite density called a singularity (an area where space-time curvature becomes infinite), which itself is surrounded by a sphere of space where the gravitational pull is so total that not even light can escape its pull – hence its name. The black hole is the result of the deformation and warping of space-time (a mathematical model where space and time are combined into a single continuum) caused by the total collapse of individual stars or by the coalescence of binary neutron stars.

This collapse occurs at the culmination of a star's life span when, under the pressure of gravity, it is compressed perpetually – unable to resist due to the nonexistence of nuclear fusion in its core – until it reaches critical mass. At this point, providing the star is over 1.4 to three solar masses (our Sun equals one solar mass) – a necessity for black hole formation instead of a white dwarf – the star will go into core-collapse supernova, expelling much of its remaining outer layers at one tenth the speed of light and leaving behind either a neutron star or, if the solar mass is high enough, a black hole. ✿

> *" A black hole is the result of the deformation and warping of space-time caused by the total collapse of individual stars or by the coalescence of binary neutron stars "*

Where's the nearest black hole?

Introducing the Sagittarius A* region, home to a supermassive black hole

At the heart of almost every galaxy lies a black hole, even our own the Milky Way, which centres on a region of space called Sagittarius A* – at the middle of which lies a supermassive black hole. Black holes like these, however, do not form directly but from the coalescence of multiple smaller stellar-mass and intermediate mass black holes, which then form a supermassive black hole such as Sagittarius A*. Supermassive black holes also often form from the slow accretion of matter from neighbouring stars, the mass collapse of large stellar gas clouds into a relativistic star (a rotating neutron star), or directly from external pressure caused by the Big Bang.

While unimaginable due to its very nature (it absorbs all light), its distance from Earth and the fact that the Sagittarius A* region is removed by 25 magnitudes of extinction from Earth (blocked from optical sight), our own supermassive black hole can only be observed by scientists through the actions of neighbouring cosmic phenomena. Indicating the presence of its existence most notably is the movement of star S2, which has been monitored by scientists following a slow elliptical orbit with a period of 15.2 years and a closest distance of less than 17 light hours from its orbit centre. From the slow motion of S2, scientists have extrapolated that the object which it is orbiting around has a solar mass of 4.1 million, which when taken with its relatively small diameter, strongly affirms that it is a black hole. No other known object can have such a large mass at such a small volume.

Sagittarius A* is a relatively small supermassive black hole when compared with others of its ilk, such as the black hole at the centre of the OJ 287 galaxy, which has a mass of 18 billion solar masses.

Sagittarius A lies at the heart of out galaxy the Milky Way. Unfortunately, from Earth Sagittarius A* is blocked from optical sight and presently scientists can only observe it through the actions of its surrounding stars*

How do scientists correlate black hole mass to stellar system mass?

1 billion

Galactic star bulges

1 million

Globular cluster G1

Globular cluster M15

1 thousand

1 million   1 billion

Stellar system mass (in solar masses)

> « *Our own supermassive black hole can only be observed by scientists through the actions of neighbouring cosmic phenomena* »

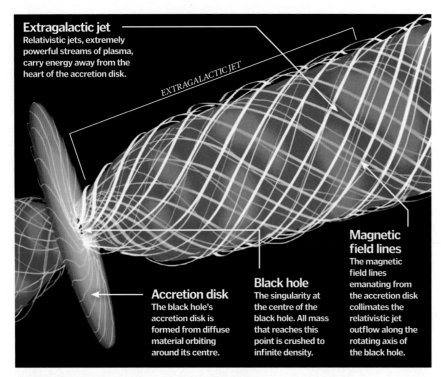

Extragalactic jet
Relativistic jets, extremely powerful streams of plasma, carry energy away from the heart of the accretion disk.

EXTRAGALACTIC JET

Magnetic field lines
The magnetic field lines emanating from the accretion disk collimates the relativistic jet outflow along the rotating axis of the black hole.

Accretion disk
The black hole's accretion disk is formed from diffuse material orbiting around its centre.

Black hole
The singularity at the centre of the black hole. All mass that reaches this point is crushed to infinite density.

What's inside our black hole?

What are its properties and structure?

To understand our Sagittarius A* black hole it is important to understand how black holes in general work. After any black hole stabilises post formation, it has only three possible independent physical properties: charge, mass and angular momentum. Now, when an object is accreted (swallowed) by a black hole its own mass, charge and momentum is equalised with the black hole's own, distributing the matter evenly along its event horizon (a one-way space-time boundary), which then oscillates like a stretchy membrane. The course that this pattern follows, however, depends on the individual black hole's properties and type.

The simplest black holes have mass but neither charge nor angular momentum, accreting mass to a point-singularity centre; however, most types of black hole formed from the core-collapse supernova of a star are thought to retain the nearly neutral charge it once possessed. Other, and theorised by scientists to be far more common, types of black holes – due to the spinning nature of stars – are rotating variants. These form from the collapse of stars or stellar gas with a total non-zero

angular momentum and can be both charged and uncharged. These black holes, unlike the totally round, static variants, bulge near their equator under the phenomenal velocity of their spin (the quicker the rotation the more deformed the black hole will be) and instead of accreting matter to a point-singularity do so to a smeared disc singularity. Eventually all black holes, however dependent on their charge or rotation, revert to a non-rotating, uncharged variant.

Unfortunately, from the measurements taken from the stars surrounding our Sagittarius A* black hole, scientists have been left unsure about its physical properties. However, recent research from the University of California, Berkeley, suggests that A* rotates once every 11 minutes or at 30 per cent the speed of light.

This information, when combined with the known proximity of the surrounding stars (a spinning black hole drags space with it, allowing atoms to orbit closer to one that is static), would seem to suggest that not only is the gravitational pull of Sagittarius A* mitigated to a degree by its rotation but also that these measurements are accurate.

How do black holes distort space and time?

The theoretical consequences of time and space distortion

The event horizon (a boundary in space-time through which matter and light can only pass through inwardly) of a black hole is one of its central characteristics, and one that brings a host of issues for any object that passes through it. As predicted by general relativity (our geometric theory on gravitation) due to the colossal mass of the black hole – which by these rules is infinite at the heart of the black hole – space-time is deformed, as mass has a direct bearing on it. Indeed, when the event horizon is passed, the mass's distortion becomes so great that particle paths are bent inwardly towards the singularity (centre) of the black hole, unable to alter their course. At this point both time and space begin to be warped.

The consequences of this, while theoretical, are mind blowing. For example, theory states that if a hypothetical astronaut were about to cross the event horizon of a black hole, then apart from being stretched physically (spaghettification), they'd also be stretched in time. So, while the astronaut would pass the event horizon at a finite point in his own time, to a hypothetical distant observer, he'd appear to slow down, taking an infinite time to reach it. Further, if the astronaut were wearing a watch, it would tick more slowly as he approached the event horizon than a watch worn by the observer, an effect known as gravitational time dilation. Finally, when the astronaut reached the singularity, he'd be crushed to infinite density and over an infinite time (to the observer) before having his mass added to that of the black hole.

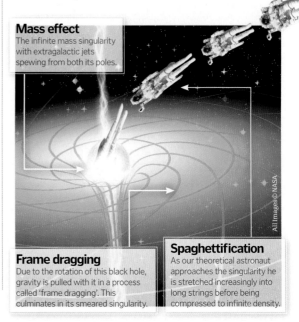

Mass effect
The infinite mass singularity with extragalactic jets spewing from both its poles.

All images © NASA

Frame dragging
Due to the rotation of this black hole, gravity is pulled with it in a process called 'frame dragging'. This culminates in its smeared singularity.

Spaghettification
As our theoretical astronaut approaches the singularity he is stretched increasingly into long strings before being compressed to infinite density.

How do ocean tides work?

Gravitational forces tip ocean waters like a bathtub

You're sitting on a beach, cooking a barbecue with the family. The Sun sets in the distance. You look around and – like the famous scene from *Chitty Chitty Bang Bang* – you're surrounded by water. The phenomenon of ocean tides is caused by gravitational forces as the Earth moves around the Sun, and the moon moves around the Earth. ✿

Earth

There are two scientific principles at work, says Iheanyi N Osondu PhD, an associate professor of geography at Fort Valley State University in Georgia. "The rotation of the Earth produces the Coriolis effect," he says. "The movement of currents of water and air is affected by Coriolis. Ferrell's law states that any object or fluid moving horizontally in the northern hemisphere is deflected to the right of its path of motion regardless of compass direction. In the southern hemisphere, it is deflected towards the left."

High tide

Moon

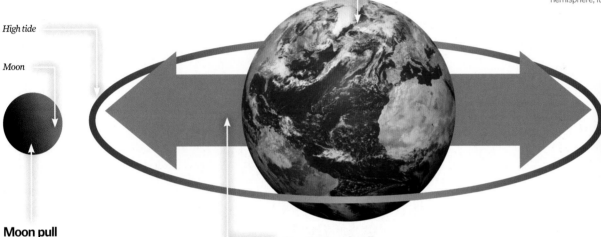

Moon pull

A second reason for ocean tides rising and lowering: the ocean tends to bulge on the side of the Earth that is closest to the moon. "The moon makes one complete rotation round the Earth every 29 and a half days," says Osondu. "On the other hand, the Sun also influences the tides. It should, however, be noted that the moon has a greater influence on tides than the Sun because it is nearer, even though the Sun is much larger."

Gravitational pull

It helps to think of the ocean as a giant bathtub filled with water: if you tipped the bathtub to one side, the water would rise. In the ocean, the water levels change when gravity pulls water to one side of the Earth, which causes the water level to lower on the other side.

Tides

There are also three kinds of tides on the planet, says Osondu. Diurnal is when the tide rises and lowers once per day, and is common in the Gulf of Mexico. Semidiurnal, common in the Atlantic coasts, has two similar tides per day. Mixed tides, where there are two dissimilar tides per day, are common in the Pacific coasts.

What's the weather like in outer space?

The weather on Earth can be terrible, but in space it can be positively cataclysmic...

Had NASA decided to launch an extra mission between Apollo 16 and 17, its astronauts would've been killed by an acute overdose of radiation caused by a solar radiation storm courtesy of a solar flare.

In extreme circumstances, you wouldn't even have to be in space to suffer the consequences of increased energetic particle activity caused by a nasty solar flare – passengers on commercial airlines would receive a unhealthy dose of radiation too. During this extreme solar weather, satellites can be rendered useless and high frequency communications would stop working near the polar caps.

Geomagnetic storms are potentially more deadly, however. Disturbances in the Earth's magnetic field caused by the Sun's solar wind have been enough to wreak havoc with power systems across the world. In 1989 an electromagnetic storm wiped most of Quebec off the power grid for nine hours. In fact, the effects were so strong auroras (the visible effects of particles interacting with the Earth's magnetic field) could be seen as far south as Texas.

There's also the thought of micrometeor showers. Space rain is actually made of tiny particles of rock and metal travelling at tens of miles per second. Micrometeoroids are remnants of the creation of the solar system and millions of them bombard the Earth from space every day. ✿

What's the forecast?

The most common forms of space weather include solar wind, raining micrometeoroids and geomagnetic storms

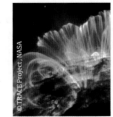

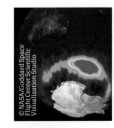

Micrometeoroids

These are only called micrometeorites once they've fallen to Earth. They can potentially destroy satellites and other space-based technology, though rarely make their way to Earth.

Solar radiation storms

Caused by solar flares rushing at the Earth, solar radiation storms could potentially kill an astronaut stone dead and even severely harm unfortunate airline passengers.

Geomagnetic storms

Ever-changing solar winds create geomagnetic storms, which could completely overload power systems and cause devastating country-wide blackouts.

What is gravity?

Surprisingly weak yet mysteriously powerful, gravity is the super glue of the universe

Everything in the universe is made of matter – the cosmic 'stuff' of creation. Mass is a measurement of the amount of matter contained in any object, from planets to protons. The Earth, for example, has a mass of 5.9742×1024 kilograms, while the mass of a single proton is $1.67262158 \times 10^{-27}$ kilograms.

When we think of gravity, we usually think of the gravitational force exerted by massive celestial bodies like the Earth, the Moon or the Sun. But the truth is that any object of any mass – even a sub-atomic particle – exerts a gravitational pull on nearby objects.

Sir Isaac Newton proved that objects of greater mass exert a stronger gravitational force. That's why we typically talk about gravity in reference to planets and not protons. But the shocking truth about gravity is that even a colossal hunk of rock like the Earth exerts an exceptionally puny pull. An infant, in fact, can defeat the combined gravitational pull of every single atom on the planet by simply lifting a wooden block off the floor.

That's what makes Newton's discoveries so amazing, even today. Gravity – this wimp of a force – is somehow powerful enough to pull the moon into orbit and keep the Earth cruising in a perfect elliptical path around the Sun. Without the constant tug of gravity, planets would crumble into dust and stars would collapse.

Gravity is also responsible for giving objects weight. But don't confuse weight with mass. While mass is a measurement of the amount of matter in an object, weight is the downward force exerted by all of that matter in a gravitational field. In the zero-gravity vacuum of space, objects are weightless, but they still have mass.

On the surface of the Earth, where the force of gravity is essentially constant, we consider mass and weight to be equal. But that same object – with the same mass – will weigh 17 per cent less on the Moon, where the gravitational pull is weaker. On Jupiter – not the best place to start a diet – that same object will weigh 213 per cent more.

Newton's Cannon
Understanding gravitational forces

1. Short-range
If a cannonball is fired from a mountain peak above the Earth's atmosphere, gravity will pull it down in the direction of the centre of the Earth.

2. Mid-range
With a higher muzzle velocity, the cannonball travels a longer horizontal distance, while falling at the same rate of acceleration (gravity).

8. Escape velocity
With enough velocity, the cannonball will escape the Earth's gravitational pull entirely. The Earth's escape velocity, as calculated by Newton, is 11.2 kilometres/second (7 miles/second).

3. Long-range
With enough muzzle velocity, the cannonball reaches the horizon. In this case, the curve of the Earth makes the Earth's surface 'fall away' slightly from the cannonball, allowing it to travel even further before landing.

7. Elliptical orbit
A little more speed produces an elliptical orbit, like the paths of the planets around the Sun.

6. Circular orbit
A little more speed results in a continuous circular orbit. Fixed positioned satellites reach a circular orbit with a launch velocity of 11,300kph (7,000mph).

5. Orbital velocity
At a precise muzzle velocity, the cannonball will balance its gravitational fall with the curve of the Earth, resulting in a circular orbit that collides with the cannon.

4. Half orbit
Here, the horizon effect is exaggerated. The surface of the Earth falls away from the cannonball nearly equal to gravity's rate of acceleration.

Falling force

Legend has it that Galileo famously disproved Aristotle by dropping two cannonballs of different mass from the top of the Tower of Pisa and showing that they land simultaneously. In 1971, astronaut Dave Scott dropped a feather and a hammer on the moon, proving that all objects fall at the same rate in a vacuum.

What's the Coriolis effect?

How our windy atmosphere gets left behind thanks to this deceptive force

It's actually all an illusion. The winds blowing in Earth's atmosphere are affected by the Coriolis effect, though that's somewhat hard to see. So what is this Coriolis effect? It's a visual effect seen, for example, when a ball rolls forward on a rotating platform, and you're on the receiving end. The ball appears to curve on the platform, when actually it's rolling in a straight line. The Earth's atmosphere has continual rising layers of hot air, predominately from the equator. The hot air later cools and settles back down to Earth, moving away from the equator to both the North and South poles.

This huge travelling flow of air moves in a straight path, but as the Earth rotates easterly, the air, as it moves from hot to cold, is left behind and falls further west. If the atmosphere was visual, the winds would most likely appear to be bending. ☼

What was Newton's contribution?

Sir Isaac Newton was born in 1642, the same year that Galileo died. While Galileo proved that objects of different masses fell at the same rate, it wasn't until Newton published his revolutionary Principia Mathematica – the most influential physics text of all time – that this mysterious force was finally given a name: gravity.

Newton's Universal Law of Gravitation was the first to explain gravity in clear, mathematical terms.

It was also the first truly 'unified' theory, explaining both earthly and heavenly mechanics. To readers of his day, it would have been completely inconceivable to imagine that the same force that pulls apples from trees could also coax the moon into orbit.

Over 300 years after their publication, Newton's elegant formulas still played a vital role in putting humans on the moon for the first time.

> ❝ According to Einstein, objects of great mass act like bowling balls on a trampoline, bending and warping the space-time fabric ❞

What is Einstein's 'space-time'?

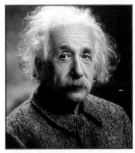

While Newton was able to mathematically prove the existence of gravity, he had no idea where it came from or how it actually worked. In the Newtonian world view, gravity was a constant, independent force that acted instantaneously. If the Sun were to disappear, Newton argued, then the planets would immediately spin off into the void.

In 1905, a young and unknown Albert Einstein postulated that light travelled at a discrete speed limit through the vacuum of space. Since nothing can travel faster than light, the force of gravity cannot act instantaneously. If the Sun disappeared, it would take over eight minutes for the loss of gravity to be felt by Earth.

But Einstein's most mind-boggling gravitational insight came in 1916 with the General Theory of Relativity. In his radical view of the universe, the three dimensions of space are merged with a fourth

dimension of time and represented as a flexible, two-dimensional 'space-time' fabric.

According to Einstein, objects of great mass act like bowling balls on a trampoline, bending and warping the space-time fabric. If a smaller object rolls too close one of these bowling balls, it will be drawn toward it. Gravity is not some mysterious independent force, but the result of the collective wrinkles in the fabric of the universe.

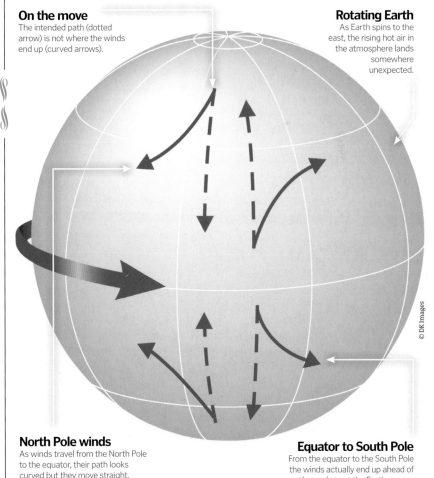

On the move
The intended path (dotted arrow) is not where the winds end up (curved arrows).

Rotating Earth
As Earth spins to the east, the rising hot air in the atmosphere lands somewhere unexpected.

North Pole winds
As winds travel from the North Pole to the equator, their path looks curved but they move straight.

Equator to South Pole
From the equator to the South Pole the winds actually end up ahead of themselves as the Earth moves.

© DK Images

> ❝ If the atmosphere was visual, the winds would most likely appear to be bending ❞

What's it like on the moon?

Understanding man's fascination with Earth's natural satellite

The average distance from Earth to the moon is 238,857 miles

Not only is the moon our only satellite, it's one of the biggest in the solar system and the only other celestial body upon which humans have stood. It's much smaller than the Earth, with a diameter only about 25 per cent that of Earth's diameter. The Earth's mass is also about 80 times that of the moon. The moon has a much lower gravitational force than the Earth – its gravity is about one-sixth that of our home planet's.

The moon is often referred to as dead, mainly because there is no life and its surface hasn't changed much over the billions of years. Temperatures at its poles can be as high as 127 degrees Celsius during the day and as low as -173 degrees Celsius at night. The moon is also covered in deep craters that can stay as cold as -240 degrees Celsius.

Its apparent glow is just light reflected from the Sun. There's no atmosphere and no air, although there is a collection of gasses above the surface known as an exosphere. The moon does have days that last about 29.5 hours, although the sky is always dark with visible stars. It rotates on its axis in about the same time it takes for it to orbit the Earth, a phenomenon known as synchronous rotation. This means that the same side – called the near side – is typically facing the Earth. The far side is illuminated by the Sun once per lunar day just like the near side.

As the moon orbits around the Earth, it goes through four phases – the new moon, first quarter moon, full moon, and last quarter moon. During the new moon, the moon is between the Sun and the Earth, so the sunlit side is turned away. Every seven days, more of the moon becomes visible. This process is known as waxing. Halfway through the lunar month there is a full moon. Then as the moon's orbit takes it further away from Earth, it wanes and less of it is visible. ⚙

1. Maria
The darker areas of the moon are cratered plains called maria (Latin for 'seas'). Originally they were thought to be water-filled, but they are actually filled with solid lava.

5. Copernicus
The moon is covered with numerous impact craters, and Copernicus is one of the most prominent. It's about 800 million years old and light in colour because it doesn't contain lava.

4. Ocean of Storms
Also known as Oceanus Procellarum, this is a massive mare covering more than 4 million square kilometres. The Apollo 12 mission and several lunar probes have landed in

> **" *The moon is covered with interesting features, including plains, highlands, and craters* "**

3. Sea of Tranquillity
Known in Latin as Mare Tranquillitatis, this mare was the landing site for the Apollo 11 mission. It looks very blue in photographs due to its high metallic content.

Could we ever live there?

Many people believe that we may someday colonise the moon. Space tourism could be a huge source of income and a permanent colony would make it easier to construct and launch spacecraft to explore other planets. It doesn't take long to reach the moon – just three days – and there isn't much delay in communications between the moon and the Earth. Many experiments that could result in new findings could be conducted there. It's an excellent site for an observatory because of its slow rotation and inactivity compared to the Earth. There also appears to be water at the poles.

However, there are some negatives to the idea of moon colonisation. The low gravity would require compensation because of its detrimental effect on the human body. The lack of atmosphere and extreme temperatures, as well as the relatively long lunar night (15 hours), would also require advanced technologies to allow for any kind of habitation.

A possible future lunar mission would include establishing a Lunar Observatory with a telescope

What lies beneath the surface of the moon?

Solid inner core
Unlike the Earth this does not provide a global magnetic field

Mantle
Extends down to a depth of 1,000km

2. Terrae
The lighter regions of the moon are called highlands or terrae (Latin for 'lands'). There are several mountain ranges and ancient volcanoes present.

All images © NASA

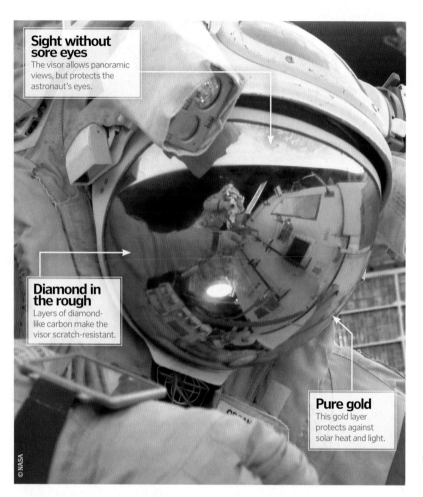

Sight without sore eyes
The visor allows panoramic views, but protects the astronaut's eyes.

Diamond in the rough
Layers of diamond-like carbon make the visor scratch-resistant.

Pure gold
This gold layer protects against solar heat and light.

© NASA

How do space suit visors work?

What do these visors do to protect astronauts against the sunlight?

Attached to the upper torso of a space suit, the Extravehicular Visor Assembly (EVA) is a transparent polycarbonate shell which gives an astronaut a panoramic view of their surroundings. The shell contains two visors; both protect against micro-meteorites, accidental impacts and solar radiation. To maintain optimal vision the visors also employ layers of diamond-like carbon (DLC) which make them resistant to scratches.

The interior visor is sprayed with an anti-misting agent for clear vision. It is transparent but contains a reflective plastic coating to retain heat emitted from the face. The exterior visor is coated in a highly reflective gold film to protect against solar heat and light. It is thickly tinted in one direction to protect the astronaut's eyes against incoming sunlight, while still allowing optimal vision. When operating in shade the sun visor is not used as visibility would be poor. ✿

> *The shell contains two visors; both protect against micro-meteorites, accidental impacts and solar radiation*

When does sky become space?

Want to turn from an aeronaut into an astronaut? Just cross the Kármán line

The Kármán line is an official boundary between the Earth's atmosphere and space, lying 100km (approximately 62 miles) above sea level. The governing body for air sports and aeronautical world records, Fédération Aéronautique Internationale (FAI), recognises it as the line where aeronautics ends and astronautics begins.

The line is named after aeronautical scientist Theodore von Kármán. He calculated that approximately 100km above sea level it was more efficient for vehicles to orbit than fly. The air thins with increasing altitude and aircraft rely on air flowing over their wings to keep them aloft so must move faster with increasing height. Above 100km they'd have to move faster than the velocity satellites orbit around the Earth.

Thin air also explains why the Earth's sky looks blue and space is black. Atmospheric gases scatter blue light more than other colours, turning the sky blue. At higher altitudes, less air exists to scatter light. ✿

How is the Earth's atmosphere layered?

Exosphere
Many satellites orbit in the exosphere – the highest atmospheric layer. It extends to 10,000km above sea level and gets thinner and thinner until it becomes outer space.

Thermosphere
'Thermos' means hot. Air molecules in this layer can be heated to over 1,000°C by the Sun's incoming energy, but we would feel cold because there is so little air.

Mesosphere
Meteorites entering the Earth's atmosphere normally burn up in the mesosphere, the coldest layer in the atmosphere that lies 50 to 80km above sea level.

Stratosphere
The stratosphere stretches from around 12km to 50km above sea level. This layer contains the ozone layer, which shields us from the Sun's potentially harmful ultraviolet radiation.

Troposphere
The atmosphere's lowest layer contains 75 per cent of its mass and almost all its weather. It varies from around 8km high at the poles to 20km over the equator.

10,000 km | Exosphere

690 km

Thermosphere | Shuttle

Aurora

100 km (Kármán line)

85 km | Mesosphere | Meteors

50 km | Stratosphere | Weather balloon

6 – 20 km | Troposphere

Mount Everest

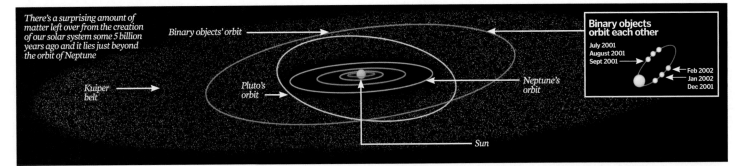

There's a surprising amount of matter left over from the creation of our solar system some 5 billion years ago and it lies just beyond the orbit of Neptune

Binary objects' orbit

Kuiper belt

Pluto's orbit

Neptune's orbit

Sun

Binary objects orbit each other

July 2001
August 2001
Sept 2001
Feb 2002
Jan 2002
Dec 2001

Where is the Kuiper belt?

If you were looking for a gigantic asteroid field and a cloud of icy particles, where would you look?

If you were to scale down the Sun and planets so the Earth sat just 1cm away from the Sun, the furthest dwarf planet would sit some 30 centimetres away. Just beyond the orbit of Neptune, however, lies a wide belt of the remnants from the construction of our solar system. The Kuiper belt contains hundreds of thousands of icy particles thought to be up to 60 miles in diameter, along with up to a trillion smaller comets.

But the solar system doesn't end there – our entire solar system is entombed in an almost perfect sphere of ice, the Oort Cloud, that lies some half a kilometre further away on our previous scale where the distance from the Earth to the Sun is just one centimetre. Lying on the boundaries of interstellar space, this shell is thought to contain up to 2 trillion icy bodies teetering on the very cusp of our Sun's gravitational grasp. ✿

How do we look for hidden planets?

Why bending light can reveal hidden worlds

It's been over 80 years since Einstein first published his general theory of relativity and he's still making headlines. Astronomers are now using a central tenet of Einstein's revolutionary theory – that massive objects like stars and galaxies can bend the fabric of space-time – to create celestial magnifying glasses called gravitational lenses.

Using Einstein's theory, scientists proved that light travelling toward Earth from a distant star bends as it passes by the Sun. The bending effect is almost imperceptible because the Sun doesn't contain tremendous amounts of mass.

But imagine if an entire galaxy sat between the Earth and a far-off star. The mass of the galaxy cluster would act like a thick lens, bending and warping the light as it passed. To someone on Earth, the effect would be multiple images of the star, or in some cases, a glowing halo called an 'Einstein ring'.

To discover one of farthest 'extrasolar' planets – a planet 15,000 light years from our solar system – astronomers have used a version of a gravitational lens. In this case, astronomers used a nearby star as a 'lensing star' to bend the light of a distant source star. They chose the lensing

star because of its size and its likelihood to have orbiting planets.

What they observed was remarkable. When the source star aligned behind the lensing star, the astronomers observed a double image of the source star. Then they witnessed two sudden spikes in the brightness of the double images. The spikes, they deduced, were caused by the gravitational pull of an unseen planet orbiting the lensing star.

Powerful gravitational lenses also act as magnifying glasses, detecting faint light from distant sources. ✿

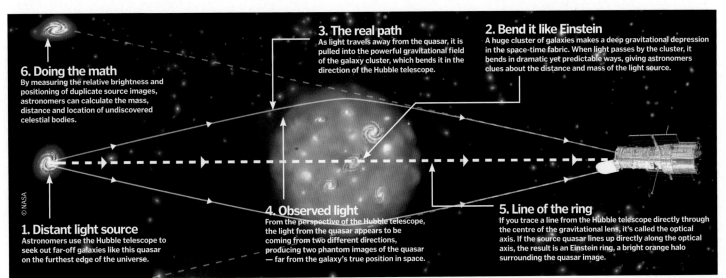

6. Doing the math
By measuring the relative brightness and positioning of duplicate source images, astronomers can calculate the mass, distance and location of undiscovered celestial bodies.

3. The real path
As light travels away from the quasar, it is pulled into the powerful gravitational field of the galaxy cluster, which bends it in the direction of the Hubble telescope.

2. Bend it like Einstein
A huge cluster of galaxies makes a deep gravitational depression in the space-time fabric. When light passes by the cluster, it bends in dramatic yet predictable ways, giving astronomers clues about the distance and mass of the light source.

1. Distant light source
Astronomers use the Hubble telescope to seek out far-off galaxies like this quasar on the furthest edge of the universe.

4. Observed light
From the perspective of the Hubble telescope, the light from the quasar appears to be coming from two different directions, producing two phantom images of the quasar — far from the galaxy's true position in space.

5. Line of the ring
If you trace a line from the Hubble telescope directly through the centre of the gravitational lens, it's called the optical axis. If the source quasar lines up directly along the optical axis, the result is an Einstein ring, a bright orange halo surrounding the quasar image.

© NASA

An image taken by the Chandra Observatory of a giant eruption

© NASA

What causes a stellar quake?

The truth behind these giant explosions that rock the universe

At the heart of a stellar quake is a neutron star, which has a highly dense mass of protons and electrons that have been forced together to form neutrons. Neutron stars have up to five times the mass of the Sun but are only about 20 kilometres in diameter. They spin on average at 400 rotations per second, but their strong magnetic fields cause them to slow down over time. The highest observed spin speed of a neutron star is 1,122 rotations per second.

As they rotate, the incredibly strong gravitational force of the star counteracts the spin of the star. The former attempts to draw in the equator, while the centrifugal forces resulting from the spin of the star try to push the equator out. This changes its shape from an oblong to a sphere, cracking the rigid iron crust. Mountains only a few centimetres tall begin to appear across the surface as the tension builds.

Eventually, the tension in the surface reaches such a level that the crust 'snaps' and a huge number of gamma rays and x-rays are released as a stellar quake. As the geometry of the star readjusts, the strong magnetic fields temporarily drop to a lower energy level. Combined with the energy released from inside the star, this creates one of the largest known flashes of x-rays in the universe. ✿

© ESO/L. Calçada

What is a magnetar?

Recent evidence suggests the primary causes of the largest stellar quakes are magnetars, large neutron stars with an incredibly powerful magnetic field. At twice the size of a regular neutron star, a magnetar can have up to 30 times more mass than the Sun, despite the Sun being 46,000 times larger. A tablespoon of mass from a magnetar would weigh the same as 274 Empire State buildings. The magnetic field of a magnetar is several trillion times stronger than that of Earth while its rigid crust is 10 billion times stronger than steel and 1.5km thick.

What is a solar flare?

The largest explosions in the solar system explained

A solar flare is a sudden, high-energy explosion of energy that extends out to the Sun's corona, or outermost layer of atmosphere. They are caused by a build-up of magnetic energy and occur in areas of strong magnetic fields around the equator of the Sun. The number and frequency of solar flares correlates to that of sunspots. These temporary dark spots on the surface of the Sun mark areas of intense magnetic activity. During the solar cycle, the number of sunspots increases and they concentrate near the equator. The more sunspots there are, the more solar flares there are.

Solar flares happen in three stages, with each stage lasting as short as a few seconds or as long as a few hours depending on the strength of the flare. During the precursor stage, the energy begins to release in the form of lower-wavelength, or soft, x-rays. Next, electrons, protons and ions accelerate nearly to the speed of light during the impulsive stage. Plasma rapidly heats to anywhere from 10 million to as much as 100 million degrees Kelvin during the impulsive phase. A flare not only results in a visible flash of light, it also emits radiation across the electromagnetic spectrum at other wavelengths. These include gamma rays, radio waves and x-rays. The final stage is decay, in which soft x-rays are once again the only emissions detected.

Solar flares are classified on a scale of A, B, C, M or X, with each classification being ten times stronger than the previous one. Within each letter classification there is also a one to nine scale; an A2 flare is twice as strong as an A1 flare, for example. This depends on their peak x-ray flux measurement as determined by the GOES (geostationary operational environmental satellite) system. ✿

What does a solar flare look like?

Each solar flare has a unique structure, and these can be quite complex, but there are a few basic structures typical to each. Solar flares cannot be observed via the naked eye (and viewing the Sun this way at any time isn't advised), but are observed via electromagnetic emissions recorded by telescopes and spacecraft.

Loop footpoints
Footpoints appear during the impulsive stage and are areas of electromagnetic emission. During the flare they appear to move due to the changing state of magnetic energy.

Magnetic reconnection
This phenomenon is thought to be responsible for solar flares. When two opposite magnetic fields are brought together, the magnetic lines of force in the Sun rearrange and energy is released.

Post-flare loops
These hot magnetic loops remain on the surface of the Sun after a flare and are observable as white areas on soft x-rays.

Coronal mass ejection
Coronal mass ejections (CMEs) are powerful ejections of plasma that sometimes occur with strong solar flares, but can also occur during other types of solar activity.

What effect do they have on the Earth?

The occurrence of a solar flare can have many different effects on Earth as well as on our space explorations. The hard x-rays emitted from a flare, as well as bursts of highly charged protons called proton storms, can do damage to both astronauts and spacecraft. Soft x-rays enter Earth's ionosphere and can disrupt radio communications. Ultraviolet radiation and x-rays also cause the outer atmosphere to heat up, creating a drag on satellites in low Earth orbit and reducing their life span.

Coronal mass ejections (CMEs) often occur along with solar flares. These ejections of a large amount of plasma can disturb the Earth's entire magnetic field, known as a geomagnetic storm. Geomagnetic storms can damage satellites in high Earth orbit as well as power grids, leading to both communication and power outages.

How do orbits work?

Why doesn't the moon crash into Earth?

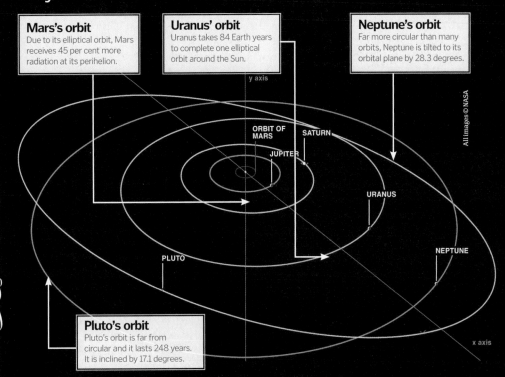

Mars's orbit
Due to its elliptical orbit, Mars receives 45 per cent more radiation at its perihelion.

Uranus' orbit
Uranus takes 84 Earth years to complete one elliptical orbit around the Sun.

Neptune's orbit
Far more circular than many orbits, Neptune is tilted to its orbital plane by 28.3 degrees.

Pluto's orbit
Pluto's orbit is far from circular and it lasts 248 years. It is inclined by 17.1 degrees.

All images © NASA

y axis

ORBIT OF MARS · SATURN · JUPITER · URANUS · NEPTUNE · PLUTO · x axis

Orbits work because two bodies of mass are attracted to each other with force and that for every action there is an equal and opposite reaction, as explained in Newton's Third Law of Motion. In terms of orbits, this means that when one object rotates around another of a higher mass it experiences continuous free fall towards the larger body, undertaking a constant gravitational acceleration towards the greater object that deflects what would otherwise be its straight-line motion into a curved trajectory. In essence, any orbit is maintained by the direction of its motion and acceleration, both of which alter constantly, thereby producing its curved orbit.

All closed orbits are elliptical in shape, the degree of which varies from a perfect circle to a stretched egg form, and is referred to as an orbit's eccentricity. Many of our solar system's orbits – such as our moon's around Earth – are pretty circular with a low eccentricity. Here, both bodies rotate around the joint centre of mass – which in the Earth/moon relationship is deep inside the Earth –

and the lesser body remains relatively circular throughout its orbit. Others, such as Pluto's orbit around the Sun, are highly elliptical and elongated, with a large gap between its perigee (its closest point of approach) and its apogee (the point where it is farthest from the orbit's focus).

In the case of Pluto and its own moon Charon, while Charon follows a largely circular orbit due to its large size and close proximity (it is roughly half Pluto's size), the mass centre of the two objects is not within Pluto but out in space between the two.

An easy way to understand orbits is to imagine a cannonball fired out of a cannon from the top of an impossibly high mountain (see p192 for a diagram of Newton's Cannon). Once fired the cannonball moves sideways and falls towards the Earth (the central body), however it has so much tangential velocity that it misses the central object as it curves away beneath it due to its circular shape and continues to fall indefinitely, caught in an equilibrium sustained by its velocity and the pull of gravity. ✿

Why is there so much space junk?

Looking at the space age junk that pollutes our planet

Since the launch of Sputnik I, which was the first man-made satellite to orbit the Earth in 1957, a vast amount of space debris has accumulated in its wake. This consists of anything from flecks of paint to discarded rocket boosters, 'dead' satellites that no longer function and equipment lost by astronauts during space walks.

The scale of the problem can be grasped by the fact that there are estimated to be several hundred million items of space junk less than 1cm in size, several hundred thousand items between 1cm to 10cm and at least 19,000 objects larger than 10cm.

In low Earth orbit (LEO) this junk travels at an average speed of 7.5km/s, which is ten times faster than a bullet. This means that even the smallest objects can damage the subsystems of a satellite. Objects from 1cm to 10cm are part of a 'lethal population' because they are big enough to do considerable damage to a satellite, but are too small to be tracked. Larger debris is tracked and can be avoided; in the case of the International Space Station, it makes at least one manoeuvre a year to divert it from potentially lethal collisions.

Last year there were 13,000 near misses and by

> ❝ *Last year there were 13,000 near misses and by 2059 it is predicted that there will be as many as 50,000* ❞

2059 it is predicted that there will be as many as 50,000. The increased need to use rocket fuel to avoid these hazards shortens the life of satellites, and increases the cost of launching satellites that need to carry extra fuel.

1,400 items of space junk were created when the first ever collision between two satellites occurred on 11 February 2009. This was between the Iridium 33 US communications satellite and a defunct Kosmos 2251 Russian satellite, 790km over Northern Siberia. Even worse, 150,000 pieces of junk were deliberately created when China destroyed an inactive Fengyun-1C weather satellite with a missile, as part of an anti-satellite test.

Radar systems are used to track LEO junk, and telescopes are employed to track objects from 2,000km to 36,000km in medium Earth orbit (MEO) and geostationary orbit (GEO) at 36,000km. Telescopes, however, are only capable of tracking objects that are 1m or more in size. Radio frequency technology can also be used to discover if satellites are operating or not.

Tracking systems help warn of possible collisions, but measures that are more drastic are being employed before it is impossible to launch manned flights, or operate the satellites that provide us with TV signals, weather forecasts, mobile phone networks and global positioning systems. ✿

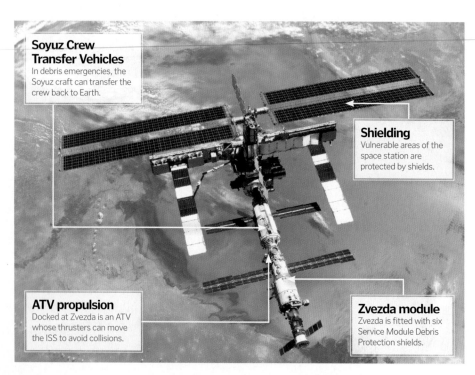

Soyuz Crew Transfer Vehicles
In debris emergencies, the Soyuz craft can transfer the crew back to Earth.

Shielding
Vulnerable areas of the space station are protected by shields.

ATV propulsion
Docked at Zvezda is an ATV whose thrusters can move the ISS to avoid collisions.

Zvezda module
Zvezda is fitted with six Service Module Debris Protection shields.

How does the ISS dodge the debris?

Orbiting at 350km in low Earth orbit, the ISS is particularly vulnerable to damage from space debris. Manned modules and other vulnerable areas have been fitted with protective aluminium shields – both during and since construction.

The ISS also carries out Debris Avoidance Manoeuvres (DAMs) to dodge space junk or micrometeorites. When warned of such dangers, the ISS is sent a few kilometres higher or lower, using a short engine thrust from a docked Automated Transfer Vehicle (ATV) or Progress spacecraft. The ATV is fitted with an automatic system that during docking procedure will abort the procedure if it detects any danger from debris.

If any debris comes within 0.75km above or below, or within 25km around it that cannot be avoided, the ISS is put into unmanned mode and the astronauts have to seek protection in a spacecraft docked with the station. In 2008 and 2009, astronauts had to seek refuge in a Soyuz craft, due to such warnings.

One line of defence for the manned modules is aluminium shielding

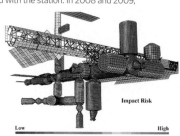

Impact Risk

Low — High

How can we deal with the space junk?

The European Space Agency is currently building a radar system to catalogue and track hazardous objects in Earth orbit. At the moment, the US military Space Surveillance Network (SSN) tracks 19,000 objects and its Space Fence radar system scheduled for 2015 expects to track as many as 100,000 objects.

To mitigate the problem of space junk the Inter-Agency Space Debris Co-ordination Committee (IADC) was formed in 1993 to produce a set of guidelines. It advocates several preventative measures, including reducing the amount of hardware ejected or rendered inoperative by a space mission. Since accidental orbital explosions have accounted for at least 200 incidents, it is recommended that explosive gasses or fuels be vented to stop this happening. The deliberate explosion of satellites should be stopped, and where possible satellites should be steered clear of debris. As LEO satellites are the biggest culprit, they should be designed to only have an orbital life of 25 years, and carry drag devices or a propulsion system to send them into re-entry if its orbit is not low enough for it to naturally re-enter. Higher satellites should be designed to enter a 'graveyard' orbit at the end of their operating life.

Several ideas have been proposed to dispose of existing junk. They range from shooting it down using lasers, scooping it up with Aerogel material or netting it with 'trawler' satellites. For the smallest debris, large panels of porous foam could slow down junk that passes through it, making it re-enter the atmosphere. For larger debris, it could be collected by the robotic arm of an unmanned spacecraft.

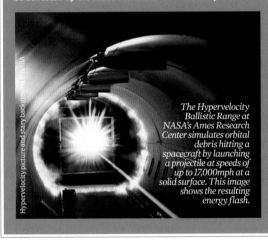

Hypervelocity picture and starry background: © NASA

The Hypervelocity Ballistic Range at NASA's Ames Research Center simulates orbital debris hitting a spacecraft by launching a projectile at speeds of up to 17,000mph at a solid surface. This image shows the resulting energy flash.

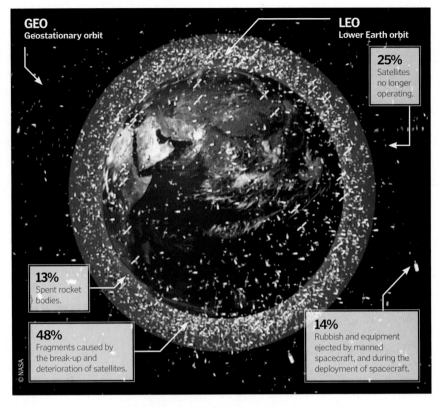

GEO Geostationary orbit

LEO Lower Earth orbit

25% Satellites no longer operating.

13% Spent rocket bodies.

14% Rubbish and equipment ejected by manned spacecraft, and during the deployment of spacecraft.

48% Fragments caused by the break-up and deterioration of satellites.

© NASA

How much debris is orbiting the Earth?

Objects in low Earth orbit (LEO) are between 160km and 2,000km above the Earth. Military satellites, Earth monitoring satellites and communications satellites operate at these orbital altitudes.

LEO satellites pose a problem because they orbit the Earth at least 15 times a day along different orbital planes to provide global coverage. This gives them more chance of hitting other satellites in contrast to those that keep to the elliptical plane of the Sun. In addition, they have shorter battery lives and are more vulnerable to the gravitational pull of the Earth than higher satellites.

The so-called Kessler Syndrome proposes that as collisions multiply they create even greater numbers of fragments that will start an unstoppable chain reaction of collisions. In this process, the debris will increase more than the amount of debris burnt up by orbital decay, and will make the use of low Earth orbits impossible.

Most objects that go beneath LEO, through orbital decay or, due to a collision, fall back to Earth and harmlessly burn up in the atmosphere. Larger space junk is more of a problem. This was emphasised by the accidental crash of Cosmos 954 in January 1978. The Soviet reconnaissance satellite carried an onboard nuclear reactor, which instead of reaching a safe orbit fell over northwest Canada. A huge recovery operation found 12 large pieces, ten of which were radioactive and one that carried a lethal radiation level of 500r/hr.

In 2001, the Russian Mir space station was deliberately made to crash into the southern Pacific Ocean. The re-entry of the 130,000kg station created a spectacular display, and metal fragments from it were recovered and sold on eBay.

So far, such crashes have been in oceans or remote parts of the world but certainly, there is a risk of a rogue piece of space junk causing serious damage to a highly populated area.

So what exactly is up there?

Glove
Lost by Ed White, the first American astronaut to take a spacewalk on 3 June 1965, during the Gemini 4 mission

Metallic spherical drinking water spheres
Started a UFO scare when they crashed in Western Australia in 1965, but were identified as coming from the Gemini spacecraft

Tool bag
Worth $100,000 containing grease guns lost by Heide Stefanyshyn-Piper during a shuttle spacewalk in 2008. It re-entered the atmosphere in August 2009

128kg of nuclear reactor coolant
Leaked from inactive Soviet Radar Ocean Reconnaissance Satellites

200 rubbish bags
Produced when the upper stage of a Pegasus rocket exploded in 1996

480 million copper needles
Launched in 1963 as part of Project West Ford to create an artificial ionosphere, it encircled Earth at 3,700km. Most re-entered the atmosphere in the Seventies

Gene Roddenberry
His ashes were released in a small capsule by a Pegasus XL rocket in 1997

Cameras
Lost during the Gemini 10 and a Discovery space shuttle mission in December 2006

When were we last on the moon?

Gene Cernan, the last human to walk on the moon, stepped off its dusty surface and onto his spacecraft's ladder in the early morning of 14 December 1972. Seventeen hours later Cernan and Jack Schmitt, his fellow moon walker on the Apollo 17 mission, blasted off from the Sea of Serenity to be reunited with their crew mate Ron Evans, orbiting high above in the command service module. Cernan had said, as he climbed the ladder, that he believed it would not be too long before people once again walked on the moon.

Well, almost 40 years on and we have yet to return. Why is this? Put crudely it is because, for those people who would have made the decision to return, there has been no need too. Project Apollo happened because President Kennedy and the US Congress wanted it to; a demonstration of American scientific and technological capability to surpass that achieved by the Soviet Union with its Sputnik and cosmonaut programs. Once Neil Armstrong had stepped onto the Moon in 1969 and been 'returned safely to the Earth', Kennedy's objective had been achieved – the space race had been won – and the political will to maintain a multi-billion dollar manned moon program evaporated. Will we return? Possibly, but whoever gives the decision will have to be happy with the huge price tag it brings with it.

Can you see light if travelling at the speed of light?

If you were travelling at the speed of light, the light would still appear to you to be going at the speed of light, therefore 'theoretically' it would look completely normal. This is an effect that is described by Einstein's special theory of relativity. Putting it into perspective, we are orbiting our Sun at an immense speed, our Sun is orbiting the galaxy at an immense speed, while all the time our galaxy is accelerating at an even more immense speed! Yet when we turn a light on it still travels at the speed of light regardless of all this motion.

Exactly how fast is our galaxy moving?

Until the 20th Century it would have been virtually impossible to reach any sensible figure for the speed with which our galaxy – the Milky Way – is travelling through space. Many scientists would not have presumed the galaxy to be moving at all. This all changed, however, when the universe was shown to be expanding from a huge explosion or big bang of creation, with the Milky Way and the billions of other galaxies seemingly spreading out across the cosmos.

But how could we measure this speed of travel for our Milky Way? Scientists in the Forties had predicted that there should be residual evidence of the big bang in the shape of cosmic background radiation infiltrating the whole of space. When this was duly discovered in the Sixties it was used as the frame of reference with which to gauge the rate at which our own galaxy is speeding through the universe. It turns out to be some 1.3 million miles per hour (2.1 million km/hr)!

What's the next nearest galaxy to ours?

The next nearest galaxy is actually inside our own galaxy. It's called the Canis Major Dwarf galaxy and eventually it will be completely absorbed by our Milky Way galaxy. It contains around a billion stars, compared to the 200 billion in the Milky Way. The nearest big galaxy to ours is Andromeda, around 2 million light years away.

Astronomers have discovered more than 400 planets around stars other than the Sun, but most of these resemble gas giants like Jupiter rather than our rocky Earth. New telescopes have revealed a handful of more Earth-like planets but it's still very hard to detect a small planet close to a star. All of the extrasolar planets so far confirmed have been in the Milky Way, as it's very difficult to spot something as small as a planet in another galaxy. But theorists reckon that there could be billions of Earth-like planets in our own galaxy, and a similar number in others. So somewhere out there, ET may be waiting...

> **It turns out our own galaxy is speeding through the universe at some 1.3 million miles per hour (2.1 million km/hr)!**

What's beyond the universe's border?

It's hard to imagine, but the universe doesn't have an edge in the normal sense. The Big Bang theory, the most widely accepted description of the universe, states that the universe is expanding from a very hot and dense initial state – but it's not expanding into anything else, as space itself didn't exist before the Big Bang. Some astronomers think the universe might be infinite. As to what shape it is, it could be flat, behaving like the geometry we are familiar with from school. Or it might somehow curve back on itself, requiring a more complex geometry to describe it. A spacecraft called Planck is currently studying the cosmic microwave background. This is remnant radiation from the Big Bang that permeates the whole universe. Small fluctuations in the cosmic microwave background provide clues as to how the universe has developed into what we see today, and Planck's results should help mathematicians refine their models of the universe's shape.

However, there is a limit to the observable universe – no matter how good our technology gets, we will only ever be able to observe areas from which light has had time to reach us since the universe started expanding. The boundary of this area expands as the universe does.

How long could you survive unprotected in space?

You might be able to survive in space for over a minute, so long as you got back to safety and medical care immediately. Following a sudden exposure to the vacuum of space, the first thing to do would be breathe out – if you held your breath, the gas expanding in your lungs due to the reduced external pressure would cause them to rupture (it's a bit like ascending after a scuba dive).

Around ten seconds in, you would start to lose consciousness and vision due to oxygen depletion. In the low-pressure environment, your body fluids would begin to vaporise, causing tissue to swell up. If you were in the sunlight, without the protective effect of the Earth's atmosphere, serious sunburn would occur. Experience from training accidents suggests that if astronauts are returned into a pressurised oxygen environment within 90 seconds, injuries are reversible. However, with so many factors at play, the survival limits are not well known.

❝ If you held your breath, the gas expanding in your lungs due to the reduced external pressure would cause them to rupture ❞

© NASA

When looking into space, are you seeing it in the past?

When you look at an object in space, say for example Jupiter, you see it as it was in the recent past – approximately 43 minutes ago. That's the average time it takes light to travel from Jupiter to your telescope (it varies depending on what time of year you are looking, as the distance between Earth and Jupiter changes during their journeys around the Sun). Light travels at a fixed speed of 299,792,458 metres per second. So, on all but the largest scales, we can detect it almost instantaneously. But over the vast distances of space the delay becomes apparent. Light from our nearest neighbour, the Moon, takes a bit over a second to reach us, while the travel time from the Sun is around about eight minutes. Our next nearest star, Alpha Centauri, is over four light years away, with distant galaxies being millions of light years away.

Even if there were an alien spaceship travelling past Jupiter, you wouldn't be able to see it from an Earth-based telescope, as it would be too small. The Juno spacecraft, launched in August 2011, will reach Jupiter in 2016. In the highly unlikely event that it had a close encounter with an extraterrestrial spacecraft, we would have to wait for Juno's radio signal, travelling at light speed, to reach Earth before we knew about it.

How would a space tether be built?

There have been many different attempts by scientists and engineers to devise a way to build a space tether or 'elevator' and yes most of them involve constructing a really long cable of some kind – 38,000km or more to be exact! The idea is that the cable would be in a geostationary orbit around Earth, one end of the cable would be attached to either a fixed or mobile platform on the Earth and the other end would connect with some kind of counterweight, high above the Earth's atmosphere.

The elevator would prove highly useful in being able to get things into space without the need for launching rockets, however such a project is not without its share of difficulties. The main technical issue to overcome in building such a cable is to keep it from collapsing under its own weight. One idea is to vary the thickness of the cable to allow for the tension to stay constant throughout, as the gravitational force on the cable increases the closer it is to the Earth. It would need to be built out of a material which is incredibly strong, yet very light. In fact the strength required from such a material would need to be at least twice that of diamond!

Currently there are no such materials which could handle this strain, however there is a lot of exciting research happening at the moment in the field of carbon nanotubes which may prove useful. Carbon nanotubes are extremely strong carbon structures which have been synthesised in laboratories and it has been theorised that these nanotubes may have what it takes to withstand the strain while still being a relatively light material.

Is it possible to knock Earth out of its orbit?

Yes, it's possible, but the impact required would be so large that the Earth would likely be destroyed in the process. Many astronomers think that around 4.5 billion years ago, when the solar system was forming, the Earth got a 'big whack', which resulted in our moon being formed. According to this theory, a Mars-sized object struck the early Earth. At this stage in the solar system's evolution both bodies would have been made mainly of molten material that had not yet solidified. Their iron-rich cores merged, while parts of their outer layers were vaporised and thrown into orbit around the Earth. This material eventually coalesced to form our rocky moon. The Earth gained angular momentum, and its orbit may have changed, although only slightly. This impact is likely to have been 100 million times bigger than the impact that wiped out the dinosaurs. If a body that size hit today's mostly solid Earth, we would be blasted to smithereens.

What is a solar corona?

The solar corona is a part of the Sun that spreads out from our star's surface. The word literally means 'crown', which is quite appropriate for the monarch of the solar system. Because the corona is not very dense, it is hard to observe.

During a solar eclipse, however, the moon blocks the glaring light from the Sun and we can see the corona in its full glory. Observatories in space keep a constant eye on this crown and send us images of its always-changing features modelled by magnetic fields and the solar wind which is made up of charged particles emitted by our star.

At over 2 million degrees Celsius, the corona is strangely much hotter than the surface of the Sun below. People are still looking for a precise explanation for this but it appears that magnetic fields are responsible for making the corona so hot.

It's nice to have mysteries like this to keep astrophysicists busy for a while!

How does the Sun burn without oxygen?

The Sun is an amazing source of energy and people have long wondered how all that energy is produced. The word burning usually means combustion and if the Sun was burning this way, it would indeed need oxygen. We're certain this isn't the case because the Sun wouldn't last for long. Nuclear reactions are the only source of energy able to keep the Sun shining for at least the age of the solar system and keeping us warm on a good day.

When physicists say a star is burning hydrogen, they mean it's joining hydrogen atoms together to obtain helium and release energy. The exact name for this process is nuclear fusion. There is no need for oxygen in these nuclear reactions but with respect to tradition, and as it sounds better, astrophysicists use the word burn. This means that you can use it as well if you want to sound like a pro... just remember the explanation to back it up.

Why is Venus referred to as Earth's twin?

Some of the reasons for this are that Venus is almost exactly the same size as Earth, just 400 miles shorter in diameter and 20 per cent smaller in mass. During the early evolution of the solar system both Venus and Earth would have been almost mirror images of each other. This, however, was not to last and differences in our atmospheres' compositions play a part in the vast differences we see today. With surface temperatures approaching 500° Celsius and an atmosphere of around 96 per cent carbon dioxide, Venus exhibits the kind of runaway greenhouse effect people are worried might befall Earth if we carry on pumping carbon dioxide into the atmosphere.

Along with more than three per cent nitrogen and the rest largely composed of sulphuric, hydrochloric and hydrofluoric acids, when it rains on Venus it's actually almost pure acid carried by weather patterns that aren't too dissimilar to those that we find on Earth. Fortunately, however, our rain isn't usually quite so harmful!

Why is Pluto not a planet any more?

Well, it's still a planet of sorts. Since 2006 Pluto has been classified by the International Astronomical Union as a 'dwarf planet'. In recent decades, powerful telescopes have enabled astronomers to discover several Pluto-sized objects beyond Neptune's orbit, and there are probably lots more out there. So, either they had to expand the list of planets (which would mean you'd have to remember a lot more for your science exams) or it was time to come up with an official definition of what counts as a planet.

After some fierce debate, the international committee agreed a condition that a planet must be the biggest thing in its orbital neighbourhood. Pluto and the newly found similar objects are all in the same neighbourhood, so that rules them out. However, the definition of 'planet' is controversial, so the 'Save Pluto' campaigners hope it will be re-instated one day.

Could we travel faster than the speed of light?

As we've established, the speed of light is 299,792,458 metres per second, which is fast enough to travel around our planet seven and a half times a second. That's pretty fast! In fact it's the fastest thing we know, but why is it so difficult to travel at this speed? Surely if we were far away from any other forces like gravity, we could just keep accelerating and eventually we would get there, wouldn't we?

Unfortunately no. One of the things which Einstein realised from his theories of relativity is that as any particle of mass increases in speed it also increases in mass. By the time the mass has finally reached the speed of light it would have infinite mass which would mean to get it to that stage would have required an infinite amount of energy and we don't know about you but there are a definite shortage of infinite energy sources in this universe!

© NASA

What's the farthest out into space we've seen?

The farther you look into space, the farther back in time you'll see. This is because light has a speed and it takes time for that light to travel across the universe. Because of this there is a limit to what we can see. It also means there are regions of space which we will never see because they are so far away, even though the light is travelling towards us, the space itself is expanding faster (nothing moving through space can travel faster than light, but the expansion of space can).

We calculate the age of the universe to be around 13.7 billion years old. Therefore we can only see light that has been travelling for this time. However, the rate of expansion of the universe has been changing. The most distant observed object is GRB 090423 which was a gamma ray burst detected in 2009, most likely caused by a star which collapsed when the universe was around 600 million years old. The light we're seeing from this object has been travelling through the universe for about 13 billion years yet we are seeing the object as it was when it was closer to the Earth, about 36 million light years away.

However, in the 13 billion years that the photons of light given off by GRB 090423 have been travelling, that distance of 36 million light years has stretched to about 46 billion light years away. As a result the light itself has become stretched, which causes it to be shifted more towards the red end of the spectrum – red shifted.

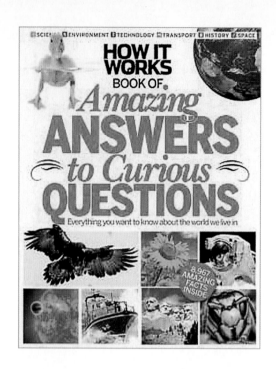